Of Gardens

Of Gardens

SELECTED ESSAYS

Paula Deitz

Afterword by John Dixon Hunt

University of Pennsylvania Press · Philadelphia · Oxford

PENN STUDIES IN LANDSCAPE ARCHITECTURE

John Dixon Hunt, Series Editor

This series is dedicated to the study and promotion of a wide variety of approaches to landscape architecture, with special emphasis on connections between theory and practice. It includes monographs on key topics in history and theory, descriptions of projects by both established and rising designers, translations of major foreign-language texts, anthologies of theoretical and historical writings on classic issues, and critical writing by members of the profession of landscape architecture. The series was the recipient of the Award of Honor in Communications from the American Society of Landscape Architects, 2006.

Title page photograph: Fred R. Conrad, *Pleached crab apple tree arbor, Oak Spring Farms, Upperville, Virginia. The New York Times*/Redux.

Published by

University of Pennsylvania Press

Philadelphia, Pennsylvania 19104-4112

www.upenn.edu/pennpress

Printed in the United States of America on acid-free paper

10 9 8 7 6 5 4 3 2 1

Library of Congress Cataloging-in-Publication Data

Deitz, Paula.

   Of gardens : selected essays / Paula Deitz. — 1st ed.

     p. cm. — (Penn studies in landscape architecture)

   Includes index.

   ISBN 978-0-8122-4266-9 (hardcover : alk. paper)

   1. Gardens. 2. Gardens—History. 3. Gardens—Design—History. 4. Landscape architecture—History. I. Title. II. Series: Penn studies in landscape architecture.

   SB465.D44 2010

   635—dc22

2010021357

For Fred, in loving memory

Wild blossoms on the river banks
sway yellow in the rising wind:
see—their images loom too,
deep in the watery clarities.

> —Frederick Morgan, "Recollections of Japan,"
> from *The One Abiding*, 2003

Contents

. . . nothing to the true pleasure of a garden.

—Francis Bacon, "Of Gardens," 1625

Introduction

*I*IN 1625, the British philosopher and empiricist Francis Bacon wrote in his seminal essay "Of Gardens" that without gardens "buildings and palaces are but gross handiworks," and that even "when ages grow to civility and elegancy, men come to build stately sooner than to garden finely; as if gardening were the greater perfection." As I reread this passage recently, my mind harkened back to the experience that jolted me into understanding landscape architecture, not just as a stepsister to architecture, as Bacon partially implies, but as the means by which man redeems the natural environment through design. The occasion was a lecture by the landscape architect and ecologist Ian L. McHarg at Rockefeller University in New York City. He had just published his book *Design with Nature*, and that evening, along with his clarion call for environmental responsibility, he coined the concept of "the reassuring landscape," defined as cherished scenes from childhood that we continually seek out or recreate later in life. This lecture struck a chord in me and eventually became the taproot of this book. McHarg was a founder of the Department of Landscape Architecture and Regional Planning at the University of Pennsylvania, and therefore it is a singular privilege for me that John Dixon Hunt, Professor of the History and Theory of Landscape Architecture in that department, selected this collection for the Penn Studies in Landscape Architecture, of which he is the inaugural series editor.

Three years after McHarg's lecture, the Whitney Museum of American Art presented the exhibition "Frederick Law Olmsted's New York." At the entrance to this show was a map of the United States with Olmsted's landscape designs pinpointed across it. Standing there I realized that my entire young life, with the exception of my college junior year abroad in Geneva, Switzerland, had been circumscribed by Olmsted's pastoral landscapes. I was raised

Facing page: Eugène Atget, *Versailles, coin de parc*, 1902.

in Trenton, New Jersey, where Cadwalader Park, with its bucolic hills and dales, was the focus of recreational and cultural events (sledding the best of all), followed by Smith College, where Olmsted designed the entire campus as a botanic garden and arboretum, with every tree and plant labeled. And finally, I settled in New York City, where I live two blocks from Central Park and walk its paths regularly. The American landscape, as I knew it, was derived from the eighteenth-century picturesque parks and gardens Olmsted had visited in England and recreated on native soil.

During the six weeks that the Smith College Geneva group spent in Paris my year, before the term began at the University of Geneva, Versailles topped the list of our orientation activities. I still have the class photograph documenting the unforgettable visit that gave us our first view of André Le Nôtre's gardens. Until then, nothing in my life had prepared me for the classical grandeur and geometric precision of those seemingly endless parterres, bosquets, fountains, and statuary set among topiary and clipped trees. Like Ian McHarg in his book, I was enthralled with the snow-capped Alpine scenery of Switzerland during the subsequent year as well as with the local farm villages, wildflower fields in spring, and vineyards cascading down mountains. But the rigorous beauty of Le Nôtre's designs became the lasting touchstone for me, linking gardens with history as well as nature. What had prepared me to understand this linkage was a lecture in European intellectual history at Smith presented during the preceding year by Elisabeth Koffka. She gave an account of the bridge between the Enlightenment and Romanticism, which has stayed with me ever since when thinking and writing about Western gardens, where, reflecting the evolution of literary and artistic movements, the earlier classicism of gardens evolved into the Romantic landscape park. Madame Koffka, as she was always called, was also our faculty adviser during the Geneva year, which gave us the constant benefit of her insights and perceptions.

Many years later, when I married Frederick Morgan, I began to spend my summers at his house on the coast of Maine. During my first week there, the local postmistress took me under her wing and gave me a list of places to visit in the area, including the Abby Aldrich Rockefeller Garden in Seal Harbor, on the nearby island of Mount Desert. She explained that the garden was open to the public one day a week. I have visited this garden every summer since, and no matter how familiar it became, the first impression of passing through the gate in the Chinese wall, through the dark woods, and into the walled garden with its three concentric rectangles of brilliant flower borders remained as startling as ever. On that initial visit, I remember thinking, "This is landscape architecture"—a garden whose plan was as intricately conceived as any major structure. It was the first of many landscapes I was to visit over the years designed by Beatrix Farrand. This was the garden that inspired me to write about landscape.

I cite these formative experiences with Olmsted, Le Nôtre, and Farrand because I realized, as I edited these essays, that references to their work recur throughout, for they figure prominently in the lives and work of many of the landscape architects and designers about whom I have written. Even the most contemporary among them draw inspiration from the basic concepts of Olmsted, Le Nôtre, and Farrand, so one might say that these three have spurred dynasties, with each generation adding a fresh interpretation.

By the time I saw the Rockefeller Garden, I already knew the campuses of Princeton and Yale universities well but did not know they incorporated designs by Beatrix Farrand. Her other major extant garden was Dumbarton Oaks in Washington, D.C., where in May 1980 its Center for Studies in Landscape Architecture sponsored a symposium titled "Beatrix Jones Farrand (1872–1959): Fifty Years of American Landscape Architecture." The surrounding Georgetown streets lined with charming Federal houses were blanketed with wisteria vines and pink dogwood that spring weekend, and yet we all sat in a dark auditorium for two days of lectures with intermittent walks in the garden and lunch in the Orangery. For me, the weekend was a turning point because it was my first foray into what we call "the garden world," where I met writers, designers, and scholars, many of whom have remained good friends ever since. I have always been struck by the generosity of members of this garden world even as the circle expanded with other such occasions over the years both here and abroad. I wrote about the Dumbarton Oaks event for the *New York Times*, and my career as a garden writer was launched.

While studying for my master of arts in French literature at Columbia University, I was naturally under pressure to proceed to a doctoral degree. But I decided instead that were I ever to write at length, I would do so for millions of people who would read my work riding the subway without knowing who I was. My wish came true when I began writing for the *New York Times*, where almost half of the pieces reprinted here first appeared. Only one, "1680 Formal Garden Discovered in the South," made the front page, on December 26, 1985; it was a story about a remarkable archeological discovery that shifted our views of Colonial gardens. At a dinner party the following week, the gentleman on my right recounted the entire story back to me chapter and verse, thinking it would interest me, though he had no idea that I had written it. I had achieved my goal. In the end, I received my doctorate anyway, albeit an honorary one in humane letters from Smith College with a citation, for which I was deeply grateful, noting that my published works on landscape design "help readers from all walks of life appreciate the historical and contemporary dimensions of our physical environment." In lieu of a thesis, I offer this book.

Many of the connections among these essays are obvious, for one feature led directly to another as I traveled across America and in countries abroad, especially Great Britain, France, and Japan. But other connections were not obvious to me until the writing stage when I would discover while preparing a piece about the New York Botanical Garden, for example, that Nathaniel Lord Britton, the garden's first director, wrote a book in 1918 titled *Flora of Bermuda* that has served in recent years as the main resource for replanting native species on an island off Bermuda, the subject of another article. Or, in writing about the Désert de Retz in France and Painshill Park in England, eighteenth-century folly gardens, I found that Thomas Jefferson visited them both in the same year, 1786, when he was minister to France.

This book records a great adventure of continual discovery, not only of the artful beauty of individual gardens and landscapes but also of the intellectual and historical threads that weave them into patterns of civilization, from the modest garden for family subsistence to major urban developments. Landscapes, ever changing and ephemeral, are an expression of our ways of taming the environment, mindful of its fragility now as we address ecological issues of sustainability. These essays, then, are also about people over many centuries and in many lands who have expressed their originality and individuality by devoting themselves to cultivation and conservation. My aim as a writer and observer has been to report accurately my descriptions and knowledge of these places so that the reader can share the experience.

A few years ago, on a winter afternoon, I made one of many return visits to Versailles, this time to view an exhibition of royal porcelain and table settings. In keeping with the nature of the show, a café was set up in one of the boiserie-encrusted salons overlooking the garden. While I sipped my tea and ate my chocolate patisserie listening to seventeenth-century music, I had an extraordinary sensation of what it actually felt like to live at Versailles. As I gazed out the window, it began to snow, with great swirls lifted by a fierce wind. It was already dusk, but I hastened to finish and went out into the garden. Because the wind came from only one direction, all the immense pyramidal topiaries were only half covered in snow. I bundled up and walked down the long avenue as far as the Fountain of Apollo when I suddenly realized that I was completely alone in the garden, and that it was now dark. Before I panicked that the gates might be closed, I was exhilarated by the awareness that, like Louis XIV, I had the garden to myself. I realized then that because gardens give structure without confinement, they encourage a liberation of movement and thought, a legacy over time and from many cultures that accounts for Francis Bacon's conclusion "nothing to the true pleasure of a garden."

Prologue

The Lure of the Porch in Summer: Privacy and Pleasure

WITHOUT A PORCH, life at my summer place in Maine seemed incomplete. A granite patio-terrace adjoining the main house suited everyone as a gathering space for eating, drinking, and socializing—until the sun went down and the mosquitoes drove us inside. Nearby, however, was a small guest cottage with a wooden deck that had a roof over it. A local carpenter constructed a screened enclosure with a door on either side, and, with three wicker rockers, I was in business.

True, it was not the wide-screened porch of my childhood on a quiet city street shaded by maples. But the very structure of this new porch gave continuity to the cherished habit of privacy on summer afternoons. As I sit there reading or writing, or just watching the day settle as the lobstermen pick up their catch, the question is always before me: What special contribution does the American front porch make to the quality of life that the outdoor patio, as conceived for modern homes, can never provide? Answering this question forces one to acknowledge how architectural design both determines social habits and is, in turn, determined by them.

In ancient Greece, the porch, or portico, was a public area, an open gallery alongside a building with a roof supported by a colonnade. Zeno's Stoic school of philosophy derived its name from the Greek word for porch, *stoa*, after the place in Athens where he taught his disciples. The Pompeii exhibition at the American Museum of Natural History shows how open-air patios—in the form of peristyle gardens and atriums—were private areas of the house within the confines of the external walls.

Facing page: Walker Evans, *Detail of a Frame House in Ossining, New York*, 1931.

With the exception of Spanish-style houses, American homes have generally looked outward, reversing the situation. The porch, architecturally, is considered inside the boundaries of the home and usually forms part of a main entrance; the patio, with little structural form except for the flagstone or concrete paving that defines the area, is outside and not particularly private.

The porch as we know it now appeared about 1840 on the Gothic Revival cottage; as the century progressed, it became larger and more elaborate, preferably on two sides of the house to give a choice of exposure. It was covered with honeysuckle or some other lush vine to add scent on warm evenings and protect it from road dust.

In his invaluable text on the American home, *The Domesticated Americans*, Russell Lynes tells us that when screening was made with fine mesh in the 1890s, porches were further protected from mosquitoes and other insects. They already were shelters from the hot sun and inclement weather and provided the family, Lynes wrote, "with a window on the world about them and ample space for relaxation, gossip, games, and interludes of romance." The couple on the porch swing in moonlight is the image that comes to mind.

Although outdoors in the fresh air, the porch is a midpoint between inside and outside, governed still by the rules of the home but with formalities of its own. Ultimately, it is these formalities that make porch life a liberating experience by offering the benefits of privacy. When a person is alone on a porch, it is assumed he wishes not to be interrupted. Others may join him, but it is not considered polite to intrude unless he makes a sign. Similarly, though passersby may greet people on a porch, they will not come up without being invited. The ability to choose whether to be alone or to be sociable gives one's time a higher value. The porch offers delicious isolation in conjunction with nature or an awareness of others, particularly where porches are close together and near the front paving-line.

On the screened porch of my childhood, I could look into all the porches up and down the street and hear, above the sound of crickets, the murmur of voices. When the streetlights came on, there was a magical quality that seemed to link all of us night-watchers. Sitting still that way for a long time, and usually unseen behind the screens. I would observe the smallest details, which for me added drama to my neighbors' lives. What was revealed to me there, as I sat on the porch, added to my experience of life.

Porches were not restricted to private homes; they were also a main feature of those enormous wooden structures, the resort hotels. Here is how Henry James described one at Newport, Rhode Island, in *An International*

Episode: "In front was a gigantic veranda, upon which an army might have encamped—a vast wooden terrace, with a roof as lofty as the nave of a cathedral. Here . . . American society . . . was distributed over the measureless expanse . . . and appeared to consist largely of pretty young girls, dressed as if for a *fête champêtre*, swaying to and fro in rocking chairs."

So highly do we value the porch and the lifestyle that went with it that even though the porch itself has been in decline, the "porch look" has survived inside the house. Wicker furniture has become increasingly expensive and is used everywhere in a way unheard of in the porch era.

That era waned after 1910. The decline of the porch coincided with the advent of the automobile, which made it both easier for people to go out and noisier on the streets. At this point, many porches became glassed-in sun parlors or were removed.

In suburban communities, so dependent on the automobile, life revolves more around the back of the house. As meals became central to sociability— an emphasis the porch era did very well without—dining moved outside in the summer, onto an area near the kitchen called the patio or terrace. And then cooking moved outside, too, and passed into the male domain.

Even though it may be carefully landscaped, because the patio has little or no structural definition or boundary it is an outdoor public space subject to another standard of behavior. Anyone sitting alone on a patio is fair game; it is assumed that he is available to anyone passing by. Patio life, with its stress on family recreation that often involves complicated equipment, like that for barbecues, may lack spontaneity. And because it is an unprotected area, patio furnishings must be covered or put away. All this, along with the insects, makes patios a great deal of trouble. They are not for me.

Two plays shown on public television this year illustrate my point. The Long Wharf Theater's production of *Ah, Wilderness!* used an actual front porch, although Eugene O'Neill's stage directions only imply its presence on the other side of a screen door. At the end of the play, most of which takes place on the Fourth of July, the young hero goes out on the porch alone to contemplate an evening that is for him momentous. Respecting his privacy, his parents advance only to the screen door, but no farther, to gaze at the moonlight.

The other example is British: the third part of Alan Ayckbourn's *The Norman Conquests*, called *Round and Round the Garden*. A seemingly endless series of conversations by various combinations of characters takes place on a patio-like area near the house. The point is made that no one is allowed to be alone for long.

This porch story does not have a sad ending. At a time when postmodern architects are rediscovering valuable aspects of the traditional house, porches are again in evidence, particularly in quiet areas with attractive views. A pair of shingle beach houses by Venturi & Rauch at Nantucket, Massachusetts, for example, has covered porches facing the bay.

And porches that have survived are now being restored. On East 92nd Street in Manhattan, there are still two wooden houses with porches set cheek by jowl, remnants of an earlier era when New Yorkers, too, sat outside in the evenings. As I walk by them these early summer days, they touch off an image of another two houses I know—two plain white ones on a rise, overlooking a bay dotted with islands, in a town called Sunset, in Maine. Every nice evening now, their residents are sure to be sitting out on the porches in black rocking chairs, silhouetted against the white. They are satisfied spectators of an annual display: the sun going down over the water on the longest days of the year.

New York Times, June 28, 1979

One

Landscape Architects
and Designers

Designing Women: In-Depth View
of Twentieth-Century Women Landscape Designers

WHEN EDITH WHARTON went abroad in 1902 to write *Italian Villas and Their Gardens,* she felt she was better known for her knowledge of seventeenth- and eighteenth-century architecture than for her novels. Reading this work gives the sense of how the American eye perceived the Italian garden and translated it selectively into the American estate garden. "In the modern revival of gardening," Wharton wrote, "the garden-lover should not content himself with a vague enjoyment of old Italian gardens, but should try to extract from them principles which may be applied at home."

One who followed her advice quite literally was her niece, the landscape gardener Beatrix Farrand, who took meticulous notes in her travels abroad and used these motifs and others of her own in the 176 landscapes she designed between 1897 and 1950. One of the twelve founding members of the American Society of Landscape Architects in 1899, she is the acknowledged dean of women landscape architects. From her New York office, she set a pattern professionally for the generation of women landscape designers who followed and attained a kind of celebrity status during the 1920s and 1930s as they traveled around the country designing estate gardens and public projects. Despite this fact, very little mention has been made of their work in the standard histories of landscape architecture.

Along with Farrand, many of these women were influenced by the writings and gardens of Gertrude Jekyll, the English landscape gardener, and they adhered to her theories on natural gardens and the compatibility of color and

Facing page: Hervé Abbadie, *50 Avenue Montaigne, Paris.*

texture and how to use color like a wash in an Impressionist painting, by gradual changes in shade rather than abrupt contrasts. (In 1948, Farrand, who had met Gertrude Jekyll on her travels, purchased her papers from the Massachusetts Horticultural Society, and they now reside along with Farrand's archive at the College of Environmental Design, University of California, Berkeley.)

Many of Farrand's most ambitious commissions went on for decades. In the East, two of these have been maintained in the intended style: Dumbarton Oaks, in Washington, D.C., formerly the home of Mr. and Mrs. Robert Bliss and now part of Harvard University, and Mr. and Mrs. John D. Rockefeller, Jr.'s Eyrie Garden on Mount Desert Island in Maine. The Dumbarton Oaks garden is the more architectural and European in influence, with its walls and stairways joining intimate terraced gardens—each with a different floral motif—to various fountains and pools.

On the other hand, the Abby Aldrich Rockefeller 1930 Eyrie Garden was specifically designed for summer. In the midst of moss-laden woods, a Chinese wall surrounds secluded woodland settings for sculpture from the Far East and, in contrast, a central, rectangular sunken flower garden, a Maine interpretation of Jekyll's style taking advantage of the brilliant seaside hues of annuals and perennials.

Because of her expertise in architectural design and horticulture, Farrand brought to each plan the specific balance required for the terrain and climate. The plant materials she worked with were usually indigenous to the region, and she selected trees, shrubs, and vines for shades of greens, autumnal reds, and seasonal blooms, and for the texture of leaves. Her designs began with formal elements that eventually merged at the edges with natural landscapes that were selectively planned for effect. She believed that formality gave the illusion of space to small properties; for large ones, she introduced a studied asymmetry: although there were strong axes, where one most expected resolution in the design, there would, instead, be subtle dissolution. In the same fashion, formal terraced enclosures would open up to natural landscapes, as at Dumbarton Oaks, where woodlands were cleared to reveal the wild North Vista beyond.

Farrand took into consideration the taste of her clients, as is evidenced by her voluminous correspondence, in particular her letters to J. P. Morgan's office during the years she landscaped the grounds of the J. Pierpont Morgan Library in New York City. While only remnants of scraggly wisteria still grow on the wooden posts linked by chains just north of the library, the intended effect of wisteria festooned along chains linking columns garlandlike is still maintained to perfection at Dumbarton Oaks. This technique of using ornamental vines as complements to architecture was a hallmark of her work, especially at Princeton and Yale, where her wall gardens on university buildings enhanced the architecture with the warmth associated with the Ivy League.

Unlike a building, whose construction may eventually be seen as complete, a garden on paper becomes a garden in reality only after a period of growth and maturity and from then on requires continual maintenance and restoration to retain the original form and scale. So crucial to design was the control of maintenance that Farrand billed her clients in two ways: accounts payable in advance for gardeners' and nurseries' bills, and a periodic retainer for herself as overseer of design and maintenance.

As Farrand and other women landscape architects hired women as draftsmen and assistants, the need for professional studies became imperative. This led to the founding of the Cambridge School of Architecture and Landscape Architecture for Women, established in 1915 by two Harvard professors, the institution with which the school eventually merged in 1942. The curriculum was distinguished by a balance between architecture and horticulture in the belief that an integrated design depended on form as well as on texture and color—a balance not always achieved in current training. Despite the difficulty women had in finding positions—the assumption being that either they disrupted office morale or could not supervise construction—by 1930, 83 percent of the Cambridge graduates were engaged professionally.

Acknowledging the success of her generation of women landscape architects, Ellen Biddle Shipman told a reporter in 1938: "Until women took up landscaping, gardening in this country was at its lowest ebb. The renaissance was due largely to the fact that women, instead of working over their boards, used plants as if they were painting pictures and as an artist would." Exaggerated as this may sound, the women proved themselves and their talents adaptable and expanded into parkway, industrial park, and housing development design when the lucrative residential work was on the wane. Their training in design and engineering even qualified the next generation for military service in World War II, where they worked in cartography, camouflage, and geographic model making.

Shipman's own talents in both engineering and horticulture were evident in her design for the seven-mile lakeshore boulevard in Grosse Pointe, Michigan, which featured a combination of flowering trees, willows, and evergreens to vary the colors and shade of green according to the season. Her own office comprised five or six women and one construction man always out on the job. She designed mostly American- or English-style gardens on an intimate scale and, like Farrand, kept in her charge, as much as possible, the gardens she planned in order to monitor their growth. She moved extensively through the South, particularly in Texas, where she created estate gardens during the oil-boom years. Outstanding among her plans was Longue Vue Gardens in New Orleans, with its oak-tree allée leading up to the house. Her influence was wide, and one contemporary landscape designer, Rachel Lambert Mellon, who sought her advice more than once, prizes Shipman's handwritten directions for making grass steps.

Marion Cruger Coffin, a 1904 Massachusetts Institute of Technology graduate, also met Jekyll on her travels and proceeded to interpret her ideas in the fifty estate gardens she designed during her career, including Winterthur, the du Pont estate in Wilmington, Delaware, and many on Long Island. Essentially Coffin's estate grounds used circulation routes and sight lines to form a plan of grand vistas, intimate walkways, and gradual descents to draw one away from the house for an aesthetic experience in controlled nature that did not relate directly to the domestic environs. One architectural element leads to another—a trellis of Ionic columns, to a rose arbor walk, to French parterres—until one arrives back at the house. On a large scale, Coffin applied her circulation routes to the campus of the University of Delaware, equivalent in scope to the work of landscaping the great grounds of country houses in England.

Annette Hoyt Flanders succeeded in reducing the scale of estate garden designs to make them compatible with the smaller gardens that were her specialty, such as the one she completed in 1929 for fellow Smith College alumnae Ellen Holt and Elizabeth H. Webster. "A momentary pause," she called it, amidst the grandiose mountain scenery in Tryon, North Carolina. A white-and-green garden, it resembles Vita Sackville-West's white garden at Sissinghurst Castle. The plan called for three symmetrical rectangular beds of myrtle surrounded by an "ivy hedge" and, along the borders, plantings of white dogwood, white azalea, and white gardenia—all within an eighty-foot-long terrace on a mountain slope. Flanders traveled so widely that it was not always possible for her to return to the small out-of-the way gardens she designed, and so she admonished Webster, "Remember, Betty, this is architecture; it must be kept to scale." Webster maintained it until she was well over a hundred years old.

Flanders completed her own studies in landscape architecture at the University of Illinois in 1928 and received the gold medal of the Architectural

League of New York in 1932 for an eighty-five-acre pink-and-green garden in the French style for Mr. and Mrs. Charles. E. F. McCann at Oyster Bay, Long Island. In addition to residential work, she specialized in industrial plants, recreational development, and exhibition gardens. She lectured widely on gardening, and when she moved her office from the Sherry Building in New York back to Milwaukee, her hometown, in 1940, she conducted a landscape school on the premises.

In October 1981, Wave Hill, a New York City cultural institution in Riverdale, sponsored a conference, "American Women & Gardens, 1915–1945," as the inaugural event in its new American Garden History program headed by landscape designer and historian Leslie Rose Close. The conference was accompanied by an exhibition featuring the architectural drawings and planting plans of prominent women landscape architects of that period who specialized in implementing the look of the private estate. Also included were vintage photographs of the gardens, many by the prominent photographer Mattie Edwards Hewitt.

The Wave Hill exhibition, a discriminating selection of documentary evidence, accurately conveyed the dimensions of these careers—and successful ones they were. It also underscored the problem of there being no repository for these valuable plans, most of which come from the original clients or their descendants. Because much of the available material had been stored in damp cellars, it was too decomposed to be included.

In addition to being a source of ideas for contemporary study, the preservation of drawings and archival material is essential to recapture the original form and scale of older gardens that now barely resemble their originals. For example, one 1920s photograph in the exhibition portrayed an East Hampton garden, designed by New Yorker Ruth Bramley Dean, which gained notoriety years later as the dilapidated Grey Gardens of Edith Bouvier Beale and her daughter. Working with the photograph, the current owners, Benjamin Bradlee and Sally Quinn of Washington, D.C., are now restoring the garden's pergola according to Dean's design.

Public designs were also highlighted in the exhibition as part of the repertory of these women, one of whom, Marjorie Sewell Cautley, designed a planting plan for one of the early "garden city" developments in Radburn, New Jersey. Exact specifications on her 1931 drawing of the entrance perspective for the Phipps Court Garden Apartments in Long Island City demonstrate her concern for balance and scale: "Tree lilacs, 10 feet tall; specimen elms, 40 feet high."

Cornell graduate Helen Bullard (not represented in the exhibition) was a landscape architect who worked almost exclusively in the public domain. During her five years with the Long Island State Park Commission, she designed flower gardens around the Jones Beach bathhouses. This position and her work as director of the annual program for flower planting in the city's parks—300,000 bulbs for spring alone—prepared her for participation in planning one of the biggest commissions around New York at that time, the 1939 World's Fair grounds. She realized that "with modern buildings we cannot depend on classic forms," meaning straight beds and pattern gardens. Instead, she elaborated in a 1938 interview, "We have no precedents to follow, but, in general, the plan will be designed in directional lines to give the feeling of motion." The color scheme for the fair was red, yellow, and blue, and the flower beds were planted to contrast with the nearby buildings. And again, it took horticultural expertise to select both well-known varieties and exotic plants for the long-blooming season of a Long Island summer.

Women were equally successful on the West Coast, where the California landscape designer Florence Yoch, working with her associate Lucille Council, was changing her style from making exact copies of Mediterranean gardens in the 1920s to more abstract forms in the 1930s. In 1952, she designed the courtyard for Robinson's department store on Wiltshire Boulevard in Beverly Hills, which is still a lush background for glamorous fashion shows.

George Cukor, the film director, remembers her as "a most distinguished woman" whom he greatly esteemed as "the artist who cut my garden right out of the side of a hill." So much did he admire her work that he commissioned her to build a complete Italian Renaissance garden in the studio as the set for his 1936 MGM film of *Romeo and Juliet*. The tall cypresses and blossoming trees, the planted urns and the reflecting pool, the balcony in the distance—it endures forever on the silver screen, no maintenance at all, and yet always fresh and always in pale moonlight.

Venerable as these women were, they and their golden era must not be glamorized at the expense of those working now, who have followed their lead. Alice Recknagel Ireys, a 1936 graduate of the Cambridge School who also studied with Flanders, concluded the Wave Hill conference. In speaking of her own work, she described design principles that have formed the critical transition in American garden history between the great estate era and the explosion of suburban and town gardens after World War II. By scaling down and reconfiguring broad terraces, flower walks, and parterres, she confers on modest properties the same sense of privilege and gracious outdoor living that had once been the preserve of country estates. In her designs, she makes a great virtue of the serpentine line to give the illusion of length and breadth.

Vistas and walkways now relate directly to the house itself, and terraced areas are created for outdoor living. Swimming pool design was the innovation of the 1940s. She predicts that, with the two-income family, property sizes will increase again, only these will feature the natural look of woodland walks and dry streams.

In general, she believes the public now knows what a landscape architect is, and most of her clients come to her by word of mouth. According to Ireys, a landscape architect in residential work must have these five qualities: imagination, an understanding of family patterns, sensitivity to detail, a sense of color, and a love of growing things. Hers was the voice of continuity.

Metropolis, December 1982

Beatrix Farrand and *The Bulletins of Reef Point Gardens*

"WRITTEN WORDS and illustrations outlive many plantations." This was Beatrix Farrand's farsighted view in 1955 when she acknowledged that her cherished gardens at Reef Point could no longer be maintained to her satisfaction. *The Bulletins of Reef Point Gardens* essentially bears out the truth of that statement. Written by Farrand and her colleagues over a period of ten years, the bulletins preserve what she referred to finally as the less important "out-of-door phase" of her gardens. One of the premier landscape gardeners of the twentieth century, Beatrix Farrand (1872–1959) created at Reef Point, her family's summer residence, a private showcase of native and naturalized plantings that evolved into the only botanic garden then in the state of Maine.

The idea for the Reef Point Gardens bulletins originated with her husband, Max Farrand, a distinguished author and professor of constitutional history. With his "disciplined scholar's mind," wrote Beatrix Farrand, he "felt that publication was an essential part of the gardens' work." Prior to his death in 1945, he even suggested a list of topics and approved a selection of material submitted, and the Max Farrand Memorial Fund became the official publisher of the bulletins. Along with Reef Point's extensive horticultural library, documents collection, and herbarium, the bulletins became an equal partner in the Gardens' mission. Distributed to botanic gardens, arboreta, and libraries worldwide and sold to local visitors for ten cents a copy, they were shaped over the years to contain the essence of the entire landscape. At the time of their publication, everyone associated with Reef Point Gardens had high hopes for its future as a public garden and educational center, organized specifically to expose students of landscape architecture to horticultural expertise and design. Now the bulletins are what remain of a horticultural adventure that came to an end in 1955.

In addition to the landscape gardener herself, four other writers are represented in this collection. Amy Magdalene Garland (1899–1996), who became the chief horticulturist of Reef Point, was born in Bishop's Waltham in Hampshire, England. She arrived in New York City just after World War I to work for Farrand's mother, Mary Cadwalader Jones, as a domestic in her Greenwich Village house. In time, she married Lewis A. Garland, the handyman and chauffeur at Reef Point, and developed into a trusted collaborator in maintaining and documenting the plant collection.

Robert Whiteley Patterson (1905–1988), a 1927 graduate of Harvard College, returned to the university in 1932 to study landscape architecture at the Graduate School of Design. He first went to Maine in 1934 as a designer and planner for Acadia National Park and met Beatrix Farrand at that time. Later, he maintained an office at Reef Point as her associate.

Marion Ida Spaulding (1908–1994) was a landscape architect who completed her degree at the Rhode Island School of Design in 1947. She worked at Reef Point for long periods between 1946 and 1952 to create the herbarium and map the gardens into sections for record-keeping purposes. Later, settling in New Hampshire, she became the resident designer at Mt. Gunstock Nursery in Gilford and was also associated with the Laconia Housing and Redevelopment Authority.

And finally, Kenneth A. Beckett (b. 1929), a young Englishman, spent six months as a skilled gardener and propagator at Reef Point in 1954 after receiving his Royal Horticultural Society Diploma from the Wisley School of Horticulture. He eventually became a prominent garden writer in Britain, and among his more than forty publications is the popular *Royal Horticultural Society Encylopaedia of House and Conservatory Plants*. Now living in Norfolk, he looks back on the two bulletins he wrote for Farrand as his first ambitious work.

Although the name Reef Point visually connotes an isolated property projecting out into one of the myriad bays along the rugged coast of Maine, the original two-acre plot purchased in 1882 by Frederic Rhinelander Jones, Beatrix's father, was actually located in the middle of Bar Harbor, the then newly fashionable summer community on Mount Desert Island. Expanded by later purchases to six acres, Reef Point lies between Hancock Street and Atlantic Avenue, two side streets that run perpendicular to the Shore Path. Like Newport's oceanside Cliff Walk, Bar Harbor's Shore Path is a long public walkway that skirts the rocky coastal ledges and overlooks Frenchman Bay and beyond to the procession of hump-backed islands called the Porcupines.

In a line with other rambling Shore Path cottages—as Maine summer houses are called after the early hotel guest cottages—the Reef Point cottage was built in 1883, one of twenty-two buildings designed in Bar Harbor by the Boston firm of Rotch & Tilden, which specialized in a combination of flat log and shingle construction with turrets, high gables, and dormer windows as well as wide verandas. By the time the house was completed, Beatrix's parents were already separated and the property signed over to her mother. Although the land is now divided among five residents, the configuration of the perimeter has remained surprisingly intact. To all appearances, it is possible to walk to the end of Hancock Street in the silence of a summer afternoon and stand in front of the granite gate pillars and finials of Reef Point under towering white spruce as though nothing had changed. A curved entrance drive leads to the picturesque Gardener's Cottage, one of the few buildings to survive the demolition of the gardens. A short stroll along the lichen-covered, white cedar boundary fence on the Shore Path gives a sense of the dramatic views across the water, which determined the axes of the fanned-out garden paths.

Preserved among Beatrix Farrand's papers at the University of California, Berkeley, is a bound journal from her early twenties with the printed title *Book of Gardening,* in which she recorded from October 10, 1893, to May 31, 1895, her observations about horticulture and garden design both in America and abroad, mostly in Italy and Germany. In addition to noting her critical impressions of a visit to the grounds at Fairsted, Frederick Law Olmsted's office and residence in Brookline, Massachusetts, and of gardens at the 1893 World Columbian Exposition in Chicago, she expressed in early entries her appreciation of the details that made Reef Point and Maine a magical place and the center of her life.

"The scarlet trumpet honeysuckle over the porch has small bunches of scarlet berries all over it which make it as effective as in the blooming season." This description of what she later called "vertical flower beds" is of a piece with the bulletin she wrote sixty years later on climbing plants. Tutored privately, Beatrix Farrand developed early on a keen sense of observation and taste as well as a distinct writing style that rendered her ideas and opinions as clearly as if she had drawn them in a detailed plan. Like many Maine summer residents, she returned to view the autumn color in a ritual not without its melancholy side. Among pressed leaves and sketches for the alignment of trees, she wrote, "I noticed the coloring of the leaves more beautiful than ever . . . this season before we left." Despite Maine's harsh climate, nature always conspires to make one's day of departure the most inviting.

Since the majority of Farrand's voluminous writings are in the quasi-public form of reports to or correspondence with clients, these journal entries provide a rare opportunity to look over her shoulder in a private moment. Her descriptions of gardens prove to what degree observation was the foundation of her education. During the early 1890s, she was guided in this technique during her training in horticulture and landscape gardening at Harvard University's Arnold Arboretum under the tutelage of Charles Sprague Sargent, its first director. The source of Professor Sargent's oft-quoted advice to her—"make the plan fit the ground and not twist the ground to fit a plan"—is found here in the final bulletin, an autobiographical account intended as her obituary. She continued to forge links with the Arboretum over the years, frequently seeking advice on the specific identification of plants, which were carefully packed and mailed from Bar Harbor to Jamaica Plain.

In traveling abroad, Beatrix was often in the company of her aunt Edith Wharton, her father's sister, who in 1904 published her own travel impressions in the quintessential *Italian Villas and Their Gardens,* many years after her niece's journal was written. During this period, the specifics of European gardens recorded by professionals and Grand Tour travelers became the new grammar of American estate gardens as designed by Beatrix Farrand and her contemporaries. Although the divorce of Beatrix's parents may have altered the path of her life in New York society, the dynamic relationship among the three women—the vivacious mother, the daughter, and the aunt, only ten years Beatrix's senior—provided the catalyst for a secure, confident, and independent life. Being different was in a sense also liberating. Her cousin and adviser, John Lambert Cadwalader, a lawyer and founder of the New York Public Library, was also part of the family equation. His picture was placed over a mantle at Reef Point, where Beatrix Farrand once showed it to a young friend, saying, "He is the person I have been closest to in my life." Cadwalader encouraged her early on to a career in landscape gardening, which she pursued for over fifty years—completing nearly two hundred commissions—with unswerving determination and efficiency.

During the winters, until she married in 1913, Beatrix Farrand lived with her mother at 21 East 11th Street. Like the gateposts of Reef Point, the five-story brick town house with its high stoop makes real the comings and goings of that early professional life, which began in a top floor office as early as 1895. (Eventually, her office was moved to 124 East 40th Street.) Often, while she worked upstairs, Henry James was their houseguest below. "My liveliest interest attends her on her path," he once wrote in a letter to Beatrix's mother.

On April 7, 1917, Mary Cadwalader Jones signed over Reef Point to her daughter by deed of gift, and from this point on Beatrix and Max Farrand began building a personal institution that married their scholarly and horticultural interests. In reviewing any one project in her range of accomplishments (which included university campuses such as Princeton and Yale and private gardens for the Rockefellers and J. P. Morgan—and for the White House during the Woodrow Wilson administration), the researcher is always struck by the single-mindedness of the correspondence and reports, implying an exclusivity, as if nothing else could have mattered in her life at the time. But the reality is that Reef Point was the permanent underlying warp of the tapestry on which the weft of her other gardens was woven. Because their winter residence shifted from New Haven, where Max Farrand was professor of history at Yale, to San Marino, California, where he was appointed the first director of the Henry E. Huntington Library and Art Gallery, Reef Point became the main home for their libraries and art works as well as their gardens.

Like creative innovators of any century who are said to be ahead of their time, the Farrands conceived of a long-range plan for Reef Point which promoted ecological objectives that today are de rigueur for any institution concerned with land use. Founded in 1939, the Reef Point Gardens Corporation established a study center "to broaden the outlook and increase the knowledge of a small group of hand-picked students who are in training to become landscape architects." Beyond the gardens and library of Reef Point, Beatrix Farrand noted that Mount Desert Island offered other laboratories for the study of New England flora and "the ecological adaptation of plants to the environment." These included Acadia National Park, along with its issues of design and management, and the private gardens of the area, over fifty of them designed by Farrand herself.

In the history of garden design, the influence of Reef Point Gardens as a personal expression of horticultural taste and design may be compared with such other pivotal gardens as Gertrude Jekyll's Munstead Wood and William Robinson's Gravetye Manor, both of which Beatrix Farrand visited in England. It was modern in the sense that its design did not allude to any historical style but was instead an enhancement or an elaboration of the natural features of Maine, such as the native bunchberry (*Cornus canadensis*), for example, which grew in dappled sunlight at the entrance to a wood. But her gardens also possessed components necessary to a botanic garden: systematic classification of plants of a single species; an herbarium of almost eighteen hundred pressed plants, created for scientific study; and micro-environments specific to the coast of Maine, such as a bog filled with purplish pitcher-plants. With the gardens charted into sections and the plants labeled, the scientific scope of Reef Point—yielding a disciplined design with its own harmonies of color, texture, and form—was akin to those early botanic gardens founded by professors and physicians at medieval universities.

To give the illusion of a larger terrain as in eighteenth-century English landscape gardens, Farrand devised a circuit of curvilinear paths that intersected the straight axial paths radiating toward the views. Guests were conducted along a preordained route so that the gardens unfolded in a succession of experiences: the vine gardens on the house; the rose terraces with the single varieties that were her passion; the rhododendrons and laurels on the way to the vegetable enclosure with its espaliered fruit trees; the perennial beds across the turf from the rock gardens; and past the pink azaleas, holly hedges, and heathers to the bog. Surrounding these areas were stands of red and white spruce, planted in tight clusters as barriers to the severe winds, while others were allowed to grow freestanding to retain the spread of their "youthful outlines." And twin Alberta spruce, one of her signature choices, stood as sentinels at the head of the paths leading to the bay. From the shore, this skyline appeared like "the great army of the pointed firs, darkly cloaked and standing as if they waited to embark," which Maine novelist Sarah Orne Jewett described so memorably in *The Country of the Pointed Firs* (1896).

Within the gardens were certain Arts and Crafts style ornaments reflecting not so much indigenous crafts but the work of others like herself, in particular Eric Ellis Soderholtz, whose tastes were formed on European travels. Born in Sweden, Soderholtz was an architectural draftsman and photographer in Boston who had made a survey of ancient art and architecture during a Grand Tour of southern Europe. After settling near Bar Harbor in West Gouldsboro, he devised a method of fashioning classical oil jars and amphorae out of reinforced concrete that could withstand the harsh elements. Hand finished, sometimes on a wheel, with slight pigment and incised ornamentation, these dramatic containers still grace many gardens in the area. (Lunaform, a craft studio in Sullivan, Maine, carries on this technique and also reproduces Soderholtz's original designs.) Two of his oil jars were positioned on either side of the main pathway at Reef Point, and his birdbath in a bed of heather was the central feature of the lower garden. In addition to rustic benches placed strategically throughout the gardens for the views, there was one formal bench positioned under the eaves of the entryway. With multiple spindles turned on a lathe, its elaborate structure blended with the architecture of the house and its vine-covered walls. In reproduction, it is known as the Reef Point bench.

Although their lives were very different, Farrand created a seaside garden that can be seen in direct relation to the flower beds Celia Thaxter cultivated next to her porch on Appledore Island off the southern coast of Maine. (In Farrand's files is a note she once scribbled to herself about Thaxter's 1894 book, *My Island Garden*.) Farrand may have crisscrossed the country and traveled abroad to design gardens for clients on a grand scale, with walled enclosures and formal garden rooms linked by naturalized plantings to woodland and wilderness areas beyond. But at Reef Point, she did what she loved most by creating a Maine garden of apparent simplicity where families of plants laid out in drifts meshed with others in a studied asymmetry. In addition to designing and constantly rearranging the plantings, she planned every aspect of the daily life at Reef Point, preparing for the big day when the establishment would stand on its own. The truth is that the pinnacle reached at Reef Point during this period was its great moment.

The annual reports she presented to her board of directors are the behind-the-scenes companion narrative to the bulletins. They included horticultural developments, the titles of books acquired for the library, and lists of seeds received from botanic gardens around the world as well as of plants culled from wilderness areas such as Mount Katahdin in Maine. In them, she never failed to thank the Garlands, her secretary, Isabelle Stover, and her French personal maid and expert flower arranger, Clementine Walter, who greased the wheels of an enterprise that valued the perfection of the domestic arrangements as much as the gardens.

The influence of Beatrix Farrand's life is still fresh in Maine, where the younger generation in her time have become leaders in the community, one that is still divided in a friendly way between local residents and summer people. David Rockefeller, who was a child when Farrand designed his mother's garden in Seal Harbor, recalls her as "the epitome of a New England grande dame in a long dark dress and hat—tall, erect, austere, sure of herself, opinionated and frightening to most people." And he remembers walking in her heather garden and how beautiful and completely unpretentious it was. The Rockefeller family still houses the four-wheeled buckboard carriage David's father, John D. Jr., drove through Acadia National Park with Farrand at his side. Beginning in the late 1920s, they made these excursions together to inspect the plantings and the design of the bridges along the fifty-seven miles of carriage roads that were his imaginative contribution to the park. Farrand responded to these outings with closely typed "Road Notes," offering suggestions in her usual no-nonsense language, with the names of appropriate trees and plants—sweet fern, wild roses, sumac, goldenrod, and bush blueberry—listed along with directions for how and where to plant them: "On the south and west sides of the road opposite the view young spruce should be used, and later on, as pitch pine is available. The north slope of the hill could be gradually planted with these giving a splendid Chinese effect to this superb northern prospect. These pitch pine will never intrude on the view any more than they do on the Shore Drive where they add a great picturesqueness to the position (November 4, 1930)."

Throughout these notes, she urged Rockefeller "to vary the road planting in height and quality and type of material, as these varieties are usually shown in natural growth." In a sense, like the eighteenth-century British landscape designer William Kent, Farrand leaped the fence of Reef Point and saw the whole landscape as a native garden. When her directions were not followed, she expressed displeasure, particularly when trees were planted in straight lines. Nevertheless she wrote to Rockefeller in 1933, "Again I want to thank you for the way in which you are so consistently upholding my judgments and helping with the ease of carrying on the work to which I look forward as one of the great pleasures of the Island days." He, on the other hand, found pleasure in the results: "For the first time [I] could understand why you are so partial to wild cherries and pear trees. The blossoms certainly are lovely."

Every six months, Farrand forwarded a detailed accounting of the number of drives and days in the field in addition to office consultations and stenography. With a few exceptions, the amount owed was always the same: "No charge." Rockefeller, of course, was deeply appreciative and enjoyed their teamwork "in the public interest" for the "beautification of Acadia National Park." "I do not know when I have spent an entire half day in so carefree and enjoyable a manner as last Sunday afternoon," he wrote in May 1929 early on in their long road correspondence. "To feel that I could talk as frankly as I did about park matters, with the perfect assurance that nothing that was said would go further, added much to my satisfaction and sense of freedom in the talk."

The collaboration was a close and dedicated one. Toward the end of the correspondence in 1941, and at the season's end, the two tried unsuccessfully to make a rendezvous for a final carriage ride up Day Mountain. Rockefeller responded with the courtly congeniality that characterized their rapport. "What ever happens to the world," he wrote, "Day Mountain will be standing next summer and I much hope we can drive up it then." Throughout their long association, however, neither abandoned a formality and reserve instinctive to them both. One August, Farrand wrote: "It was only with what I thought great self-control that I passed you the other day on your way homeward from an evidently brisk walk. I wanted to stop and say how do you do to you and to tell you what a pleasure it has been to work over the lodges and their surroundings [in the park]." Horticulturists on the island have observed what may still be traces of her handiwork in such selections as the American bittersweet (*Celastrus scandens*) around the bridges that serve as overpasses for the carriage roads, now being restored after years of neglect.

Involving though their work in Acadia was, their main project together, which entailed hundreds more letters written between 1926 and 1950, was the garden Farrand designed for Rockefeller's wife, Abby Aldrich Rockefeller, in a spruce forest below The Eyrie, their hilltop house in Seal Harbor. One of Farrand's major designs, The Eyrie garden is still in family hands. Although Farrand worked directly with Abby Rockefeller, the correspondence confirming verbal arrangements was always with her husband. In 1921, the couple had traveled to China for the opening of the Peking Union Medical College, which was supported by the Rockefeller Foundation. Culturally, the voyage was a galvanizing event in their life. Yellowing newspaper articles in a scrapbook at the Rockefeller Archive Center show the tiled pagoda-style roof of the college entrance, which confirms the influence of this architecture on the structures of the garden. Inside a pink stucco wall coped with yellow tiles from the Forbidden City, the contours and harmonies of mossy woodland settings for sculptures from the Far East are juxtaposed with a Maine interpretation of an English flower garden in brilliant seaside hues. Passing from cool green paths through a Moon Gate into a two-level walled enclosure of concentric rectangular borders provides one of the richest garden experiences in America today. The Abby Aldrich Rockefeller Garden, as it is now called, continued under the stewardship of David and Peggy Rockefeller. They reinstated the central greensward in its present form, and Peggy Rockefeller monitored the borders imaginatively by introducing new perennials and annuals.

Although no longer as complete as the Rockefellers', the garden Farrand designed at The Haven in Northeast Harbor for Gerrish H. Milliken and his wife, Agnes, beginning in 1925, possesses a special aura today. Agnes Milliken was a close friend of Beatrix Farrand and consulted with her on matters concerning Reef Point; it was she who aided Farrand in the acquisition of Gertrude Jekyll's papers in the late 1940s. In designing the Millikens' garden, Farrand incorporated, more than in any other private commission, many of the themes that made Reef Point so distinctive. Looking out today over a field of purple heathers to glimpses of blue water between stands of pointed firs—and to white sails that appear and disappear behind the trees—one gets an exact sense of what she sought as perfection for Maine. Now owned by Gerrish H. Milliken, Jr., and his wife, Phoebe, the garden comes the closest to how Reef Point itself must have appeared in its prime. Along the entrance path to the rambling shingle house, there is another Reef Point touch: borders of heliotrope by the porch and white nicotiana along the path, the former with a heavenly fragrance by day, the latter radiant by night. Like her own terraces of native single roses at Reef Point, there is a long rose path leading to an open terrace and a vine-covered pergola with modified Tuscan columns, where Agnes Milliken would take tea in the afternoons. These pergolas also became a characteristic feature of Farrand's gardens on Mount Desert Island.

Following Max Farrand's death in 1945, his wife began taking measures to adapt Reef Point architecturally for its future. Robert Patterson was the architect, and in 1946 he completed the Gardener's Cottage for the Garlands, employing many of Rotch & Tilden's decorative motifs from the main house. Beatrix Farrand describes other renovations and additions in the bulletins themselves, including the new Garden Club House given by the Garden Club of Mount Desert, of which Farrand was the founder in August 1923. By the summer of 1947, the establishment was at a peak of activity: books and papers were catalogued daily; herbarium specimens were collected and pressed; new species arrived to be recorded and planted; and, of course, visitors were coming on a regular basis. In the end, over fifty thousand people visited Reef Point on its open days. On one occasion, young sailors from a warship in dock came for tea and cakes in the garden. Despite the depression and World War II, Reef Point survived in a mode that combined the most advanced thinking in scientific and educational techniques with a kind of gracious Edwardian summer life.

Donald E. Smith, a gardener at Reef Point during summers in the early 1950s while he was a horticulture student at the University of Maine, recalls the routines as everyone did his or her tasks in the garden overseen by Amy Garland. Often Farrand surveyed the scene from her balcony. "She always wore Harris tweeds even in the summer and walked around the gardens with a cane and a shawl over her shoulders," he said. "She was very erect, very pleasant though stern, but we got along fine." Clementine Walter was the first one out in the early morning to hear the bird calls, and even Farrand herself kept track of the birds' nests, especially a mockingbird's in the Alberta spruce. After his early training, Smith went on to work at Dumbarton Oaks, where he eventually became superintendent. Now in retirement, he lives in his wife's family's house down the street from Reef Point.

The event that caused a slow but not so subtle transition in this way of life came suddenly on October 17, 1947, when a fire that began smoldering in a cranberry bog spread fiercely with the wind to devastate the town of Bar Harbor and many of its elegant summer cottages. Although Reef Point was not affected physically, and daily life appeared to go on as usual, the character of the town began to change. Visitors more and more came as tourists in search of amusement rather than with notebooks in hand to look and learn. At that time, Farrand wrote in her report to the board, "Those who see the garden's visitors from the windows occasionally wish that fashionable scarlet coats would not pause too long minutes in front of lavender and pale pink flowers—but mercifully fashions change."

The Garlands, too, were getting older and becoming less active. In her search for someone with experience who could take over Amy Garland's responsibilities in the garden, Farrand sought the advice of, among others, Thomas H. Everett, the chief horticulturist of the New York Botanical Garden. Everett, an Englishman, was on a speaking engagement at Wisley when he met Kenneth Beckett and subsequently recommended him to Farrand. Beckett came to Reef Point for six months during the season of 1954; and in the annual report of that period, Farrand praised him for his excellent propagating work in the greenhouse. But he never felt at home in Bar Harbor and eventually returned to England. During her California stay the following winter, Farrand, then eighty-two, took realistic stock of her position. Costs were mounting, no guarantees could be made on a perpetual tax exemption or on the status of Reef Point Gardens as a foundation until after her death (Bar Harbor had lost much of its tax base as a result of the fire), and finally, and even more urgent, she feared the deterioration of the gardens.

From Farrand's perspective in the early spring of 1955, if Reef Point Gardens with its ephemeral nature could not be maintained to her standards, she would rather see it destroyed. As usual, she made the courageous decision and took action immediately by writing to Robert Patterson to set the wheels in motion. Some of her colleagues, including the lawyers, were incredulous, but Farrand was as determined now to put an end to the Gardens as she had been to create it. Together, the house and the gardens were sold for $6,500 to Patterson, who maintained a desperate hope that the gardens could be saved. There was no way of knowing then that Reef Point Gardens was ahead of its time by only fifteen or twenty years. A renewed interest in landscape architecture and environmental issues—the greening of America—got a fresh start in the 1970s on the heels of the consciousness-raising Earth Day celebrations. And the first major review of Farrand's work came in May 1980 at a symposium at Dumbarton Oaks.

Having made her decision, Farrand began to disperse possessions to friends. The young David Rockefellers, who badly needed furniture for their new houses, went to see her. "We told her of our plight," recalled David Rockefeller, "and she gave us first crack. We took almost 90 percent of what she had." Now scattered among many homes, they have become treasured mementos of the family's long friendship. Several pieces of fine glassware and furniture also went to the Milliken family. (And just how fine they were was proven with time. One Milliken daughter finally decided to sell the Philadelphia Chippendale wing chair with elaborate hairy paw feet which she had stored in her barn for many years. When it came on the block at Sotheby's in January 1987, it went for $2.75 million, thereby setting a record for the most expensive piece of furniture ever sold at auction. It had been ordered from the maker Thomas Affleck by General John Cadwalader, Farrand's ancestor, and the carving was attributed to James Reynolds.)

The heart of Reef Point, as Farrand called it, was the 2,700-volume horticultural library, along with its collection of documents and garden prints, and the herbarium. When Farrand acquired the archives of Gertrude Jekyll, with over three hundred garden plans, plant lists, and photograph albums, she called her "one of England's best horticultural writers and artist gardeners of the last hundred years." The Reef Point collection also included a donation made by Mary Rutherfurd Kay, a Connecticut garden architect, of her own notes, books, and valuable slides. Farrand was painfully aware that even were the collections to remain in the house, the conditions were damp and the facilities not fireproof. During the forties and early fifties, after receiving an honorary degree from Smith College in 1936, she donated to the Smith library over three hundred horticulture and landscape architecture books and many volumes each of more than one hundred periodicals in the same fields. One rare book, in John Evelyn's 1693 English translation, was *The Compleat Gard'ner; or, Directions for cultivating and right ordering of fruit-gardens and kitchen-gardens* by Jean de La Quintinye, the gardener of Louis XIV's kitchen garden at Versailles. In addition, she gave the college almost eight hundred literary titles, among which Jane Austen figured prominently. From 1932 to 1942, the Cambridge School of Architecture and Landscape Architecture in Cambridge, Massachusetts, was an affiliated graduate school of Smith College.

As the future home for her collections, Farrand sought an institution offering courses in "landscape art" and discovered that there were relatively few. Finally, to begin what she called their "new life under other skies and with wider opportunities for use," she selected the Department of Landscape Architecture at the University of California, Berkeley. The College of Environmental Design Documents Collection is located in Wurster Hall, the headquarters of the Departments of Architecture and Landscape Architecture. Today, the life in this building is extremely active and exciting, with a constant parade of student projects and exhibitions pinned to the lobby walls. Here, in an educational institution where young people address environmental issues, the heart of Reef Point beats on.

After she sold Reef Point, Charles K. Savage, a member of Farrand's board, came forward with an imaginative and ambitious solution for the future not of the gardens per se but of the rare plant collections, which he considered the finest in Maine. Savage was the owner of the Asticou Inn in Northeast Harbor. He was a special person in an unusual position. Deprived of a college education by the early death of his father, who was innkeeper before him, he sought every opportunity to educate himself in art, music, and literature. His aesthetic interests and ambitions were recognized by the intellectuals among the summer residents, who lent him books and invited him to cultural events. Finally, he developed a talent for landscape design by reading widely in the field and becoming knowledgeable in all its aspects.

In a paper simply titled "The Moving of Reef Point Plant Material to Asticou," Savage proposed to document and then transport the Reef Point collection of azaleas, rhododendrons, laurels, and heathers, along with other plant materials, across the island to a site around a reflecting pond across the road from the Asticou Inn. Noting that "many features of the natural scenery of Mount Desert have similarities to the Japanese, particularly in the parts of the island where bold ledges, rocks and pitch pines prevail," he was inspired to create a stroll garden in the spirit of the famous water garden at Katsura Imperial Villa in Kyoto, which had "the same low stone slab bridge, mown lawns to the water's edge, azaleas and pines." This proposal was made to John D. Rockefeller, Jr., who paid the greatest tribute to Beatrix Farrand, his old friend and adviser, by supporting this project with an initial $5,000 to purchase the plants and with additional funds during the next few years to create the Asticou Azalea Garden and enhance the terraces and gardens at Thuya Lodge. Savage was already involved in developing the Thuya property above the Asticou Inn. This had been the home, library, and garden of the Boston landscape architect Joseph Henry Curtis, who had died in 1928.

Charles Savage and his sixteen-year-old daughter, Mary Ann, made many trips together to Reef Point with a book of paint samples and colored pencils to list the azaleas and record their colors with a color chip or pencil mark. In one letter to Rockefeller he reported, "A great deal of my thought has been given to the arrangement of the trees and shrubs in this garden—mass, line and color, as well as the progression of azalea bloom—with the hope that the effect from the road as people pass by may be, (I hope), an outstanding one." Lewis Garland chauffeured Farrand over in the dark blue Dodge every two weeks or so to view the progress of the garden, and she would get out of the car, remove her shawl, and stand to talk with Savage for awhile.

Even the Alberta spruce were brought to the new homes. At Thuya, they have retained their natural form, while at Asticou, one has been saved by expert pruning in the Japanese style. Many of the perennials were also planted in the Thuya garden, so that together the two places have become the successors to Reef Point in an extraordinary feat of plant preservation. In early spring, when the azaleas are in bloom, the paths in the Asticou Azalea Garden wind through clouds of pastel pinks muted by melancholy mists from the sea. But Asticou is equally beautiful in summer, with its cool sand garden inspired by Ryoan-ji, also in Kyoto, and its subtle range of greens, and in autumn with its brilliant leaf colors.

Farrand's gardens also continued in a more direct way. When the main cottage at Reef Point was dismantled (her old friend and executor, Judge Edwin R. Smith, lives on in the Gardener's Cottage), Robert Patterson incorporated entire sections of its interior into a new cottage he designed for her adjoining the farmhouse at the Garland family farm on the main road near Salisbury Cove, where Lewis and Amy Magdalene Garland had retired.

The team then stayed together, for Clementine Walter lived with Farrand in her house. The charming white clapboard cottage with peaked roofs had three major rooms—two bedrooms with a sitting room between them—that faced the back, and the tripartite rear facade reflected this arrangement. Each of the three rooms had French doors that opened onto its own section of the garden terrace. Outside the bedrooms, perennials from Reef Point were planted in rectangular beds with annuals around the edges, and heather mixed with lavender thrived along a serpentine path leading from a millstone by the sitting room door. The gardening continued, with a subdued palette of pink, lavender, and gray outside Farrand's window, and brighter colors—red, yellow, and orange—outside Clementine Walter's. The balustrade from the Reef Point vegetable garden with carved oak leaves formed an elegant barrier between the garden and the wild cherries and fields beyond.

Farrand brought all of her favorites from Reef Point, including the *Hydrangea petiolaris,* which thrives today more than ever, covering the whole back of the barn. And her beloved single roses are crammed in wherever possible. Donald Smith remembers well his visits to her at Garland Farm, where she surrounded herself, just as she did at Reef Point, with myriad vases each holding a single rose. Even her local dressmaker, Mary H. Barron, continued to serve her at Garland Farm, although there was no more need for dresses like the one she made for Farrand's sojourn to Boston in the 1930s to take tea with King George VI and Queen Elizabeth. "The Scotch tweeds she brought with her each summer for suits," Barron recollected, "were so rough the briar burrs were still in them." Most of her suits were in a mixture of black, white, and gray, although there was one exceptional soft purple tweed, and all of the blouses matched the jacket linings and were made with sleeves full enough so that when she pointed, the fabric would not fall back and reveal a bare arm. In later years, she was never without her distinctive black ribbon choker.

When Beatrix Farrand died on February 27, 1959, her service, by her own request, was attended only by Robert Patterson and the small loyal band at Garland Farm. Her ashes were scattered, like her husband's. But the garden at Garland Farm, her only truly private garden, has survived. The Goff family, who lived there between 1970 and 1993, were meticulous in overseeing it. Helena E. Goff, who was president first of the Bar Harbor Garden Club, and later of the Garden Club Federation of Maine, Inc., took on the mantle of responsibility to maintain Farrand's last garden, with occasional visits from Amy Garland. When the house was sold after the death of his parents, Jerome I. Goff became guardian of Farrand's last remaining papers in the house, including her treasured collection of seed packets from botanic gardens and plant societies around the world. The current resident of the cottage, Virginia Dudley Eveland, has engaged two local women landscape gardeners to maintain the gardens in pristine condition, including the fenced-in rock garden in front with its profusion of ginger and other Far Eastern–style plantings. Although the Garland Farm garden is small, a review of the plant labels indicates that all the important ones are there—a microcosm of the much larger world Beatrix Farrand inhabited.

The memory of Reef Point Gardens as it was, though, is guaranteed only by the written record. Publishing the bulletins as a collection is tantamount to re-creating in depth the multifaceted endeavor of Reef Point, which was supported by a devoted staff whose standard of excellence gave her joy. Read together, they constitute a descriptive account that both restores the gardens in their visual form to the mind's eye and summarizes the knowledge and experience of a lifetime.

Beatrix Farrand lived by a Latin motto from Psalm 119 inscribed first in the hallway at Reef Point and later at her Garland Farm cottage: *Intellectum da mihi et vivam* (Give me understanding, and I shall live). Her own intellect is at the center of the bulletins' texts, and her goal was simply to impart knowledge that would increase the reader's appreciation of gardens and natural landscapes. "The added happiness to life given by an interest in outdoor beauty and art has a very distinct bearing on a community," she wrote in her 1939 prospectus for Reef Point. There is also in these essays an echo of a frequent expression found in her letters from Maine: "At last I have reached home again . . ." For within the pages of the bulletins, the gates to Reef Point Gardens are always open.

> Introduction, *The Bulletins of Reef Point Gardens,*
> The Island Foundation, Bar Harbor, Maine (Sagapress, 1997)

The Private World of a Great Gardener: Rachel Lambert Mellon

UPPERVILLE, VIRGINIA—"Part of creating is understanding that there is always more to do; nothing is ever completely finished," says Rachel Lambert Mellon, whose landscape designs grace such varied places as the White

House, Jacqueline Onassis's summer home on Martha's Vineyard, and Hubert de Givenchy's chateau, Le Jonchet, in France.

In the same tradition as an earlier landscape designer, Beatrix Farrand, Mellon is one of those inherently talented women, who, though not formally trained, has read her way through the subject and observed and learned in her travels both horticulture and landscape design. Recalling their work together at the John F. Kennedy Presidential Library on Boston Harbor, I. M. Pei says, "Mrs. Mellon has the combination of sensitivity and imagery with technical knowledge that you only find among the best professionals." It was she who suggested for the library grounds the dune grass that now bends in the wind— symbolic of the Cape Cod terrain where the president loved to walk.

This past year Mellon has been occupied overseeing the completion of her own new garden library, a building designed by Edward Larrabee Barnes on the grounds of Oak Spring, the farm here, southwest of Washington, where she lives with her husband, Paul Mellon, the art patron and philanthropist. The library houses her extensive collection of botanical and gardening books amassed over the years, which she considers her working library.

Oak Spring, a U-shaped complex of whitewashed buildings with trees espaliered against the walls, is the residence that the Mellons consider "home." Like their other properties—city houses in New York, Washington, and Paris, country houses in Cape Cod and Antigua—Oak Spring has a distinctive garden, designed by Mrs. Mellon, this one in a series of parterres in the French style. Crab apple trees square off one area, and a single cordon of McIntosh apple trees border the cool beauty of blue-and-white flower beds. Nearby is a vegetable garden planted in perpendicular rows edged in boxwood. The garden slopes gently, and descending on either side is the main house, with the peaked roofs of the linked structures, giving the impression of a small white village.

Settled into a hillside, beyond an orchard, is the new whitewashed fieldstone library with the pitched shed roof silhouetted against the sky. In his design, Barnes sought to convey a vernacular farm building in a contemporary geometric form. The entire facade facing southwest is an immense sundial with steel gnomon and strokes. The building includes the main book room, underground stacks, a book-processing room, a kitchen, and a cubical tower, which is Mellon's workroom and where her collection of botanical porcelain will be installed.

Inside, the white walls are awash with light and shadow from strategically placed square windows, one of Barnes's signature motifs. "I wanted a modern exterior with large openings to let the outside in," Mellon confirms.

Between the library and the main house, a pleached arbor of crab apple trees leads to the double greenhouse where Mellon experiments with unusual and rare plants. Working greenhouses they are, but Mellon has added her touch: the storage shelves of the entryway are concealed by trompe l'oeil doors depicting other shelves arrayed with garden paraphernalia. Not the least of which, hanging on a "hook," is the riding raincoat from her days at Foxcroft School, which she still wears.

One area of the greenhouse is reserved for her miniature herb trees, a form that she originated thirty years ago in this country. Using rosemary, thyme, myrtle, or santolina, she grows them from small slips. "They are living objects," she says, "and although they have a medieval quality, they complement a contemporary interior as well."

Her miniature herb trees sit on trestle tables inside the galleried library where the bookshelves rise to the ceiling. The white linen shades on the window wall blow like sails in the wind, and the patterned floor, a hallmark of every Mellon interior, is a diagonal checkerboard in blue-gray and beige squares that blend with the paving stones of the adjoining library terraces.

Most of the interior fittings have been hand-crafted on the farm to Mellon's specifications. "All the materials relate to the earth: clay tiles, hand-woven linen, and the wood is from our own trees," she says. The seventy-five-foot-long room, with its white stone walls and juxtaposition of old and new, has the comfort and ease of a spacious living room. Couches upholstered in off-white are scattered with botanical-print pillows from old French fabric. The homespun blue linen covering the desk chair matches the peasant dresses in a Pissarro painting next to it. Even on a gray day, the brilliant yellow of a Mark Rothko painting lights the space.

In her tower workroom, Mellon continues to design landscapes and gardens that take their inspiration from Le Nôtre, as well as from modern artists, paintings by Mondrian and Diebenkorn, and collages by Anne Ryan. Despite her active life, she has always found time to design and feels close to the long tradition established by other women landscape designers.

As a child, Mellon was fascinated by gardens. She watched the landscape man from the Olmsted company in Boston who came down to Princeton to work on the grounds of her family home. Fairy tales, especially those illustrated by Arthur Rackham and Edmund Dulac, were beloved childhood reading. She studied prints in old books of Italian and French gardens and then built miniature ones in wooden boxes incorporating small stone steps, real soil, and tiny topiary trees from sponges, glue, wire, and wood.

"One of the first gardens I did outside the family was for the designer Hattie Carnegie," said Mellon. "I was twenty-three then, and I went to her salon, but could not afford any of her dresses myself, though I loved them," she tells the story. "Miss Carnegie suggested I do a garden in exchange for a coat and dress, and so I designed and planted a garden for her."

Since then, Mellon has created numerous landscapes for private residences and for public projects. In some instances she has received payment, which she donates to a horticultural or medical cause. But most of her clients, frequently her friends, are creative personalities themselves and savor the experience of their collaboration with her.

Looking out the window of her workroom to the Virginia fields stretched out between the Blue Ridge Mountains and the Bull Run Mountains, Mellon comments, "My two horizons." "I always design a landscape with fixed horizons," she explains, "whether it be mountains or a stone wall around a twenty-foot-square plot." If there is no set boundary, she will create one. "On the other hand," she says, "the sky is a free asset in design and nothing unnecessary should be planted that takes away the sky."

She shapes the terrain and uses trees as sculpture. Trees are the bones of her garden—always systematically pruned, frequently in topiary forms or espaliered against walls—and they become the focal points from which flower, vegetable, and herb beds evolve. She selects indigenous plant material so that her planned landscapes will flourish. And she knows the forms of trees intimately and whether they cast dark shadows or dance like firelight.

On the drawing board now is the landscape design for Jacqueline Onassis's new house on Martha's Vineyard, which includes a grape arbor and an apple orchard of several varieties of apple trees with here and there a gap—"as if a few old trees had died," Mellon explains. Mrs. Onassis and Mrs. Mellon began their close friendship by working together on the floral decorations for the White House. Mellon, given President Kennedy's suggestion for a ceremonial outdoor space at the White House, designed the now-famous Rose Garden.

Hubert de Givenchy, the designer, refers to his gardens at Le Jonchet in France, which Mellon helped him design, as "a delicate piece of embroidery," that is, after he heeded her advice to "take out a hundred trees and straighten up the lines." Now a row of forty linden trees runs the width of his seventeenth-century chateau. In the park she planted lapis-blue scilla underneath a hundred-year-old oak tree, filling in the exact area where the tree casts its summer shadow. When the flowers bloom then in early spring, their blueness is like a memory of that shadow.

For the small garden of the New Jersey home of Charles Ryskamp, director of the Pierpont Morgan Library, she had removed a somber wall of hemlocks around the garden in favor of a low split-cedar fence in order to treat the surrounding properties visually like a unified park. Then she planted a sugar maple that echoed one in a neighbor's yard, thereby extending his horizon to include the tree beyond.

Currently she is a consultant to River Farm, the headquarters of the American Horticultural Society on the Potomac. According to the executive vice president, Thomas W. Richards, she has begun "with plantings that give our driveway the appearance of a country road."

Although each garden or landscape she creates is as distinctive as the person for whom it is designed, Mellon envisions them all as one immense garden of her own. And where are the horizons of *this* garden? As far, indeed, as her imaginative inner eye can see.

New York Times, June 3, 1982

"Make the Land Work for You": Russell Page in America

In the United States a limited and provincial European culture
was already outdated a hundred years ago by the rapid growth
of a new people in a new continent. Now styles from all over the
world chase each other through the American scene, to be tried,
accepted, modified and then discarded.
—Russell Page, *The Education of a Gardener*

WHEN RUSSELL PAGE began his travels to the New World, he brought with him the mental images and experiences already accumulated in a lifetime of planting and design. Once in America, he found fresh challenges and a variety of opportunities that spanned the public and private sector and that also introduced him to an intriguing array of new plant materials—and new friends. Like an itinerant salesman or a magician with a bag of tricks, he had ingenious solutions to offer from abroad; but at the same time, he embarked on an important learning process that remained in force until his death in 1985.

Page's commute to America commenced in the fifties in the years before publishing his book, *The Education of a Gardener.* Among the more than twenty-five gardens and landscapes he designed in the United States only a handful remained as unrealized projects. In viewing drawings of this latter group in his archives at the Kalmthout Arboretum in Belgium, one realizes how his ideas on a grand scale would have permanently changed the face of many American institutions. For example, in 1966, at the behest of Mrs. Vincent Astor, he made a Beaux-Arts elevation sketch in pencil of New York's Metropolitan Museum of Art embellished with elm trees and lawns, low ilex hedges, and magnolia trees surrounding spouting fountains. A railing detail of a bronze owl was modeled on an Athenian coin from 400 to 500 b.c. By the next year, the museum's director, Thomas Hoving, launched the proposal for the Metropolitan's master plan, and Page's gardenesque Fifth Avenue facade disappeared into oblivion.

Years before he advised Mrs. Albert Lasker on her gardens in Greenwich, Connecticut, she asked him to draw a new fountain to be placed at the end of the Central Park Mall in New York. The result in 1969 was a simplified version of a fantasy fountain from Hieronymus Bosch's *Garden of Earthly Delights*, with pink plastic parts that would have added a delicious touch of humor to the park. And, near the end of President Lyndon B. Johnson's administration in 1968, Page proposed a National Rose Garden for Washington, D.C.'s West Potomac Park, with three hundred geometrically shaped planting beds and over a hundred thousand roses, that would have been a major contribution to Lady Bird Johnson's movement to beautify the cities of America. In all of these projects from the sixties, Russell Page was ahead of American planners in his thinking about civic landscapes, but fortunately he remained on the scene into the next decades and the revival of interest in greening American cities.

In the meantime, there were his private clients, the first of whom was Mrs. William S. Paley, at her Long Island residence, Kiluna Farm. The design received its greatest accolade in a 1980 article titled "Water in a Woodland Setting" that appeared in the British magazine *Country Life*, written by Lanning Roper, an American who made his career in England as a garden designer and journalist. He described the large oval pool in a natural setting of trees and shrubs and the grass steps that rose gently through a wooded area under a canopy of dogwood trees. Barbara Paley's daughter, Amanda Burden, remembers walking from the house and looking over a mound and down the incline of steps to the surprise view of the still pond that reflected a rare assortment of pale orange azaleas. On the far side was a woodland walk lined with fritillaria. Regrettably, under its recent ownership the garden has reverted to a jungle of trees with little evidence remaining of its romantic setting.

Thomas and Iris Vail, who live in Hunting Valley, Chagrin Falls, Ohio, near Cleveland, first contacted Russell Page through William Paley, who was a former chairman of the Columbia Broadcasting System. Thomas Vail himself was the publisher and editor of a prestigious newspaper, the *Cleveland Plain Dealer*. After a first meeting with the Vails in London, Page began to work at their home, an old stable block called "L'Ecurie" that had been moved to the top of a hill from lower in the valley where they had originally lived in it. As was Page's custom, he stayed with the Vails while he designed the garden at various stages, and in his working habits—taking long walks in the morning and then rapidly drawing in the late afternoon (always with some time out for tea)—can be found the secret to his extraordinary productivity. His focus and concentration on the land and garden at hand would yield the creative idea within a day rather than later in an office somewhere. Sometimes the moment of inspiration and decision would come when he was actually working with the bulldozer driver shaping the land, as he did in flattening the Vails' front courtyard. This efficiency made it possible for him to move quickly and unfettered between commissions, always retaining his clarity of thought for the next place.

The Vail garden, composed of eight garden areas surrounding the house, incorporates images Page had retained from various European garden traditions, and yet reduced in scale, they blended perfectly with the typically American wilderness landscape viewed in the distance. In creating a gravel courtyard, he treated the stable block as if it were a small rustic chateau, say in Normandy. One day, after driving up and down the access road with Iris Vail, he conceived the idea for an entrance allée of a double grove of clipped and pleached linden trees underplanted with myrtle. Viewing them lined up on a grid, they are as satisfying in appearance as the long rows of clipped lindens at the Palais Royal in Paris, and yet they retain a domestic flavor.

The regularity of these trees is reflected in the swimming pool garden behind the house by twin rows of clipped hawthorns and by tall hemlock hedges that enclose garden rooms with long beds of roses or lilacs planted with peonies. Reflecting their mutual interest in Spanish gardens, outside the library window he designed a rill garden with fountains at either end bubbling away to his specifications, which were always explicit on this matter. Among his drawings for this garden is a sketch of a water jet shaped in wood on a lathe to be used as the form for the final jet in beaten copper. Thanks to a rigid maintenance program, except for occasional storm damage, these gardens have matured over the years without losing any of Page's precision or inspiration. Within the last year, the Vails planted the last segment of his original plan—hemlock hedges in U-shaped patterns enclosing single dogwood trees. Thomas Vail recalls the time they planted seventy thousand white pine seedlings on open land beyond the house according to Page's directive to "make the land work for you."

Paris was the inspiration for Russell Page's best known urban garden in America, the small enclosed terrace on East 70th Street behind the Frick Collection, the choice museum of old master paintings located in the Fifth Avenue mansion in New York City that once belonged to Henry Clay Frick. Nothing is more tantalizing or inducive to fantasy than a beautifully trimmed garden with a refreshing fountain in an enclosure that no one may enter. Passersby pause and press their faces against the iron gates to enjoy this quiet respite from the noisy streets. Because Page understood that people cannot judge distances over water, the rectangular lily pond that stretches across the central lawn creates the illusion of great depth in this shallow space. With its low green hedges, balls of box, and asymmetrically planted trees, the garden is not unlike one he designed on the rue de Varenne in Paris and evokes the same sense of catching a glimpse of a private French garden. New Yorkers consider it as one of the masterpieces of the Frick Collection.

"He regarded this garden as his calling card," says Everett Fahy, the former director of the Frick Collection who oversaw the garden's installation in 1976 and 1977. The opportunity for the garden presented itself when the Frick purchased and dismantled the last of three town houses adjoining the museum. Although there was talk of a temporary garden and future expansion, the garden has in fact become a permanent visual amenity. Reassembling architectural fragments that had been removed from the mansion's interior during an earlier renovation, the architects were inspired by the Grand Trianon at Versailles to design a garden pavilion facade of arched niches and Ionic pilasters to surround the garden.

During the planning stage of the Frick Garden, Page was introduced to Powers Taylor of Rosedale Nurseries in Hawthorne, New York, who had already been involved in other plantings at the Frick. From this meeting came one of the most important partnerships of Page's career in America. The men would spend hours roaming the acres of gardens at Rosedale, where Page learned about the hardy plants and trees of the region. For his part, Taylor enjoyed the challenge of working within the rigid architectural framework composed by Page. At the Frick, trees—like the *Sophora japonica* and the *Koelreuteria paniculata*—were placed and rotated into position for the best view from the street. A *Metasequoia* commands the northeast corner, linking the lower garden with an upper planter of pear trees that were intended to conceal the Frick's library building next door. And in the niches, dark green trellises support wisteria and clematis vines.

Although the border plantings change seasonally to introduce new colors and textures, what makes the scene alluring even in winter snow are the strong forms that Page cherished in his gardens. During recent warmer winters, the beds are carpeted with blue pansies that make a strong contrast with deep evergreens like the *Cryptomeria japonica* 'Lobbii' that grow in the foreground. No doubt Page also saw his enclosed design as an antidote to the rustic openness of Central Park across the street.

He used similar motifs in designing a sculpture garden in 1978 for the Columbus Museum of Art in Columbus, Ohio—only here the inspiration was Italian. Taking into account the museum's building in the Italian Renaissance style, he wrote in his comments, "I have therefore thought it best that the whole effect of the gardens . . . should reflect the garden developments which such a building might have acquired over the last three or four hundred years." And in suggesting an eighteenth-century landscape treatment along the main facade, he cited Veronese and Giorgione as two Renaissance painters who used "romantic landscape elements in relation to classical buildings."

In 1984, Page was finally given the opportunity of designing a monumental civic landscape when he was engaged by the Friends of the National Arboretum in Washington, D.C., to select the site and design the installation for twenty-two Corinthian columns that had originally supported the east central portico of the United States Capitol building, where the presidential inaugurations take place. Although the architect B. Henry Latrobe incorporated these columns in his 1806 plan for the Capitol, their design was derived from Sir William Chambers's 1759 *Treatise on Civil Architecture*. Chambers himself had borrowed the motifs from a sixteenth-century Italian book illustrating the combined capitals of columns from the Temple of Jupiter Stator and the Pantheon. Carved from local sandstone, the Capitol's columns were dismantled in 1958 and replaced with marble.

In a sense, the project was like creating a ruin as grand as the Roman Forum, since the columns' formation in a rectangle with the hint of a portico suggests the remains of a grandiose building. He selected a vast knoll with a prospect overlooking the surrounding meadows, and a rill from a low bubbling central fountain in the marble floor of the structure cascades down a rise into a reflecting pool, thereby echoing the settings of other great monuments in the nation's capital. Herbs were planted in the interstices of the marble floor. Once he drew up the plan, only the first column had to be sited and the rest could be mathematically deduced, not unlike the formation of the pleached linden trees at L'Ecurie.

In many ways, all of his work—including the country houses of England—served as a prelude for his most ambitious achievement in America—the Donald M. Kendall Sculpture Gardens at the PepsiCo World Headquarters in Purchase, New York. In an effort to pull his company together under one roof, Donald M. Kendall, who was chairman of the board and chief executive officer of PepsiCo, gave up the company's several offices in New York for a rural location, thus spearheading the creation in America of the corporate park. He had achieved two major goals before he met Russell Page—the first was the completion in 1970 of a new low-slung building of inverted ziggurats designed by the architect Edward Durrell Stone, and the second the accumulation of a major collection of contemporary sculpture that was placed both in courtyards framed by wings of the building and in an open landscape. These outdoor areas had been designed by Edward Durrell Stone, Jr.

When Kendall first saw the gardens Page designed for Augustine Edwards in Chile (where Edwards had worked for PepsiCo), he realized the greater possibilities offered by the 168 acres of former polo grounds surrounding the headquarters. They now include more than forty sculptures by twentieth-century artists. There was an opportunity in the New World for corporate America to replace the landed gentry of the Old World in the scope of cultivating the landscape. This was the ideal canvas for the kind of eighteenth-century landscape devised in England by "Capability" Brown and Humphry Repton.

When Russell Page began working at PepsiCo in 1978, the team included Powers Taylor and the Carmine Labriola Contracting Corporation. Like the historic circuits that were established in Romantic folly gardens in England, he laid out a winding "golden path" that linked the sculptures and the plantings he designed to complement their forms and sometimes their colors, as in the case of a stand of blue spruce positioned behind a red Calder. He became enamored of American trees and once wrote to a friend: "We're using American trees of course. Your Northeast has some of the most beautiful forests I've seen in my life. I'm using pines and cedars and junipers, lots of maples, liquidamber, called sweet gum here."

But the jewel of this extravagant landscape with ornamental grass and woodland gardens were the mirror-flat rectangular lily ponds bordered by a sloping perennial garden in a right angle of the building. Richard A. Schnall, now vice president for horticulture at the New York Botanical Garden, remembers the day when Page arrived to plant this perennial bed. Schnall was working for Labriola and was at the garden to receive the order from White Flower Farm. Page directed him to lay out the plants in strict alphabetical order; and when he arrived, he began with "A," pointed his cane for the placement, and went on to the next letter until they completed the alphabet. "He was simply the most knowledgeable plantsman I have ever known, and he could visualize exactly how the border would look in every season," recalls Richard Schnall. On one of his PepsiCo plans, Page drew a pedimented trellised arbor taken from a drawing by Humphry Repton and wrote next to it: "I'm tired, it's raining and I am not a waterlily." Page worked at PepsiCo to the end of his life; after he died, the corporation built the arbor with the inscription in his memory.

During most of the years Russell Page worked in America, his correspondence and plans bore the London address of his flat near Sloane Square at 12 Cadogan Gardens. This charming residential enclave around a garden is well known to American visitors who frequent the hotel around the corner at 11 Cadogan Gardens and share what must have been his own pleasure in the garden's year-round interest. One cannot help but think of him when the winter flowering cherry is in bloom and how a cloud of gray-pink blossoms would have filled his window.

When he published the new edition of *The Education of a Gardener* in 1983, he gave a copy to Powers Taylor with an inscription that sums up their long collaboration: "To my friend Powers Taylor, who over the years has taught me the ins and outs of making gardens in America." It is a story simply told. For many years now, Powers Taylor and other gardeners, designers, and contractors who were devoted to Russell Page have maintained this peripatetic British garden designer's rich legacy in America.

Russell Page: Ritratti di giardini italiani,
American Academy in Rome and Electa, 1998

Profile of Dan Kiley

NEARING NINETY, Dan Kiley has lost none of the irreverence (nor the long hair) he acquired at Harvard University's Graduate School of Design, 1936–1938, when he rebelled against professors in the landscape architecture division who showed reams of slides turning students off European garden history. Instead, he and fellow students James Rose and Garrett Eckbo looked to the architecture department, under Walter Gropius, for inspiration and fresh breezes blowing across the Atlantic from the Bauhaus.

Kiley was raised in an old quarter of Boston, and his earliest experience of landscape was roaming alleyways between houses, crossing the Arnold Arboretum on his way to school, and ambling through Frederick Law Olmsted's Emerald Necklace of parks along the Charles River. Visits to his grandmother in New Hampshire left impressions of fragrant pine woods in summer and stark maple tree trunks above strewn leaves in the fall. As a golf caddy, Kiley retained images of modeled green courses, and as a skier, the clean ski tracks across an expanse of white snow.

When Kiley entered Harvard, he was already employed by the landscape architect Warren H. Manning, known for his grand estate gardens. Manning had been a young associate of Olmsted and was one of the founders in 1899 of the American Society of Landscape Architects. When Manning died in 1938, Kiley left Harvard to work on housing projects in Washington, D.C., with the architect Louis Kahn. During World War II, Kiley joined the new Office of Strategic Services, where he replaced Eero Saarinen as chief of design. In this capacity, he was sent to Germany in 1945 to transform the Nuremberg Palace of Justice into a court to try Nazi war criminals. It was his first trip to Europe, and it changed his life.

Reminiscing in the sunroom of his farmhouse-cum-office in East Charlotte, Vermont, he described those days "when France became my first love." With his limited free time, he visited Versailles and the Château de Sceaux and discovered that those boring slides he had seen at Harvard had nothing to do with the breathtaking reality of André Le Nôtre's creations: the formal geometry, the allées of trees, the axial views, the terraces and fountains. He was smitten. Later, he recalls, on a more extensive European tour: "I would simply go to a railroad station in Paris and board the first train going anywhere. I felt so free spirited and connected to France, and crazy things would happen to me. I would often end up dancing with young people in a bar somewhere."

While other young American landscape architects were seeking fresh designs in abstract land formations, Kiley immediately grasped the grids of Le Nôtre's classicism and applied them, as he says, "to the open-ended, dynamic simplicity of Modernism." As the sleek, axial interiors of International Style buildings like Mies van der Rohe's 1929 Barcelona Pavilion merged with the landscape through glass walls, Kiley saw a harmonious way to continue the architecture through ordered plantings in private gardens and public plazas. In brief, he wanted to express the classicism in Modernism without losing the mysterious dynamics of nature—perpetual growth, seasonal transitions, flow of water, and, crucially, the effects of light and shadow.

His first modernist garden was for J. Irwin Miller of Columbus, Indiana, the manufacturer who commissioned a whole group of contemporary architects to build in Columbus, making the city a veritable museum of twentieth-century public architecture. The Miller garden reflected the same geometric grid of the 1955 house designed by Eero Saarinen, and the honey-locust allée, with the Henry Moore sculpture at its end, has become an iconic landscape in American garden history. Kiley despairs of landscape architects like Olmsted who mixed varieties of trees in clumps in the picturesque tradition, and with a wave of his hand to his own woods he demonstrates how maple trees are massed along a boardwalk path. Though he seeks to plant grids of trees close together—"the better to squeeze between them as in nature"—he has conceded to spacing them farther apart for his public work.

While Kiley has collaborated with almost every major contemporary architect in America, each landscape has been individually conceived to suit the spirit of the site. In Tampa, Florida, Harry Wolf's 1988 tower for the North Carolina National Bank, for example, is complemented by squares of the perennial grass zoysia between paved strips, a grid of *Sabal palmetto* and swaths of *Lagerstroemia indica* with brilliant pink blooms. Over the garage, a glass-bottomed canal (illuminated at night) feeds nine rills that terminate in bubbling fountains. Versailles with a difference.

For the two-acre plaza of I. M. Pei's 1986 First Interstate Bank Tower in Dallas, Texas, Kiley envisioned the cooling effects of a swamplike water forest. The geometric waterfalls of Fountain Place, as it is called, are enlivened by 263 bubbler fountains and 440 native bald cypress (*Taxodium distichum*) in planters. He describes landscapes like these as "dancing in space."

In New York City, the towering trees and fountains of Rockefeller University on the East River are an urban oasis, as are the interior gardens of the Ford Foundation and the grid of trees in planters behind Lincoln Center for the Performing Arts. He has traveled worldwide to design his award-winning landscapes—but best of all, he returned to his beloved Paris to add his minimalist touch to the public spaces around La Défense.

Among the many modernists in the field who have trained with Kiley is Cornelia Hahn Oberlander, the Canadian landscape architect. She can remember his Vermont office within the family house also occupied by Kiley and his wife, Anne, and their eight children in the 1950s. Kiley once told her: "Through the woods, walk softly, feel the ground." One of Kiley's oft repeated principles is that man *is* nature, that design and the environment are inseparable. As he told a New York audience a decade ago: "One sets the design in motion, and it makes its own growth—an organism continually in a state of dynamic equilibrium trying to find its place in the universe."

Gardens Illustrated, September 2001

Grounded in History: Deborah Nevins's Landscapes

BACK IN THE summer of 1988, just after the crest of the boom years, a columnist for the *Independent* in London conjured up the ultimate fantasy of a new stately home and pleasure ground for a figure he called the Thatcher-era millionaire. For the house design he turned to a young British architect who drew on "ancient values," alluding to classicism without imitating it. For a garden plan, however, he tapped an American, Deborah Nevins, the New York landscape designer who during the past decade has earned a solid reputation creating lush gardens and timeless landscapes, mostly for families of the Fortune 500.

Thoroughly grounded in art history, Nevins emerged in 1976 as a curator of the exhibition "200 Years of American Architectural Drawing" at New York's Cooper-Hewitt Museum. One of the most illuminating offshoots of the Bicentennial, the show and catalogue established Nevins as a perceptive historian of architecture—a field that soon led her to the related area of landscape architecture. After stints as an adjunct professor in landscape history at Barnard College and a museum lecturer, she decided, she says, "to create landscapes rather than write about them."

Her classic survey lecture, a grand tour of landscape history, is still part of her repertoire, though now it helps her to brief potential clients as well as architects, with whom she often collaborates. One recent afternoon Nevins set up her slides for architects at a SoHo firm near her own office. "History," she began, "is a source, not a pattern book." With that, she launched into a stream of images—fields divided by hedgerows, circular clearings in woodland, groves of trees, orchards, and allées—to explain a vocabulary she appropriated for her designs without ever making direct quotations. "Some of our strongest forms in landscape design," she says, "are references to primary forms that evolved from agriculture and from community or religious practices." As examples of plantings harking back to traditional configurations she shows a single majestic tree positioned above stone steps at Hidcote in the Cotswolds and a grove of chestnut trees in the Place Dauphine in Paris.

Nevins describes the gardens she designs, often suites of intimate open-air enclosures, as "private territories within the exterior world." Her sensibility to regional character—both in plant selection and in formal composition—binds the private realm to its context. Proposals for new commissions are presented as a mix of site plans, relevant historic views, and photographs of indigenous flora—all mounted on fine paper in bound volumes that rival Humphry Repton's "Red Books" for sheer beauty and clarity of organization. The idea of the garden becomes as exciting as the garden itself.

By defining a progression through a series of spaces, Nevins can make even a small property appear filled with visual incident. In one Long Island garden, for example, a buttressed brick wall separates a geometric arrangement of square parterres of herbs and standard roses from an apple orchard underplanted with spring bulbs and summer wildflowers. On a New England estate, the lawn between luxuriant yet muted herbaceous borders in the Arts and Crafts manner becomes a green corridor to a simple hedge-ringed circle. At a new town in Florida, the repeated verticals of cypress trees unite several townhouse gardens by a single skyline. On a working farm in the Midwest, Nevins will plant clumps of full-grown trees in the middle of vast corn fields as confidently as "Capability" Brown deployed copses in English parks. "I love dense trees," she allows with a smile, as if she knows her passion is self evident.

Nevins's landscapes work on several visual levels, from low rills of water and borders framed by hedges or stone walls to apple orchards with clouds of spring blossoms. Recently, Nevins has embarked on a series of garden enclosures surrounding a new Caribbean hideaway that involves an imaginative adaptation of different cultural traditions: vine-draped slat houses, a mandarin grove in continuous bloom, coral-stone paving, a lotus pond based on one in Bali, and a courtyard of citrus trees like those in Seville. Fragrance is the client's mandate, and the night air will be tinged with the scent of jasmine and stephanotis.

If a single image can sum up Nevins's landscape sensibility, it is a treasured photograph by Henri Cartier-Bresson that hangs in her dining room from a collection of photographs she has amassed by selecting one a year.

Having lived in France, she senses the connotations of this 1955 park scene, *Près de Juvisy, France,* akin to Seurat's *A Sunday on La Grande Jatte* in its inherent quality of formality mixed with fantasy. On one side of a hedge, two boys play on a path leading to a river, while on the other, two girls in tutus turn toward a sunlit opening like sprites. "The photograph shows how minimal forms—a hedge or a path—can create intimate spaces within the larger landscape," Nevins says. She could just as well be talking about one of her own gardens.

House & Garden, September 1992

Private Visions: The Gardens of Michael Van Valkenburgh

AS A CURATOR himself in the 1980s of exhibitions on American landscape architecture, Michael Van Valkenburgh has explored the private garden in the twentieth century—both real and visionary. "Like the house in architecture, the garden is a succinct design statement, offering a concise view of each designer's philosophy," he wrote at the time. In his world, the private garden is more than a setting or an appendage to a house. It is an independent laboratory of ideas, a synthesis of art and craftsmanship. If the experiment succeeds, the forms may be applied to the larger world of parks and public spaces, but the fresh inspiration belongs to the original compressed version.

"Ideas spring from our hearts and minds and are informed by history and culture and tempered with a keen knowledge of how the world is built," is how he describes the creative confrontation with a new space. Drawings reveal the immediacy of this experience and serve as the repository of ideas which may take years to execute. He views design on the land, even with natural materials, as an artifice tempered by the dimension of time.

Van Valkenburgh's expansive imagination incorporates his knowledge of historical precedents—what he calls "revisiting ideas from the past"—and an ability to respond to the uniqueness of a site and of how it relates to a regional environment. Private gardens allow him personal control, and their scale makes possible a complete exploration of design. Sometimes he refines an experimental idea in the backyard of the gray clapboard house in Cambridge where his office is located next door to a former Laundromat that serves as the drafting room for Michael Van Valkenburgh Associates.

Growing up in an agricultural community, Van Valkenburgh says, provided him with the comfort and ease to let landscapes look legible and manmade. He recalls first fantasizing about the land as a boy when he brought the cows home from pasture in the Catskills to his family's modest dairy farm in Lexington, New York. Today, his work retains what he sees as "the deliberate simplicity of that remembered agrarian landscape," as in the way a plantation of trees is angled into the hillside. For him, beauty and elegance are found in the straightforward solution rather than in the contrived picturesque. His search for a realistic approach, he believes, complements the abstract ideas he develops in his academic life at Harvard University, where design is taught as an art form.

At the beginning of his career, he was inspired by the book *Design with Nature* by Ian L. McHarg, the University of Pennsylvania landscape architect in the vanguard of the ecology movement who describes man-made landscapes as a picture of nature devised by both conscience and art. McHarg also offers the theory that we continually seek out or recreate "reassuring landscapes," images made memorable through past associations. In his own work, Van Valkenburgh refers to memory and narrative. Seen in succession, his gardens are woven together by threads of repeated themes and images that recall in minimal forms archetypal models.

In these private landscapes, he combines horticulture—both as a strong element of design and as a transition to natural plantings at the fringes—with a seductive use of mineral elements—stone, water, and metal—that bring a cool, tangible veneer to the settings. Finally, he adds levels, dramatic changes of level that suggest passage and journeys through the gardens. As at the Potager du Roi, the king's kitchen garden at Versailles, steep staircases and slopes make abrupt shifts in the viewer's perspective and repeatedly alter the experience of space.

In the birch garden he designed in Chestnut Hill, Massachusetts, he drew on his agrarian sensibility to resolve the problem of a sloping terrain behind the house by creating a grade change that was even more pronounced. From a flat terrace above, defined by a brick-and-bluestone retaining wall, a plain flight of wooden stairs plunges into the lower-story woodland garden. The steps evoke for Van Valkenburgh the rickety ones leading down to docks on Martha's Vineyard, where he spends weekends and summers, and they function visually like a drawbridge lowered as a connector.

Planted along the steep slopes on either side is a thick grove of multistem gray and white birch trees whose trunks angle out into linear designs against

44

lush underplantings of rhododendron, mountain laurel, ferns, vinca, common periwinkle, and European ginger. In this deliberate quotation from the garden Fletcher Steele designed in 1926 at Naumkeag in Stockbridge, Massachusetts, Van Valkenburgh pays tribute to Steele's ideas about massing with subtle irregularity and about grading land in sculptural rather than natural forms.

While at Naumkeag the birch trees are seen in counterpoint to a series of curving stair rails of white pipes, in the Chestnut Hill garden the birch grove is bisected by a traditional Japanese temple path of diamond-shaped stepping stones set into bluestone gravel scattered with pine needles. Similar to the long granite stones that line Japanese paths, like one at Nanzen-ji in Kyoto, Van Valkenburgh has edged his path with black brick manganese, two dark lines that lead serenely not to a temple pavilion but to a stele-cum-fountain of polished green granite. Visible through a slit on the face of the stone column are overlapping plates of stainless steel that step up so that the flow of water cascades down over them as a fluid surface. At night, neon lights attached vertically in pairs to the brick piers at the top of the stairs cast an eerie glow akin to moonlight. This garden goes beyond pleasure by offering ideas and images that heighten one's experience of traversing what is otherwise a simple grove of trees.

As if designed as a continuation to the birch garden, the Pucker Garden, in nearby Brookline, evolved as a hillside embankment that creates an ascent in the shallow space of a suburban backyard. Calling on references to Roman antiquity, the garage at one side now appears like a ruin of an old tomb that has been excavated out of the adjacent hillside. Echoing the wooden steps, a staircase in high-tech galvanized steel checkerplate floats up like a shiny ziggurat across the myrtle-covered hillside. Curved like an amphitheater and planted with single-stem shadblow trees, the embankment becomes an ideal foil for displaying abstract sculptures on pedestals. The arrangement calls to mind the 1962 exhibition of David Smith's Voltri sculptures arrayed on the steps of the ancient coliseum in Spoleto, Italy.

Like the modernist architects of this century, Van Valkenburgh subscribes to the aesthetic principle that new materials and the latest technology dictate new forms. Without relinquishing classical garden features, he introduces hard-edged structures and industrial surfaces that at first appear more practical than ornamental, except that in the end their trimness and suitability make them a perfect blend with the flat green expanses that are to his gardens what sleek glass is to architecture.

At the entrance to the Pucker Garden, and on axis with the floating stair-case across the lawn, a progression of Japanese-style stepping stones has been abstracted into rectangular stones of varying lengths embedded into exposed aggregate concrete. Running crosswise between these pavers are inlaid bands of irregularly set black pebbles that mimic Japanese stepping-stone patterns. Further on, the rendered surfaces of gray stucco for the retaining wall of the formed hillside and the garage exterior complement the galvanized steel post-and-wire-mesh trellis for Boston ivy that screens the back of the viewing path around the top of the hill. Guests usually complete the garden circuit on the flat terrace roof of the garage with its balustrade also of galvanized steel and wire mesh. From this overlook, the Japanese stone entrance patio below resembles a Mondrian painting in tones of gray.

In the lee of a 1950s modern house on a waterside estate in Greenwich, Connecticut, Van Valkenburgh continued the play of hard and soft surfaces in another sculpture garden he created to display important works by Barbara Hepworth. Concealed from the outer drive by a brick serpentine wall that provides slots for the carpark, the bluestone path inside the enclosure swings around a central island of *Vinca minor* in what the landscape architect calls a gestural curve. Except for an existing cutleaf maple he retained to preside over one corner, the sculptures are the main vertical features in the landscape. With the sound of low spouting fountain jets along the center of a rectangular goldfish pond, the scale recalls old cloistered gardens, fresh but simple, with dark beds of ivy around the perimeter.

Some of these same qualities are present in his Black Granite Garden in Los Angeles, only here the inspiration might be Italian cypress allées or Moorish rills. Even where the images refer to historical precedents, the forms are classically minimal. This is a linear garden, a 120-foot avenue of twenty-foot-high columnar Italian cypress trees set in beds of needle point ivy along a central spine of rosy gray manganese brick pavers that appears infinitely long, channeled as it is between the tall trees. At the edge of a small rill parallel to the path, another granite stele fountain has a monolithic quality—the water pours down the created "washboard" side, while the rough side, dry, faces the sun. A wall of thick-trunked ficus trees forms the boundary along the entire length of the garden. Length like this in a defined landscape is a liberating quality. The reason why avenues in general are so inviting is that they appear to go on forever.

One of Van Valkenburgh's wittiest designs is for a client in St. Louis who collects art from the commercial memorabilia of American highway strips—

the real Pop Art. Among his treasures is a red metal Pegasus, the mythological flying steed that is the logo for the Mobil Company. As the myth goes, Pegasus with a single stroke of his hoof could bring forth the waters of Hippocrene, the sacred fountain of the Muses on Mount Helicon that brought them poetic inspiration. This is a symbolic garden ornament for all times. Van Valkenburgh has treated it as the pinnacle of a garden experience that begins with a long granite walk on the street side that passes under a connecting passageway between two house structures and continues as a bridge across a sunken garden to the terminus, the flying Pegasus soaring appropriately across a fountain pool on a metal arch.

Four years ago, Michael Van Valkenburgh began working on Martha's Vineyard and fell in love with its magical landscape of agricultural fields and stands of oak trees stunted by the force of prevailing winds. After coming to the island and eventually buying a house there, he came to see the natural landscape as more powerful than anything he could possibly do to change it. His own house is protected from the road by a picket fence and an unclipped lilac hedge as well as a new swing gate he designed across the drive after spending the better part of one summer in research by looking at everyone else's gate. By isolating architectural features of the New England landscape in their pure form—like a white gable-peaked arch he designed at the end of a double herbaceous border—Van Valkenburgh forces others to see in them associations with and memories of other places and other times.

For one client who owns houses across the road from each other on Martha's Vineyard, Van Valkenburgh's additions made it possible for their surrounding spaces to be experienced with fresh eyes. On the oceanfront property, the new cobblestone drive with runoff troughs that impede erosion is a forceful design in itself. But the major innovation, Wrightian in its dynamic form, is an extended stone terrace wall that juts out into the lawn like the prow of a ship. Extending far beyond the weathered Colonial house, it functions as a viewing platform looking out to the panorama of the sea. In the afternoon, it casts a dramatic shadow on the sweep of lawn that circles around it. On the boundary of the property, Van Valkenburgh planted an equally arresting long border of white hydrangeas.

On the land side, the property around a Victorian clapboard house had to be cleared of scruffy growth to carve out a landscape where the lawn again becomes the central focus for the rest of the garden. From the roadside, granite steps framed with indigenous day lilies look like an ordinary entrance, corresponding to porch steps at the end of a bluestone walk. The house is screened from the road by a woodland growth collected from woods including pitch pine, hollies, azalea, and woodbine.

Only after turning the corner of the house is the plan revealed: joined bluestone pavers suddenly become stepping stones embedded in grass. It is a stark design in contrast to the turquoise carpenter's lace of the house. Then simply by using the multiple entrances at the side of the house to determine axes, Van Valkenburgh made a repeated design out of a set of granite steps leading up the slope of the lawn to a terrace and two of the doors. A stone path from the third door crosses the lawn at right angles to the stepping stones; its line is reinforced by a parallel border of Russian sage. And in the corner of the house, a linden viburnum turns brilliant crimson against the green lawn in autumn. Two more sets of granite steps, cut into a fieldstone retaining wall at the far end of the lawn, lead to shaded paths through a dense growth of maples, sweetfern, bayberry, and wild roses.

Though this landscape bears Van Valkenburgh's imprint of hard-edged forms, the shapes and textures of stones as pavers and steps and a typical New England wall crafted by a New Hampshire stone mason, it reflects the nineteenth-century aesthetic where each house was surrounded by lawn and modest gardens that blended on the fringes with wilderness areas beyond.

On a beachfront property, he designed a peaked-roof open pavilion on the path from the house to the sea as a front porch, where the family congregates after dinner, only apart from the main house. He calls it a rain house because of its copper roof and his own recollection of boyhood afternoons sitting on the farmhouse porch listening to the deafening but soothing sound of a summer shower on the old tin roof.

In contrast to these severely architectural designs and because of his extensive work with the photographs of Gertrude Jekyll, Van Valkenburgh is a strong proponent of planted borders. What interests him is the design of borders that direct as well as please the eye. Fascinated with the seasonality of Jekyll's floral selections and the progression of plantings along her garden paths, he reproduced these theories in a plan for a hypothetical corporate garden, a three-hundred-foot herbaceous border, with hundreds of ten-foot-square beds set on the diagonal, separated by grass walkways. Each bed is planted with one kind of flower in shades of pale pink to deep red; the border blooms sequentially, so that color washes over it slowly like a wave from one end to the other, with, for example, a light pink iris, 'Vanity', in June, to a deep burgundy dahlia, 'Black Narcissus', in July, and on to a silvery pink Japanese anemone, 'Robustissima', in August.

For several gardens, he has designed raised parterres with granite curbs. At a house in Minnesota, he planted these with vegetables, herbs, and flowers, while at another garden in Greenwich, for clients seeking plant diversity, he filled them with several varieties of roses and divided one bed from the other with rows of espaliered fruit trees. The beauty of the parterre form is that in winter, covered with snow or even barren, the open rectangles of stone make a pleasing design on the land.

What is engaging about following Michael Van Valkenburgh's career as a landscape architect and teacher is that his ideas build with his commissions and exposure to new places. For example, a new landscape he designed within a traffic circle for General Mills in Minneapolis could easily have been planted in lawn, "captured lawn," he calls it. But instead he created a prairie encircled by 162 Heritage River birch trees, and each year the grasses are burned off to invigorate future growth. Similarly, although he did not finally win the competition to restore the Tuileries Garden in Paris, his study of Le Nôtre's geometric plantings and his innovative plan—to introduce the topiary cones of Sceaux in a series of grids that would have linked the Tuileries to the Place du Carrousel—will continue to affect not only his designs but our own perceptions of that historic space.

Extracting the essence of this French classical garden vocabulary, Van Valkenburgh has created a small interior walled garden for an office building in Paris at 50, avenue Montaigne. Although placed in a contemporary setting, the elements, new and spare—rows of pyramidal hornbeams and espaliered lindens in alternation with long basins of water—evoke the spirit of a young seventeenth-century garden. What gives it away as a Van Valkenburgh landscape are the stainless steel water columns that terminate the basins as well as the steel runway and viewing platform, and benches designed by Judy McKie in the form of jaguar cats. Where Van Valkenburgh differs from the landscape architect Dan Kiley, who has also acknowledged the influence of Le Nôtre, is in disrupting the geometric order and linear symmetry. Because of some irregular spacing that is his trademark, a crossview of the garden makes the symmetrical arrangement dissolve into a simple bosque of trees. But still, the minimal form of this garden conveys the richness of centuries of French culture.

Van Valkenburgh achieved a similar effect with a birch bosque he designed for a property in Redding, Connecticut, where he planted sixty white spire birch trees in four rows on a slight incline at the edge of some woods. Like the linear Black Granite Garden and the courtyard of 50, avenue Montaigne, the experience of walking among the trees gives the sense of order dissolving only to become ordered again. The only other experience in art that compares with this is watching a corps de ballet dance Balanchine's choreography—just as the dancers give visual satisfaction by lining up, they break ranks into new groups in a constant pattern of resolution and dissolution.

All of this leads to the commission which may be the summit of his career to date, the new Master Plan for the Harvard Yard Landscape. As a sacred space in American history, it compares in importance to the Tuileries in Paris. Van Valkenburgh admits that to alter either of these spaces is like being asked to repaint the Mona Lisa. Still Harvard is home to Michael Van Valkenburgh, and he speaks of the Yard—a word that has all the connotations of a workaday enclosure attached to purposeful buildings—as an aesthetic unto itself representing Yankee parsimony and elegant frugality. The challenge for him is how to intervene without making the landscape look significantly revised.

Essentially, the landscape is composed of a ground plane of grass crossed with paths under a high canopy of deciduous trees, a combination, according to Van Valkenburgh, that provides a unique sense of place, a New England commons. The firm's sketches for the project demonstrate that Van Valkenburgh's extensive knowledge of tree planting will be as important to our century as Le Nôtre's was for his. Drawings of the Old Yard show how the central axis will be reinforced with tulip poplar trees and how the general replanting will look with rows of unevenly spaced trees. In the part of the yard called Tercentenary Theater, he plans to develop a central halo of light in the deciduous canopy by planting honey locusts in the center with red oaks and red maples at the periphery.

A view of these gardens and landscapes provides an anthology of a sensibility that is intensely original, modernist, and respectful of the past. I met Michael Van Valkenburgh and first saw a garden of his in 1986 at the Urban Center in New York during an exhibition called "Transforming the American Garden: 12 New Landscape Designs." We stood together next to his submission, a model for a visionary corporate garden called Eudoxia: A New Civic Landscape. It was spatial and sculptural, and it used elements of private gardens, like hedges and herbaceous borders, in colorful hues that related to the city. But what I remember most was the tissue-paper model for the twenty-five-foot-high ice and water wall and what he said about the sounds of water and the fragrance of moisture. The image of the ice wall is lodged in my imagination as if I had seen it. I missed the real ones he constructed in Radcliffe Yard in the winter of 1988, but I have the newspaper photograph

of him in front of them—a spare white glistening veneer. In a kind of magical alchemy, Michael Van Valkenburgh can take old elements and transform
them into new visions.

> *Design with the Land: Landscape Architecture of Michael Van*
> *Valkenburgh,* Harvard University Graduate School of Design exhibition
> catalogue, Princeton Architectural Press, 1994

A Cultivated Civilization: Barbara Stauffacher Solomon's Drawings of Classical Gardens

IN 1904, Edith Wharton set out to reveal what she called "Italian garden-
magic" in her book *Italian Villas and Their Gardens.* Wharton laid the ground
rules by saying the "garden must be adapted to the architectural lines of the
house" and provide "shady walks, sunny bowling-greens, parterres, and orchards." All this happened, of course, only after castle walls disappeared. Before that, the garden was like an interior room, a respite set within the parapets. What Wharton did for the Renaissance house and garden in elegant yet
direct prose, California landscape architect Barbara Stauffacher Solomon has
achieved in delicate colored-pencil drawings that are masterworks of technique. By limiting herself to a small eight-and-a-half-by-eleven-inch format,
she bears out her own thesis that within a disciplined environment, here the
classical garden, the imagination can achieve the greatest release.

By now, Solomon has produced more garden plans on gallery walls than
in the ground. Nevertheless, her composite drawings and photographic
collages, which convey the essence of place and time in historic landscapes,
have made her an influential scribe and seer in the field of garden design.
It is not surprising that the wall is fertile ground for Solomon; starting
out as an artist in the 1960s, she gained immediate fame as the inventor
of supergraphics when her bold stripes and huge letters in blue, red, and
black became murals at William Turnbull and Charles Moore's Sea Ranch
condominium in Sonoma.

Then, as she worked toward a master's degree in architecture at the University of California, Berkeley, "the grand scale was boiled down to simplicity,"
she explains, and her new format in a new medium was born. She remembers
learning how to draw trees in a plant materials course. Since then, from a stu-

dio in her native San Francisco and on sojourns abroad, she has been turning out magical combinations of plans and elevations with maps and scenery— only now these elements are executed in compressed images.

She draws on a desk in front of six crocks of colored pencils of many different brands, including one from Switzerland, to obtain the fullest range of colors. These drawings can be compared to the experience of garden visits as preserved in memory, which is indeed the basis for her technique, along with historical research. Sudden shifts of scale and dotted sight lines reproduce the sensation of travel or of a passing train of thought. In her "manifesto" drawing, she follows the garden as it moves outside: two identical grids, one dotted in brown, the other in green, demonstrate how the grid of the garden became the grid of the house. The caption: "There is a garden which is neither forest nor farm."

Writing about the Villa Lante in Bagnaia, Wharton describes a natural woodland as "boldly worked into the general scheme, the terraces and garden architecture skillfully blent with it . . . its recesses . . . pierced by grass alleys leading to clearings where pools surrounded by stone seats slumber under the spreading branches." From this passage, one turns to Solomon's drawing of the twin pavilions at Villa Lante, attributed to Tommaso da Siena, who also designed the gardens she depicts stretching out to the woodland. All her drawings are accompanied by brief passages verging on prose poems, a stream of consciousness that includes her own thoughts and those she has gleaned from literature. Of Villa Lante she writes, "through gardens parting palaces," and she describes the natural woodlands there as "pinewoods become pergolas." Villa Lante's axiality and perspective owe much, it is frequently said, to the architectural theories inaugurated by Donato Bramante. The integration suggested by Wharton is here rendered with great clarity.

At first, Solomon's drawings appear to be of fantasy gardens because they are composites of various views and vistas, including elevations, axonometric projections, and site plans, all within one flat plane. Every line, however, is real, based on historical and photographic research and on Solomon's own observations during leisurely walks through gardens. As a result, they also function as a personal account of her own impressions, for she singles out a point of reference, a particular vista or allée of trees, or an entrance revealed in a single vignette. With finely drawn sight lines, she leads the eye from a small detail in the general plan to its enlarged image or a secondary view of it. The effect is of gardens as they are recalled in memory. Each written phrase unlocks in her readers' minds myriad images of other remembered landscapes.

A collection of her drawings of French and Italian Renaissance gardens along with written descriptions is the focus of an exhibition called "Green Architecture: Notes on the Common Ground." Originated by the Walker Art Center in Minneapolis, it is currently on view in New York at the Urban Center under the sponsorship of the Architectural League. As the title suggests, Solomon explores that margin where controlled nature and structure coexist, where the inside and the outside merge. (The word *garden,* she tells us, derives from the Indo-European root *gherd,* meaning enclosure.) The garden that is expressed architecturally (romantic English gardens and herbaceous borders are not her subject) extends the protective privacy of the home. It expands the house like a porch or even an awning or canopy.

Evocative, then, as the drawings are of place, they also raise the philosophical question of defining inside and outside. Swiss critic Jean Starobinski, in his essay on this topic, writes that "philosophers and biologists alike have stated that an outside begins at the point where the expansion of a structuring force stops. One could just as rightly say that an inside comes into being the moment a form asserts itself by setting its own boundaries." Though exposed to the natural forces of the out-of-doors, gardens still relate to the life of the interiors—boundary is the key word.

Solomon's study of the European formal garden as derived from the classical garden is presented chronologically, from 1545 to 1723, in the exhibition catalogue, and over time the garden structure becomes increasingly complex, a view that has rarely been given with such precision. Beginning with the simple rectangular lawns and intervening pathways of Ancy-le-Franc in Burgundy, the pergolas, arbors, topiaries, mazes, and colonnades of trees multiply over the centuries. But green architecture is only half the story. The other half is the pale blue-green of water, in fountains, canals, basins, and pools, adding music to the gardens. "Water descends on axis or circuitously," she writes in tribute to those engineering feats that conducted water from terrace to terrace with only the law of gravity to give it force.

In her drawing of Marly, also called Marly-la-Machine, one sees the grand waterworks that were planned by Louis XIV with Hardouin-Mansart to feed the waters of Versailles between 1677 and 1714. Here, architecture gives the water shape as well as direction.

Palladio's Villa Barbaro (1560) was in essence a gentleman's farm, and in Solomon's drawing the symmetry of the agricultural fields reflects the symmetrical wings of the villa itself. She carries through the semicircular portico of the Villa Giulia in Rome from the villa to garden to water basin. The number of architects and landscape architects who had a hand in this plan would comprise a *Who's Who* of sixteenth-century Rome: Vasari, Michelangelo, Bartolomeo Ammannati, and Giacomo da Vignola.

By contrast to the hillside terraced gardens of the Italian villas, the more open French gardens of Gaillon and Vernueil offer broader horizons. For the latter, she draws the four grand terraces of promenades and parterres reflected in canals that hark back to the castle moat. Gaillon is a garden and chateau now in ruins, but form and symmetry survive in her drawing. There is nothing static about these; the viewer is always on the move into the farthest recesses of the gardens.

She ends with a drawing of the Portico of San Luca at Bologna, the arcaded walkway from the city to the eleventh-century Santuario della Madonna di San Luca on a hill. Here the inside becomes a pathway through the outside: "a promenade open to the vistas and closed to the rain."

Although the Continent may have provided Solomon with the historical images for her drawings, her memories of garden architecture began with childhood walks on San Francisco's Marina Green, the grass rectangle that runs along the bay near the Yacht Harbor. She defines this personal archetype in her idealized drawing of it, set within a grid: "The Urban Garden: The green rectangle equals paradise," or *pairidaeza*, the ancient Persian concept of enclosure. This greensward, as a basic component of the formal garden, became her "reassuring landscape," a term employed by another landscape architect, Ian McHarg, to denote a landscape that becomes meaningful from an early association and that one seeks thereafter to recreate or rediscover in other environments. From this bit of urban paradise, she has traced garden history back to the basic form of the tilled field, the agrarian garden. The straight lines of man's first holding become for her the origin of the architectural grid.

Although Solomon's drawings have become an art form in their own right, she puts her theories to practice as a landscape architect of real projects, in particular, for the proposed Turia Gardens in Valencia, Spain; for an estate in Oregon; and for four gardens in Omaha, Nebraska. Closer to home, she has applied the principles of Renaissance architecture and Bramante axiality to a series titled "Crissy Field and the Palace of Marina Green," a proposal based on her childhood haunt. The focus of this plan is the Crissy Field area, an unused Army airstrip along the bay that lies between Marina Green and the Golden Gate Bridge and is separated by a major road from the Presidio, an 1860s military garrison originally built in the Italianate style. On first view, the site plan resembles the configurations of the Renaissance gardens, but a closer inspection reveals elements suitable to contemporary California life, retaining nevertheless the traditional axes.

Solomon also continues to observe history, colored pencils in hand, most recently on a fellowship at the American Academy in Rome, an experience that culminated in a series of nine drawings of Roman streets and the patterns that originated the Western city. She began with the handout map of Rome given to all Academy fellows during orientation, and traced this map in as an overlay, a theme in all the drawings, with a wide serpentine line, the Tiber, as a motif. This juxtaposition records the passage of time from the original inception of the architectural plans to the progressive realization of structure and landscape.

In looking at these drawings, one is reminded that before Bramante was an architect, he was a painter, and, as British critic Stephen Gardiner writes in *Inside Architecture,* Bramante "saw architectural design in terms of planes and spaces as he might have seen a painting." These drawings are like the paintings he might have seen. "Rome is Rome still," Henry James wrote in *Roderick Hudson.* Here the pergolas, arbors, and garden walls of green hedges have given way to masonry facades that wall in narrow streets and piazzas that lead to vistas of other classical or baroque facades. The outside, the open space, now becomes the inside, the interior.

"The sky is a precious commodity," says Solomon. "Needing this rare light, Romans have persistently used clearings to catch the sky's brilliance. Places, piazzas, voids—the city is a network of inhabited walls enclosing the mirror images of streets." One remembers emerging from just such a narrow street and coming upon the Fontana di Trevi for the first time.

In some of the drawings, architectural details float in a surreal fashion above the canyonlike streets; Annibale Carracci's *Blue Mercury* is in flight over the Piazza Farnese. A sign reading "Lollypops" gives away the century in another one that includes the Teatro di Pompeo. In the Piazza del Popolo, she captures the effect of that great open space with the obelisk; the twin image of the church forms a gateway to the streets of Rome. And she writes on the drawing of the Piazza S. Eustachio: "A landscape is a place enclosed by buildings." The reversal is complete.

Solomon knows everything about the color of stone. The grays and terracottas of Roman buildings turn into multishades of beige in her latest drawings of San Francisco houses cascading down the grid of hilly streets there.

Essentially all the drawings, of Renaissance gardens or of contemporary city streets, are about passageways from interiors to exteriors and the individual's private experience of borders—cafés under trees, shops under awnings, and fishing piers are some of her border images. But also as the body moves in a disciplined pattern, the mind is free to wander. "Order encloses magic," is how she expresses it, as muted colors and blurred edges in her drawings evoke the qualities of gardens and places remembered.

Some of the memories she jogs are of literary gardens, those lawns and allées fixed in the imagination with a reality equal to experience. Seen through her eye, Henry James's description of the memorable lawn that stretches out behind the gabled brick house at the beginning of *The Portrait of a Lady* takes on a deeper significance: "Privacy reigned supreme, and the wide carpet of turf that covered the hill-top seemed but the extension of a luxurious interior."

"There is magic," concludes Solomon in one passage, "when illusion is reality and opposites merge." For her, the common ground, where the inside and outside meet, has become the stage for civilization—civilization, that is, at its most cultivated.

Metropolis, March 1984

Planting Plastic: Martha Schwartz
Looks to Art for Inspiration

IN EXPANDING the concept of what makes a garden, the landscape architect Martha Schwartz defines it as a place that is "conducive to contemplation and understandable on a human scale." It need not necessarily contain plants—"Certainly many fine Japanese gardens do not," she explained. And even when gardens are "filled with plastic or other strange objects," Schwartz said, "I think they are still real gardens." Such a garden is the one Schwartz created several years ago at her mother's home outside Philadelphia.

Admittedly, Schwartz does not come to landscape architecture with a horticultural orientation. She is drawn instead to the fluidity of outdoor spaces and the possibilities of various other media. Her concern is the synthesis between art and landscape, a concern she shares with Peter E. Walker, formerly her professor at the Harvard Graduate School of Design and currently her partner in The Office of Peter Walker Martha Schwartz Landscape Architects, of San Francisco and New York. It is an approach that would not be foreign to the great landscape architects of the seventeenth century, like André Le Nôtre, who brought all the arts to bear on garden design, employing sculptors as well as gardeners. In fact, Walker sees minimalists like Carl Andre and Donald Judd as contemporary interpreters of the flat planes and systematic order of Le Nôtre's gardens. He adds another dimension with his definition of a garden as "any place out of doors one really cares about and transforms into something memorable."

"Instead of dealing with the old clichés of garden design," said Schwartz, "we examined the artists and their sensibilities to determine what their work reflected about today's culture that could be translated into landscape architecture." During their explorations, Schwartz was especially influenced by the early exhibitions of Frank Stella's metal relief paintings in the late 1970s. These were wall constructions of corrugated aluminum and other materials in arabesque and linear motifs painted in Fauvist colors with a smattering of glitter. In high relief against background patterns resembling those in Matisse paintings, the crowded elements were hooked onto a metal grid, and there was just enough open space at the sides to invite the possibility of the viewer's being inside them.

"I was bowled over by these relief paintings," she remembered, "and I was intrigued by the notion of 'more is more.' It was an additive process that ran counter to the modernist tradition I had been trained in, of paring down to the essential idea. He was layering banal shapes with more layers of paint and glitter and building them up to the point where the whole transcended the junk to become richly beautiful. I decided then to try to make a garden like that." The site for the Stella Garden was her mother's dreary twenty-foot-by-twenty-foot yard behind a semidetached house outside Philadelphia. Her mother's name is Stella Schwartz, so the garden was named for her as well.

Martha Schwartz began the garden by collecting junk. First she made weekly excursions to Plexiglas outlets around Boston, where she then lived, to purchase odd pieces by the pound. They came prewrapped, so she did not even know what colors she was getting. Next, she drove up to Marblehead, Massachusetts, for fishnets, then went to tropical fish stores for aquarium gravel, which comes in two-pound bags, each of a different color.

After carting the stuff to Philadelphia, she culled more objects from the assortment in her mother's garage. Once organized, she built a small study model of her ideas as a guide. The mirror-image yard next door to her mother's house provided a sufficiently verdant background for the Stella Garden, and the neighboring trees that towered above cast down dramatic shadows. Schwartz removed all the scraggly remains of a previous garden—her mother not having a notably green thumb—and laid a sheet of Visqueen plastic to prevent further growth. She then filled in the entire area with gravel.

Schwartz created a formal portal, with two tall tree trunks supporting a cloud of white chicken wire. To "dematerialize" the trunks so that the clouds might appear to float alone, she painted them white with red and green dashes, which also blended in with the visual chaos she sought for the rest of the garden. The height of the trees was balanced by a ladder placed surrealistically against a garage wall. Schwartz also repainted the house with a light lavender base to make it an effective backdrop.

The big moment arrived when she unwrapped the Plexiglas. She and her sister, Megan Reid, then a student at the Pennsylvania Academy of Fine Arts, assessed the various sizes and colors and determined an arrangement of the slabs in a border around the garden, gradating them from clear to hot to cool colors. Standing in staggered rows, these sheets of Plexiglas served both as a visually spectacular fence between the backyards and as "flower" beds, with taller varieties in the rear, some shooting out in different directions as flowers are wont to do. The pieces were set in a trench of clay, which was pliable enough to allow ongoing adjustments even after the Plexiglas was in position. As some colors were seen through others, the palette became even richer in shades, and in early morning, the sun shining through the panels cast colored shadows across the gray gravel.

The garden also had a kind of central "water" feature. "Having water in a garden," Martha Schwartz said, "is what brings the sky down to the ground plane." Since she is always seeking new ways of translating elements, she introduced into the design, instead of water with its inherent maintenance problems, a four-foot-square wire-glass table on concrete block supports. Like water, the glass reflected light and the color of the sky. The table, in turn, was placed on a six-inch-high wooden plinth or platform painted green, with a grid across the surface containing aquarium gravel in a pattern of amorphous colored shapes that appeared to reflect the jewel-like tones of the Plexiglas. Finally came a canopy of dyed-pink fishnets, stretched like sails above the whole composition.

One aesthetic drawback remained. Old garbage cans stood along the access route from the garage to the garden. Schwartz replaced them with five brand-new galvanized ones, which she covered with glitter and epoxy. "I figured that if my mother had to walk past garbage cans to get to the garden, at least they were going to be beautiful garbage cans," she says.

Though her mother had the garden for less than a year before she moved from the house, the Stella Garden was built to last, with a minimum of maintenance—primarily an occasional raking of the gravel. Over the long term, cleaning and repainting would have been required, and eventually some of the Plexiglas might have had to be replaced because of fading.

So far the Stella Garden has been unique in her oeuvre as an experiment. "It was a difficult process," she said, "because I kept feeling I shouldn't add one more thing, but then I felt that I should, for the exercise of it—the more, the better." The experience of the garden was like walking through the picture plane of a collage. And what it lacked in fragrance, it made up in glitz.

The Stella Garden reflected what Schwartz's partner Peter Walker describes as the historical tendency of gardens to exploit the artistic and theatrical attitudes of their age. At present, under the influence of what Walker calls "the park movement," he feels that landscape architects generally tend to create natural landscapes; as a result, he believes, the magical, make-believe element of gardens has disappeared.

But that could not be said of the Stella Garden, where, in the black of night, the lights shining through the transparent columns of neon colors created what seemed like an imaginary city somewhere in outer space, and the isolated ladder against the garage wall, a stairway to the stars.

New York Times Magazine, September 22, 1985

Resurrection: The Built Landscapes of George Hargreaves

WALKING AND THINKING, to breathe the site. This is how the landscape architect George Hargreaves works best to achieve his mission of weaving ideas and spaces into masterful combinations, reconnecting cities with their postindustrial derelict lands. And because his designs are perceived as figurative, rather than scenic, to experience them also evokes clarity of thought and observation. The promenade or circuit becomes the tangible thread connecting people to a series of events in these sculpted landscapes that retain a sensitivity to their environments and to their previous histories. Where others see destitution, Hargreaves sees restitution.

Hargreaves found his vision through his own circuitous route, one that began with an epiphany on the summit of Flattop Mountain while backpacking in Colorado's Rocky Mountain National Park. Emerging above the tree line onto a summer snowcap dotted with flowers, he looked out over Bear Lake to a view of the peaks beyond. It was a spatial experience that made him feel at one with nature and the landscape. When he recounted the feeling to an uncle, who was dean of forestry at the University of Georgia, the older man responded, "Have you ever heard of landscape architecture?"

From then on Hargreaves traveled in a straight line. After completing his bachelor of landscape architecture at the University of Georgia School of Environmental Design, he earned his master's degree at Harvard University's Graduate School of Design, where he has taught since 1986 and now chairs the Department of Landscape Architecture. During graduate school came a second revelation. He discovered earthworks of the 1970s like Robert Smithson's *Spiral Jetty* in Great Salt Lake and *Amarillo Ramp* in Texas. While artists like Smithson and Michael Heizer, whose *Double Negative* cut trenches on a Nevada mesa, saw their works purely as sculptural objects in the landscape, Hargreaves explored them as new elements exposed to the shaping effects of water, wind, and gravity. He further developed these concepts in workshops devoted to landforms—spheres, cones, pyramids—that would serve as space makers the way other designers would insert walkways or plantations. In his 1996 entry to the Festival International des Jardins at Chaumont-sur-Loire, France, he compressed these ideas into something akin to poetry. On a small site, he constructed a spiral mound alongside serpentine beds of grasses and perennials, suggesting agricultural furrows, and an abstract forest of fiberglass rods. The arrangement invited a promenade to the top of the mound for an uplifting view of the Loire River.

While traveling abroad as a young professional, he embarked on another formative experience, that of appreciating the complexity of history and culture that marks places like Stowe Landscape Gardens in England and Courances in France. Stowe provides the most evocative long walk in England through a vast property that was shaped in succession in the eighteenth century by Charles Bridgeman, William Kent, and Lancelot "Capability" Brown, who became head gardener in 1741. On the circuit around fields and lakes and across bridges and into small temples and monuments, there is a moment at Stowe when suddenly the majestic scheme, though based on disparate influences, comes together. The enchanting seventeenth-century park at the Château de Courances, said to have been designed by André Le Nôtre and repaired in the late nineteenth century by Achille Duchêne, is planned on a more domestic scale than Le Nôtre's grander designs for Vaux-le-Vicomte and Versailles. It is fed by ten natural springs that establish such diverse water features as a moat, a horseshoe fountain, a mirror lake, a stepped canal, and—the culmination—the striking image of a long, somber canal lined navelike with black poplar trees. The fact that the landscapes of both Courances and Stowe have survived the centuries in a composite, readable form indicates a respect for their individual parts.

Cumulative history rather than complex theory is what most affected Hargreaves's view of landscape design. And yet, looking closer at work by "Capability" Brown and Humphry Repton during his travels in Britain, he found that their smooth approaches to grading and tame clumps of trees sanitized rather than invigorated the surrounding nature. Instead, Hargreaves preferred the richness of the wilder approach in New York's Central Park, where Frederick Law Olmsted and Calvert Vaux unleashed nature by scattering plants and trees and by creating a geological basis with rocky outcrops. Many landscape architects, Hargreaves believes, "lift" the substance of Olmsted without truly understanding his style. (Like many of Hargreaves's own projects, the idealized landscape of Central Park itself was constructed on vacant swampland, as was its inspiration, Birkenhead Park near Liverpool, the oldest free-entry municipal park in Britain, designed by Joseph Paxton.)

Hargreaves followed the forcefulness of nature one step further as he witnessed the destructive powers of a hurricane destroy a beach in Hawaii. He saw in this disorder a beauty that countered the static norms of American landscapes and recognized the greater possibilities of kinetic potential in a human rapport with the land.

Since 1983 Hargreaves Associates of San Francisco and Cambridge, Massachusetts, have traveled the world with their original concepts of engagement and narrative in rediscovering the underlying essence of landscapes. The plaza for the Sydney Olympics 2000, a waterfront park on landfill for Lisbon's Expo '98, and landforms tying Japan Science World to Tokyo Bay are only a few of their international commissions. But for Hargreaves, northern California was like the Land of Oz, a magical but somewhat bizarre, windswept country where anything was possible. Following his professional path in the Bay Area, where he lives, reveals not only the historical evolution of the land itself but also the continuity and fluidity of a practice that has developed, as he says, into three different stages. He describes early work, like Byxbee Park in Palo Alto, as abstract and bare, pushing beyond the limits of normal ideas about landscape and relying for materials on dirt and the remaining detritus on the site. The middle period, represented by Guadalupe River Park in San Jose, brought a dramatic turnaround to fringe or marginalized areas closer to populous downtowns and demonstrates a full command of the requisite supporting technologies. And the third and most recent stage addresses locations at the very heart of a culture, requiring ever more complex solutions, like Crissy Field in San Francisco. At the interface of land and water, all of these remnant sites were also the edges inhabited by Native American tribes whose spirits can be reimagined as people once more promenade along these shores.

Byxbee Park was a garbage mound before it became a park in 1991. Now, paths of crushed oyster shells weave through a series of landforms that blend with adjacent baylands and encourage the return of wildlife. A walk there is similar to hikes in the English Lake District, where the natural hills form an immediate horizon that dissolves when one approaches the next rise. This perceived increase in space and distance through valleys and elevations is something that Olmsted understood when he created the illusion of deep perspectives with undulating paths leading toward a near horizon crested with trees. There are no trees, though, in the thirty-five acres of Byxbee Park, for fear that the roots would disturb the one-foot-thick impenetrable clay cap sealing the landfill under two feet of soil.

In collaboration with two environmental artists, Hargreaves has made a powerful combination of elements that integrate the reclaimed site with its history and location. Waves of nonirrigated native purple stipa grass give the landscape a velvety appearance, changing from green in early spring to a rich golden hue by May. Surrounded on two sides by water, the Mayfield Slough and the Mayfield Marsh, the park may be isolated on a peninsula, but it also meshes visually with the larger landscape beyond.

Striking out across the northern slope, the visitor climbs along a series of eight massive chevrons, formed by concrete highway barriers embedded at right angles as a directional motif for airplanes heading to the nearby municipal airport. From there the path proceeds through a narrow pass between two landforms that open into the park's protected area. Here clusters of hillocks (reminders of Ohlone Indian shell heaps) planted with lupines and other wildflowers offer both shelter from the wind and a lookout over the long vistas.

On the descending slope, five berms of compacted soil and rock infill, set in ever larger arcs for erosion control, give the impression of rippling water. A sculpture installed at the head of this procession, called *Wind Wave Piece*, echoes the rippling motion—a square arc with hanging ropes that wave in the afternoon northwest wind. The path proceeds along the slough and passes the flare needed for burning off methane gas from the underlying garbage. The thick hedgerows lining the banks of Mayfield Slough are interspersed with triangular, cedar-plank viewing platforms for birdwatching over the wetlands.

As the walk continues around the point, a conceptual forest comes into view, a dramatic grid of weathered green cedar posts. These create an exciting visual rhythm as the grid shifts and finally disperses into randomness as one turns the corner. The patterns recall the experience of passing telephone poles on a drive in the country and reflect as well the processional aspect of power pylons across the slough. The pole field, as it is called, is sliced off at the top in a slanted plane gesturing down to the marsh.

Hargreaves's design for Byxbee Park includes a small gem of architecture: the triangular restroom at the parking lot entrance. An unmistakable reference to Louis Kahn's famous 1950s Bath House for the Jewish Community Center of Trenton, New Jersey, it is elegantly simple and practical. Hargreaves's crisp little pavilion has a translucent roof for natural light, thereby eliminating the need for electricity, while the gap between the roof and cedar walls provides ventilation.

A few miles south in San Jose, Hargreaves engineered an entire series of parks around the Guadalupe River that have transformed and rejuvenated the city. The river, a valuable water source, has also been an instrument of vast destruction during periodic flooding. But Hargreaves brought to the assignment an understanding of both natural and man-made landforms that provided the solution to the hydrological challenge. In a sense, he has designed a string of city parks as a vast controlled water garden. Few landscape architects since Olmsted have had the opportunity to work on such a grand scale in one urban location.

Downstream from the city, the river flows innocently through its narrow bed, but on the embankment of Guadalupe River Park the braided network of alluvial berms resembles in accentuated form the buildup of striated sediment in a river delta. Intermittent channels contain the periodic overflow before redirecting it to the riverbed. In dry periods, the graceful undulating landscape along serpentine paths with plantations of oaks and bay trees belies the technological precision of the engineered landforms that are narrowed on the upstream ends to reverse the torrents. The woody plant habitat on the riverbanks—cottonwood trees, scrub willow, snowberry, and gooseberry—possesses the wildness that Hargreaves believes brings richness to the landscape and also guarantees low maintenance.

In San Jose itself, where the Guadalupe River meets Los Gatos Creek, Hargreaves designed Confluence Park as a meeting place for crowds converging on the San Jose Arena for sports events. Stately rows of poplar trees along the green are like those seen in the French countryside. The sloped Arena Green amphitheater is configured with pyramidal landforms and pocket spaces for picnicking within groves of trees. It recalls the green amphitheater at Claremont Garden in Surrey, designed by Charles Bridgeman. The park crosses the creek via a pedestrian bridge to Confluence Point, a cool, wet naturalistic woodland on a spit of land formed by the two rivers. The handsome Cor-Ten steel bridge has all the stately elegance of the Palladian Bridge at Stowe.

In downtown San Jose, with its combination of old Spanish-style and contemporary office buildings, the threat of the Guadalupe River was even more dangerous, as it flowed through the heart of the city. Hargreaves secured the riverbanks with a wall of terraced gabions that have filled up with enough soil and pioneer plants to sprout a genuine riparian plant community. (Gabions—metal cages filled with rocks used in roadway fortifications—have become one of the most attractive and useful industrial products available to landscape architects.) These terraces combined with long serpentine steps along the riverbank, allowing the water to rise step by step, both control and speed up the river as it travels through the city. A new corporate headquarters constructed by the Silicon Valley giant Adobe on the riverbanks is proof of renewed confidence.

Hargreaves's Plaza Park is San Jose's main square, crisscrossed daily by pedestrians on angled paths typical of town commons. Its central promenade retraces the historic Camino Real, the route that led to the California missions. Here, water has been captured and tamed in the first fountain the landscape architect designed. Its spouts, at intersecting points of a grid of glass blocks, are flush with the ground. They produce mist in early morning, provide playful geysers for children at midday, and at night, illuminated through the glass blocks, glow in a magical terrain. A grid of jacaranda trees recalls the satisfying beauty and regularity of orchards that once dotted the region; mature redwoods, live oaks, and sycamores shade pathways lined with park benches. Hargreaves also leaves his mark with the angled green walls of an informal amphitheater.

While accommodating every aspect of outdoor enjoyment, Crissy Field, now a national park in San Francisco, redefines the process of a public landscape. George Hargreaves and his associates, particularly his longtime collaborator Mary Margaret Jones, peeled back layers of the site's natural and man-made history to discover a configuration of elements that overlap in time. Hargreaves often speaks of the poetry of landscape, which suggests a compression of language and forms that reveal ideas without overelaboration. Urban parks are never natural landscapes, but they may be designed to enhance appreciation of nature. Waterfront parks, like Crissy Field on San Francisco Bay, have the added advantage of facing the beauty and unpredictability of the sea.

Located at the bottom of the Presidio, the old Spanish garrison turned U.S. military post, Crissy Field was originally a tidal marsh where the Ohlone Indians harvested shellfish. In 1912 it was filled in as an automobile racetrack for the upcoming Panama-Pacific International Exposition of 1915; in 1921, as a grassy meadow, it became an airfield for biplanes named after the aviation pioneer Major Dana A. Crissy. The airfield was paved over in 1935 and remained in use by the military until 1974. Since then, the beach has become a haven for windsurfers who appear even today to fly through the waves on glinting Mylar sails like a flock of low-flying seabirds.

Crissy Field extends one hundred acres from east to west, from a stand of cypress trees just beyond Marina Green to the Golden Gate Bridge. The major elements of the park are a vast tidal marsh, a lagoon fed with seawater, and, overlooking it, a lush kidney-shaped grassy meadow of an airfield. Running the entire length of the park along the sandy beach and boulder-strewn shore is a 1.3-mile windy esplanade, wide enough never to appear crowded even on a holiday. The airfield itself is a giant berm of red fescue grass that rises several feet above the promenade at one end and slants down to ground level at the other. The parking area at the eastern end, for windsurfers and visitors, fades into a meadow with finger-splayed mounds and a grid of trees. At the far end, red-roofed structures with weatherboard siding in groves of palm trees preserve a bit of Army vernacular but also serve as a refreshment area. Complex swirls of berms protect picnic areas and challenge children more than most conventional playgrounds do. In general, though, the flatness of the landscape makes richer all the fine details: the wisps of color of thousands of native plants growing in the dune gardens or the boardwalk leading to a standing grove of Monterey cypress on the beach.

But what is public may also be private. While the flow of people proceeds along the esplanade, anyone can walk out on the bridge crossing the lagoon and quietly watch the birds settle in the twilight as the rosy clouds of sunset gather over the Golden Gate Bridge. Hargreaves has no doubt been walking and thinking there himself to breathe in the site, motivated to re-create in other people's lives the sensation of his existential experience at Flattop

Mountain, "to make moments and places more than what they are in a redefined picturesque for the twenty-first century."

In every era, individuals emerge with a singular creativity—part genius, part opportunity—that takes their art or science to a new level of realization, but without departing entirely from the cultural past. Stowe, Courances, Central Park, and countless other sources have played a role in Hargreaves's education.

In architecture, spectacular results are achieved by variations of form and function combined with new materials and advancements in engineering. The challenge has always been greater, though, in landscape architecture, where the substance of design remains the same: earth, water, stone, plant life, and sky as a source of light and shadow. Add to this list time, memory, people, and the natural history of a site. And more often than not, today these sites represent cultural wastelands depleted of both character and characteristics, abandoned brownfields at the edges of cities. George Hargreaves's goal is resurrection.

> The Changing Garden: Four Centuries of European and American
> Art, exhibition catalogue, Iris & Gerald Cantor Center for Visual Arts,
> Stanford University, University of California Press, 2003

A Twinkling Terrace that Reaches for the Stars: Kathryn Gustafson in New York and France

PARIS—ZOOMING UP the Champs-Elysées in her Saab, Kathryn Gustafson, an American landscape architect, stopped to admire bouquets of roses tightly arrayed in the rear window of a florist's truck. "That's a garden, too," she said, and she drove on.

New Yorkers had better prepare themselves for such judgments. Gustafson, forty-seven, has been handed her first American project, the Arthur Ross Terrace at the American Museum of Natural History, scheduled to open in the spring of 2000.

Her new, nearly one-acre urban garden will be just outside the moonlike sphere, designed by Polshek & Partners, that will house the new planetarium. Gustafson's terrace, on the 81st Street side of the museum, will echo what's inside, with a long slanting shadow of dark granite—meant to evoke a lunar eclipse—that will glisten with rivulets of water and twinkle with fiber-optic stars depicting the constellation Orion.

James Stewart Polshek, architect of the planetarium, said Gustafson won the competition to design the terrace because "she understood that the design must be metaphorically linked to the planetarium."

Ellen V. Futter, the museum's president, said she found Gustafson's spare design for the terrace "elegant yet simple, harmonizing both with nature on earth and with the universe beyond, in a physical context." She expects that crowds will be drawn to the pristine quality of this public space, and to Gustafson's fantasy of fiber-optic starlight that will sparkle at night.

Gustafson is always in tune with the sights, sounds, and smells of her environment, especially in France, where, until 1997, she lived and worked. Now she is back in her native Washington, on Vashon Island in Puget Sound, but she still commutes to Paris and London for work. Her studio offers the tranquility to create the plaster models that are the basis for the sweeping landscapes and vast movements of land that have become her signature style. Her projects remain best known in Europe, and it is necessary to understand what she has done abroad in order to comprehend her vocabulary for the museum terrace, which is only beginning to take shape.

Having left the fleeting world of fashion, she completed her landscape architecture degree at the École Nationale Supérieure du Paysage at Versailles and opened an office in Paris. She sees herself as part of a historical movement in transition from agriculture to pleasure gardens, and from the architectural garden rooms of the Renaissance to the picturesque. Although she seeks to mix and unify these traditions, her aesthetic veers toward abstract and minimalist forms and was shaped in France by her mentors there. These included the well-known landscape architect Jacques Sgard ("I never drew a curve before I worked with him"), the sculptor Igor Mitoraj ("He gave me the tools to sculpt my clay models"), and Peter Rice, structural engineer of the Pompidou Center. Walks among the systematic beds and the glasshouses of the Jardin des Plantes in Paris influenced her planting designs.

What has evolved is a vision of landscape as an immense canvas to shape and manipulate. Gustafson takes into consideration the movement of people through these spaces and the environment beyond: not only buildings, but also shifting sunlight and shadows throughout the day or, at night, landscapes made vivid by her lighting designs.

Since 1980, she has been involved in three dozen important public projects: town squares, corporate landscapes, and city parks. The Parc de la Villette, in Paris, is on her roster, as are a number of projects for corporations and governments, clients she feels are more accepting of her bold approaches to nature.

In the summer of 1997, when the city of Lausanne, Switzerland, invited landscape architects to enhance its narrow streets and broad esplanades for an International Festival of Urban Gardens, Gustafson redesigned the Esplanade de Montbenon, an undefined expanse of lawn overlooking Lake Geneva. By placing swathes of silvery leafed plants next to long blue beds, she linked this plaza visually with the gray-blue waters and the Alps rising beyond. Then, with the composer François Paris, she suspended glass chimes and gongs from metal arches along the adjacent walkways. Their soft tinkling sounds in the wind were reminiscent of the clock chimes that add a pervasive music to Swiss townscapes.

A few months ago, Gustafson was in the London offices of Sir Norman Foster, the architect of the Great Glass House for Britain's newest botanic garden, the National Botanic Garden of Wales in Llanarthne. It will open next year. The elliptical structure, 330 feet long, will be the largest single-span glasshouse in the world. Gustafson is designing the interior, best described as the Grand Canyon under a glass sky. With deep, sharply cut stone chasms and crevices, a sixteen-foot waterfall, and a flood plain at the bottom, the landscape, to be planted with Mediterranean flora from the Northern and Southern Hemispheres, will be a milestone in botanic garden design.

In presenting the model, Gustafson held high a light on a long wire and moved it in orbit like the sun to demonstrate how in the course of a day deep shadows will be cast by the sheer walls of the gorge. The landscape in real stone will be softened by the grays, yellows, and greens of the planting palette. "The atmosphere will be permeated with the fragrance of damp earth and crushed thyme and the crackling sound of real pebbles on the paths," she forecasts.

But France has been her stronghold, especially the town of Rueil-Malmaison on the Seine, eight miles west of Paris, where several corporations have built new homes nestled among the quiet residential streets lined with linden trees. Those corporations wanted to add to, not detract from, suburban neighborhoods already filled with gardens. Gustafson gave Shell Petroleum rolling green lawns that are bermed up against the headquarters building. One can understand why she says, "I'd love to design a golf course." The lush lawns, separated by sharp-cornered limestone walls, are like a green lava flow.

Her complex designs for corporations are comparable in scope to gardens designed around palaces and chateaus in the seventeenth century, though her work is closer to that of contemporary land artists like Michael Heizer or James Turrell. Behind Shell's buildings, Gustafson switched from a bold to an intimate, almost domestic, scale. A canal-cum-water garden separates the two main buildings, which are joined by a series of glass-enclosed bridges. Along the water, plantings of dogwood, magnolia, azalea, and rhododendron are arrayed in color patterns from white to purple. Along the canal, a low boardwalk with steel handrails barely skims the water.

In a simpler but no less elegant vein, Gustafson laid out a series of rills in marble troughs in front of the Esso headquarters just blocks away. The troughs stretch like ribbons of water between rolling lawns and a grove of willow trees. From each side, these channels empty into a shallow cascade that flows gently toward the Seine. On the banks of the Seine, in view of the railroad bridge at Chatou, a favorite subject of the Impressionists, she fashioned an overlook with modern steel benches and ample space for skateboarding.

Her ideas about history, culture, and memory are summed up in her park for the medieval town of Terrasson in the Dordogne. It redefines the meaning of gardens. On a steep hillside next to a fifteenth-century fortified abbey, Gustafson created what she describes as "history fragments of gardens," or what the town calls "Imaginary Gardens." One mysterious feature of the park is how streams, fountains, and cascades rush into the open—and just as quickly disappear. It is possible to walk through her forest of fountains there and, on a still day, not get wet. And when asked about the undulating trellises of steel bars over the rose garden, Gustafson described the configuration by flipping an imaginary sheet in the air.

Gustafson is also in tune with Paris, and with what makes it the City of Light. Driving by the Place de la Concorde one night, she pointed out how the numerous lampposts are placed at different heights. "If you squint your eyes," she said, "it is like driving through a galaxy of stars."

New York Times, January 7, 1999

Landform Future: Laurie Olin and the Integration of Architecture and Landscape

IN 1964, when Bernard Rudofsky wrote of "the challenge of topography" in his seminal work *Architecture Without Architects*, little did he imagine the import that topography as an organizing principle would exert on twenty-first-century architecture. In a recent book *Landscrapers: Building with the Land* (Thames and Hudson), Aaron Betsky, director of the Netherlands Architecture Institute, has heralded the joint engineering of the land and structure as a "utopian form of architecture." In what appears to be a movement, architects, given the opportunity of a spacious site, have an increased awareness of the importance of melding their design with the existing environment. And gone are the days when landscape architects were viewed only as enhancers of surrounding settings.

Now architects and landscape architects are collaborating in designing buildings that are essentially landform structures in and of themselves. In describing his long collaboration with architect Peter Eisenman, landscape architect Laurie Olin speaks of "the relationship between buildings and site—and our exploration of ways that the two might be considered as aspects of the same thing." As he elaborates, "This is a bit more than thinking of architecture and landscape as being commingled or working in harmony, but rather thinking (and making) each an extension of the other, conceived and built as a continuum." This form, Olin acknowledges, grows out of the topography of place.

Although Eisenman and Olin have been working together since completing the Wexner Center for the Arts in Columbus, Ohio, in 1989—drawing buildings and landscapes as one integrated unit—only two of their twenty-some projects have been built, the other being the recently opened Memorial to the Murdered Jews of Europe in Berlin. As in any long creative process, even unbuilt projects serve to solidify ideas and lead to new ones. Their current collaboration on the City of Culture of Galicia, above the medieval pilgrimage town of Santiago de Compostela, is a true culmination of their long partnership combining theoretical concepts once nurtured separately.

Anyone who saw the first models of the City of Culture exhibited at the Spanish Institute in New York in 2001, or heard the architects in a dialogue on "The Processes of Santiago" at the Architectural League of New York last February, understands to what degree this complex of six undulating ribbons of buildings emerging from Monte Gaiás and a mass of trees surpasses earlier projects and expresses new concepts in urbanism. Since the purpose of the City of Culture—with two libraries, an audiovisual center, a photography bank, a history museum, and an opera house—is to capitalize on the intersection of technology and information systems with art and culture, the buildings themselves on the 173-acre site are tangible proof of the possibilities that can be achieved through technology without losing the memory of the land.

Although the City of Culture appears to be a long way from Eisenman's squared-off House III (1973), which rotated one cube inside another, he has remained true to abstract Modernism destabilized by other figurative programs related to the site. Olin is also a modernist, but with a touch of Le Nôtre, the seventeenth-century landscape architect for Versailles. If Olin is known for such orderly, populous, urban sites as Manhattan's Bryant Park and the just-completed renovation of Columbus Circle (a Place de la Concorde for New York, brimming with fountains), he also adds other dimensions to his work through his eye for what Frederick Law Olmsted valued as natural scenery.

For the Galicia project, cultural and geological elements merge in a solution that combines nature and urbanity. The architects began by overlaying the site with the figure of a furrowed scallop shell, symbolic of James the Apostle, whose relics have drawn pilgrims to Santiago since the twelfth century. Then they transposed onto the site plan the medieval streets from the historic core of Santiago, warped by the computer, according to Eisenman, as if the topography of the hill were somehow pushed through them. Finally, a Cartesian grid was superimposed to create a variable tartan of unequal intersecting lines. From this three-dimensional model resulted the distorted, tilting, undulating ensemble of buildings and red sandstone walkways with a large plaza. "Instead of the ground being conceived as a backdrop against which the buildings stand out as figures [read the Acropolis], we generate a condition in which the ground can rear up to become figure, and the buildings subside into the ground," Eisenman explains. The interiors reflect the same folding and fluid surfaces.

Cast over the site plan is a grid of cork oaks recalling agricultural plantings in social centers of Spanish towns. Local grasses and wildflowers creep up the sides of the apparently "excavated" structures of the hilltop to meet roof cladding of native granite slabs. In this northwest corner of the Iberian peninsula, these wavelike volumes are unintentionally reminiscent of the ancient robust granite storehouses for corn described by Rudofsky.

Olin likens the ensemble to the ruins of Etruscan tombs at Cerveteri, north of Rome, where the structures emerge from the landscape at different levels so that they all become one. To complete the illusion here of the mountainous landscape, the plan includes a new forest of Galicia along the steeply terraced slopes descending from the City of Culture. Though Olin has initiated plantings of oaks, birches, mountain ashes, and hawthorns placed on a grid, he knows that the percentages have to be right in order for the natural selective process to turn them eventually into a true hillside forest.

In a different approach to landform architecture, the constructed topography of Seattle Art Museum's Olympic Sculpture Park by Weiss/Manfredi Architects offers a means of healing a divisive rift of urban infrastructure along the derelict site of a former fuel storage and transfer station. In 1976, sculpture had already begun to encroach north of this shoreline area with Michael Heizer's massive *Adjacent, Against, Upon* on landfill with railroad tracks running behind it.

Clearly, the openness and abundant light on waterfronts present coastal cities as ideal locations for displaying the kind of oversize sculpture difficult to house in museums. In their design for the Olympic Sculpture Park, Marion Weiss and Michael A. Manfredi were faced with a forty-foot drop from street level to the water's edge at a location divided by the same railroad tracks and a four-lane highway. Drawing on earlier experiences in mechanically stabilized earth, they created a wide, descending zigzag of a park that bridges seamlessly over the transportation "gorges." The firm's design for the Museum of the Earth in Ithaca, New York, incorporates a series of berms that conceal parked cars but also purify runoff water through plantings of equisetum; eventually, the overflow of clean water discharges into Lake Cayuga. A similar technology will carry excess water from Olympic Park into Elliott Bay.

In this case, a glass pavilion with galleries at street level acts as an extension of the landscape, and a cut through the sloping roof opens to spectacular views over Puget Sound. Along the first descent, a forest of conifers and redwoods surrounds an upper-level sculpture garden; from there, the landscape unfurls along grassy paths above sheered slopes planted with fragrant wild roses and supported by concrete slabs that double as screens for video art. The architects are restoring the shoreline into a new recreational beach.

Working with local landscape architect Charles Anderson for horticultural materials, the architects have designed an intimate, aerial park that offers appropriately open settings for the museum's extensive sculpture collection, with works by David Smith, Alexander Calder, Toni Smith, and Mark di Suvero. The level changes and sloping platforms provide an opportunity for distant viewing from different angles that adds to a critical appreciation of three-dimensional objects that cannot be perceived in a flat space.

As a totally constructed environment, like the City of Culture, the Olympic Sculpture Park qualifies for Laurie Olin's definition of landform architecture as simply a set of built structures that end up being a landscape. What may have begun as a gesture to energy conservation or sustainable development has evolved into a new aesthetic that shapes inside and outside as a continuum, to use Olin's words. As the architectural firm Weiss/Manfredi has turned to landscape to devise architecture by sculpting the land with felicitous results, Eisenman, in his long collaboration and discussions with Olin, has discovered in local topography a means of merging multidimensional concepts into a veritable eruption of the land. As Olin remarks, "The history of architecture is not over; there is still more to come." Landscape architecture is definitely in its future.

Architectural Record, October 2005. Reprinted with permission from *Architectural Record* © 2005 The McGraw-Hill Companies. www.architecturalrecord.com

A Feminist View of Landscapes: A Partnership with Nature

WHAT DO WOMEN who are landscape designers really want? A new landscape architecture that is ethical as well as aesthetically pleasing. That was the conclusion at a symposium, "Women, Land, Design," sponsored by the Radcliffe Seminars to celebrate the twenty-fifth anniversary of its landscape design program. At the symposium, a feminist view emerged, not like the ponderous and theoretical gender studies that have dominated art history and literary studies in universities, but rather a lively discussion that focused on practical applications for shaping the future of the environment.

Setting the theme, Elizabeth Meyer, a landscape architect who teaches at the University of Virginia, dispelled the long-held image of landscape as merely a "soft or feminine frame" for architecture. In the traditional view of culture versus nature (which she equated with male versus female), man's relationship to the land is one of stewardship rather than partnership, she pointed out. What she called for was a new definition of landscape architecture that would foster a land ethic as well as an aesthetic that would operate between culture and nature.

Because the Radcliffe program has traditionally attracted to its graduate seminars in landscape design women who already play a planning role in their local communities, the message created a context for new and sometimes revolutionary ideas. "Control" was the word used pejoratively by Deborah E. Ryan, a landscape architect on the faculty of the University of North Carolina, to describe the Louis XIV school of landscape design, epitomized by Versailles. "It expresses man's dominance over the land," she said. "The majority of design work is still based on historical precedents rather than on an ideology that takes ecology and nature as process into consideration." Eco-feminism is the word she used for her new value system where ecology and design coexist.

One successful historic example cited was the Fens in Boston, a waterway within the seven-mile spine of parks designed by Frederick Law Olmsted, known as the Emerald Necklace. People who enjoy the Fens for its beauty are not aware that this created landscape has now become an important ecosystem.

Because conventional gardens and landscapes can also be cost prohibitive, today's landscape designers are challenged to use found materials, as Ryan did in the Playful Forest adjoining an elementary school in Charlotte, North Carolina. In a woodland devastated by Hurricane Hugo, she and her students designed a series of friendly pathways, incorporating pebble puddles and tree ladders that helped the children overcome their fear of the woods. (Another speaker, Margaret Dean Daiss, pointed out that in fairy tales, children are often being abandoned and frightened in the forest.)

Gina Crandell, who teaches landscape architecture at Iowa State University, amused the audience with a slide show that identified water motifs as either male (for example, a geyser, which is "predictable") or female (a "mysterious" swamp). "Is a geyser superior to a swamp?" she asked, getting participants to consider wetlands not as murky swamps but as national treasures that are more valuable ecologically than Old Faithful. In fact, some local commissions are regulating the work of landscape architects even on private wetlands to protect these endangered areas and their native plants. One example of wetland landscaping shown at the lecture was a pond "planted" by Karen McCoy, a Williamstown, Massachusetts, artist, with a grid of submerged arrowhead leaf plants whose delicate blossoms and spiky leaves cut a design across the surface of the water. "The danger," Crandell said, "lies in overdesigning wetland areas and thereby converting them from natural to pictorial landscapes, like the geysers.

In conjunction with the symposium, photographs of the work of women who are landscape architects and designers are on display on four floors of exhibition space at Schlesinger Library on the Radcliffe Yard. Co-curated by two faculty members, Elizabeth Dean Hermann and Eleanor M. McPeck, the show reveals innovative ideas from the past as well as for the future. Included among the historic exhibits is the 1923 plan for the garden community of Oakcroft in Ridgewood, New Jersey, by Marjorie Sewell Cautley, who Nell M. Walker, one of the symposium speakers, said was the first American woman landscape architect to enter city planning. At a time when developers built houses in uniform rows, her design of a communal green with six houses separated by gardens of native plants and trees was considered revolutionary.

It was the precursor in the East of what became known as the "garden cities movement," where plantings and houses are merged in the landscape.

The show, whose focus is New England, displays several projects for the greening of cities, especially Boston, where new open space will result from the submersion of Interstate 93, a major road. A study by Catherine Oranchak proposes new parkland that would be an extension of Olmsted's Emerald Necklace. To make the ten-year construction period attractive to pedestrians, Sheila Kennedy has designed elegant frame passageways for the Interim Bridges Project, which look in silhouette like New England covered bridges. (A prototype of this airy structure has already been built in a Boston parking lot.) As a studio project, the Radcliffe students themselves have been working on a proposal for a conservatory and a botanical garden on land that will be reclaimed with the submersion of I-93.

But the show isn't limited to the library. There is a touch of magic right across the common from Radcliffe. Steam and mist that emerge on city streets from underground ducts have inspired the designer Joan Brigham with an idea for a fountain on the Harvard campus. In the center of Peter Walker's Tanner Fountain, a concentric circle of boulders, she has produced clouds of mist that shroud passersby like a deep coastal fog.

As another interpretation of what women seek in gardens, the graduate students presented a separate exhibition called "Strangers in Paradise," located in Cronkhite Graduate Center. Student members of the Radcliffe chapter of the Boston Society of Landscape Architects used their impressions of a 1990 Canadian women's film titled *Strangers in Good Company* as the basis of their projects. In the cult hit, a group of elderly women are stranded at a house in the wilderness. As they learn to cope with the environment, they reveal their life stories. The students designed models of imaginary gardens and landscapes suitable to the characters in the film. Using mostly collage art, they created windows on private worlds—a call for landscapes with poetry as well as ecology.

New York Times, April 29, 1993

Two

Parks and Public Places

A Bouquet of British Parks: Liverpool, Edinburgh, and London

THE SLANT of late afternoon sun enhanced the spring green of New York's Central Park as I walked home along its winding paths and around the still, dark waters of the reservoir. Although I had walked this route hundreds of times over the years, the experience was enriched by having recently walked in the public park in England that gave Frederick Law Olmsted, Central Park's creator, the idea in the first place.

Writing in 1852, Olmsted described taking a ferry from Liverpool to Birkenhead on a spring day. He stopped to eat some buns in a baker's shop, and it was the baker "who begged of us not to leave Birkenhead without seeing their new park." Olmsted proceeded to the entrance, an impressive stone archway with Ionic columns (it still exists) and into a "luxuriant and diversified garden" with "winding paths," "varying surfaces" planted with shrubs and flowers, and "a greensward, closely mown," where gentlemen were playing cricket.

In general, Britain's public parks and gardens stem from two traditions. One is the conversion to public use of royal hunting preserves and gardens, frequently known as the Royal Parks. The other is the creation by city governments, mostly in the nineteenth century, of recreational parks and open spaces to improve the health of those who lived in congested urban slums.

There is no one season to visit parks, for they are like museums with changing exhibitions; each season has its own particular charm, color, and fragrance. But if you walk in parks at home to feel a respite from the pulse of

Facing page: Cervin Robinson, *IBM Garden Plaza, New York.*

the city, you will love them in Britain, as I did during a week's visit to public parks in London, Liverpool, and Edinburgh.

Liverpool

I began with Liverpool, at the park that inspired Olmsted, now known as Birkenhead Park. It was laid out from 1844 to 1846 by Sir Joseph Paxton, architect of the Crystal Palace in 1851 and head gardener to the Duke of Devonshire at Chatsworth in Derbyshire. Strolling through it, one has a sense of déjà vu, with its hilly contours of land, random arrangement of trees, and outer circular park drive ringed with villas. Swans glide across a pond lined with willows. Outside the Birkenhead Park Cricket Club, a Victorian chalet-style pavilion, spectators on green benches watched one of the last matches of that season.

From Birkenhead Park, one crosses the Mersey River to Liverpool's newest park, Riverside. It was created as part of last year's International Garden Festival and includes a splendid esplanade, punctuated by lampposts, stretching out along the estuary.

Riverside was built over a garbage dump and oil tanks. In only two years, landscapers have shaped an undulating terrain with distant views across the Mersey to the Welsh hills on the south. It will be years before the oak and beech trees are mature, but the outlines are there—rivulets cascading into an oxbow lake and embankments of wildflowers. Among the features that remain in the 125-acre area are the new Festival Hall and the excellent garden paths created by the Japanese. The festival's international theme gardens, inside the park, were so successful that they will be open again this year.

At least a ninth of Liverpool is parkland, with an emphasis on the botanical tradition that began in the late 1700s when travelers and sea captains returned to the city with exotic plants for the conservatories of the wealthy. The centerpiece of Sefton Park, the city's largest, is the triple-tiered Palm House, an 1896 octagonal structure that houses a central display of palm trees of many varieties. An elaborate spiral staircase winds around to an upper walkway, and the inner perimeter is lined with colorful flowering plants, some actually planted in beds. Hanging vines, including a pink bougainvillea, trail along many of the walls. With rose beds planted outside, there is a rich profusion of color and fragrance. An inscription from William Cowper reads, "Who loves a garden loves a greenhouse too."

Deeper in the residential district is Calderstones Park, with an extensive Botanic Garden near the main entrance. One passes from ornamental flower beds to a Japanese garden and finally into a typical English cottage garden that has the intimacy of a series of private terraces. Each circular section has four pergolas dripping with grapevines. It all exudes a comfortable charm that is surprising for a public place. Elsewhere, espaliered trees line the garden walls.

Edinburgh

Standing on any of the hills surrounding Edinburgh, one is impressed by how thickly treed the city is: the gray stone buildings are interspersed with rich patches of dark green. Another noteworthy fact: there are thirty-two golf courses within the city limits. Seeing them, one realizes how much golf links all over the world are made to resemble the natural Scottish landscape—the rough terrain of the hills and waterways. The network of burns (or streams) running through Edinburgh covers a distance of almost a hundred miles. The gradual greening of the embankments and walkways along these burns is creating a continuous waterside park throughout the city.

The most recently planted area—along the Water of Leith near the harbor—can be reached from steps off Great Junction Street. The slopes, artfully planted in a seemingly natural arrangement of rugosa roses and firethorn with brilliant reddish-orange berries, have already earned this new kind of park a major British prize.

Another good starting point is the seventy-acre Royal Botanic Garden in the city's Inverleith section. Though it is smaller than the Royal Botanic Gardens at Kew, the landscaping here is perhaps more interesting. The economical use of space leads to greater diversity in brief compass, and the plantings, though always of scientific interest, have an exotic beauty.

The Botanic Garden's nineteenth-century palm houses are landmarks in the annals of greenhouse architecture. The octagonal Tropical Palm House has a conical roof; when the original palm trees outgrew it, a second greenhouse was designed, adjacent to the first. This building, the Temperate Palm House, is a sandstone structure with arched windows and a curved glazed roof. Both are now juxtaposed against the newer Exhibition Plant Houses, designed in 1967, with a suspended roof and walls supported by external pylons, thus creating unimpeded internal spaces. Inside is a series of successive environments—including an aquatic house, a fern house, and a cycad and orchid house—no gimmicks, just exquisite plantings using peat beds as supports. It is a research collection in, quite simply, a wonderland.

From the highest point of the Botanic Garden, one has a panoramic view of Edinburgh and its salient features, including the castle that dominates the city. Having seen the castle from a distance, one cannot resist visiting the city park beneath the palisade on which it is perched—a small public garden in a deep ravine called West Princes Street Gardens—with a belle-époque fountain, abundant flower beds, a small café, and an immense floral clock. Imagine a summer evening, sitting with thousands of people listening to Tchaikovsky's *1812 Overture* when in addition to the fireworks at the finale a waterfall cascades over the castle wall. But its quiet pleasures on a weekday afternoon suit just as well, for it is an oasis between the old city on the hill and the new Georgian town beyond.

Other parks in Edinburgh, like The Meadows, near the West Princes Street Gardens, have evolved from village greens, and the crisscrossed paths under the cherry trees facilitate pedestrians as well as casual strollers and spectators of the local croquet teams. The Inch Park is where plantings for the rest of the parks are begun in three-quarters of an acre under glass. Saughton Park has extensive formal gardens with Italianate topiary.

Finally there is the city's Royal Park, called Holyrood Park, next to the Palace of Holyroodhouse, where the Queen stays when she visits Edinburgh. Holyrood Park is the city's largest, more like open countryside. Swans swim in St. Margaret's Loch, and a peaked ridge, Salisbury Crags, towers above an area called Hunter's Bog.

London

Henry James was a great man for the parks of London—especially the area of central London he describes in *The Princess Casamassima* as "that barely-interrupted expanse of irrepressible herbage which stretches from Birdcage Walk to Hyde Park Corner." This expanse—consisting of St. James's Park, Green Park, and Hyde Park—constitutes the core of the Royal Parks: it was through here that Hyacinth Robinson and Millicent Henning, two characters in the novel, passed on their way to Kensington Gardens.

Though physically linked, each of these parks has its own distinguishing characteristics in a spectrum ranging from greenswards and avenues of plane trees to flower beds. What all the Royal Parks have in common are 5,500 beechwood and green nylon canvas deck chairs, scattered invitingly throughout. For a pittance, one can rent a chair from early morning until closing time.

Even in the dead of winter, these parks stay green. But the freshest moment comes in March. While New York is still fighting off winter, the London parks become dense fields of Wordsworthian daffodils. In St. James's Park, where the willows around the lake are turning the palest green, one can sit for hours watching the pelicans and ducks, a frequent pastime of the seventeenth-century diarist Samuel Pepys. In those days, the park had more rigid French lines with a central canal; it got its romantic form in the early nineteenth century. The flower beds cluster around shrubberies in an informal manner, and crossing the lake on the small bridge, one is suspended in a charmed world between Buckingham Palace at one end and Whitehall at the other.

The parks are quite heavily used in comparison with preceding years, especially on Sundays, and restaurants at either end of the Serpentine are popular watering spots. No radios are allowed, and live music is by special permit only, based on its merits.

On a Sunday in May, the flower walk in Kensington Gardens provides rich visual pleasures. At the end of the walk, one comes to the Serpentine Gallery, which offers exhibitions of contemporary art. The two experiences make an aesthetically pleasing day.

For gardens on the grand scale, however, one goes to Queen Mary's Gardens in Regent's Park, which was laid out in the early nineteenth century by John Nash, whose neo-classical terrace facades lend an elegance to the park surrounds. The time to visit is the rose season for the acres of rose beds, but more to my taste are the intimate hillside rock garden with lavender spilling onto the pathways and the ornamental shrubs and alpine plants on a small island in the lake, reached by a wooden bridge. Not to be missed at the Zoological Gardens is the park's wire-mesh aviary, designed by Lord Snowdon.

Parks in London also include the squares—most of them privately owned—that keep the residential areas green and add enormously to the freshness of the streets. For the visitor they are a visual amenity, and a fragrant one in spring when the lilac bushes cascade over the iron railings. In autumn, at dusk, as the squares are prepared for winter, the London air is filled with the heady scent of burning leaves like any country town.

Finally there is Holland Park, originally the private estate of the family and descendants of the seventeenth-century Earl of Holland, with interruptions here and there. Essentially, this is a woodland park, with picket fences along the paths and intermittent fields of wildflowers. Occasionally one hears the crowing of a rooster. In the nineteenth century, the original stables were converted into a garden ballroom that now houses a restaurant, the Belvedere, overlooking the Dutch Gardens. Near the formal gardens are beds of dahlias, a reminder that Lady Holland is said to have introduced the dahlia into England in the nineteenth century.

As in most British parks, the handsome teak benches alongside the flower beds in Holland Park, weathered to a silver gray, are given as memorials to friends or family members and bear such inscriptions as this one: "In memory of Doris Wheeler who found joy in this garden." One day, I hope someone will remember me with a bench with this inscription: "For Paula Deitz who on many occasions found joy in the British parks and public gardens."

New York Times, April 7, 1985

Central Park's Bethesda Terrace and Its Restoration

IN JUNE 1859, after he had left Wall Street early to explore the park then under construction uptown, the distinguished New York lawyer and astute diarist George Templeton Strong wrote: "Central Park . . . will be a feature of the City in five years and a lovely place in AD 1900, when its trees will have acquired dignity and appreciable diameters. Perhaps the city itself will perish before then, by growing too big to live under faulty institutions corruptly administered." What struck him that afternoon amidst the roads and paths that "twist about in curves of artistic tortuosity" was how "a broad avenue [the Mall], exceptionally straight (at the lower end of the park) with a quadruple row of elms, will look Versailles-y by A.D. 1950."

Even in its embryonic state of lakes without water and mounds of unshaped dirt, the plan that was emerging for Central Park in 1859 showed a fresh genius combining several different traditions in landscape design. All too frequently the park is compared only to its ultimate ancestor, the eighteenth-century picturesque English park. In fact it encompasses all the advantages of the Victorian sensibility, which borrowed from a long line of historic architectural styles and exotic decorative motifs and fused them in a setting that was always romantic, whether rustic or formal, and echoed an adventurous past. In Central Park one can pretend to be anywhere. Even Strong could imagine himself in Versailles as he promenaded under the elm trees—and although he foresaw the splendid maturity of the park, he could not contemplate its decline during recent decades.

Completed in the 1860s, the Mall was the only formal axis in the park plan, a pathway leading north from about 67th Street into the rustic landscape beyond. Originally, at the end of the promenade one could see above the forested Ramble a distant castle on a craggy hill. Like a medieval folly in an English picturesque landscape, Belvedere ("commanding a view" in Italian) Castle is but a fragment of architecture that nevertheless suggests all the possibilities of the whole. A grand staircase at the end of the Mall leads under the 72nd Street carriage road to an underground arcade, which in turn opens onto a large plaza called the Terrace, the enchanting centerpiece of the park. Two balustraded staircases lead down directly from the carriageway, in the seventeenth-century Italian style, and paths come in from the sides to this shallow bowl of a plaza with a central fountain in a large round basin of water. At the northern edge of the plaza, shallow steps create a landing for boats in which, in the last century, visitors could set off to explore the far shores of the gracefully shaped lake and its inlets.

In the European park tradition, architecture in the landscape usually consists of the remains of a great house and its surrounds, including garden structures, staircases, and fountains and other innovative waterworks that bespoke the aristocratic life. To create this illusion from a wasteland of space in the middle of a burgeoning American city required a visionary imagination—in this case the result of a collaboration in which the individual experiences of two men were forged to create a unique park that perhaps neither one could have conceived of separately.

By the time Frederick Law Olmsted became superintendent of Central Park in 1857, he had already made a chance visit to Birkenhead Park across the Mersey River from Liverpool during a trip to England in 1850. Carved out of swampland in the 1840s according to a plan drawn up by Sir Joseph Paxton, Birkenhead is generally considered the oldest free-entry municipal park in Britain. Olmsted describes his impression of Paxton's interpretation of the picturesque style, with tree-studded hills and serpentine lakes, in *Walks and Talks of an American Farmer in England*: "Five minutes of admiration, and a few more spent in studying the manner in which art had been employed to obtain from nature so much beauty, and I was ready to admit that in democratic America there is nothing to be thought of as comparable with this People's Garden."

When the competition for a master plan for Central Park was announced in 1857, Olmsted only decided to enter after Calvert Vaux, an English-born architect recently settled in New York, suggested a collaboration. Andrew Jackson Downing, who had been America's preeminent landscape gardener, had discovered Calvert Vaux in 1850 through his drawings on exhibit at the Architectural Association in London, and had invited him to join his office in Newburgh, New York, to design country houses in the picturesque European styles for which Downing was known. After Downing's untimely death in 1852, Vaux stayed on, eventually moving his practice to New York City. In 1857, he had just published his seminal work, *Villas and Cottages,* with thirty-nine designs of houses and their plans. In his introduction, he makes several comments that become relevant to the parks design: first, he believed that until then America as an emerging republic had rejected the Beaux-Arts tradition because of its association with European aristocracy; secondly, that most architects practicing at that time in America were not born and bred in the United States; thirdly, that in domestic architecture, the irregular Italian and Gothic were the most useful types to analyze; and finally, that the great charm of natural landscapes can be explained by the irregularity of their forms.

Olmsted and Vaux, both then in their thirties, held complementary views, and their plan for Central Park, signed anonymously "Greensward," was selected by the park commissioners on April 28, 1858. Happily for Olmsted, one of the advisers to the commission was Edward Kemp, the supervisor of Birkenhead Park, who had worked under Paxton.

The design of the park was based on sound observations about architecture and its practice in a democratic environment, although aristocratic is the word that best describes the Terrace, now resplendent again after a $4.5 million, four-year-long restoration that was completed last year. After many seasons of overuse—as the site of a restaurant in the 1960s and 1970s—and disuse—as a center for the drug culture in the 1970s—the architecture and the landscape have been returned to their original condition, albeit mellowed by age, by the Ehrenkrantz Group as the architects and Philip N. Winslow as the landscape architect. Among their guidelines were more than three hundred working architectural drawings for the Mall and Terrace alone, now stored in the New York City Municipal Archives. These were rediscovered not long ago, damaged by water, in a basement of a building in Sara D. Roosevelt Park on Manhattan's Lower East Side. These are working drawings with detailed renditions of tracery designs, and, as several notes and pin pricks indicate, many appear to have been used at the site itself.

It was decided early on that the ornamental stonework would symbolize the cycles of nature, and the man who rendered these decorative designs was another English architect, Jacob Wrey Mould. For eight years in London Mould had worked with Owen Jones, the author of *The Grammar of Ornament* (1856), in whose colorful pages are laid out hundreds of decorative motifs from different cultures. Drawing from Greek, Persian, and Celtic motifs, Mould rendered stylized and abstract designs of flowers, plants, birds, insects, and other animals to be carved into the tracery panels of the staircase landings, the balustrades, and the piers. The designs for each of the four sides of the two grand staircases represent a season. The cycle begins with spring on the east side, represented by birds twittering in tangled arabesques of dogwood in the style of William Morris's foliated motifs, crocuses and jack-in-the-pulpits on the balustrade posts, and a bird's nest with an emerging chick in a medallion on the pier below. Summer is symbolized by sunflowers and honey; autumn by stags, grapes, and apples; and winter by holly, pine cones, ice skates, and snowflakes—and always birds among twisted tree branches. All of these are set within a framework of stylized leaf-and-scroll designs, and crests encircled with vines recall medieval chivalry.

On the piers terminating the Mall south of the 72nd Street carriage road are allegories of the hours of the day: a wise owl and a witch on her broomstick for night; a crowing rooster and a brilliant sunrise for morning. Vaux intended that the themes be completed by bronze allegorical statues representing Day and Night (as well as Sunlight, Moonlight, Starlight, and Twilight), the seasons, the ages of man, Art, Science, and aspects of geography—the Mountain, the Valley, the River, and the Lake. In marble beneath the arcade would be a group of statues depicting Nature, and at the center of the fountain was to have been a figure of the spirit of Love. However, the figure that was installed in the fountain was not the one Vaux proposed.

Until 1863, when Vaux submitted his master iconographic plan for what he called this "open air reception for dress promenade," the central fountain was a single spout. In 1864 the board of commissioners named Emma Stebbins, the sister of the park board's president, Henry G. Stebbins, to create a central bronze figure for the fountain. Working at that time in Rome. where Biblical subjects were as much in vogue as the classical and allegorical (remember the Adam and Eve of Henry James's sculptor-hero in his 1875 novel *Roderick Hudson*), Stebbins sculpted a sublime yet energetic image of a striding angel, the one in the Gospel according to John, 5:4: "For an angel went down at a certain season into the pool [called Bethesda, near the sheep market in Jerusalem], and troubled the water: whosoever then first after the troubling of the water stepped in was made whole of whatsoever disease he had." This healing image, *The Angel of the Waters*, was cast in bronze in Munich and unveiled in May 1873, and thereafter the place was called Bethesda Terrace.

Below the angel with outspread wings, and seen through a curtain of spray, are four putti representing Temperance, Purity, Health, and Peace. (In general, in the nineteenth century, city fountains celebrated the advent of pure drinking water from the reservoirs to which they were ultimately connected.) From the architectural drawings, it appears that the columnar base for these figures was designed by Olmsted, Vaux, and Mould in 1872, and as installed it elevates the angel high enough to be seen from the Mall, while the spray from the fountain is so delicate that only when there is a breeze does the water in the basin ripple. It is both a grand and a soothing image.

According to Jean C. Parker, who was project architect for Ehrenkrantz until 1984, their object was to "to restore crispness to the unornamented areas of the stonework and not to tamper with the decorative sculptures except to replace missing parts"—mostly birds' heads and finials. The mustard-olive stonework is made from Nova Scotia or New Brunswick sandstone originally from eleven different quarries. Because it is a porous stone affected by extreme climatic changes and pollution, it was already weathering by 1890, while the recent graffiti posed other cleaning problems. The only quarry still supplying the stone is in Wallace, Nova Scotia, where new stones were selected and shipped to Indiana for fabrication, along with molds for replacement parts and drawings for the design motifs of balustrade screens and scrollwork and finials that had long ago disappeared from the piers.

Weathered and damaged stones were removed by methods called honing or retooling, while existing surfaces were stabilized with preservatives, so that the architecture has recaptured its original form without being so perfect that the benefits of aging have been lost. This is particularly true of the diaper-patterned stone panels, which have weathered unevenly on the walls of the staircase that leads down from the Mall to the arcade under the 72nd Street carriage road.

The arcade itself is a forest of Romanesque arches and columns. Lining the walls are twenty-four arched niches originally intended to house fountains alternating with diaper-patterned panels of marble and granite—none of which were ever realized. Mould, who designed these, originally came to New York as the architect for All Souls' Unitarian Church (which was executed in striped stone) and its parsonage. He was known for his vibrantly colorful designs, and the ingenious ceiling he executed for the arcade had predominantly blue and white Minton encaustic tiles with Islamic-style motifs. The forty-nine nine-foot-square panels into which these tiles were set featured designs adapted from an Islamic arabesque shown against a white field. The effect was that of a Moorish pavilion. Some sixteen thousand tiles were bolted into cast-iron plates with brass bolts that had been affixed to the back of each tile. Unfortunately, the metals have so eroded that the tiles have all been removed and are now in storage until a new method can be devised to reinstall them.

In the meantime a new design to complete the wall niches was proposed and will be executed by the Italian artist Lucretia Moroni, who specializes in trompe-l'oeil painting. She has suggested *The Flowing of Time* as a theme for new murals to be painted on thin marble panels. With the texture of the marble showing through, the effect of the murals will be of marble intarsia. These murals will depict the months in twelve of the twenty-four niches. Each month is to be represented by a woman in a flowing classical robe holding a symbol of her month. In alternating niches will be painted trompe-l'oeil panels repeating Mould's original marble diaper design in paint but with the addition of a sign of the zodiac in each central medallion.

Originally, the landscape surrounding the Terrace was planted in the gardenesque tradition as a Victorian showcase of exotic large-leafed or spiky plants. Great clumps of water lilies were planted in the fountain basin itself, and wide lawns emphasized the sloping grade of the valleylike space which rose up to the hills and rock outcroppings that framed the Terrace: Cherry Hill to the west and Pine Hill to the east.

What in essence finally destroyed this open, formal landscape was the planting in 1947 of twenty-four pin oaks on the slopes to commemorate the major naval battles of World War II. Not only were the perspectives narrowed, but as the trees matured the roots infiltrated the stonework, causing cracking at the seams. Also, as the slopes eroded, dirt piled up the sides of the balustrades. For all intents and purposes Bethesda became a romantic ruin. Jed Devine recorded those years of the tangled, overgrown landscape in a series of early-morning photographs (palladium prints) published in a portfolio called *The Bethesda Terrace* in 1986. The results suggest the photographs of the park at Saint Cloud near Paris made by Jean Eugène Auguste Atget in the 1920s.

Many see the park as an unspoiled wilderness rather than a man-made creation to be kept to scale; and although the bird watchers' lobby was difficult to overcome, enough pin oaks were removed to reshape the lawns and excavate the balustrades. "Historic landscape restoration is difficult," Philip Winslow points out, "because even though old plant lists exist, many of the original plants no longer grow in the city or are even available." So in replanting the hillsides he evoked the palette and feeling of the historic plan with dense groups of flowering shrubs such as long-blooming abelia with its subtle pink blossoms, yellow-orange kerria, forsythia, and abundant azalea and rho-dodendron.

As with any romantic architectural environment, to see the Terrace obliquely from a distance across a naturalistic landscape—as one does here through trees and over shrubs—enhances its beauty. According to Winslow the paths Olmsted laid out across these hills are experiential, passing through the landscape rather than around it, with plantings at each end, where they meet and merge with others. Along the way plantings are spaced as focal points to direct the eye to a distant view. At the edge of the lawns and the Terrace itself, Winslow has selected showy plants such as oakleaf hydrangea to recall the original plantings.

The final dramatic touch was the restoration of the two gonfalons—long banners such as those carried in medieval Italian processions—which are sus-pended from the crosspiece of newly fabricated bronze poles with decora-tive bases and finials in openwork designs of rosettes and arabesques. Seen from the north side of the lake, the flowing green and red-orange gonfalons anchored at either corner of the waterside landing define the proscenium, as it were, of the Terrace's stage. High in the distance a flag also flies from the battlements of Belvedere Castle, but here time has wrought the great-est change, for the mature trees have completely obliterated the view of the castle from the Terrace.

Nineteenth-century photographs and paintings of the Terrace show how its architecture was complemented by the elegance of people's dress. In many stereoscopic views the men wear hats and natty day attire, and the women, corseted in long dresses, are as rigid and stylish in appearance as the archi-tectural stonework. This is particularly evident in a painting by William Mer-ritt Chase called *Early Morning Stroll* (c. 1887–1891): a woman standing in nipped-in jacket and ruffle-edged skirt echoes the silhouette of the Terrace pier, while the small child dressed in white bending over a red ball has the fluffiness and grace of the swan gliding across the water.

As late as 1971 an unforgettable magazine advertisement for Drambuie featured the fountain at night with the angel's wings dark against the trees and still waters below. In the photograph a couple in evening dress leans against the basin (she in flowing pink chiffon); as their carriage pulls away, they are left alone under soft lamplight (the lampposts, incidentally, have not been replaced). "Evenings that memories are made of . . ." reads the advertisement. Now that Bethesda Terrace has been restored, and the waters spout and spill lyrically in the glint of late afternoon sun, one wonders, looking at the crowds milling about the fountain, whether our current denim culture can measure up to this architecture of the past.

Antiques, April 1988

Summer in Central Park

FOR A New Yorker like myself, nothing equals the tranquility of a summer's afternoon after a sudden rainfall has cooled the air. I live two blocks from Central Park, which I think of as the city's courtyard, ringed by a wall of skyscrapers, apartment buildings, and museums. Before I walked in the park today, I stopped to set my window boxes to rights after the rain. As I live in a ground floor maisonette, my windows are protected by decorative grilles that double in summer as trellises for vines. This summer the boxes were planted by a Connecticut landscape architect friend, Susan Cohen, who drove into the city one afternoon with a carload of potting soil, young plants, and seed packets. Morning glories have become the traditional twining material around the wrought iron bars and scrollwork, but Susan had discovered *Evolvulus*, the same heavenly blue as morning glories (both also of the same family, *Convolvulaceae*), for the main planting, and all summer long I look out on the world through a curtain of bright green spiced with blue and a touch of white moonflower for the evenings.

The closer one gets to Central Park, the more the buildings are consciously linked to it. My window boxes are a small example, but, in profile, one sees the larger green of the park beyond them. Along Fifth Avenue, the eastern boundary of the over two-mile-long park, buildings are set back behind narrow strips of fenced garden usually with a few flowering trees. In recent years, there has been a vast improvement in the plantings that surround these trees—gone is leggy box in favor of oakleaf hydrangea and mixtures of grasses and astilbe. Lynden B. Miller is the cause of this new awareness. As director of the Conservatory Garden in Central Park, she has shown New Yorkers how to plant public gardens with long, mixed borders in the English style, emphasizing the texture, color, and contour of foliage combined with traditional and unusual flowering plants.

Most of the mansions that originally lined Fifth Avenue at the turn of the century had extensive gardens. Andrew Carnegie built his mansion in 1902

89

uptown in order to have enough land for a generous garden. Fortunately, this mansion with its own conservatory has survived as the Cooper-Hewitt Museum, and its balustraded terraces and borders frame a small neighborhood park with chestnut trees that appears to adjoin Central Park across the avenue. Recently revived with new plantings by Lynden Miller and landscape designer Mary Riley Smith, the gardens look particularly abundant in late summer with *Coreopsis* 'Moonbeam' and *Sedum* 'Autumn Joy' among such gray foliage as *Helictotrichon* and *Helichrysum.*

This link between the city and Central Park was understood by Frank Lloyd Wright when he designed the Solomon R. Guggenheim Museum on Fifth Avenue, a block below the Carnegie Mansion. "Garden and building may now be one," he told a London audience in 1939, six years before his drawings of the Guggenheim were unveiled. "In any good organic structure it is difficult to say where the garden ends and where the house begins or the house ends and the garden begins—and that is all as should be," he further clarified. In his original drawings and renderings of the spiral-shaped museum, Wright brought elements of the park across the street, as it were, and planted trees, either columnar-shaped or with spreading canopies, in a moat along the facade. Shrubberies and vines spilling over from the tiers above created the effect of a folly in a landscape park.

When the Guggenheim reopened in 1992 after a major restoration, one of these renderings was used to announce the event. But, alas, a year has gone by and no trees or shrubs are in sight—only a ground cover of ivy planted in the moats like an afterthought. The building may be sculpturally pristine, but this was not the intention of an architect who believed in merging inside and outside. The saddest part is that no one else appears to have noticed.

But I pass it daily, especially in the evenings when I walk around the reservoir in the park. The reservoir, an irregularly shaped lake, filled with birdlife, in the middle of the park, not only refreshes one with its lapping sounds and cool breezes, but has become one of the most dramatic elements in this nineteenth-century pastoral landscape. As of last spring, it no longer serves as a source for the city's water supply, which unfortunately gives park planners the option of replacing it with playing fields or other popular amusements. But for now, in the morning mists, when the city skyline disappears, one could be at Stourhead in England, and the small, rusticated pumping stations along the reservoir's green rim could be follies or eye-catchers, and at dusk, when the skyline reappears in silhouette, twinkling lights make the distant towers appear like fairy-tale castles. With fireflies illuminating the glades and dells, it is a magic moment in Central Park.

Gardens Illustrated, August–September 1993

For This Movie, Step into the Garden

*I*F THE WORLD of film is to make trickery appear solid, then the Australian film director Peter Weir was faced with unusually difficult sleight-of-hand for his newest movie, *Green Card,* filmed last spring entirely in New York City. The script called for three gardens, all integral to the storyline, to be created either in the streets or on the rooftops of a glittering Manhattan. As in the past, for his production designer he called on Wendy Stites, who is also his wife, to create these illusions.

The plot centers on a French national (Gérard Depardieu) who enters into an arranged marriage with a New York horticulturist (Andie MacDowell) to obtain the treasured green card that will allow him to work. What she gets out of the deal is a penthouse apartment with a Victorian-style conservatory available only to a married couple.

Brontë Parrish, the character in the film, a Parks Department employee, is an advocate of the Green Guerilla community garden movement, so one garden—a neighborhood plot on the Lower East Side—was easy to devise. Stites chose a festive look with structures in bright Caribbean colors. More difficult was the treed garden for either a roof terrace or an Upper East mansion belonging to a friend's parents, where Parrish mingles at a cocktail party on a fundraising prowl.

Stites likes best to create something out of nothing. Her own tropical garden that weaves around paths and pergolas at a beach house near Sydney was inspired by their trips to Bali. "From my outpost in Australia," she says, "my lifeline to the real world is through magazines where I glean ideas that fuel my imagination."

Since moving mature trees to a selected site was prohibitively costly, Stites opted instead to enclose nature to give the illusion of a garden. She selected one of the picturesque allées of crab apple trees in Central Park's Conservatory Garden on Fifth Avenue and 105th Street. Along one side she constructed a garden wall facing, on the other side, the first story of a brick and masonry mansion. With a pergola, a central reflecting pool, and a trellis closing off the far end, this avenue of park trees embellished with planters of topiary was transformed for a few brief days into a romantic formal terrace akin to one at the Frick Collection or the Carnegie Mansion.

"We photographed architectural details up and down the side streets of the Upper East Side," explains Stites, "and the facade facing the garden with its grand entrance staircase and tall balustraded windows is a composite structure representing those motifs that best portray New York in the Beaux-Arts era."

By day, one could see the temporariness of fake building materials and their supports, as well as a tree limb that pierced the mansion wall, albeit camouflaged by leaves. But during one long night of filming, under the soft glow of lamplight from the "windows" and strategic lighting under the trees, the aura of an old garden on a summer's night was complete, especially with elegant party guests milling about.

The main place of enchantment in the film is the penthouse's rooftop conservatory, which was actually built on a soundstage in mid-Manhattan with only one facade constructed on a rooftop for exterior scenes. As Stites poked through stores of old tiles and windows for the greenhouse, she came up with some authentic leaded sidelites for the door surrounds. "A bit of genuine old among the new is what makes the whole composition ring true," she says.

This is the conservatory of everyone's dreams, with a trickling wall fountain in the shape of a shell under a whitewashed brick arch, and an oval skylight large enough to allow a shaft of light across the leaves. The hexagonal floor tiles, scuffed with dirt, look as if they had been there since the first owner built the conservatory. With a bit of classical frieze and transom windows above the glass-paned walls for authenticity, it is a perfect setting for the dense collage of tropical foliage, reminiscent of Stites's garden in Australia. (No one notices the tree fern so tall it was planted below the floor.)

Since the main action of the film takes place over a three-day weekend, and since leaves brown quickly under bright lights, the trick was to maintain this exact look of lush tropical growth over a three-month period. The film crew included a real horticulturist, Joni Brockschmidt, who maintained a nursery holding area where she grew new flats of grass every two weeks, refreshed baskets of hanging orchids, and even aged duckweed to replace the scum in the fountain pool.

When the sprinklers went on in the conservatory, the atmosphere was of a miniature tropical rain forest. Standing in the damp fragrance, one fantasized, as with a doll's house or a period room, that it could become what Stites calls "one's own peaceful retreat." When the filming was over Andie MacDowell, a plants person herself, gave in to the fantasy and relocated the conservatory to her own home in upstate New York.

New York Times, December 23, 1990

Rooftop Formal Gardens at Rockefeller Center

AS HOLIDAY CROWDS swirl around Rockefeller Center's fiftieth annual Christmas tree, few watching the glittering, festive scene are aware that above them, unseen from the plaza level, are rooftop terraces with formal gardens of great calm and symmetry.

Looked down upon from hundreds of office windows, two of these rectangular gardens appear to have wide green lawns with hedges, deep pools, and twin juniper trees, and the absence of people along the flagstone paths adds mystery to their beauty. Because of the heat generated from the buildings below, the lawns, like English parks, stay green most of the year. Designed strictly for the pleasure of viewing, the gardens are not for public use, although visitors may see them on guided tours.

There are four such terraces on the rooftops of the center's six-story buildings along Fifth Avenue. Their origin and purpose are integral to the philosophy of the architects and developers who nurtured the powerful concept of Rockefeller Center into existence fifty years ago.

No sooner had the Industrial Revolution destroyed the pastoral element in cities than responsible people rose up to encourage the planning of parks and green spaces. Raymond Hood, one of the more visionary architects of Rockefeller Center, was no doubt familiar with Edward Bellamy's 1887 utopian novel, *Looking Backward,* in which the hero, Justin West, looks out at a city of the year 2000 and sees "public buildings of a colossal size and an architectural grandeur," with "large open squares filled with trees, among which statues glistened and fountains flashed in the late-afternoon sun." This could pass for a description of Rockefeller Center itself.

One day in 1931 Hood was standing with John R. Todd, of Todd, Robertson & Todd, managers of the Rockefeller Center project, looking down on rooftops from the Graybar Building. "Mess, isn't it?" he said. "Look at all those roofs down there cluttered up with bulkheads, ventilators, chimneys, elevator penthouses, water tanks, and God knows what else." He let that sink in and then said, "I was wondering if office space that looked out on a garden would be worth any more." The response from Todd, perhaps apocryphal, was "A dollar a square foot," and so the greening of Rockefeller Center's low rooftops was introduced as a visual amenity for those working inside. Hood wrote in 1931 that "the city architect can no more afford to neglect the roofs that continually spread out below him than the country architect can afford to neglect the planting about a house."

What he saw in his mind's eye was terrace joined to terrace by walkways bridging streets, a park in the air, with fountains and luscious plantings akin, he said, to the "fabled living tapestry of the Hanging Gardens of Babylon." John Wenrich, the accomplished architectural renderer of that period, caught the spirit of Hood's vision in his romantic drawings for these gardens. The utopian feeling is unmistakable. By 1932, the plan called for a tea garden, formal gardens, and a conservatory.

The four gardens on the Fifth Avenue rooftops and a fifth one on the eleventh-floor setback of the RCA Building, gardens that were eventually constructed between 1933 and 1936, are in reality closer in form to the well-protected walled gardens of medieval castles, contained as they are within the Indiana limestone parapets. Economic realities and Raymond Hood's death in 1934 curtailed the original conception, but the nearly two acres that remain are still more than had been attempted before.

Upon the completion of the Maison Française and the British Empire Building at 610 and 620 Fifth Avenue, the landscape architect Ralph Hancock of Montclair, New Jersey, a fellow of the Royal Horticultural Society, designed the gardens and supervised construction. Tons of specially selected soil were loaded into wheelbarrows and transported at night by elevator to build up plots ranging from eighteen inches to twenty-four inches in depth over a layer of coarse gravel. Additional steel girders were placed in the buildings to support the weight of the gardens.

Hancock's design for both gardens called for a central rectangular lawn framed by privet hedges in a series of U's. The lawn is sloped slightly on either side, creating a saddle effect that increases the surface area and thereby makes the lawn appear wider from above. Similarly, by painting aquamarine the 12-by-6-foot two-inch-deep fountain pools at the ends of the lawns, he created the illusion of depth. Those fountains still splash into the pools during the warm months. "It is also where the first spring crocuses bloom in Manhattan," said Robert C. Marville, executive vice president of Rockefeller Center, who speaks of their "village-green atmosphere."

The Mediterranean settings of the north gardens, on the Palazzo d'Italia and the International Building North, were designed by A. M. Van den Hoek, chief horticulturist of Rockefeller Center in 1936. The 229-by-52-foot gardens are made more dramatic by the near presence of the spires of St. Patrick's Cathedral. The original grass lawns are now solid beds of ivy bordered by hedges in an undulating design with oversized terra-cotta planters set in symmetrical patterns. The cobblestones for the walkways around the central area are from Italian streets, and two stone plaques come from a courtyard fountain in the Roman Forum.

Flanking the end of the Palazzo d'Italia garden and set against the background of the cathedral are two bronze statues of a maiden and a youth by Paul Manship, also the sculptor of the Prometheus statue in the lower plaza. The two in the garden represent "historical and mythological background," part of the general theme that inspired all of the art for the center: "man's progress along successively higher planes of civilization."

The fantasy gardens Ralph Hancock created on the RCA Building in 1934, called Gardens of the Nations, were in Spanish, French, Japanese, and Dutch motifs with similarly costumed hostesses. They were illuminated at night, and the central section had Z-shaped raised Art Deco flowerbeds.

In 1938, when the "Sky Garden Tour" of these gardens was no longer profitable, they were dismantled. Lost gardens they are, like those of Babylon itself, but their existence is confirmed in a fine photographic record. The three-quarters-of-an-acre rooftop park remains adjacent to NBC offices. Structurally, some of the plan survives in the dry bed of the 125-foot-long meandering stream and the goldfish pond.

Satisfied in 1934 that these lush "gardens in the sky" were a realization, albeit a partial one, of the utopian ideal, Hancock pronounced, "The days of penthouse gardening are over, and miles and miles of roof space in every metropolis in this country remain to be reclaimed by landscape gardening." His message is equally valid today in a city where landscape architecture too often refers to concrete plazas and not frequently enough to grassy areas and trees.

New York Times, December 16, 1982

Hortus Conclusus: The Gardens at the Cloisters

SHADY CLOISTERS on a wooded hilltop overlooking a wide, silvery river below; soft strains of twelfth-century polyphonic music waft on a breeze that flutters the pale pink quince blossoms in a medieval herb garden. This scene could be a Benedictine abbey in the French countryside—except for the George Washington Bridge over the Hudson River that comes into view from the south. Located in Fort Tryon Park at the northern tip of Manhattan, this is the Metropolitan Museum of Art's medieval branch, called the Cloisters—one of New York City's greatest treasures.

Having begun my pilgrimages there as a graduate student in medieval French, I continue to find refuge in its cloistered gardens throughout the year, from that moment in spring when the quince blossom takes flight in the wind to the stark beauty of the winter months. The genius of the place—the true architectural flow of a monastery—was created in a tasteful composite of old European cloister arcades and chapel ruins from the Romanesque period to the Gothic.

The medieval stonework, first collected by the American sculptor George Gray Barnard in the early years of this century, was ultimately purchased by the Metropolitan Museum of Art with funds provided by John D. Rockefeller, Jr., who also supported and oversaw the construction of the Cloisters, which opened in 1938. No attempt was made in the blend of old and new to conceal the fragmentary nature of the architectural elements, and yet the space acquired an integrity and spirit that have endured and deepened with time. The Cloisters is now well known for its collection of precious objects and tapestries, and it is also a place where medieval arts, including music, drama, and gardening, continue to thrive in halls that resound with those haunting intonations of the past.

Although Saint Fiacre is usually considered the patron saint of gardening, the spirit and know-how of the ninth-century monk gardener Walahfrid Strabo (A.D. 809–849) presides at the Cloisters. An abbot of the Benedictine Abbey on the island of Reichenau in Lake Constance, he was renowned for his Latin verses, and in particular for his poem about the pleasures and difficulties of gardening titled *Hortulus* ("The Little Garden"). Whenever Susan Moody, horticulturist at the Cloisters for the past seventeen years, speaks about the gardens, she carries with her a well-worn copy of the poem as translated in

1966 by Eton classics scholar Raef Payne. In the distillation of his verses ("your land cannot fail to produce / Its native plants"), including descriptions of twenty-nine plants and their uses, and from her own visits to remaining monasteries and agricultural schools in the same region, she has discovered the guiding principle of her endeavor to give "a twentieth-century face to the ninth-century."

The gardens, comprising three separate cloisters, were originally laid out by the medieval art scholars James J. Rorimer and Margaret B. Freeman, who both in turn served as early curators of the Cloisters. They based the design on existing archival materials such as the famous Carolingian plan (A.D. 830) of the Benedictine Monastery of St. Gall, with its cloister garth, an ornamental garden at the heart of the monastery, as well as its herb and physic gardens. As a guide for selecting plant materials, they also used the *Capitulare de Villis*—the decree passed down by Charlemagne in A.D. 812 as a directive about agriculture and horticulture in his royal domains, in which he listed 150 recommended plants in cultivation.

Medieval gardens derive their beauty from a sense of order that ultimately reflects the rigid regimen of monastic life. This minimalist simplicity, so akin to Modernism, is just as satisfying in a twentieth-century context. More horticultural than simply decorative, the appeal of the medieval garden lies also in the freshness and harmony of plantings within the preordained designs, highlighting individual foliage and blossoms.

This sense of order and harmony is immediately apparent in the Saint-Michel-de-Cuxa Cloister, whose architectural remains come from the Pyrenees. The paths dividing the four quadrants of the garden are symbolic of the four rivers to the corners of the earth. In each green quadrant of this garth grows a single tree—Cornelian cherry, pear, crab apple, and hawthorn—and they bloom in sequence as a constant reminder of the ephemeral nature of spring. "Throughout the season, along the borders of the inner paths, we maintain an early summer palette with an emphasis on fragrance," explains Susan Moody on an autumnal day. To blend with the rose marble and stone of the surrounding columns are *Spiraea japonica* 'Shirobana', *Sedum* 'Autumn Joy', and *Dianthus* 'Bath's Pink'. These are offset by a rich blue *Salvia guaranitica* and white *Malva moschata* var. *alba*. The plantings gradually ascend to the height of the prerequisite fountain in the center, this one originally from a neighboring French monastery.

Set in the archways of the Cuxa Cloister are old terra-cotta pots of jasmine growing through elaborately woven grapevine supports. These are made from the woody stems of grapevines, demonstrating how medieval techniques have been developed into contemporary forms at the Cloisters. To supply these highly decorative yet utilitarian supports, grapevines, hanging like living tapestries, are grown in abundance on the rampart walls surrounding an exterior courtyard. This is also the staging area where plants are grown from seed in cold frames.

The Bonnefont Cloister encloses its own herb garden, which every year reveals another successful quest to acquire seeds for plants documented in herbals of the period. The horticulturists have managed to track down, for example, seed for such plants as the rare field pea, 'Blue Pod Capucijners', developed by the Capuchin monks in the 1500s. They send for seeds from places as far-flung as Warsaw, Geneva, and Utrecht, to add to the 250 fragrant, culinary, or medicinal plants already growing in designated beds surrounded by low woven wattle fences in the herb garden. They also grow plants that would have been used in medieval times for dyeing tapestries and painting illuminated manuscripts: woad (*Isatis tinctoria*) for blue, pallid iris for green, weld (*Reseda luteola*) for yellow, and madder (*Rubia tinctoria*) for red. This is a garden that could cure bad humor or pain with the right root or leaf, but the sight of it alone could also do the job.

The pure whiteness of the Bonnefont's central Venetian wellhead under the quince trees is echoed elsewhere in a mountain of *Rosa alba* blooms and more than a hundred Madonna lilies. On the hillside below the garden's supporting wall grow crab apple trees, like the orchards of yore, and across the Hudson River the Palisades, the high cliffs on the New Jersey side, are forever green and undeveloped, thanks also to the generosity and foresight of the Rockefeller family.

Adjoining the Bonnefont garden is the Trie Cloister. Here, the horticulturists have created a fantasy garden based on the *mille-fleurs* backgrounds of the famous series of seven sixteenth-century Flemish tapestries, "The Hunt of the Unicorn," which hangs in one of the inner galleries of the Cloisters. Like "The Lady with the Unicorn" tapestries at the Cluny Museum in Paris, the figures depicting the hunt and capture of the unicorn are set against a deep blue background covered with myriad flowering plants whose symbolism, both religious and secular, adds to the drama of the story. In these tapestries, no season is observed, and trees burgeon with fruit and flower at the same time. In 1941, two botanists from the New York Botanical Garden published a list identifying eighty of the almost one hundred plants illustrated in the tapestries, and it is this list on which the planting of the Trie garden is based. For anyone, like myself, who considers these tapestries one of the highest art forms, these gardens of dark green with points of color—strawberries, violets, columbine, dandelions, according to season—fulfill the wish to enter the magical world of the unicorn.

As full and fertile as the gardens are in summer, my favorite visit to the Cloisters is during the Christmas season, when the Cuxa Cloister has been glassed in and the arcades are filled with a spicy hothouse fragrance of assorted potted trees and plants—orange, oleander, myrtle, rosemary, and acanthus. Sometimes an arrangement of plants is moved to the interior Saint-Guilhem-le-Désert Cloister, with its Corinthian capitals of acanthus leaves. My first visit to the Cloisters was in late winter, and I recall the joy of seeing there early spring blooms of lily-of-the-valley and paperwhite narcissus.

From mid-December until the Feast of Epiphany, the halls are decked in a quietly festive manner. In the Langon Chapel, bay laurel garlands, based on those depicted in frescoes at Assisi, are draped from the twelfth-century ciborium, a fifteen-foot-high marble-columned canopy over the altar. In the entrance-hall rotunda, a great wheat wreath made from Kansas wheat, eight feet in diameter and weighing nearly forty pounds, symbolizing the nativity, is suspended horizontally, like the Romanesque chandeliers that hung in the cathedrals of Aachen and Hildesheim. The four Romanesque archways in the entrance hall are framed with branches of boxwood intertwined with thick-leafed ivy and decorated with clusters of lady apples, hazelnuts, rose hips, and pine cones. New York may appear to be an unusual place to celebrate the Middle Ages, but for a few moments here each winter, when the cloisters are filled with polyphonic music and sweet fragrances, and the hellebores bloom outside, one can suspect the presence of Brother Walahfrid, whose poem speaks so eloquently of "the joy that comes of devoting himself to a garden."

Gardens Illustrated, December–January 1996–1997

The IBM Garden Plaza

AT 8:55 A.M. on Saturday, March 14, 1981, Larry Tatum, the American Bridge superintendent overseeing the steel erection for the IBM tower at 57th Street and Madison Avenue, called out to his signal man, Bobbie Snow, "Give me an easy swing to the left." Snow radioed the order to Bob Portland, who was controlling the derrick guyed out from the twenty-third story of the IBM tower, and by 9 A.M. the first of the gigantic hollow-pipe triangular-section steel trusses that form the saw-toothed roof of the four-story greenhouse was set down on columns. It was seventy-eight feet long and fourteen feet high, and it weighed twenty-one tons. The ironworkers had begun their shift at 1 A.M. that morning, having already worked fourteen hours straight the day before unloading the four trusses from a barge. These were floated down the Hudson River, through late-winter ice floes, from Newburgh, New York, after having been fabricated by Quickway Metal Fabricators, Inc., in Monticello. A city permit had been issued to bring the trusses across town in a convoy of steerable dollies from the West Side dock in the middle of the night—two on Saturday, two on Sunday.

Having seen these huge white linear forms lumbering through the razzle-dazzle of New York City streets on a freezing night—traffic lights were temporarily removed to gain clearance at corners—and having stood by for long hours until they were unloaded at dawn, I retain a memory of a unified effort and of a camaraderie that enriches the experience now of sitting in the completed greenhouse on a quiet sunny afternoon. When the work was over that night, the general contractor, Turner Construction Company, to loud cheers from all, treated the ironworkers to breakfast. By 5 P.M. Sunday, near the end of an eighteen-hour shift, the second truss, 113 feet long, was raised into place, and sparks from the welders' torches sprayed their last light into the dusk. Larry Tatum and Lee Saunders, his assistant, sat in their trailer office. "We did a stroke of work this weekend," Tatum said—the skeletal structure of the greenhouse was partially in.

What gives this greenhouse its special allure? It is an interior world of light and air defined by a structure but not restricted by it from its exterior surroundings—the tracery of its framework creates only a veil-like separation. It is a place to be inside without surrendering the outside, and yet from out-of-doors the interior appears to have a fixed life, a quiet orderliness that is becoming to good architecture. At night, the structure glows jewel-like on the city street; the roof, facets of light against a dark sky.

Many years have gone by since midtown Manhattan had a public glass-house structure—New York's Crystal Palace, inspired by its London predecessor, was completed in 1853 on the present site of Bryant Park only to burn down in 1858. While it stood, millions of visitors filed through to see the exhibited wonders of art, science, and mechanics. There was a dual tradition of nineteenth-century glasshouse architecture. The great botanical conservatories, for cultivating the horticultural exotica of the world, have survived in public parks and on private estates. In the urban winter gardens, on the other hand, the decorative flora was only incidental to pleasurable pastimes cultivated for people. With pathways through luxuriously landscaped interiors, and with music and cafés, there were no better retreats in Europe from noisy, bustling streets. Their heights grew to cathedral-like proportions to accommodate the increasingly popular palm trees.

"What I wanted," says Edward Larrabee Barnes, the architect of the IBM tower, "was a structure that would look like outdoor space and that would appear to be a separate building—a brilliant crystalline form next to a prismatic tower, a stone shaft that comes right down to the paving." The big moment in the design, he says, came with the idea of putting the greenhouse on the diagonal behind the tower.

The completed structure is a house within a house, a conventional truss system anchored to a glass-and-black-anodized-aluminum curtain wall (the aluminum is the same as for the tower's own window mullions). The trusses are painted white. "I think from the inside all greenhouses should be painted light so that the structure melts into the sky—all of the great old ones, like those at Kew Gardens in London, are painted white," explained Barnes.

To describe the effects on a neighborhood of quality public space, Barnes likes to cite the experience of leaving behind the din of Wall Street as one enters the calm of Trinity Church. Tranquility as a paramount characteristic of public space is a no less valid requirement than the circus atmosphere prescribed at the other end of the spectrum. More on this later.

Beyond the aesthetic and philosophical reasons behind the design of the eleven-thousand-square-foot, four-story greenhouse, its existence is motivated by zoning regulations that offered bonuses in the form of additional floor area for the building in exchange for amenities that benefit the public. Reading the greenhouse then in terms of what it accomplishes gives other interpretations to the form. According to Armand P. Avakian, who was the associate architect-in-charge during the design and working drawing periods, the basic component was the covered pedestrian space. In those days, the old Fifth Avenue Bonwit Teller backed up to the property and provided the necessary retail presence (the story of how Bonwit's was then sold, relocated to 57th Street, and slipped back in behind the greenhouse is for another time), and from an early date, the New York Botanical Garden had opted for space in the greenhouse as a midtown plant information center. Also, continuing the long tradition of providing tasteful exhibitions in their former building on the same site, IBM planned a Gallery of Science and Art for museum-quality loan shows on the subterranean level just below the greenhouse. In keeping then with the grand tradition of the Crystal Palaces themselves, the IBM greenhouse would become the foyer of an exhibition hall one flight down.

Finally, a through-block arcade between 56th and 57th streets at mid-block was originally foreseen with open entrances until wind-tunnel tests proved the necessity of the great rolling doors at the mid-block points of both streets to avoid the effects of high winds on the tower base and the greenhouse. A constant pedestrian flow through the arcade area adds to the life and activity of the greenhouse and retail spaces.

The most dramatic aspect of the structure is the sixteen-foot-high saw-toothed or folded roof, with the six ridges running north to south. The total height of the greenhouse is sixty-eight feet. Although this resembles the ridge-and-furrow glasshouse roofs devised by John Claudius Loudon and Joseph Paxton in nineteenth-century England to regulate the intensity of direct and indirect light, the purpose here is contemporary: "Maintenance was one of our considerations," says Barnes, "for the slanted glass is easier to clean, and the ridges create an interior space for vents, lighting, and catwalks, making a kind of stage tower." There are three kinds of lights: incandescent for general illumination, colored-gel theatrical spotlights, and special growing lights for the trees, which are illuminated between 2 and 7 a.m.

As in the gables of traditional greenhouses, there is a system of louvered vents that open automatically to let out overheated air as it rises, and these vents are also maintained from the catwalks. The greenhouse has an "intermediate climate" between the street and controlled atmosphere of the offices. Coming in from the street, one will always feel warmer in the winter and cooler in the summer. Barnes achieved this by redirecting into the greenhouse, through louvers, the percentage of air that by law has to be exchanged from the tower's interior; and because this air has been filtered, it is cleaner than outside air, and has been heated or cooled as well. Thus a climatic zone—between 40 degrees and 90 degrees—similar to that of Virginia and North Carolina is maintained. Also, the temperature would be lower at night (on the night-cycle), which is conducive to plantings accustomed to the outdoors and a requisite quiescent period.

At that point, the project's landscape architect, Robert Zion of Zion & Breen Associates, came up with a suggestion for plantings that was pure Southern romance in contrast to the hard-edged city: magnolia trees. This idea waned due to the difficulty of finding trees in the nurseries with a significant horizontal spread. While driving around North Carolina in the quest for magnolia trees, Alistair Bevington, another Barnes associate, had noted the large stands of bamboo trees growing wild in the region and added them to his list of possibilities. About the same time, Carlton B. Lees, then vice president of the New York Botanical Garden, showed Barnes some photographs of bamboo groves in the Los Angeles State and County Arboretum, and Barnes liked the sculptural effect of the tall stems with a canopy of light feathery tops. He later told me that he could see the tight groves of bamboo, in the seven-foot-square sunken planters set on a grid, resembling the massive columns of the temple at Karnak. The decision was soon made in favor of bamboo: *Phyllostachys pubescens*, from North Carolina.

On March 10, 1981, I spent a day in North Carolina with Turner's expediter, Guido T. Garbarino, to see the bamboo and to verify the ready state of some of the material being fabricated for the tower. We drove to the largest open-faced granite quarry in the world, the North Carolina Granite Company in Mt. Airy, which was providing the paving stone for the greenhouse in five-foot squares as well as the round granite refreshment kiosk. Guido counted the paving slabs, and then the owner, Ed Corder, drove us out to the quarry flats. By then it was night, and the granite glowed almost white in the pale moonlight—Indian tribes understandably were attracted to these plateaus for ritualistic ceremonies. At night, in the greenhouse, one sees the granite as it looked that night in North Carolina.

On November 17, a team including Richard C. Keller, Barnes's field architect, Leo Plofker, the structural engineer from The Office of James Ruderman, Daniel Millman, a project manager for IBM, and others traveled down to the Construction Research Laboratory alongside a highway in Miami, Florida, for the stress tests on the garden enclosure. The laboratory, an outdoor area around a warehouse, looks like a movie lot with a main street of fake building facades, which in reality are two- and three-story test mockups of buildings under construction from all over the world. The greenhouse mockup, an end section of one saw-toothed element, was constructed next to the ruins of the former two-story granite mockup of the IBM tower itself. The man who oversees the testing of this unusual empire for the vicissitude of climatic conditions—wind, rain, heat—is A. A. Saknovsky, or simply Sak.

The subcontractor for the garden enclosure curtain wall had built the full-size mockup of aluminum framing and heat-strengthened triple-laminated glass for the slanted panes of the saw-toothed roof. Early in the testing, they first increase the air pressure, then suction the air out of the enclosure—now a closed chamber—to test the framing for deflection and the effect on the glass in imitation of wind pressure conditions. They found, unfortunately, that they could do neither with success, and it was not the fault of the machinery. There must be leaks, and to see where they were, they exploded a smoke bomb in the interior. There were more curlicues of smoke coming though seams than I could count.

Everyone went home until the sealant and gasket problems were resolved. On the return in January to complete the tests successfully, the most dramatic moment came when a one-hundred-pound leather bag filled with lead shot was raised high over the slated panes by a hydraulic crane and dropped from ever increasing heights to test the amount of force required to fracture and then fully penetrate the roof panels. At thirty seven and a half feet the shot bag finally broke cleanly through a previously intact roof panel, leaving less than half a teacup of fine powdered glass. There were no long or sharp knifelike shards, as had been feared, from any of the drop tests; some of the panels were repeatedly pounded, with the same results.

Later, as actual construction proceeded, it took six glaziers to install the large trapezoidal panes, two on ladders at either side with suction cups, three at the bottom, and one man underneath on the scaffolding planks, balancing as if he were on a surfboard. It took eighteen glaziers to install the seven-and-a-half-ton, thirty-three-foot-high rolling door at the 56th Street entrance to the pedestrian walk-through. At times, the scene looked like Philip Henry Delamotte's evocative photographs of the reconstruction of the London Crystal Palace at Sydenham Hill.

On October 13, 1982, the bamboo was delivered by truck, and the event generated an unusual amount of excitement, for in the public imagination, winter garden or no, a greenhouse is for plants. "Birnam Wood has come to Dunsinane," quoted Dick Keller as we watched the forty-five-foot-high trees unloaded, the enormous balls wrapped in burlap. Zion was there to counsel on the arrangement, and after a few days the interior was transformed by the eleven groves, which made the space seem less high. The outlook from the third-floor employees' cafeteria, which wishbones around the upper reaches of the garden, was now onto feathery pale green. The best view of the bamboo is from the northeast corner of Madison Avenue looking across the street through the main entrance and the three open elevator lobbies, and seeing from a distance the groves and their waterlike reflections in the lobby ceiling and on the polished granite walls. The fact that Barnes designed a visually porous main floor creates some unusual vistas into the greenhouse.

Recently, William H. Whyte, the author of the book and classic film *The Social Life of Small Urban Spaces*, has been called in to study the activity in the greenhouse—too little of it and too quiet, in the opinion of many people, now that both the Trump Tower atrium and the new Bonwit Teller main floor exist as competing razzmatazz environments. As of now, inside the greenhouse on the 56th Street side, there are twenty fixed round tables of honed Vermont marble and sixty Knoll Bertoia side chairs with the wire mesh painted dark green and green vinyl seat cushions. Whyte is right; people do move the chairs about to sit in the sun and also to make their own social groupings. He wishes the tables could move too. "I would like to see the number of tables and chairs doubled," he said, "and the critical mass moved to the center," The refreshments are reminiscent of a French patisserie, and a handsome polished stainless steel ring, like a halo, over the kiosk gives digital time in four directions so everyone knows when to go back to work.

One of the fears expressed by critics in recent years is of overmassing due to the new towers in the East 50s. The greenhouse brings a character of its own to these cavernous streets. One feels it most after a stroll through the Trump Tower atrium into the greenhouse through Bonwit Teller. The quiet hits like a breath of fresh air—"Going from Trump's seraglio to New England," is how Whyte describes it. Why not? Or from Wall Street to Trinity Church?

About 11 A.M. on December 16, 1982, Ed and Mary Barnes came over to the greenhouse together. (As part of the firm, Mary Barnes has been associated with the interiors of the tower as well as the selection of granite and other decorative materials.) In a low-key way, this was the opening day of what IBM now officially calls the Garden Plaza. It was the first day the Bonwit Teller doors into the garden area were opened—their four show windows were decorated for Christmas. The New York Botanical Garden's Shop in the Garden, tucked into the tower base, was doing a land-office pre-holiday business. The unveiling of Michael Heizer's sculpture *Levitated Mass* on the plaza outside the Madison Avenue entrance was about to take place. It was raining hard, and water streamed down the glass walls.

Barnes spoke to me again of his earlier concept for the bamboo, the columns at Karnak, but he was pleased now with the lighter, more airy look, with the bamboo—about twenty trees to a well—resembling a series of church organ pipes. At that moment, a musical entertainment began with the Barnard–Columbia Chorus singing "Angels We Have Heard on High" accompanied by the St. Paul's Chapel Brass Ensemble, and people began to crowd in from the streets to listen Everything was still except for the music; and when the last note was sounded, it reverberated in the air. Ed Barnes looked surprised and then pleased. He walked over to Mary Barnes. "There's a five-second cathedral echo—the acoustics are wonderful." No one had ever thought about the acoustics. It was good luck.

The weekend before this it had snowed, and I went there alone at dusk on Sunday evening. I remembered that other Sunday evening now long ago when the second truss was raised at the end of the ironworkers' marathon weekend—where were all those men now? This evening the snow glistened on the slanted glass panes of the saw-toothed roof. I felt sheltered and comfortable within, yet I was surrounded by cold gleaming streets streaked with the red and white lights of moving cars, which were also reflected like streamers of light in the mirror-finished stainless-steel laminate ceiling in the tower's main lobby. Suddenly the vastness of the interior and the quiet repose intimated the atmosphere of a great European winter garden—a place in which to be alone and yet feel the pulse of the city.

The same chorus was filing in slowly for rehearsal and quite suddenly struck up a rousing rendition of Giovanni Gabrieli's *Plaudite omnis terra*. As they sang, one word rang out for me above the others. This word says it all for the return of the winter garden to midtown: Alleluia!

Architectural Record, May 1984. Reprinted with permission
from *Architectural Record* © 1984 The McGraw-Hill Companies.
www.architecturalrecord.com

A Crystal Palace: Final Portrait of the Palm House

ONE DAY last winter, after a fresh snowfall, the arched glass walls of the Palm House at the Royal Botanic Gardens at Kew rose up beyond the frozen pond, with only a swooping flock of black-headed gulls and yellowed weeping willows to tinge the pristine landscape. Frosted with snow like sugar icing on a tiered cake, the Palm House became for a few hours the crystalline palace of fairy tales, of Hans Christian Andersen's *The Snow Queen*. It glistened in the pale golden morning light for its final portrait, as it once was.

When I arrived in the early hours after a night flight from New York, Lord Snowdon, his head wrapped in a scarf under his cap against the bitter cold, was already poised and concentrating by his tripod. There was complete silence in the little group that stood near him on the far side of the pond, marveling at the unusual cast of blue-gold light in the clear air. Then quickly Lord Snowdon began to photograph. By 10:30 that miraculous light would be gone, and a gray London sky would take its place.

These historic photographs commemorate the last days of the revolutionary nineteenth-century glass-and-iron Palm House before a controversial restoration that has already begun to replace the dangerously corroded wrought-iron glazing bars with stainless steel ones in prefabricated panels and to install sixteen thousand individual panes of curved, tempered glass—a process that can be carried out only by dismantling and rebuilding the entire structure. The Palm House will gradually disappear and then reappear in the same form. The story behind the restoration provides a fascinating chapter in the annals of landmark preservation.

On the March day a few years ago when I first saw the Palm House, a damp, cool mist hung over Kew, and the daffodils were already in bloom. As I approached the immense curvilinear building along the Broad Walk, it appeared to loom up out of nowhere like a phantom structure in the misty atmosphere, so airy that it might take off in the manner of a nineteenth-century balloon. In fact, after seeing the Palm House illuminated from within at dusk, and reflected in a pond the full length of its facade, the British poet Herbert Lomas described it as a fragile "balloon of light" in a recent poem. Fortunately, the Palm House was not an illusion, and the hour I spent wandering along its pathways in the midst of a lush tropical rain forest—so humid one could hear the falling droplets of water—was a time of enchantment.

Never has form followed function with better results—height for the lofty palms and abundant light through arched glass walls, set off by the classical symmetry of two apse wings. Like the Parthenon or a great Gothic cathedral, the Palm House has been part of the vocabulary of the architectural imagination—"the heritage of magical space, the fantasy of transparent architecture," says James I. Freed of I. M. Pei & Partners, whose own designs have been inspired by it. Created first as a scientific greenhouse, the Palm House soon evolved into a picturesque setting that came to epitomize the Victorian era. Artists' renderings in the *Illustrated London News* of the early 1850s depicted fashionably dressed families, dwarfed by towering potted palms, walking along the stone-paved paths of an interior paradisiacal garden. To the Victorians, the palm tree was a romantic reminder of faraway places, and the Sunday promenade at Kew an expedition into a secret world of make-believe. These two images of the Palm House—as an ongoing scientific collection of plants in a world-renowned botanical garden and as a fixed interior landscape, an intact remnant of Victorian life—have been at the heart of the controversy in England over restoration.

The Palm House in an important survivor. The glass structure that inspired it, the Great Conservatory at Chatsworth, was dynamited for lack of funds to maintain it. Designed by Joseph Paxton, head gardener to the Duke of Devonshire, the Great Conservatory, completed in 1841, had perhaps its finest moment one gala evening when Queen Victoria and Prince Albert rode through the central allée in an open carriage to the light of twelve thousand lamps. That same year Sir William Jackson Hooker, first director of the Royal Property of Kew Gardens, wrote the duke to arrange to see this conservatory with its curvilinear roof of glass and wooden frames. Queen Victoria had given Kew forty-five more acres, on which Sir William intended to build a new glass structure to house the tropical plants from around the empire, overflowing the antiquated greenhouse of Kew. In Sir William's report of 1844, he boasted, "This noble structure, which . . . will be second to none in Europe, possesses advantages of both form and structure, and the means of filling it with the choicest and most valuable productions, which will render it perfectly unique."

The day Queen Victoria visited the newly built Palm House in 1848, a specimen was cut for the occasion: a "gigantic truss of fruit from which hangs a wonderful kind of velvety Victorian bell-pull, always removed before the fruit reaches the greengrocer." Sir William's explanation of this bunch of spectacular bananas was so long-winded that Thomas Meehan, the young gardener holding them, finally had to put his hat back on in order to grasp the bananas with both hands—an act of disrespect that put him forever in bad odor at Kew.

The Palm House was a technological breakthrough, made possible by the invention of rolled wrought iron and the repeal of the glass tax in 1845, and carried out by a construction engineer and iron founder from Dublin, Richard Turner, who drew up the final designs for the lofty heights and the large unsupported expanses of curved glass. He worked out of the office of the architect Decimus Burton, whose name was signed to the drawings of record.

The use of glass and iron signaled a new era in architecture, a marriage between engineering and architecture not fully realized until the modernist buildings of the International Style. One observes the close relationship between the I-shaped arch supports of the Palm House and the I-shaped beams in Mies van der Rohe's glass-and-steel buildings. In a sense, the Palm House was the first modern structure, though the Beaux-Arts tradition would carry over into the twentieth century. As architects caught up with the vision of engineers, the results became evident around the world. "Essentially," James Freed points out, "the technology of glasshouse architecture is no further advanced today than in the last century."

What is most memorable about the structure of the Palm House is its profile—one writer calls it a Victorian jelly mold. With its sixty-foot-high double-tiered central court balanced by two apse wings that stretch the structure to a length of 360 feet, the Palm House resembles an overturned ship with the six-foot-high clerestories cresting it like a giant keel. Turner designed the support arches and the ten miles of glazing bars to such a thinness that where they radiate out from corners they themselves resemble the veins of large tropical leaves.

Almost every component, including the glass, has a structural purpose. The central roof is supported by tubular cast-iron columns that serve as drains for rainwater; wrought-iron tie-rods, drawn taut through horizontal wrought-iron tubes, or purlins, brace the elliptical ribs. Only the occasional ornamental rosettes and scrolls of iron indicate the Palm House's era. Decorative iron palmettes on the balusters around the central gallery suggest the building's purpose. Ascending through the green, up one of two open spiral staircases, one discovers that the structural iron, painted white, disappears as one looks to the sky. For all its strength, the building appears delicate and fragile. "But the beauty of the building," says Kew's curator, John Simmons, "is that it has always functioned properly as a palm house from the very beginning." And therein lies the crux of the controversy.

In preserving the Palm House, the question is not the usual one of adaptive reuse of an antiquated building, for the greenhouse operation is thriving. But the hot, moist environment, after almost 140 years, has been the structure's undoing. The building must be repaired simply for reasons of safety (Kew has had to replace five hundred panes of glass a year) and the plantings made more manageable in light of a 20 percent cut in the maintenance budget.

The controversy has centered on two main issues: replacing the corroded wrought-iron glazing bars with stainless steel (wrought iron is no longer made in sufficient quantity), and the introduction of deep planting beds throughout in lieu of the potted palms and the propagating plant shelves that lined the perimeter. The deep planting, according to the horticulturists, will make it easier to prune and to keep the beds moist; as a result the plants will be able to flower and fruit as well as reach their full height. But the preservationists mourn the loss of the individual pots and tubs that made the potted palm the signature of an age, and point out that part of the pleasure and mystery of palm houses derives from the sense of being lost along narrow paths among the towering trees of a central palm court.

It is the internal changes that have aroused most opposition. The initial proposals were challenged by the Victorian Society and other preservationists, and their views have had an influence on aspects of the final design. Potted palms and plant shelves as ornamental showcases for exotic plants, for example, will be retained at the apse ends. One controversial innovation strenuously opposed by the preservationists, a display tank of tropical marine plants planned as the centerpiece of the new Palm House, will now be submerged, to be viewed only from the basement level.

The ironwork of the Palm House was originally painted ultramarine, and the glass tinted a pea green, but the entire structure has been reglazed at least three times. Toward the end of the nineteenth century the color of the ironwork was changed to a creamy white rather than the present bright titanium white. The arches and columns will be restored and strengthened, for the intent "is only to replace those components which have reached the end of their useful life." Vents in both the clerestories and the masonry base will be made operable for effective airflow, and a glass vestibule will be added to the south apse end to conserve energy in winter.

The question of whether the Palm House is a restoration or a replica remains alive. But as greenhouses in botanical gardens around the world shut down, as tropical rain forests are overwhelmed by encroaching civilization, the responsibilities of Kew become more crucial. The Palm House will remain in full use as a botanical laboratory. In the end, for preservation to make sense, the building had to be adapted to the goals of Kew. Fortunately, wherever in the world potted palms grace a single interior, the memory of the Victorian-style Palm House will linger.

As the natty and energetic curator, John Simmons, says, "People in England feel that they own Kew, that it's their garden." And the controversy, now at an end, has been a lively one. Charmian Lacey, the government architect overseeing the project, promises that "we will return the Palm House as frilly as we found it."

The process of dismantling and numbering each piece has begun. Last year, in a slow procession, two thousand plants were removed in nine days, most of them to a temporary palm house, where the fronds are now pushing against its upper limits. Included was a two-and-a half-ton rare cycad (*Encephalartos longifolius*) that has been at Kew since 1775.

Once the palms were removed, the atmosphere within was cool, and the eye moved along the soaring ribs to the clerestories, every detail etched distinctly against the sky. Without the contrast of the dense tropical green, the structural elements, white on white, will remain in memory like the finest lace unfurled to infinity—in a glass dome of the imagination.

Vanity Fair, December 1985

Gardens Fit for a Queen

LIKENED TO an ark keeping the world's plant specimens afloat while they disappear elsewhere, the Royal Botanic Gardens, Kew, is also one of the prettiest places to walk in England. Its 330 acres appear almost rural, and the Thames, which provided transportation to this London suburb when the gardens were first laid out in 1759, still flows peaceably by its western boundary.

During frequent visits, I tended to return to the Palm House and widen the circle each time to include the other half-dozen greenhouses, including the Beaux-Arts Temperate House and the Waterlily House, and the intermittent landscapes. But each time, I came away with a map showing vast areas of green, and a feeling that there was an eighteenth-century landscape I had yet to explore. And so, on a late summer Sunday, I set out for what amounted to a five-hour walk of every pathway at the Royal Botanic Gardens, interrupted of course by a delicious ploughman's lunch at the Pavilion Restaurant, set outdoors under grape arbors (each of the forty-seven grape varieties carries a botanical label), and afternoon tea at the Orangery with scones, strawberry jam, and clotted cream.

Walking the few blocks from the London Underground station to Kew gives a taste of cheerful residential streets with meticulous front gardens. At Victoria Gate, a configuration of garden walls and pergolas of London brick guides visitors through an entrance area of shops and information booths to the first spectacular view of the Palm House. This time, I routed myself away from the Palm House, past the Temple of Arethusa, tucked away in a green glen, and the domed Temple of Aeolus, raised up on a mound—restored follies of the eighteenth century. By plunging directly into the systematics garden, where the plants are arranged according to scientific order, I came immediately to the heart of the botanical display. With over twenty-five thousand species of plants at Kew, representing 10 percent of the world's species, all of the gardens, though ornamental, basically make up a scientific collection. But in the order beds, bisected by a picturesque pergola of roses, the disciplined arrangement yields its own harmony of form, texture, and color.

Each path in this garden leads to another: first, the extensive rock garden that inspired the fashion for them in the United States at the end of the nineteenth century, then to the aquatic garden with its symmetrical pools filled with water lilies, pickerelweed, and British marsh plants. At the Duke of Cambridge's former house, a rambling brick structure now converted into the Kew Gardens Gallery with its own cottage garden, there was an excellent exhibition of botanical drawings, one of the arts encouraged at Kew.

The newest greenhouse at Kew, the peak-roofed Princess of Wales Conservatory, is just beyond the rock garden. While it may not possess the poetic structure of the Palm House, its vast interior encompasses ten climatic zones, from arid to moist tropical. While tiny orchids are on display here, the visitor does not see the behind-the-scenes orchids in the Sainsbury Orchid Conservation Project that are being replanted in the wild. Kew has collected widely, but it also gives back to wild areas of the world through its ambitious programs in conservation and preservation.

To the north stands the Sir Joseph Banks Center for Economic Botany, with its environmentally correct berm and barrel-vaulted glass enclosure surrounded by a landscape of plants useful to people, for food, medicine, shelter, and clothing. And at nearby Kew Palace, a charming reconstructed seventeenth-century garden is a favorite of mine, with clipped hedges, an avenue of hornbeams pruned into severe geometry, and a laburnum walk that is transformed into a golden tunnel in May. A sunken nosegay garden is filled with fragrant flowers and herbs, for use in small aromatic bouquets. From the Bee Garden, with its active hives behind a wattle, or woven fence, there is a first glimpse of the Thames.

But mainly I struck out on the broad grassy avenues that meander through the park, first from the Palm House along the Pagoda Vista to the ten-story Chinese pagoda. Families were seated in the shade of gigantic trees planted in pairs along the walk—purple beeches, zelkovas, and chestnuts. I stopped by King William's Temple, a neoclassical folly designed for William IV by Sir Jeffry Wyatville in 1837, and then entered the Temperate House sheltering plants and trees from the temperate zones of the world. There is an otherwordly beauty in these exotic landscapes within glass walls, and on this occasion I noticed for the first time the graceful lead shepherdess by the eighteenth-century sculptor John Cheere. Because the special gardens throughout the park for heather or bamboo or azaleas are miniature landscapes of their own, with hillocks, glades, and dells, it is always a surprise to turn a corner of a path and come into their midst. At times, I was completely alone on a distant path, with the river again coming into view.

After discovering the serpentine lake on the west side of the park, I marveled at the picturesque contour of its islands and at the monkey puzzle trees near its banks. By shifting over to the next path, I was suddenly on the straight vista that joins the Palm House with Syon House across the Thames, the Duke of Northumberland's patrician house. Five minutes later, I was in deep woods where the bluebells bloom in spring. Once I did come here in early February to see the scattering of snowdrops, the first to flower after winter in the woodland garden. And then, for a moment of repose, I stopped into Queen Charlotte's cottage, where the Picnic Room, painted green with flowering vines, was set as it once was for tea.

I had reached the western limit of the garden. On the way back to Victoria Gate, I passed through the Ruined Arch to visit the Marianne North Gallery, constructed in 1882 and paneled with the 246 different types of wood that this intrepid Victorian artist collected on her travels to every continent. On these voyages, she created an extensive record in her botanical paintings of tropical and exotic flora. All 832 of these glowing paintings cover the walls, only one of the many testaments at Kew of personal devotion and dedication to the field of botany.

The royals who lived at Kew in the eighteenth and nineteenth centuries were responsible for encouraging the enlightened and fashionable views on landscape gardening and plant collecting that have given the Royal Botanic Gardens and its park their essential character.

When Henry VII occupied a palace in the old deer park nearby, Kew was known by its older spelling of "Kayhough." Alexander Pope, a neighbor with a superb garden on the Thames, wrote with humor of attending a gardeners' meeting at Kew held by Princess Caroline in 1719 at Richmond Lodge, where she and the future George II had taken refuge from troubles at court. She made the most of this exile by acquiring surrounding lands and later hiring Charles Bridgeman and William Kent to improve the landscape and construct the neoclassical and pastoral follies that became destinations on royal outings.

In the meantime, their son, Frederick, Prince of Wales, and his wife, Princess Augusta, moved to another property at Kew, also to escape hostilities in town. After his untimely death, she forged ahead with William Chambers, who, fresh from visits to China, was eager to introduce a chinoiserie overlay by constructing in 1761 the first pagoda in Europe—a fantasy with tiered roofs and red lattice balustrades. Still a focal point of Kew, the pagoda, as well as his romantic temples, a ruined arch, and the Orangery (now a restaurant), added another historic layer to the grounds. By then, plant collecting from territories all over the world had enriched the reputation of this royal enclosure.

Through inheritance, George III consolidated the properties and engaged "Capability" Brown to add his trademark of undulating lawns and artfully placed clusters of trees to the enlarged landscape. Sir Joseph Banks, an amateur botanist, was appointed to manage the gardens following his plant explorations on Captain James Cook's first voyage to the South Pacific on the *Endeavour*. Two residences of this period, Kew Palace, the gabled brick edifice constructed as the Dutch House in 1631, and Queen Charlotte's rustic cottage, a 1772 thatched house for summer teas, still surrounded by woodland, continue to give a domestic focus to Kew Gardens.

In the early years of Queen Victoria's reign, pressure mounted to convert the Royal Gardens into a national science institution, and in 1841 Kew was opened as a public botanic garden with Sir William Hooker from Glasgow at its helm. (The current director, Sir Ghillean Prance, spent twenty-five years previously at the New York Botanical Garden.) From that time on, with the construction of the innovative Palm House surrounded by a new landscape by William Andrews Nesfield, the garden took the shape of today without ever losing traces of the royal pleasure ground it once was.

Some years ago, I bought a botanical drawing by Margaret Stones, an artist who lives near Kew Gardens, of a blossom with leaves from a *Sophora japonica* (Japanese pagoda tree) planted at Kew in 1759. During my long walk, I was hoping to spot the actual tree. When, finally, I came across it just outside the Princess of Wales Conservatory, bent and gnarled, held aloft by several supports, I realized it had been planted a year before George III ascended the throne. No doubt Fanny Burney, one of my favorite writers, had passed the young tree when she was Second Keeper of the Robes for Queen Charlotte. I thought too of Alexander Pope, who frequently visited here. More than anyone he understood the beauty of the site. Strolling on the footpath along the Thames watching the current curve around grassy tree-lined banks in the summer haze, I recalled his own image of "a River at my garden's end."

New York Times, June 16, 1996

Hartford's 1896 Rose Garden, Whose Ancestors Were Born in France

IN 1896, a young Swiss landscape architect named Theodore Wirth became superintendent of public parks in Hartford. Within a year, he began work on what became the first municipal rose garden in the United States, a decidedly Continental touch within a park system fashioned mostly in the English style of the Olmsted Brothers firm. Today, after a five-year period of restoration, the Rose Garden, on the corner of Asylum and Prospect avenues, is still the elaborate centerpiece of Elizabeth Park, and for the next few weeks it will be at its peak of bloom.

The word "municipal" has a stalwart ring, signifying that the city was willing and able to create in the public domain a rose garden on a scale that had previously existed only on great private estates. The large municipal rose garden, developed and maintained by public funds, is a late-nineteenth-century European idea. The Hartford Rose Garden, with its arched pathways and rustic summer house, predates even the famous 1912 Roseraie in the Parc de Bagatelle in Paris, and though many American rose gardens are larger than Hartford's two acres, few are as exceptional in design.

The ancestor of the multivariety rose garden was born in France, the inspiration and passion of Josephine at Malmaison, the chateau she acquired in 1799 after her marriage to Napoleon. She collected 250 varieties from as far away as China and Japan, and soldiers returned from military campaigns bearing rose plants for the Empress. In his book *Gardens, Plants, and Man*, Carlton B. Lees, the recently retired senior vice president of the New York Botanical Garden, tells how Josephine's garden became "the turning point in rose history, and breeding experiments started there became the foundation upon which modern rose varieties developed." The artist Pierre-Joseph Redouté immortalized her garden in his seven hundred paintings of her roses.

By 1903, saying, "The public in general would appreciate nothing so much as an enlargement of that special feature, the rose garden," Wirth submitted to the park commissioner a final planting plan, the one still in evidence, which included eight arch-covered walks emanating from a round center like the spokes of a wheel. In this wheel-like formation, it resembles the Botanical Garden at Padua, the first in Italy, founded in 1545, a historic garden certainly known to Wirth from his Swiss training.

In Hartford, the central garden is a perfect square with an entrance in the middle of each side leading into the four fourteen-foot-wide turf walkways on north–south and east–west axes, with the main entrance on the west side by the park drive. Narrower diagonal paths, eight feet wide, lead to entrances at the corners.

All the walks are arched over by single wood and iron arches, seventy-eight in all, covered with climbers and ramblers. Only one variety of rose is used per path to provide a unified appearance as one looks through them: red Crimson Rambler and Excelsa for the crosswalks and White Dorothy and pink Dorothy Perkins on the diagonals. The walks intersect at a rustic summer house, an open, octagonal log structure on a circular elevation from which the pattern of the entire garden may be surveyed. The four openings of the pavilion correspond with the wide paths, and the balustraded sides overlook the diagonal walks.

A lush Virginia creeper vine covers the summer house as well as the birdhouse that adorns its roof like a cupola. Rugosa roses surround the structure, and the hill is banked with arc-shaped beds of polyantha and floribunda. Otherwise, the remainder of the 132 beds of the main garden are rectangular with turf walks in between. Generally each bed contains a single variety, the majority Hybrid Perpetual roses, which have been in place since 1903.

The total budget for Wirth's 1903 proposal was $2,200, with $200 allocated for the summer house. He specified "the work to be done in all its details to perfection so as not to cause expensive repairs for a long time to come." So the rose garden has survived, in recent years with the help of the Friends of Elizabeth Park, who, according to their president, Anne P. Pinto, have raised $86,000 since they organized in 1977 with a five-year plan to restore the garden. James T. McIsaac, the foreman of Elizabeth Park, has the help of nine full-time workers, two temporaries, and ten more from a government job program. The annual budget for the rose garden is $50,000. McIsaac is usually on the premises to explain how they care for the roses, particularly the trailing ones on the arches, which are untied each fall and laid on the ground for pruning.

In 1912, a semicircular area added to the south side of the garden became one of the original test gardens for the All-American rose selections—there are now twenty-five such sites—where new rose varieties undergo stringent testing for such factors as color, scent, and hardiness before they go on sale. Another semicircular plot was added in 1936 to balance the design, bringing the present number of rose plants to fifteen thousand, with fifteen hundred different varieties.

The long vistas created by the arched pathways and the vine-covered summer house are suffused with a romance, particularly on misty days. In the Hartford Rose Garden there is the sense of entering another world, an enchanted one separated by a rose-covered fence from the cares of the real one. It never fails to work its magic.

One frequent Sunday visitor for almost forty years was the poet Wallace Stevens, whose wife, Elsie, was an expert on roses. He also walked through the park during the week on the way to his office at the Hartford Accident and Indemnity Company. How well the poet understood the rightness of the rose garden's symmetrical orientation when he wrote these last lines of "Vacancy in the Park": "The four winds blow through the rustic arbor, / Under its mattresses of vines."

New York Times, June 24, 1982

2,700 Roses Re-create Old Garden: The Peggy Rockefeller Rose Garden

THE LAST OF 2,700 roses are being moved this week from a propagation range where pots had been tucked into every corner of the greenhouses and temporary shelters. They will join the masses of roses that have already been installed in a new two-acre garden at the New York Botanical Garden. The rose garden is a reconstruction of a plan that lay dormant for seventy years.

The original rose garden was designed in 1915 by Beatrix Farrand. But architectural elements of her plan, including an iron latticework enclosure to protect the roses and other features to display them, were never built because of a lack of money. The original garden's estimated cost—$10,000—is a fraction of the $1 million being spent on the current restoration. But despite the support of such donors as J. P. Morgan, W. K. Vanderbilt, and Andrew Carnegie, sufficient funds were never raised. A less ambitious rose garden was planted in 1918 but was dismantled in 1969 as a result of a cutback in city funds.

Next Wednesday, Peggy Rockefeller is to turn the key in the lock of a lattice gate and open the Peggy Rockefeller Rose Garden. She has had a longstanding interest in horticulture and is an honorary member of the Botanical Garden's board of managers. The restoration is supported by a

$1 million gift from her husband, David. Since 1960, she has overseen a garden designed in the 1920s by Farrand for the Rockefeller family in Seal Harbor, Maine.

"As with any garden," said Carl A. Totemeier, the New York Botanical Garden's vice president for horticulture, "this one will never be completely finished. We will always be striving to develop a collection with the best of old and new roses that are both attractive and well adapted to the site."

Beth Straus, the chairman of the garden's horticulture committee and a member of the board, saw the original sketches of the garden for the first time in 1985 at an exhibition at Wave Hill called "Beatrix Farrand's American Landscapes." She decided to embark on the project to reconstruct the rose garden the way, she said, "it had never existed before," with all of its structural elements.

With the approval of New York City's Art Commission came the stipulation that the planting beds be perpendicular to the main radial paths in keeping with the more scientific divisions of a botanical garden and to conform to Farrand's own idea of the garden as a library of species.

Those active in planning the rose garden have remarked on its resemblance to the dark green lattice enclosure, arched entrances, and triangular shape of a rose garden in France designed in 1899 by Edouard André for the great rosarian Jules Gravereaux at l'Haÿ-les-Roses, just south of Paris. Conceivably, Farrand may have seen the garden on a visit to her aunt Edith Wharton in France; but in her correspondence, she cites as being helpful her visit to the 1896 Hartford, Connecticut, rose garden in Elizabeth Park. Both its slightly raised central summerhouse and beds in circular formation are incorporated in her design.

With the architectural framework for the roses now in place, there is a clear impression of the grandeur that lies ahead. Set in a valley, the garden, which is triangular, has paths of crushed bluestone that meet at a seven-sided arbor. This domed lattice structure sits within a circular trellis. There are stone piers at the main gate that are topped with Edwardian urns overflowing with Fairy roses. The piers tie in visually with a grand staircase that leads to an upper level.

Gardeners are now hosing down the seventy newly planted rose beds. Following English fashion, climbing roses on the central arbor as well as on the perimeter trellises will eventually be entwined with clematis. Beyond the arc-shaped beds of miniature roses surrounding the central arbor is a circle of posts linked by sloping chains, which were used frequently by Farrand in her designs. The roses climbing the posts will eventually spread along the chains, which will be underplanted with pansies in shades of blue.

The beds running perpendicular to the paths hold a collection of hybrid teas and grandifloras, including Ivory Tower and Queen Elizabeth. While the long inner perimeter beds will eventually exhibit a series of floribundas like Sunsprite and Fancy Talk, the outer perimeter beds along the fence will be devoted to climbing and old-fashioned shrub roses as well as newer varieties behind a cloud of hazy blue nepeta. With wide areas of grass between the formal beds, the roses will be seen in relief against a sea of green.

Some roses ordered from English nurseries are still in quarantine at the National Arboretum in Washington, and others will be selected from the Joseph Kern Collection in the Heritage Rose Garden at the Ohio State University Arboretum in Wooster, Ohio.

The restoration has sometimes been difficult. Farrand's sketches captured the spirit of the garden but lacked construction details and specific dimensions. "The problem we faced in restoring a garden that had never been built," said Robert E. Meadows, the architect for the restoration, "was how to interpret Beatrix Farrand's flat sketches by three-dimensional units, not only of the correct scale but of sufficient strength to support the long spans of trellis without their tipping over." The architectural elements, painted dark green, are constructed of rustproof galvanized steel, instead of iron, as Farrand had planned. Seen head on, the architectural elements look exactly like Farrand's drawings, though a sideways view reveals the ingenious way the intermittent arches have become stabilizing cross hoops.

Covering the sloping hillside outside the formal enclosure are naturalized plantings of other species of the rose family as Farrand pictured them, including cotoneaster, potentilla, and rugosa roses. From here one has an overview of the whole garden and its open-air architecture equal in splendor to the Enid A. Haupt Conservatory's glass-enclosed spaces.

In preparation for opening day, every tree in the woodlands rising on the far side of the rose garden has been pruned to perfection, except for one scraggly tree. As a home for honeybees, this tree cannot be touched until after the first deep frost so as not to impede the bees' good work. In a botanical garden, beauty is secondary to science.

New York Times, September 22, 1988

A Victorian Gem Restored:
The Enid A. Haupt Conservatory

FEW MOMENTS equal the steamy calm after a tropical storm, with the soft music of water droplets being shed by hundreds of saturated trees. During just such a charmed moment of horticultural theater in the New York Botanical Garden's newly restored Enid A. Haupt Conservatory, it was transfixing to stand still and listen. Clouds of moisture from the high-tech misting system had recreated the lushness of the jungle among the mahogany and kapok trees, the banana plants and chocolate trees of the Lowland Tropical Rain Forest.

The forest is one of four "biomes," or environments, in the splendid Victorian greenhouse in the Bronx—the largest of its kind in America. Reopening to the public after a four-year, $25 million rehabilitation, the conservatory is the centerpiece of the Botanical Garden's seven-year plan for renovation and renewal. Its seventeen thousand panes of glass were replaced by hand. The huge plant collection, now numbering three thousand, in this museum of horticulture has also been reinstalled, with some new plants and new settings, and a spacious café now stands in the spruce grove near the conservatory.

A World of Plants, as the new installation is called, begins dramatically in the Palms of the Americas Gallery, under the ninety-foot-high dome of the entrance rotunda. Visitors move from there through ten connecting pavilions and four environments—from lowland and upland rain forests to deserts of the Americas and Africa. Here, the intimate contact between visitors and plants is greater than ever; brushing away the banana leaves as they make their way through the rain forests and smelling the sweet scent of jasmine in the subtropical pavilion takes them about as far from New York's urban bustle as it is possible to get.

Essentially, the exhibits constitute scientific laboratories in the guise of a trip around the world, and their beauty and drama derive from the patterns found in nature by the scientists who have traveled to the Amazonian rain forests or African deserts to collect plants for research. (The Botanical Garden counts at least a thousand such expeditions in its history, and its role as a scientific institution is at least as important as its role in providing a green haven for the public.) Frequently, the botanists themselves talk about their experiences on the informative taped tour.

Under the conservatory's curved ceilings of glistening new glass open to scudding clouds and blue sky, one recalls Dr. Johnson's words of 1750 saluting the invention of glass: "A Body at once in a high Degree solid and transparent, which might admit the Light of the Sun, and exclude the Violence of the Wind . . . enlarging the Avenues of Science, and . . . enabling the Student to contemplate Nature." The conservatory in the Bronx, after a four-year rehabilitation, fulfills all these expectations.

Little did Dr. Johnson know that in the century following his essay, England itself would produce two monumental glass structures, ancestors of the one in the Bronx—Richard Turner's 1848 Palm House at the Royal Botanic Gardens, Kew, and Sir Joseph Paxton's 1851 Crystal Palace in Hyde Park—constituting a revolution in architectural technology that has informed every similar structure since. Conceived as a storehouse for the conservation of tropical plants collected on expeditions all over the world, the Palm House, in particular, became a romantic setting establishing a Victorian fad for palm-filled conservatories.

Fortunately for this country, two young members of the Torrey Botanical Club of New York, a Columbia professor, Nathaniel Lord Britton, and his wife, Elizabeth, took a belated honeymoon to England in 1888 and roamed around Kew Gardens for many pleasurable hours. Her longing for a garden "just like that" translated into the founding in 1891 of the New York Botanical Garden, with Nathaniel Britton becoming its first director.

In Europe, leading botanical gardens found their genesis in royal properties or major universities; but in New York City, the club started its garden from scratch in Bronx Park, a 250-acre site that included the former estate of Pierre Lorillard, the tobacco merchant. Beginning with virgin territory—a forty-acre seventeenth-century forest is one of the Botanical Garden's major scientific and scenic assets—the first master plan included the Lord & Burnham Conservatory, which was completed in 1902 (the restoration architects are Beyer Blinder Belle). The conservatory, with its prominent domed Palm House, balanced the 1901 Museum Building, with its central dome, designed by Robert Gibson, architect of the Cartier building on Fifth Avenue in Manhattan. Both structures display leafy Corinthian pilasters. Generally, visitors are so focused on the gardens and greenhouse displays that few are aware of the Botanical Garden's architectural legacy, from nineteenth-century industrial buildings and cottages in fieldstone to these magnificent Beaux-Arts designs.

This year, as part of the 1993–1999 master plan (which includes a children's adventure garden to open in 1998), under the direction of Gregory Long, the energetic president, the Botanical Garden has added a new building to this complex. Designed by Jacquelin T. Robertson and John Kirk of

Cooper, Robertson & Partners, this simple, solid brick orangery with immense arched windows to the ground houses the café that seats two hundred indoors and out; it replaces the historic Snuff Mill, which will be used for banquets and meetings. Adjoining the restaurant is a spacious terrace room for private entertaining (and a new source of income for the Garden). The public garden designer Lynden B. Miller has already created a garden here against the brick facades, with hollies, borders of box, climbing hydrangeas, and a rose of Sharon trained into a blind arch.

When half of the conservatory first opened in 1900, Nathaniel Britton is reported to have spent only $100 on the inaugural display of plants. Many survive today (a kapok tree, for one) at the completion of this restoration (the fourth such project in the building's history, and the largest), during which the glass, steel, and wood structure was stripped to its skeleton and rebuilt with aluminum glazing bars. Unlike stabilization programs of the past, this one involved scraping and repainting every nut and bolt.

The suite of display houses—five on either side of the rotunda—form a C-shaped pattern around outdoor tropical and temperate pools, retaining the balloon-shaped silhouettes that belie their new state-of-the-art interiors. Mist and fog are created on demand, and vents automatically admit fresh air as long as the wind permits.

In the Palms of the Americas Gallery, a visitor begins to understand the dimensions of this undertaking when Joe Kerwin, the manager of the conservatory, who masterminded the plant reinstallation, points out the *Euterpe oleracea* that has crossed the Pacific by barge from Hawaii to take its place here among the slender columns and umbrella canopies of at least one hundred species of sister palms and cycads. A pond has been added and, along with rivulets, waterfalls, and pools in other houses, enhances the quality of sound and reflected light.

Walking into the Lowland Rain Forest, one sees through a curtain of vines the massive branch of a kapok tree that has been hurled, archlike, across the path during the "tropical storm." Kapok trees, among the tallest in the forest, are what make rain forests so dark. But here the kapok is an artificial, completely convincing creation, the stuff of dioramas; the top of the forest has been brought down to eye level with bromeliads thriving on the tree bark, and the sun pours through the gap to nourish the forest floor. It's a good script made more real by the excellent eye of the tropical plant curator, Francisca Coelho, who was raised in Trinidad. The remaining trunk of the tree, buttressed like a cathedral, is found further along.

Emerging from the underground tunnel linking this section with the dry regions of the Americas, Africa, and Australia, one focuses on the sculptural quality of plants in these more open pavilions. Along the way are places to sit under a canopy of hanging plants and seasonal displays, as well as plantings of subtropicals such as camellias, olive trees, and scented geraniums. At every turn, intelligent signs entice even the casual visitor to learn about the Garden's larger missions in environmentalism and economic botany, discovering the uses of plants—including medicinal properties that are being learned firsthand from local healers in places like Belize. The thatched healer's hut near the great tree trunk gives an immediacy to the Garden's work.

The conservatory's popular seasonal flower displays will continue in two galleries. For the reopening, in a tribute to another New York institution, the Cloisters, the exhibit will consist of a garden of flowers from the sixteenth-century unicorn tapestries, based on the eighty species of plants identified in the Flemish tapestries by two of the garden's botanists in 1941. Scenes from the tapestries will also be recreated in the conservatory.

From the Botanical Garden's new entrance at the Conservatory Gate with its "lollipop" standing clock, the visitor is now led through a triangular circuit described by Gregory Long as "the garden within the Garden." Spring is a particularly good time to make the circuit, when showy tulips—there are twelve thousand here—and flowering trees are coming into their own. Beginning with the herb and perennial gardens just starting to bloom, one walks past the conservatory to borders ablaze with tulips and domestic-style demonstration gardens, which serve to help people reimagine their own.

Turning the corner at the new café, the walk continues under a broad avenue of tulip trees before shifting to the Rock Garden and Native Plant Garden on the hypotenuse. Spring is the peak season in the Rock Garden, with brilliant alpine flowers nestled among the boulders. The more adventurous can strike out for the wooded valleys where crab apple trees are in bloom or walk to the picturesque bridge over the Bronx River to view the waterfall that once powered the Snuff Mill.

Over the next few weeks, the clear glass of the Enid A. Haupt Conservatory will gradually be shaded from the sun with a wash of luminescent pale green. And during celebratory evening events when the interiors are softly illuminated, the dome will glow against the night sky—a newly opalescent jewel in New York City's crown.

New York Times, April 27, 1997

A Centennial Bouquet:
The Botanic Garden of Smith College, 1895–1995

AMONG THE most enduring of botanic gardens are those linked with universities, where the strictly scientific displays required for the study of plants possess a perpetual beauty based on order and the changing seasons. Originating in medieval monasteries and Renaissance universities, botanic gardens are still a priority in education, particularly in those institutions where they have survived and continue in force today. Public botanic gardens are another matter. Founded in the first great eras of plant exploration, they serve an advanced scientific community wrestling with problems of conservation and the environment, but like other urban parks, they are designed to entertain. Plant collections arranged in nineteenth-century glass conservatories and their surrounding gardens are meant to be decorative as well as scientific, forming an attractive background for Sunday promenades.

These introductory thoughts are meant to place in context the remarkable foresight of a New England educator, Laurenus Clark Seelye, who, as the first of the "gardener presidents" of Smith College, created a botanic garden that has distinguished the College and enriched campus and community life for over a century. Located in Northampton, Massachusetts, in the rolling countryside of the Connecticut Valley, Smith College was founded in 1871 with the fortune and determination of Sophia Smith, who wished to give women the means of obtaining a higher education equal to that offered by the elite men's colleges. (Smith remains a women's college today.) Although other women's colleges developed in this era of educational reform were housed in large institutional buildings that allowed for greater supervision, the enlightened founders of Smith selected a bucolic site at the edge of town, with two important houses on adjoining farmsteads with orchards and pastures sloping down to a mill pond that provided water to local factories.

Even as industrialization was overtaking New England, the concept of the village and the community remained a utopian ideal. From the beginning (and to some extent today), Smith students lived in domestic-style cottages along the main street, and the campus grew as an integral part of the town. (The word "campus," incidentally, was first used in America to describe the grounds of Princeton University in 1774.) From the earliest days, landscape gardeners were hired to improve the grounds; but even more significantly, in addition to

describing walks and drives that commanded "one of the most beautiful prospects in the Connecticut Valley," the young college's circulars listed botany
among the sciences taught at Smith.

New college buildings constructed of red brick in the Victorian Gothic
style were trimmed with brown sandstone, some with floral motifs in the Aesthetic tradition that would have been approved of by John Ruskin. In contrast,
one of the original stately homes, Dewey House, columned in the Grecian
Revival style, appeared like a small white temple in a rural landscape of wildflower meadows. Although one of the landscape firms planted the numerous
elm trees that became a signature of the college, comprehensive planning for
a cohesive landscape architecture was still an emerging concept in America.
Also, what began at Smith as an experiment for two hundred students quickly
grew in size, demanding a different set of requirements.

By 1890, when the college finally engaged Frederick Law Olmsted's landscape architecture firm in Brookline, Massachusetts (a suburb of Boston), Olmsted had for a long time been a national figure as the designer in the 1850s of
New York City's Central Park. He had been directly influenced in this earlier
endeavor by a chance visit to Birkenhead Park across the Mersey River from
Liverpool, England's oldest free-entry municipal park, planned by Sir Joseph
Paxton in the 1840s. But Olmsted was also known for designing university
campuses that upheld the community ideal of the New England village, according to Lisa Chase, whose essay on the subject, "Imagining Utopia: Landscape Design at Smith College, 1871–1910," summarizes his concept of campuses designed on the domestic scale of a suburban community surrounded by
parkland.

Seelye's inspiration, as expressed in his report to the college of 1891–92,
concerning the Olmsted plan, may also have been derived from his visit to the
Royal Botanic Garden in Edinburgh: "The idea of these plans is to lay out the
grounds so that they shall be not only most serviceable for our ordinary use,
but shall also provide an ornamental botanical garden, the plants and trees being selected and grouped according to scientific as well as aesthetic demands."
A campus designed as a botanic garden and arboretum with lofty trees, open
greens, and curvilinear pathways would not only reflect Olmsted's pastoral
themes, but also enhance the mission of the college to provide rigorous studies in science, especially in botany.

The Olmsted firm submitted the plan in 1892; within two years a collection of twelve hundred shrubs and trees had been planted in the college
grounds, and to this day they bear labels with their botanical names and na-

tive regions. A site on the banks of Paradise Pond was then selected for a conservatory complex. The former mill pond now served as a serpentine water feature as picturesque as any found in the eighteenth-century English landscape gardens Olmsted had admired on his travels. The firm of Lord & Burnham in Irvington, New York, was hired to build the range of glasshouses (now numbering twelve) in the balloon style inherited from mid-nineteenth-century English conservatories. (As an aside, the Lord & Burnham salesman who dealt with Seelye eventually sent his daughter to Smith, and she still recalls accounts of the transaction.) Lord & Burnham greenhouses, advertised by catalogue, have been frequently referred to as "cookie-cutter architecture" from their similarity to one another. However, their mild brand of Victorian Gothic, with white framework and decorative fleur-de-lis metalwork along the ridge line of the central Palm House, has proven to be exceptionally functional and by now possesses a timeworn beauty. At Smith the multiple glasshouses, including tasteful contemporary additions, each one articulated by its own form, cluster in the landscape as a unity that yet hints at its labyrinthine interior voyage into exotic worlds. At night, when they are illuminated from inside for special occasions, the glasshouses glow from a distance like a crystalline brooch set into the hillside.

Named in honor of the mother of the local donor Edward H. R. Lyman, whose family owned one of the original farmsteads, Lyman Plant House was constructed in 1895, and in addition to a Palm House included a Temperate House, a Stove House, and a Succulent House. To oversee the completion of the Botanic Garden, Seelye had the year before hired William Francis Ganong, a young botanist from Harvard University with a Ph.D. from Munich, to be the garden's first director as well as a professor of botany. That same year, the college engaged as head gardener Edward J. Canning, who had been both trained and employed by the Royal Botanic Gardens at Kew, thus beginning an ongoing association with Kew through gardeners trained there. On return visits to Kew, Canning would select plants to bring back to Smith.

Fortunately, Canning had been at Kew during the construction in 1882 of its innovative rock garden, a mode of gardening evoking mountainous regions on the Continent burgeoning with alpine plants that had become popular in Britain. At Smith in 1898, Canning designed one of the first rock gardens in America, on a southern slope near Lyman Plant House. Following the pattern of Kew's rockery, the garden, which is planted around the low bows of a grafted Camperdown elm, has embankments rising on either side of a dry stream bed. Paths lead through secluded areas of this miniaturized landscape, where among the over fifteen hundred taxa of plants native to alpine regions all over the world, primulas, penstemons, campanulas, gentians, and edelweiss grow like scattered jewels nestled among the rocks.

The broad lawn adjacent to Lyman Plant House is patterned with the radiating island beds of the herbaceous or systematics garden, the outside laboratory for students. An older system of classification has been replaced in recent years with plantings divided between simple monocots and the more highly developed dicot families to illustrate (according to botany professor C. John Burk, the Botanic Garden's historian) "evolutionary relationships" and "modern concepts of taxonomic relationships." This walk through evolutionary time begins with the primitive buttercup family and progresses through the lily family into specialized grasses. At the higher end of the spectrum are the asters, the snapdragons, and the mints. But within each family, care has been taken to represent species that are either economically important, botanically interesting, or simply ornamental, so that tomatoes are grouped with petunias, and corn with grasses.

What makes this garden enticing even to the casual visitor is the pleasure of the process, a lesson in design demonstrating that disciplined order yields its own harmony of form, texture, and color. To see it in bloom may be spectacular, but there is also beauty in its gradual decay, and it is often then that students are seen, sketch pads and pencils in hand, tracing a plant's final days. Botanical drawing is one of the arts that has blossomed at Smith along with the science, especially in recent years under the auspices of the Mortimer Rare Book Room in the college's Neilson Library, where drawings for its collection have been commissioned from students and alumnae. The rare book room has also played an important role in collecting rare botanical and horticultural texts and prints for the library. Moreover, the college has acquired over the years a substantial herbarium, with about sixty thousand mounted dry plant specimens housed in metal cases, many dating back to the mid-nineteenth century. In addition to serving as a reference collection for the identification of plants and as a source for illustrative material, the herbarium continues to grow, with new specimens collected on field trips to document ongoing studies of, for example, the local ecology of marsh vegetation along the Mill River that flows into Paradise Pond. Since the protection of wetlands is an important national concern, another pond, a small decorative water feature in the systematics garden, has also become an important source for the study of native marsh and aquatic species.

In 1900, Smith introduced into the curriculum its first course in horticulture, including studies in ornamental planting; in 1914, landscape gardening was offered by the botany department; and in 1919, Kate Ries Koch was appointed the first professor in landscape architecture. By 1928, landscape architecture was transferred to the art department, where it remains, as part of an introductory studio in architecture. In addition to graduates who have distinguished themselves in botany and horticulture, the bridge Smith has provided between the arts and the sciences has also motivated an impressive number of its alumnae to enter careers related to landscape design—as landscape architects, garden designers, or environmental planners.

In another important period, from 1932 to 1942, the Cambridge School of Architecture and Landscape Architecture, then in its last decade, became an affiliated graduate school of Smith College. (The Cambridge School was founded in Cambridge, Massachusetts, in 1915 as a place where women could receive professional technical training in the field.) During this time, Dorothy May Anderson, who trained at the Cambridge School, came to Smith as a resident landscape architect, and she headed a successful search for a new head gardener and horticulturist that resulted in the appointment in 1937 of William I. P. Campbell, a Scotsman trained at the Royal Botanic Garden in Edinburgh, who was working in New York City on the new rooftop gardens at Rockefeller Center. Since the campus had rapidly expanded beyond the original Olmsted plan, the challenge for Campbell during his long tenure, as for Gregory D. Armstrong, his successor in 1971, was to restore neglected areas and develop new plantings in the spirit of the original plan. The current director of the Botanic Garden, Richard H. Munson, has recently chaired a search committee to select a new team of landscape architects (which included two Smith alumnae) to draw up a landscape master plan for the college reflecting the historic Olmsted tradition.

Although every planting made over the years is considered to be part of the collection, currently numbering 4,500 taxa, the college has also developed ornamental gardens that can be visited on a walking tour of the campus. Unlike other public botanic gardens, these gardens have retained the domestic, even personal scale of the college architecture. In 1921, Smith acquired on an adjoining side street another white Greek Revival mansion, this one occupied by a preparatory school founded by Bessie Capen, who had earlier taught botany at the college. The gardens adjacent to Capen House (now a dormitory) were then redesigned by Kate Ries Koch in the style of other estate gardens of this period. The main attraction of this garden is a long rustic pergola entwined with many varieties of old roses, and beneath it a grass walk lined with mixed borders. On either side of this central spine is a series of garden rooms. One is a cutting garden that supplies flower arrangements to the college. A later addition is a medieval knot garden with *Buxus, Berberis thunbergii* 'Crimson Pygmy', and *Santolina* forming the knot. For the rest, there are cold frames and beds of annuals, where students practice their record keeping, and islands of perennials, which they learn to divide. Beyond the pergola and through a dramatic hedge arch is another enclosed garden where spring bulbs and summer annuals are planted for seasonal displays.

Although the President's House, above a steep embankment overlooking Paradise Pond and a distant view of Mount Tom, was built in 1920, the gardens surrounding it were laid out in the 1970s and 1980s. The herb garden next to the house, designed in the traditional four quadrants and paved in brick, contains culinary, medicinal, and aromatic herbs and is enclosed by a fence draped with grape vines. Below, on the grassy slopes, the President's Rose Garden is planted in stepped terraces with fieldstone retaining walls where aubrietias bloom before the roses. Some rose varieties, like 'Sea Foam', last until the first frost. And on the far side, a trail leads into a deep woodland ravine—a cool respite in summer—where under a canopy of white pines and sugar maples, species of the genus *Rhododendron* have been planted among ferns and native wildflowers, which, according to John Burk, may have been growing on this site since before the founding of the college.

Another addition to the campus is the Japanese tea hut and garden in the woodland area at the edge of Paradise Pond designed by David Slawson, who was apprenticed in Kyoto to Nakane Kinsaku. The rocks, of many different geologic origins, were collected from the hills bordering the Connecticut River and arranged in patterns that mark events in the life of the historical Buddha. Also in the 1980s, Richard Munson (who specializes in cultivating heaths and heathers) added a wildflower garden for plants native to the region, arranged in a natural setting along a dry stream bed created for effect.

Although the original plan for the arboretum has undergone many changes for better horticultural management, the campus is still crisscrossed with graceful tree-lined avenues, where oaks, lindens, or sugar maples planted in groups arch over their respective paths. So valuable are the trees to campus life that one president, Mary Maples Dunn, held a candlelight service when the largest American elm tree in New England succumbed to disease. Many early acquisitions to the arboretum originated in the Far East, but by far the most rare is the dawn redwood (*Metasequoia glyptostroboides*), considered extinct until a grove was discovered in a remote region of China in 1941. In 1947,

Chinese botanists sent seeds to Harvard University's Arnold Arboretum, which presented some to Smith. The size of the tree, now growing behind the library, has established a U.S. record. The college also maintains its own tree nursery, on the outskirts of Northampton, to provide a continual supply of mature trees for replacement purposes, and young *Metasequoia* raised there are offered to botanic gardens in the region. From the beginning the college has exchanged seeds with other botanic gardens, and the *Index Seminum,* published annually, lists seeds (more than twelve hundred varieties in 1995) gathered by the staff from plants in the wild or from the collection.

But the magical center of the Botanic Garden is Lyman Plant House. Usually visitors to botanic gardens must walk outdoors between conservatories, but here, in one interior world, the visitor walks from climate to climate as if on a fantasy journey. Scientific it may be, but great attention has been given to the internal landscape, which appears to change on each viewing depending on what is in bloom. A profusion of vines covering the walls and underplantings of Kenilworth ivy (*Cymbalaria muralis*), inch plant (tradescantia), selaginella, and fittonia give the impression that the planting benches are floating in a sea of green. There is a grottolike quality of enclosure combined with brilliant light that makes it one of the most pleasant places to be at any season.

Everyone chooses a particular route. One favorite is to enter the Warm Temperate House, with its collection of citrus, gesneriads, and begonias, and travel through to the Stove House, which features orchids and bromeliads and a tank filled with tropical water lilies and aquatic plants like papyrus and rice. The original Palm House retains its humid junglelike atmosphere with exotic fruits hanging from on high—the *Theobroma cacao* from which chocolate is made is a particular attraction, with its reddish seed pods. Mediterranean plants dominate the Temperate House, with olive, pomegranate, and fig trees, and, in mid-winter, a garland of bougainvillea swaying under the roof. The route continues through the Fern House with its central exhibit a tall tree fern, *Dicksonia antarctica,* native to Tasmania, and on to the Cold Temperate House with ornamental plants, salvia, and pelargoniums, and an old flowering olive (*Osmanthus fragrans*). In contrast, the desert floras from various regions give the Succulent House a more open and structured appearance.

In 1904 and 1915, Katherine Elizabeth McClellan, an early Smith alumna who became a professional photographer and, eventually, the official photographer of the college, photographed a series of Lyman Plant House interiors, including horticulture students clad in their long checked smocks working at planting benches. The clarity and artistry of her prints, in particular of the dense rain forest of tropical plants under the arching glass roofs of the Palm House, evoke the mysterious beauty that gives glasshouses their timeless quality.

Separated from the production houses by a corridor of camellia trees is the Show House, where each year the Botanic Garden mounts two exhibits that have become popular public attractions. The Spring Bulb Show, during the first full week of March, displays—and this is only a partial list—many varieties of tulips, hyacinths, and narcissi as well as crocuses, snowdrops, and scillas, and the Chrysanthemum Show, held the first week of November, is famous for its cascades of blooms on wire trellises and for hybrids bearing the names of the horticulture students who developed them. The college begins early to educate its students about its botanic garden tradition: each year, the Friends of the Botanic Garden sponsor a program to distribute ivy plants to more than eight hundred entering students. Cuttings for propagation are taken from the annual pruning of the ivy that covers the walls of campus buildings.

"We ought to keep this part of the world green no matter what happens elsewhere," commented Thomas C. Mendenhall, another Smith president devoted to the Botanic Garden and its role in conservation. Even during frigid New England winters, with skaters on Paradise Pond and yellow willows silhouetted against snowy banks—when Chinese witch hazel (*Hamamelis mollis*) comes into full bloom and *Fothergilla major* branches knock against the frosted panes of Lyman Plant House—the Botanic Garden of Smith College offers students and visitors the moist fragrance of its glasshouses and walks in a pleasure ground with labeled trees.

Hortus, Summer 1995

The Rose Garden at the White House

WHEN I FIRST went to England years ago, I recall complimenting a friend on her charming "backyard," only to be corrected that this term meant a rather disconsolate paved area for dustbins and the like. Be that as it may, for Americans, the backyard is a special place. Located behind the house, the elements of a backyard include a lawn bordered by a garden and, perhaps, a patio area for sitting. It is where family life takes place out of doors in summer, and children left on their own to play carve out secret domains under the shrubberies. More important, it is a ceremonial space for significant events like weddings and graduations, where family and friends gather to celebrate.

Even at the White House in Washington, D.C., when President Bill Clinton has an important announcement to make, or an honor to confer, he steps out of the Oval Office into the Rose Garden, where his associates and their families await him, along with the press corps. Since the first year of any administration is a heavy time for news-breaking events and appointments, almost weekly front-page news photographs appear of the president standing outside in his bucolic garden.

Just as the *levées* of Louis XIV influenced the architecture of the bedroom, Clinton's appearances *en plein air* affect the way people think about and use their own gardens and backyards. The idea for the Rose Garden was actually President John F. Kennedy's in 1961. He had just returned from a triumphant tour abroad and a string of state visits to the Schönbrunn Palace garden in Vienna, the garden of the Palais de l'Elysée in Paris, and, finally, the Buckingham Palace gardens. He was chagrined that the White House did not have an attractive garden for official occasions.

On a summer visit to his friends, Rachel Lambert Mellon, the landscape designer, and her husband, the art collector Paul Mellon, Kennedy asked Rachel Mellon to design the new garden. At that time, all she found of interest in the garden area was an old *Magnolia grandiflora*, planted by President Andrew Jackson in the 1830s. (President Woodrow Wilson's wife transplanted the first roses from her garden in Princeton in 1913.)

Mellon, who designs gardens with what she calls "bone structure," distinct outlines that can be broken down into subdivisions, was inspired on an autumnal evening in New York as she walked by the front terrace of the Frick Collection with its three stately, but then leafless, magnolia trees. She saw how *Magnolia soulangeana*, set at all four corners, would enhance the garden even with bare branches to catch tufts of snow in winter.

Having seen so many snippets of the Rose Garden in recent news photos, my curiosity got the better of me, and I arranged to visit the garden, during one of Clinton's trips abroad, to see how it had fared during the last thirty years. The tall trees and wide green lawns surrounding the White House still make it appear like a mansion of the Old South. The West Wing for offices is a low, L-shaped addition with a Doric colonnade around an open courtyard, which is the Rose Garden. Since there is no interior passage, the president leaves the White House every morning and walks under the portico around the garden to the Oval Office at the other end. By then, the gardeners have already done their day's work.

Mellon's elegant design, with its flavor of an early Virginia garden, is intact. On each side of the fifty-by-one-hundred-foot rectangular lawn (that accommodates one thousand people) are twelve-foot-wide borders framed by tall holly-leaf osmanthus on the outside and low-growing boxwood along the lawn. Within each border, like a crisscross of green ribbons, Mellon outlined five diamond-shaped beds with English boxwood and set a Katherine crab apple tree in each one. All of the trees are delicately pruned. Heavy-blooming iceberg roses reflect the whiteness of the colonnade, and summer plantings suggest a patriotic palette with a preponderance of red and white geraniums, white begonias, heliotrope, ageratum, and blue salvias. At the far end, by a grove of *Magnolia grandiflora* (including Jackson's, now supported by a steel pole) is a flagstone patio with wrought iron garden seats and a central Lutyens bench in white.

Just thirty years ago, Clinton, as a student delegate to Boys' Nation, met his hero Kennedy at a ceremony in the Rose Garden and decided then and there on a career in public service. Other memorable garden occasions include Tricia Nixon's wedding and a dinner for Queen Elizabeth II. But President Lyndon B. Johnson, returning from a trip, caught the real spirit of the place in his remarks at another function there: "The best thing about going away is to come back home and find so many old and dear friends here in the backyard." The Rose Garden at the White House is the backyard of America.

Gardens Illustrated, October/November 1993

A New Memorial Squanders a Sparkling Opportunity

ON MEMORIAL DAY weekend this year, I attended a family burial in a small New England cemetery on the coast of Maine. As we arrived, several young men from the town jumped out of pickup trucks with stacks of American flags and proceeded to place them in metal holders by designated graves—an annual ritual to honor those who served their country. We requested one for the fresh grave of our relative, a veteran of World War II, thus entering him on the list of those to be remembered or memorialized in perpetuity by the community.

The next day, driving back through the countryside, we observed these flag-dotted cemeteries repeated in every town and village, to say nothing of monuments and plaques commemorating the war dead in public squares. As we passed by these tranquil local scenes of remembrance that stretch across America, the world was given its first views of the more grandiose national World War II Memorial at its dedication on the Mall in Washington, D.C. Although this project, controversial in the design stage, had been in the works since 1993, when Congress authorized the creation of the memorial, the stark reality of its presence raises serious questions about both its design and appropriateness.

A few words first about the site. With the exception of the Washington Monument, completed in 1885, the creation of the Mall on former marshland was a twentieth-century concept (though originally envisioned in Pierre Charles L'Enfant's 1792 plan). In 1901, the Senate Park Commission located Henry Bacon's Lincoln Memorial at the west end and called for a long Versailles-like canal with a crossarm and a terminal pool. By the time the tree-lined Reflecting Pool was constructed in 1923, temporary War and Navy buildings installed along the Mall eliminated the possibility of a cross canal. However, the final ellipse was built and called the Rainbow Pool for the showy effects of sunlight on its tall jets of water. In 1995, the Commission on Fine Arts selected it as the location for the World War II Memorial.

First designated for presidential memorials, the Mall, including the adjacent area surrounding the Tidal Basin with the Jefferson and Roosevelt Memorials, was subverted into war memorials with the completion in 1982 of Maya Lin's understated, contemplative Vietnam Veterans Memorial. Secluded in the ground with its list of names, this memorial took on a private nature for mourners of loved ones lost in an unpopular war little recognized by their communities. When another memorial was built for Korean War Veterans, the pressure to seek national recognition for World War II was inevitable, despite ample community ceremonies honoring the war dead of that period.

Before arriving at the World War II Memorial, it is instructive for the visitor to begin at the Jefferson Memorial, itself only completed in 1943 in John Russell Pope's Roman style. From there, following the cherry tree promenade around the Tidal Basin, one approaches a path that flows through the Franklin Delano Roosevelt Memorial integrated into the parkland. Before it opened in 1997, its designer, the landscape architect Lawrence Halprin, had worked for twenty years sketching the rough pink granite walls of open rooms representing Roosevelt's four terms. A series of waterfalls increase in chaotic ruggedness and torrential foam to form a crescendo in the "War Room Fountain." Inscribed in stone is Roosevelt's "I have seen war. I have seen blood running from the wounded . . . I have seen cities destroyed . . . I hate war." The last phrase is repeated on broken stones piled on the ground.

With this grim reality of war in mind, it comes as a shock a short walk beyond to encounter the pristine blandness of the facing pylons that form the main structures of the World War II Memorial: two semicircles of slotted pillars, representing states and territories, with central triumphal arches symbolic of the European and Pacific theaters of the war. These are set around an immense elliptical two-toned granite plaza with, at its center, a sunken reincarnation of the Rainbow Pool and its waterworks. Designed by Providence, Rhode Island, architect Friedrich St. Florian, the quasi-classical architecture he chose to employ celebrates victory more than it commemorates individual sacrifice—a morale booster for a country that was never to know that kind of clear-cut victory again.

One need only recall the dignity of the Tomb of the Unknown Soldier in Arlington Cemetery or the subtle architectural expression of Sir Edwin Lutyens's Cenotaph in London, both drawn from the classical tradition, to know everything that the World War II Memorial is not. Though some have likened its scale and form to the overbearing public architecture of Germany and Italy between the wars, in truth, St. Florian's design lacks any sense of style or imagination. For example, whether classical or modern, architecture should articulate or modulate through contour a sense of light and shadow to achieve a modicum of elegance. The characterless, blocky surfaces of the memorial's structures and the oversized open plaza radiate a blinding whiteness, particularly notable in Washington's humid summer heat. Whereas the Roosevelt Memorial allows the visitor to think between inscriptions and episodes and the Lincoln Memorial offers the cool majesty of a Greek temple interior, here there is no relief from the onslaught of words and symbols.

An architecture professor at the Rhode Island School of Design, St. Florian tends to exaggerated, overscaled designs that may succeed in locations like Waterplace Park in Providence, where he joined three department stores under one roof in his Providence Place Mall with its three-story-high Winter Garden. But despite the efforts of the Commission on Fine Arts to scale down the war memorial to something less monumental, the effect is still overly heavy. It might have been better to leave the original arcade that was transposed into meaningless elevated pillars tied together by a bronze rope and ornamented with heavy door-knocker-like bronze victory wreaths of wheat or oak leaves.

An even larger wreath of laurel appears under the arches suspended horizontally by the beaks of four bronze American eagles, forming a kind of canopy or baldacchino. These are the work of architect/sculptor Raymond J. Kaskey, as are the bronze bas-reliefs depicting the mobilization of war along the entry walk that were inspired by those at the former Pension Building, now the National Building Museum.

For all St. Florian's stated objective to respect the "utopian spirit" of Washington's "preeminence of Classical architecture," the design misses by a wide mark that breathtaking creative artistry and spirituality required for so important an occasion. Also, he chose to open the elliptical formation of pillars onto a slanted esplanade to 17th Street, thus turning the memorial's back on the Reflecting Pool, entry from which would have been the more poetic solution. Where hushed reverence is called for, there is instead a vast playground of a plaza with children wading in the pool between jets of water. And tour bus groups line up to be photographed beside their state pillars.

With regard to the Freedom Wall that encloses the memorial on the west side, it features a panorama of four thousand gold stars on a dark blue ground representing the 400,000 service people who lost their lives. During World War II, every family that lost a father, husband, or son was given a square navy blue banner with a single gold star and gold fringe to hang in the front window. That star became an expression of grief for an entire neighborhood and made everyone, including school children passing by each day, sad witnesses to the sacrifice of war. Multiplying it into a field of stars is an effrontery that dilutes the power of that remembered symbol.

For comparison, a properly elegiac example of a suitable Washington civic monument and landscape can be found close by in the U.S. National Arboretum, where in 1984 the British landscape designer Russell Page was asked to reassemble the twenty-two 30-foot-high sandstone Corinthian columns that had been replaced by marble ones on the east portico of the U S. Capitol. He set them in a simple rectangle with the hint of a portico on a vast knoll overlooking meadows; a single rill fed by a bubbling fountain in the marble floor of the structure cascades down a rise into a reflecting pool, an echo of the Mall.

Is there anything good about the World War II Memorial? Yes, some of the surrounding landscaping by James A. van Sweden, with greenswards at the sloping entrance as an attempt to marry the architecture to the Mall, and including the restoration of the double allées of elms along the Reflecting Pool that make it as grand as the tree-lined canal at Courances in France. But also the double flag poles at the entrance that would have been sufficient unto themselves with nothing more than a dramatic water feature tumbling into the Reflecting Pool. Like twin masts, they are set into circular granite bases with the seals of the branches of the armed services in bronze and a simple inscribed message: "Americans came to liberate, not to conquer, to restore freedom and to end tyranny." That says it all. Perhaps a dark blue flag with one gold star could have been flown beneath the stars and stripes. Given such a lone inspirational image, one would almost hear the bugler sounding taps. But for now, the Roosevelt Memorial, with its contemplative atmosphere and symbolic representation of war and sacrifice, would appear to be the true World War II Memorial, as is that rural seaside cemetery in Maine and its like across America.

Architectural Record, August 2004. Reprinted with permission
from *Architectural Record* © 2004 The McGraw-Hill Companies.
www.architecturalrecord.com

The Green Gardens of Jerusalem: Parks, Squares, and Promenades

AS THE HEAT of the day turns to cool dusk in Jerusalem, families and friends emerge for an evening's stroll in one of the thousand or more parks, gardens, and green spaces of every size throughout the city. Yet when Teddy Kollek was elected mayor of Jerusalem in 1965, there was scarcely a single park or playground. After the city was united in 1967, he gathered an international committee of architects, landscape architects, writers, and professors to establish guidelines for city planning. As a result, the greening of this ancient city has also preserved its character.

An ordinance requiring that all buildings be constructed of Jerusalem limestone—a legacy of British rule—is responsible for the mellow pinkish cast that unifies the cityscape. Regulations limiting the height of buildings (in certain areas they can be no more than eight stories) make it possible to see the whole city from many vantage points as it swoops up and down the hillsides under an open sky. One of the first tasks was to clear away the ramshackle housing leaning against the ancient walls and create a green belt around the Old City that gives it today, with its more than thirty grass-covered archaeological sites, the biblical appearance of a city on an open plain.

Throughout Jerusalem every new community and housing development built to accommodate immigrants has a right to a park—the backyard, as it were, of the neighborhood— where Arab and Jewish mothers sit side by side for long hours watching their children splash in fountains. Creating parks in this semi-arid region has taken fortitude and imagination. More than 350 of these landscape projects, proposed and maintained by the municipality's Gardening Department, were developed by the Jerusalem Foundation established by Teddy Kollek in 1966 to seek donors for his programs. Among these new oases in the city are several major gardens, parks, and open landscapes carved into the hillsides like giant earthworks. Their beauty and ingenuity rival the more traditional sites for the visitor's attention and enjoyment. Now Teddy Kollek's business card can display on the reverse a photo of a tree-laced city of handsome squares that could be Edinburgh were it not for the red-tiled roofs. (His term ended in November 1993, when a new mayor was voted into office.)

During the last decade a dramatic promenade, almost a mile long, was built across a watershed ridge south of the Old City. Built of Jerusalem stone, it can be perceived visually as a new city wall traversing the countryside; but more than that, the promenade represents an ingenious concept of what constitutes an urban park. It follows the route of the ancient aqueduct that brought water from Solomon's Pools south of Bethlehem to Jerusalem from 100 B.C., during the days of the Second Temple, into this century. (A mosaic in the pavement of an adjoining neighborhood park in East Talpiot maps the route of this aqueduct.)

The first segment, called the Walter and Elise Haas Promenade, was designed by Lawrence Halprin, the American landscape architect responsible for the land-planning at Sea Ranch, north of San Francisco. Under one portion of the promenade he incorporated an arcade recalling the Romanesque arches that supported the original viaduct. From a distance, they look like the clasp in a necklace of stone pathways that, funds forthcoming, will stretch even farther around the city.

By a quirk of fate, Halprin lived on this site as a boy when his parents brought him to Israel, and he remembers gleaning wheat from the neighboring fields after the harvest (shades of the Book of Ruth). From this early memory of the land grew the idea that the slopes below the promenade should be planted to suggest the fields and olive groves surrounding local villages. Essentially, Jerusalem has a Mediterranean climate, although plants are still nourished by the extensive use of drip irrigation. The trees symbolic of

Jerusalem are the olive and the cypress, according to Gardening Department personnel, rather than the stereotypical palm tree of desert oases. On the slopes of the ten-acre Ana and Moise Trottner Park below the Haas Promenade, clusters of cypresses planted along circuitous pathways evoke romantic hill-town landscapes, and olive trees in rows echo the aged plantings among the gravestones on the Mount of Olives across the valley. Below, in the valley, the Peace Forest forms a lush carpet of deep green.

Structurally, the promenade is designed to blend with the architecture of the Old City, as if the two places had a shared history. Capping the intermittent piers of the low promenade wall are smooth half-round stones that reflect the grandeur of the gilded Dome of the Rock, the mosque that dominates the view of the walled city. Picturesque wrought-iron light fixtures and railings along the promenade and its vast belvederes are like those fashioned in the Armenian Quarter hundreds of years ago. On Sundays, Israeli army units come here to be briefed on the ancient history of the land as they sit in the shade of pine trees and overlook the panoramic view.

The second segment, the Gabriel Sherover Promenade, weaves through a hilly landscape with fields of wheat, rosemary, and lavender and the furrowed groves of more than seven hundred olive trees. The Israeli landscape architect Shlomo Aronson, who oversaw this design, also sought to place the elegant urban promenade in a rustic agricultural setting. Most of the plants, including jasmine, limonium, and thyme, are selected for their early morning and late evening aromas. Like stations on a pilgrimage, there are shady places to rest on stone steps under latticed wooden pergolas, whose complex designs cast intricate shadows at midday across pale limestone paths. Surrounded by beds of santolina and sweet pea and by stands of carob, fig, or pomegranate trees, these lookouts could be set in a primeval biblical garden.

Souvenirs are not large in my life, but I could not resist a small rough-cotton bag of fragrant dried lavender from the slopes of the Sherover promenade. It sums up the experience of this vast silver-green landscape, particularly in the evening. To the east, the soft Judean Hills are cloaked in a rosy haze, while in the valley below, lights twinkle from the windows of nearby villages, and beyond, from the Old City itself. Entering from the far end around the steep wall of St. Claire's Monastery, with its tufts of caper plants growing in the interstices, I was witness to the ease with which people came together in this innovative, indigenous park. Serious joggers took to the paths, and local village girls and their mothers, heads covered in their crisp kerchiefs, played and conversed quietly in the central belvedere, a structure akin to an ancient Greek theater with flintstone steps leading down to the site of the old aqueduct. It took only moments before a breeze wafted the scent of lavender, rosemary, and a touch of pine on the evening air.

While the promenade is a contemplative park at the edge of the desert, Liberty Bell Garden in downtown Jerusalem, just west of the Old City, is an active seven-acre, open-air social center, designed by Ulrich Plesner, a Danish-born Israeli architect, to celebrate the American Bicentennial. From residential streets lined with jacaranda trees, the visitor comes into the park through a belt of flowering oleanders. At the core is a replica of the Liberty Bell donated to Israel by citizens of Philadelphia. (Observing the crack, one installation worker was afraid to touch it lest he be blamed for the damage.) The processional route to the bell is shaded under an unusual and fragrant arcade. From a long colonnade of earth-filled concrete drums, a profusion of flowering vines—bougainvillea, honeysuckle, wisteria, and morning glory—climb over a filigree network of dome-shaped trellises composed of glass-fiber rods with netting.

In addition to the customary playgrounds, an amphitheater, and a bandstand for the police band and Punch and Judy shows, Plesner has introduced along the central arcade individual pocket rose gardens that offer privacy and quiet in a bucolic setting. Each activity area—say, for folk dancing or basketball—is divided from the rest of the park by flowering shrubs that create a great sense of intimacy and enclosure in a very public garden. And a wide expanse of serpentine lawn shaded with olive trees, an urban necessity for family picnics and recreation, also offers a traditional setting for a Henry Moore sculpture.

Like the White House Rose Garden, Jerusalem's official outdoor reception room for visiting dignitaries is a rose garden near the Prime Minister's office called the Wohl Rose Park. But this is a rose garden with a difference. Its collection of rare and old-fashioned roses, along with six hundred modern varieties, forms a kind of botanical library of the world's existing species. With low maintenance a high priority, most of the roses covering the twenty-five acres are hardy ground cover varieties with plentiful blooms. Even the shrubs and standard roses require very little pruning. A favorite variety is the coral pink Ferdy rose, cultivated in France, that cascades over the stone walls that define the ceremonial area.

Between the rose garden and the home of the Knesset, Israel's parliament, is a new area known as the Garden of Nations. Several theme gardens have already been built. The Parisian garden features rose-covered trellises;

in the Viennese garden, Austrian roses grow on a striking blue pergola; and the Toledo garden surrounds a Miro sculpture with chrysanthemums. (Each year, the Dutch government donates a hundred thousand tulip bulbs to Jerusalem, which the Gardening Department plants throughout the city.)

Not far from the Knesset, in a long valley next to the Givat Ram campus of Hebrew University, are the Jerusalem and University Botanical Gardens, the city's newest public garden. An important feature of Hebrew University's original campus and botanical gardens on Mount Scopus were the stands of cedars of Lebanon from their collection of Middle Eastern flora. Plans for the new gardens began soon after access to the old campus was cut off in 1948, and currently thirty of the planned sixty-five acres of landscaped gardens have been completed.

Because Jerusalem's geography and climate are hospitable to plants from most of the world, the new plan is an ambitious fusion of design and science. Rather than being grouped systematically, the nearly ten thousand different plant species are being presented in settings that recall their native lands. The earthworks molding these regional topographies, including rivers and waterfalls, require a million cubic feet of soil. Pathways weave in and out of the Canary Islands and the steppes of Central Asia on the way to open meadows with magnolia trees from North America, and in a few years they will lead to newly created landscapes of China and Japan. At the crest of this imaginative hillside terrain designed by Shlomo Aronson is the Dworsky Tropical Greenhouse.

In a valley below the South African section, the Gardens' Hank Greenspun Entrance Plaza, set around a lake, has become a popular place for an outing, with its restaurant and Visitors' Center. The steps and retaining walls of Jerusalem stone set against the green landscape give this new urban space the same timeless quality as the city at large.

In 1996, Jerusalem will celebrate the three-thousandth anniversary of its founding as the City of David, the capital of the new kingdom. New parks and projects for this event include the restoration of old garden sites and valleys where layers of ruins recall the sequence of civilizations that have inhabited Jerusalem. The hope is to return these historic places to the conditions seen by nineteenth-century travelers. There can never be too many parks, Teddy Kollek believes, and in light of recent political reconciliations, they also serve a purpose, for, as he says, "You can't dislike people if you walk with them everyday in the same park."

New York Times, January 8, 1995

Garden Letter from Greece: The Agora

But on a well-banked plot
Odysseus found his father in solitude
spading the earth around a young fruit tree.
      —Homer, *Odyssey* (24.226–27),
            translated by Robert Fitzgerald

MANY YEARS AGO, on our first visit to London together, my husband and I spent hours studying the Elgin marbles at the British Museum, particularly the sculptures from the east pediment of the Parthenon. On the left, Helios, the sun god, rises with his horse-drawn chariot at daybreak; the central figures depict the birth of Athena; and to the right, Selene, the moon goddess, descends with her chariot, closing the arc of the composition at the far end. So taken were we with the beauty of these figures that we bought from the museum shop a life-size replica of the head of the horse of Selene, the final figure in the sequence, straining visibly against the efforts of his night's run. Now mounted on driftwood at the end of my lawn in Maine, overlooking Blue Hill Bay, he presides over the watery path of the August full moon. Living with him each summer filled me with the desire to visit the sculpture's original setting on the Acropolis in Athens.

But it was another occurrence that finally propelled me to Greece last spring. In 2000 and 2001, respectively, I read the obituaries of the eminent archaeologists Homer A. Thompson (93) and his wife Dorothy Burr Thompson (101). The two died in Hightstown, New Jersey, almost exactly a year apart. Their romance began in 1934, when Homer was the acting deputy (he later became the director) of the excavation of the Agora, the civic center of ancient Athens, and Dorothy the first woman appointed a fellow of the excavation. His obituary told how her research on ancient gardens was eventually used to fulfill her dream of replanting the Agora. Although I tried to meet with her after learning this, her advanced age had closed the door to outsiders. Nevertheless, I followed up by reading *Garden Lore of Ancient Athens,* the booklet she prepared with Ralph E. Griswold, a prominent Pittsburgh landscape architect. In the 1950s, based on their research, Griswold undertook the replanting, transforming the Agora into a tree-lined archaeological park ornamented with indigenous shrubs and flowers.

While the buildings and monuments of ancient civilizations crumble under the desecrations of time, which often buries their remains under new settlements, the landscapes that give these historic sites their sense of place—the contour of the terrain, the native vegetation—often endure. In the end, although I went to Greece to experience these ancient sites, I became equally entranced by exceptional contemporary gardens built in our own era by those who had wrested from this arid climate cultivated environments of singular beauty and purpose.

My embryonic knowledge of Greek gardens was first expanded in the unlikely setting of the Athens airport, as I awaited my flight to the island of Skiathos. The Airport Museum was hosting a prize-winning archaeological exhibition, "Mesogeia, Attica: History & Civilization." The show documented the excavation of the rural townships or demes of Attica now occupied by the new international airport and its landing strips—excavations that exposed the many layers of development from 3200 B.C. through the eighteenth century. After admiring the handsome collection of terra-cotta pottery from several periods, I concentrated on site models of Hellenistic-era country houses that were built, according to the catalogue descriptions, next to cultivated fields or at the far end of gardens, in landscapes that can't have been very different from those I would soon see for the first time.

Having arrived in Skiathos late at night, only the next morning did I experience waking up amidst a hillside olive grove that swept down to the sea. The gnarled and irregular branches, some interlocking with neighboring trees, formed a solid canopy over a dry terrain. I longed to be there at harvest time after hearing the owners describe how an army of workers would swoop down to gather the ripe fruit and deliver it to the local presses, sending some of the olive oil back in exchange.

Views from the high cliffs of this pine-fringed coast to nearby outer islands, like Skopelos, reminded me of Robert Fitzgerald's travel notes to Homer's *Odyssey* (eighth century B.C.) in which he describes how he recreated the voyages of Odysseus, in order to translate accurately the Greek descriptions of the clustered islands and their landscapes. At night, brilliantly lighted ferryboats connecting these islands glide across the dark waters, illuminating each island port in turn.

I soon learned that Skiathos possesses an active garden club, its members including both seasonal and resident gardeners. In making a round of visits, I discovered how enterprising these women were in cultivating a kind of lush beauty alongside the practical. Christina Kofinas, who lived at the end of a dirt road on a cliff, had constructed a series of arcades, massed with climbing roses, leading up to her low-slung house with its ample veranda. An orchard of oranges, lemons, and apricots, the source of her renowned confitures, shaded the surrounding garden areas, including a kitchen garden. While there was a marked difference between the cultivated areas and the scruffiness of the parched landscape, I found that this contrast between wild and tame added to the beauty of Grecian gardens.

At the end of another dirt road, Chantal Prieux and her husband had made a single long house out of three huts that had originally provided temporary shelter for shepherds grazing their sheep and goats on the high cliffs. The compound was painted gaily in the typical Grecian palette: pure white walls set off louvered shutters, doors, and windows in cerulean blue. The patio, which hugged the perimeter of the house, was covered with flowerpots and ceramic bowls of the same vivid hue. These overflowed with a variety of tropical plants, all shaded by a pergola draped in wisteria vines that extended the entire length of the patio. Lavender fields terraced into the hillside provided Chantal with the raw material for her own special brand of lavender oil, which she packaged in elegant small bottles and sold locally.

On walks along the cliff roads, I could look down into gardens below—and in one instance catch glimpses of the most prominent rose garden on the island. Even from a considerable height it revealed trim beds with dense patches of deep red and pale pink roses. Though not native to Greece, roses have been grown there at least since Herodotus wrote about them in his *Histories* in the fifth century B.C. But beauty is often trumped by practicality in Greece; I found myself spending one day helping others gather basketsful of humble Saint-John's-wort, the small, five-petaled, yellow flower that has proven to have prodigious healing powers when stored in olive oil.

✿   ✿   ✿

Though it was close to midnight when I arrived in Athens from Skiathos, I left my hotel in the Plaka, the old city, to visit the Acropolis. After climbing through narrow back streets, I suddenly faced a sheer wall of glowing rock rising to classical grandeur under a sliver of moon. That held me until morning, when I began the true ascent. First I entered the new Acropolis Museum at the base of the mount, designed by Bernard Tschumi, who won the commission in a fourth round of international competitions. Worth the wait, in my opinion: it is a streamlined glass, steel, and concrete structure that hints at the classical by its delineated vertical sections. The top-floor exhibition gallery that is intended to house the Parthenon sculptures is rotated slightly off the base to face the object of its study. The museum was not yet officially opened with fully installed galleries; nevertheless, visitors were permitted to view the building's grand entrance area, which turns out to be a museum in itself, perched over the ancient landscape. Through interior and exterior floors of fritted glass, people can examine the excavated ruins of the earlier neighborhoods that once clustered around the Acropolis as they walk above them. Recently planted olive groves will be the main feature of the landscaped gardens surrounding the museum.

No photograph does justice to the physical sensation of approaching the monumental scale of the Acropolis along the Dionysiou Areopagitou, the promenade that runs parallel to the powerful buttressed walls as it winds its way upward past the Dionysus Theater to the top amidst plantings of cypress and pine. Although visitors pass quickly between the Doric columns of the Propylaia, the ceremonial gateway, this edifice it is in fact the only classical structure on the Acropolis that may be entered, and therefore an experience to be savored both coming and going. Unlike the ancient Romans, who constructed their buildings on direct axes derived from military installations, the Greeks preferred more circuitous routes. Hence the Parthenon is deliberately situated to one side of the Propylaia, providing an early example of their indirect site planning.

Although I had read copiously about the Parthenon, I still found myself counting the fluted marble Doric columns as I moved slowly around to view the east pediment. I knew that the original of my horse's head, that of one of the four horses drawing Selene's chariot, was lowered from the pediment on May 10, 1802, under the aegis of the permit or *firman* Lord Elgin received from the Turkish government. As I turned the southeast corner, I saw to my astonishment Selene's horse's head, like mine, straining over the edge of the pediment. There, too, were Helios's rearing horses and the reclining figure of Heracles at the opposite end. I discovered later that these casts of the originals were placed within what remains of the pediment by the Greek Archaeological Service. I was unprepared for this realism; nevertheless, the casts convey how details of the sculptures would have been starkly articulated in the searing light of the noonday sun.

Before I left the stony landscape of the Acropolis, I lingered for a while near the caryatids of the Ionic temple called the Erechtheion. As I watched, restorers worked feverishly to raise marble blocks on ropes, using a system of cranes and pulleys. They were filling in missing elements of the Parthenon to make it whole once more. It could have been 440 B.C., when the Parthenon was being constructed in the age of Pericles, except for the white beach umbrellas that had sprouted up all over the temple to protect workers from the sun. It was an engaging, industrious sight.

While this sacred summit was stunning in its architectural detail, I was anxious to descend to the Agora—literally the gathering place, the center of civic life. Though I could imagine the religious processions celebrating Athena on the Acropolis, my heart beat faster as I followed the paths once walked by Socrates. Because the teachings of the Greek philosophers are integral to our own culture, they feel closer in time than pagan rituals of the same period. Once, in writing about porches, I cited the *stoa* (an open gallery with a roof supported by a colonnade) as an early example of this inside/outside form, and pointed out that Zeno's austere Stoic school of philosophy had been named after the Stoa Poikile on the north end of the Agora, where he taught his disciples. Now I could stand there.

I entered the Agora from the south end to find not the dry panorama of sun-baked ruins I still half expected, but a city park filled with wildflowers and families. Systematic excavation of the Agora by the American School of Classical Studies at Athens began in 1931. Before Dorothy Burr Thompson's study of the plants of antiquity in the Agora, however, scholarly interest in the ten-acre site related to its unique importance to the history of Athens' planning and the placement of its governmental, religious, theatrical, and commercial buildings. These would have been laid out in harmony with the natural landscape and established pathways, rather than superimposed on the site. It wasn't until 1953 that Ralph E. Griswold—who had been trained in landscape architecture at Cornell University and the American Academy in Rome, and designed Pittsburgh's Point State Park—arrived in Athens to draw up a landscape plan for the Agora and execute Thompson's vision. Realizing the pioneering aspects of the undertaking, he wrote in his report, "It is as unique in modern archaeological practice as the Agora was in its historical significance and will add new interest to its ancient traditions."

Fortunately, Griswold's elegant watercolor renditions of proposed plantings, painted over earlier photographs of the site, have been preserved and published in Craig A. Mauzy's *Agora Excavations, 1931–2006,* a pictorial history celebrating the entire project's seventy-fifth anniversary. The plant list, based on writings by ancient authors and inscriptions referring to the Agora, included only indigenous plants or others acclimatized to the area. According to the notes I took that day, most of them are still in evidence, although the trees have grown to a stately size, providing welcome groves of shade.

Griswold's plan, which was the result of his observations of tourist routes and his study of irrigation pits and aqueducts, has an intrinsic beauty that is structural as well as horticultural. Large trees—plane and oak—were planted along paths that frame the major antiquities; smaller laurels and carobs provided background for important structures; cypress and pine emphasized boundaries; and dark evergreens punctuated the landscape, replacing the myriad missing heroic statues that had once been a part of the panoramic view. For the rest, there are olive and almond trees, and an abundance of wildflowers and plants in open spaces: oleander, rosemary, tree heather, and yellow jasmine, to name a few. There is also, of course, acanthus, which gave its leaf form to the Corinthian column. (Thompson and Griswold point out that in antiquity wreaths were fabricated for every honorific occasion; their ubiquity in art and literature provided Griswold's team with additional guidance concerning plant material.)

Simultaneously with the landscape restoration, the American School rebuilt the Stoa of Attalos II (king of Pergamon in the second century B.C.) along its eastern boundary to be the Agora Museum. A shopping arcade in antiquity, the *stoa* now contains sculpture and artifacts from the excavation that portray the Agora's political and commercial life. Its verticality and long double colonnade of Doric and Ionic columns for the display of sculpture provide a welcome sense of scale, helping one to imagine how the now-mature landscape would have embraced buildings of comparable size.

Among the most challenging aspects of the excavation relating to landscape was the discovery of the planting pits around the Temple of Hephaestus, which stands on a hill overlooking the Agora. Begun in 449 B.C. by one of the architects of the Parthenon, the Temple of Hephaestus is the most intact Doric temple in Greece. Once surrounded by foundries, the temple is dedicated to the god of fire and the forge, who played a pivotal role in Greek mythology: Zeus commanded Hephaestus to alleviate his severe headache by striking him with a forging hammer, thus splitting open his head to give birth to Athena—the scene depicted on the east pediment of the Parthenon.

It was customary in the fourth century B.C. to stick terra-cotta pots filled with earth on the ends of tree limbs; once the limbs took root, they were cut off and placed into tree pits with the pots broken underneath. In this case, the trees were planted in two rows, one on either side of the temple, with each tree in line with one of the temple's columns. Instead of reproducing the original design, Griswold created a starkly classical planting: a double hedge of pomegranate and myrtle surrounding the temple on three sides. Seeing the temple with its clipped hedges today, so complete in appearance itself and in balance with the landscape, makes the scene feel contemporary with antiquity.

This is what the restoration of landscape produces: a sense of continuity that the ruins themselves cannot convey alone. In the Mauzy book, there is a photograph of Ralph Griswold participating in a Greek circle dance with his male workers in May 1955, after completing the planting of these splendid spaces, so significant to Western democracy and philosophy. I felt like dancing myself after I saw the Agora.

❀   ❀   ❀

On the plain of Mesogeia, an agricultural and wine-growing region east of Athens extending to the Aegean Sea, three contemporary gardens preserving local traditions in horticulture have influenced and even inspired the wider world of gardening. In 1962, after spending many summers in Greece, Mary Jaqueline Tyrwhitt, an Englishwoman and professor of urban design at Harvard University who specialized in the evolution of human settlements, purchased land near Peania. She had spotted the location on a walk down Mount Hymettos, the mountain that dominates Athens and the surrounding area, and her knowledge of shifting populations told her that this site would not soon be suburbanized, although it offered her easy access to the city and the airport.

Thus was born Sparoza, "the hill of sparrows," a four-acre garden (purchased in narrow strips called *stremata*) that gradually climbed up a hillside. Tyrwhitt constructed a simple house of local stone, with a high-ceilinged living room furnished with tall bookcases and a southern glass wall shaded by a covered veranda. Entwined with wisteria vines, the veranda leads to a sunken walled garden partially shaded by a jacaranda tree. Tyrwhitt's purpose was to create a garden of drought-resistant indigenous plants capable of surviving strong winds and the unrelenting heat of stifling summer months, when the concrete-hard dirt had to be blasted to plant new trees.

After retiring from Harvard in 1969, she lived there full time, and before her death in 1983 she wrote a book titled *Making a Garden on a Greek Hillside* that includes a monthly journal of events, chores, climate, fauna, and native plant lists totaling around five hundred species and subspecies. Penelope Hobhouse has pointed out that this number of plants is practically the same as the one found in *De Materia Medica* by Pedanius Dioscorides, a Greek physician in the first century who traveled the Mediterranean with the military forces of the Roman emperor Nero.

Bequeathed to the Goulandris Natural History Museum, the garden had one interim tenant before the knowledgeable and energetic Sally Razelou became the resident gardener in 1991. With intermittent advice from a few professional designers and a loyal volunteer corps, she has maintained the garden to perfection ever since. In 1994, Razelou and her associates, meeting at Sparoza, founded the Mediterranean Garden Society. The society, which now has twenty-three chapters in eleven countries (including three in California), spreads the garden's horticultural message through its informative quarterly journal, *The Mediterranean Garden,* and frequent meetings and plant exchanges.

By the time I arrived in late May, the brilliant wildflower season was over, and the garden was a lush silvery haze. It was entering what Razelou calls the estivation or dormant period of summer, characterized by little or no rainfall, and no watering. And although interns were already cutting back plants, the outlying gardens and three descending terraces along the east facade of the house had retained their layered appearance: canopies of trees, including olive, Mediterranean oak, and pomegranate with tiny red blooms, provided shade for the undergrowth of shrubs, grasses, and aloes, vines clinging to stone walls, and a preponderance of long-stemmed plants blooming in subtle shades of white, lavender blue, pink, and yellow—salvia, larkspur, iris. The hillside beyond was punctuated with dark cypress trees, and tucked in everywhere were decorative terra-cotta pots and jars overflowing with foliage. Sparoza is the mother lode of Mediterranean gardens.

From there I traveled north. At the base of Mount Penteli, after a circuitous route along suburban Socrates Street, the road narrows to the sort of dirt trail that typically signifies an approaching dead end. But one more bend lands the visitor in a forested wilderness at 6 Asclepiou Street. This is Nea Penteli Phytorio, probably the most serious and specialized nursery in Greece. Fortunately, the owner, Chryssanthi Parayios, exudes a cheerful enthusiasm for her calling despite her embroidered black cotton widow's weeds. While other Greek nurseries sell typical resort flowers, like petunias and geraniums, Parayios combs the mountainside and the beaches for rare and unusual native plants, like *Saponaria officinalis* and *Bupleurum flavum,* which she grows from cuttings and seeds. She lays them out in unlabeled pots so closely packed together that the three acres of extensive clearings at the forest's edge are like a fantastic pointillist landscape. The nursery stretches out on either side of a mountain stream, which can be crossed on a wobbly but serviceable suspension bridge.

One of Parayios's customers is Eleni Martinos, who owns an elegant gallery of antiques in Athens and gardens on a grand scale in Pallini, halfway between Sparoza and the nursery. When the Martinoses bought the land in 1991, the eight-and-a-half-acre site was covered in pine trees and had spectacular views of the foothills of Mount Penteli and of the Mesogeia plain. A devastating series of fires left the land barren and vulnerable to the fierce winds, while the new airport destroyed the view.

Nevertheless, in 1992 Martinos made a fresh start with the American architect Charles Shoup, who lives in the Peloponnese, where he has built his own series of houses and gardens in the classical style. Though ample in size, the fieldstone house Shoup designed feels like a garden pavilion. It has arcaded outdoor rooms for family occasions and wide staircases that lead directly into an elaborate and seemingly endless series of walled gardens that bear the direct influence of other Mediterranean landscapes: the water gardens of the Generalife at the Alhambra, and the garden Nicole de Vésian designed near Bonnieux in Provence, with its clipped green globes using every imaginable plant conducive to the form.

Water is plentiful here. Green expanses of lawn, often ornamented with a pond, a fountain, or a piece of sculpture, are surrounded by borders burgeoning with plants and flowers, some with elaborate color schemes. The high point is a long canal, bordered by olive trees trimmed into cubes, with underplantings cascading romantically over the water's edge. Levels are constantly changing as one climbs up and down the many stone staircases; distant views lure the visitor to outer gardens with ornate examples of topiary—an exuberant variety of shapes and shades of green juxtaposed one against the other. It is a masterful design that also has its hidden corners, like a secret garden where Cavafy's famous poem "Voices" recalling the voices of those who are departed has been inscribed.

While each of these three gardens represents a different approach to the landscape of Greece, their success derives from an understanding and appreciation by their overseers of the challenge of maintaining the rich selection offered in this arid climate. Over the centuries, the possibilities inherent in cultivating the harsh terrain of Greece have remained constant. In a final touching scene in the *Odyssey,* Homer relates how Odysseus, desperate to prove his identity to his father after returning to Ithaca, resorts finally to this shared memory:

> Again—more proof—let's say the trees you gave me
> on this revetted plot of orchard once. . . .

You gave thirteen pear, ten apple trees,
and forty fig trees. Fifty rows of vines
were promised too, each one to bear in turn.

(24.336–37, 340–43)

This could be a garden today, say, on the island of Skiathos.

Site/Lines, Spring–Summer 2009

The Moonlight Garden at the Taj Mahal

ACROSS THE river from the Taj Mahal in Agra, India, there was once a pleasure garden filled with the fragrance of white night-blooming flowers and blossoming trees. But the Moonlight Garden, as the twenty-five acres were called, was neglected even in the mid-1600s, after its builder, Shah Jahan, was imprisoned. Soon, its marble fountains, aqueducts, pavilions, and watercourses, its flowers and trees, were buried by three feet of silt from the flooding Yamuna River.

For hundreds of years, people were intrigued by the idea of the existence of the Moonlight Garden, documented in paintings and manuscripts. They knew approximately where it was. What they did not know were the garden's exact dimensions, how the fountains worked, where the watercourses were, and what exactly was planted in this classic imperial Mogul garden.

Indian and American experts have begun to uncover the answers to these questions through scientific research and archaeology. And the new information about the Moonlight Garden has solved another mystery, this one about the Taj Mahal itself: why was it built at the bank of the Yamuna River, with its garden to the south, when most great Mogul tombs were constructed in a garden at the junction of four waterways?

One theory holds that the Moonlight Garden is the missing half of the original Taj Mahal gardens and that the Yamuna, one of India's sacred rivers, was the central watercourse that divided two equal gardens. "Symmetry was everything in Mogul gardens," said Elizabeth B. Moynihan, an architectural historian who is the head of the American team that is researching the garden. She was sitting in David L. Lentz's lab at the New York Botanical Garden. Lentz, a paleoethnobotanist on the team, had used an electron microscope to identify the macroremains of apricot and jujube trees among the charred specimens he unearthed last summer in the Moonlight Garden.

This is the first excavation of a Mogul garden to benefit from scientific research beyond that of the archaeologists and historians. Previously, experts guessed at plantings based on what could be found in miniature paintings or narrative descriptions of the period. Surviving gardens today, like those around the Taj, have been planted not in the Mogul fashion but with British-style lawns and tidy flower beds.

Moynihan began working in India twenty-six years ago, when her husband, Senator Daniel Patrick Moynihan, was the U.S. ambassador to India. As one of three Americans permitted to do archaeology there, she excavated the Lotus Garden of the sixteenth-century Mogul emperor Babur. Her book, *Paradise as a Garden: In Persia and Mughal India* (George Braziller, 1979), recorded imperial gardens that served as open-air palaces for the nomadic conquerors. She also chronicled the development of traditional Islamic four-river gardens, or *charbaghs*, which were densely planted with blossoming fruit trees and aromatic plants and flowers.

Historic maps of Agra indicate a series of pleasure gardens and noble residences along the Yamuna as it curves between the Red Fort and the Taj Mahal. The river provided transport from one garden to another; in the Moonlight Garden a pavilion on a raised terrace received visitors.

The Chronicle of the King of the World, a manuscript from the time of Shah Jahan, contains several brilliantly colored paintings that show how these gardens with their dense trees and marble pavilions appeared from the river. In one scene from 1637 titled "Shah Jahan honoring Prince Awrangzeb at His Wedding," the pavilions and trees across the river can be seen silhouetted against the night sky and illuminated with festive bursts of fireworks in red and gold floral displays.

But the Moonlight Garden (known in Persian as the Mahtab Bagh) was on the low side of the river and was doomed by periodic flooding. Even in Shah Jahan's lifetime, in December 1652, Prince Awrangzeb reported to his father that water had completely submerged the garden. "Consequently, it has lost its tidiness," he wrote.

In 1994, excavations by the Archaeological Survey of India confirmed that the Moonlight Garden was built by Shah Jahan in the 1630s. The Taj Mahal was built at the same time; and although tradition holds that it was constructed as a tomb for his wife, scholars now believe that he built it as a tomb for himself. Mark Twain was quite taken by this spectral vision of carved and filigreed white marble, which he described as "man's architectural ice-storm."

Moynihan first visited the Moonlight Garden excavation in 1995. "When we got there," she recalled, "children from the villages were playing, goats were grazing, and camels were being led across the terrain." In January 1998, she visited again after the silt had been bulldozed away. She plans to go back this fall with James L. Wescoat, Jr., the landscape architect who has traced the water courses at the site.

What intrigues her, she said, was that "this half of the Taj Mahal garden, unlike the garden behind the Taj Mahal, which was part of a tomb, was strictly a pleasure garden." Shah Jahan would come down the river from his fort and visit the Moonlight Garden and look at the Taj Mahal under a full moon. (The Taj Mahal has always been most seductive by moonlight, so much so that a recent proposal has called for bathing it in simulated moonlight from hidden floodlights on moonless nights.)

"No Mogul garden has ever been reconstructed and planted in an authentic manner," said Milo C. Beach, the director of the Arthur M. Sackler Gallery in Washington, D.C. Next year, the Sackler and the University of Washington Press will publish a report on some of the work on the Moonlight Garden.

As a first step in restoration, a group in Agra has planted some six thousand trees in the Moonlight Garden, all based on a list of Mogul flora. Visitors to the north bank of the river today will find remnants of a 200-foot, two-level octagonal pool with twenty-five fountain jets, which was uncovered by Indian archaeologists. (Red sandstone coping below the pool, in a lotus foliage design, is intact.) Sandstone niches, also uncovered, held fresh flowers by day and colored lamps for sparkle at night. According to Wescoat's hypothesis, water was transported from wells upstream to an aqueduct that supplied a holding tank from which water flowed under pressure through terra cotta pipes to the fountains.

Some of the marble arches from the Moonlight Garden's entrance pavilion, which had been buried by sand, have been put into storage until the day when a complete restoration of the garden is possible. And one of the four octagonal brick and sandstone towers at the corners of the garden remains. It is possible at sunset to stand by this tower, look at what has always been considered the "back" side of the Taj Mahal, and imagine what the garden was once like and may yet be again.

In the end, Shah Jahan was imprisoned in Agra Fort by his son Awrangzeb, who murdered his older brother and claimed the throne, and one can only surmise with what melancholy the former emperor would sit at his window and gaze out upon the Taj Mahal and its double gardens by moonlight.

New York Times, July 15, 1999

A Rare Garden in Barbados: Andromeda Gardens

AFTER THE first delicious blast of tropical air, what strikes a visitor most upon arrival at Grantley Adams International Airport in Barbados are the long moist beds of tropical plants that run the length of the covered concourse. Credit for this fragrant welcome mat is due to one of the most distinguished gardeners of the Caribbean, the late Iris Bannochie. By providing plant material and design suggestions to both public and private gardens in Barbados, she greatly enhanced the island's horticultural heritage.

At the center of her extraordinary achievements—including several gold medals at the Chelsea Flower Show in London, which she attended regularly—was her own five-acre garden in the parish of St. Joseph, on the rugged Atlantic coast of Barbados, which today is open to visitors and administered by the Barbados National Trust. There, sweeping down a steep hillside among giant fossil-encrusted coral boulders, deposited during a geological upheaval, the garden is a cascade of brilliant colors and lush tropical foliage. It is laid out along the axis of a meandering stream that empties into the sea near Tent Bay, a quaint fishing village below. The garden is called Andromeda after the mythological maiden who, like this landscape, was chained to a rock. The house, also built high up on a rock, is a pink-and-white coral stone bungalow with a wide semicircular veranda overlooking the sea. It is still the home of Bannochie's second husband, John, and is not open to visitors.

Bannochie, the daughter of an Anglican priest, was born in Grenada while her father was posted there. The family did not return to their native Barbados until she was eight years old. She began her garden in 1954 on land that the family had owned since 1740; and except for periods when she traveled, as an inveterate plant explorer and collector, she was in her garden working every morning by five. Cool mornings in Barbados before the sun rises too high are quite magical, as pale pinks disperse gray wisps of cloud and the lyrical sound of tree frogs provides a quiet music. In the summer of 1988, Bannochie, age seventy-three, had a stroke and died shortly after. With forty thousand visitors in 1990 alone, Andromeda has quickly become the Barbados National Trust's biggest income producer—and no wonder, since the displays of orchids, heliconia, bougainvillea, hibiscus, ginger lilies, and palms, among others, make up a fascinating tropical plant collection.

Bannochie viewed Andromeda as a botanical garden, where plants were collected and usually placed according to groups, and each newly acquired plant was listed in her accession book, with its name and source. Among the thousands of plants in the garden, more than twelve hundred species are represented. As she often pointed out, since the forests in Barbados were cut down over 250 years ago to clear land for sugar cane, the native flora of the island is very thin.

She and John Bannochie, an Oxford-educated Scot who taught French on the island, traveled all over the world and brought back exotic plants not only for their garden, but later, through propagation and their commercial nursery, for other gardens all over the island. While walking along the garden paths, she would often recall the place and even the day when an orchid was selected, say, in northern Malaysia, or a cutting taken from a brunfelsia at the Royal Botanic Gardens at Kew near London. At the entrance near the house is a spectacular jade vine, a brilliant green plant with long racemes of jade flowers that originally came from Luzon in the Philippines.

People also came to her from far away to select plants for themselves. Just before Queen Ingrid of Denmark, a famous gardener herself, visited the garden for the first time in 1971, the Bannochies built a charming gazebo, an overlook to the sea where they served her refreshments. And when the Andromeda Gardens exhibit would be dismantled at the Chelsea Flower Show, curators from Kew would be among those carrying off her rare palms for their own collection.

It may be unusual for such a methodical garden to be in private rather than in public hands. Here, though, the garden also has an ornamental feeling, planted as it was with great individual taste along paths that wound around the hillside boulders so that every area is an adventure.

Most official botanical gardens have as one of their components an herbarium, a collection of dried plants, mounted and labeled for scientific use. In a very witty interpretation of this custom, the Bannochies had a local mason devise a method of imprinting concrete paving stones with leaves from the garden, which then were placed along one of the paths.

Hurricanes have been Andromeda's greatest enemy, and the reason why the Bannochies had to fill in and reshape the landscape periodically. The configuration as it stands today takes the visitor past the orchid house, a screened enclosure of Iris Bannochie's most valuable specimens in brilliant hues (she compared these to pedigreed racehorses) and up the hill to the heliconia path, which features the yellow tipped bright red parrot's beak heliconia. Red ginger lilies, grown nearby, were also being promoted locally by Bannochie as an export crop because of their popularity abroad in flower arrangements.

Flower beds run along paths in secluded glades against a background of jungly trees that create an impression of deep forest. At the center of the upper garden near a grottolike lily pond is the majestic native banyan or bearded fig tree, with its tangle of hanging roots. Local people say it was because of the banyan that the Portuguese who sailed here called the island Los Barbados (the Bearded Ones).

In a sense, Andromeda is like an oversized rock garden overtaken by tropical growth, and the sound of water trickling as it cascades from level to level adds a mysterious pleasure. The rocks themselves are hosts to several small plants, especially succulents nestled into crevices. Shade from above is provided by a canopy of tall trees, including old breadfruit and coconut trees planted along the stream that remain from the time when the land grew sugar cane and banana trees. Among the visual surprises of a tropical garden is the variegated foliage that ranges from shades of yellow green to deep red, and the thickness of growth that can turn a simple white begonia into a lush hedge.

Along the descent lies the orchid garden, practically a field of pale lavender orchids called Vanda Miss Joachim 'Agnes', and below, the main lily pond with ferns overhanging the coral stone rim. Floating on the water are excellent specimens of the *Victoria amazonica* and *Victoria cruziana* lilies from Longwood Gardens in Pennsylvania. Beyond the pond is the palm garden containing over sixty different species of palms; eighty-five pots in the nursery are still to be planted.

When tropical trees blossom, they look like a showy fireworks display, a sudden burst of color. This is especially true of the Andromeda trees, including those bordering the lawns: the deep red flowers of the frangipani tree, the yellow of the flamboyant, and the mauve of the Queen of Flowers. Barbados cherry trees, with their sour fruit, grow along the escarpment in front of the house.

During Bannochie's time, a monthly guide was distributed listing over a hundred specimens keyed to numbered plants in the garden. John Warrington, formerly the curator of the tropical department at Kew and now general manager of Andromeda for the Barbados National Trust, is currently distributing a list of the twenty-one most important plants and groups of plants; for now plants will be labeled throughout the garden. In addition to hopes of expanding the garden with a new arboretum, Warrington has already established near the bearded fig tree a collection of bougainvillea with forty varieties, freestanding so that their arching sprays of flowers trail over the ground. Next to the new entrance a hibiscus garden has replaced a former one that became blighted. According to Warrington, about 75 percent of all the plants in the garden, and 90 percent of the palms, were first introduced into Barbados by Iris Bannochie.

Long before the National Trust took over the property, garden enthusiasts were welcome visitors to Andromeda. Many of them became friends of the Bannochies, sometimes ending the day with them on the veranda with a rum punch or a homemade ginger beer.

At this hour, the dusky clouds overtook the pale pink sky, and in the rapidly fading light one could still see the whole sweep of the garden out to the wall of casuarinas planted to break the course of the trade winds. Beyond them was the sea.

On one of these occasions, Bannochie remarked, "True gardeners like anything that is different." Her search for the rare and the unusual is the legacy of Andromeda.

New York Times, February 17, 1991

Along a Nature and Garden Trail in Bermuda

IN 1609, when Sir George Somers and his crew sailed from England to the Virginia Colony on the *Sea Venture,* they were shipwrecked between two reefs just off the coast of Bermuda, and thus were among the first to lay eyes on the lush primeval forest of cedar and palmetto that covered the subtropical archipelago. As Bermuda was one of the few island clusters in the world without a native population, early botanic observers had the opportunity to record flora untouched by human habitation before the seventeenth century—with the exception of the occasional shipwrecked crew that either perished or stayed on shore long enough to build a ship out of cedar and sail on.

News of Sir George's thrilling adventure, reported back to London in 1610 after he reached Virginia, is generally credited with providing Shakespeare the setting—a mysterious, densely green, uninhabited island—for *The Tempest,* first performed in 1611. (Ariel calls it "the still-vexed Bermoothes," and the cedars are also mentioned in the play.) Though the first recorded visit by the Spaniard Juan de Bermúdez was in 1515, the name "Bermuda" already appeared on a map dated 1511, suggesting an earlier voyage to this coral cap of an extinct volcano in the mid-Atlantic that in its isolation had developed a unique botanical and avian culture.

In time, it was discovered that there are seventeen endemic plants on the island (those that grow naturally nowhere else in the world), including the Bermuda cedar (*Juniperus bermudiana*), the Bermuda palmetto (*Sabal bermudana*) and the olivewood (*Cassine laneana*). Landowners' wealth was judged by the number of cedars on their estates, and the handsome antique cedar furniture in the old mansions is a testament to the artistry of local cabinetmakers. Sadly, in the 1940s two different scale insects decimated 80 percent of the island cedars, destroying the remaining forests and altering forever its landscape and ecology. (A few surviving stately cedars in the Old Devonshire Church cemetery on Middle Road hint at their former grandeur.)

But in the wake of this disaster has emerged over the years an island conscious of its environmental and horticultural heritage, with a rich selection of public gardens and nature reserves, where a recurring theme is an attempt to recover the primordial landscape. Bermuda is an island without highways or rental cars, where every inch of available arable land is farmed. Among the picturesque sights are the cultivated fields of vegetables and orchards that line the narrow roads in alternation with brilliantly hued hibiscus hedges intertwined with morning glory vines. To follow Bermuda's garden and nature trail, which I have done on a number of occasions, is deeply rewarding not only for seeing but also for understanding the island's enlightened approach to the future.

This trail begins in Hamilton, Bermuda's main town, laid out on a grid along the harbor. In 1962, the city of Hamilton appointed George F. Ogden, a young British horticulturist newly trained at the Royal Horticultural Society's garden at Wisley in Surrey, as its parks superintendent. These days, nattily dressed in Bermuda shorts for his daily rounds, Ogden remembers applying for the job as a lark, but during his thirty-nine years at the horticultural helm he has transformed the capital city of this British colony into a wonderland of gardens and parks. During his tenure, Ogden has more than doubled the number of trees along the eight miles of city streets and reorganized Hamilton's main parks—Victoria Park, with its towering trees and nineteenth-century bandstand, and

Par-la-Ville Park behind the public library with its central pergola draped in bougainvillea. He also created Barr's Bay park, a waterside esplanade for evening strolls under coconut palms and picturesque lampposts.

Ogden's crowning achievements are the terraced gardens built within the ramparts of Fort Hamilton and the woodland garden he planted in the twenty-to-thirty-foot-deep dry moat that surrounds the city's pentagonal fort overlooking the harbor. A fortification with underground ammunition storage chambers, Fort Hamilton was constructed between 1868 and 1888, originally out of fear that the American Civil War might spread to Bermuda. After removing generations of rubbish and tangled shrubbery from the moat, in 1966 Ogden began planting a luxuriant subtropical woodland in the thirty-foot-wide gorge. A year later it was opened to the public.

Walking within the narrow confines of the moat under towering palmettos, allspice trees, palms, and bamboo, one has the impression of moving at the bottom of an ocean. And the pathway weaving in and out heightens the mystery by making it impossible at times to see ahead or behind at a glance through the thick foliage. Each turn presents a surprise: a giant staghorn fern or Spanish moss hanging from a tree; masses of orange red blooms of the Bermuda firecracker cascading down the stratified moat walls; the fragrance of night-flowering cestrum. This rich collection of plant life demonstrates what can grow in Bermuda under shady conditions even in poor shallow soil nourished mainly by dead leaves brushed off the pathways. The experience seems both endless and timeless, although in reality the distance is only a quarter of a mile.

On the terraces above, Ogden has artfully planted trees and shrubs within the walled embankments, including the match-me-if-you-can (*Acalypha wilkesiana*), with its copper-and-green leaves; variegated pittosporum; a lignum vitae with blue blossoms; and a magnolia grandiflora. A corallita vine with pink blooms grows along the walls. In the plant house covered with shade cloth near the old guard house, Ogden arranges ornamental seasonal displays of, say, Eucharist lilies, bromeliads, and hanging ferns.

Since last fall, the public has been welcomed on weekly excursions to view an exceptional island nature reserve in Castle Harbour Island National Park at Bermuda's eastern end. In this ambitious project, David B. Wingate, Bermuda's conservation officer from 1966 to 2000, selected Nonsuch Island for his experiment to restore Bermuda's native flora and fauna. The fifteen-acre island is just large enough to incorporate in microcosm features of almost every Bermuda habitat of precolonial days, and its isolation from the main island by water excludes the possibility of invasive plants, except for the seeds dropped by birds (notably those of the Brazilian pepper-tree). Unthreatened by most of the exotic species, the endemic trees, shrubs, and plants have reproduced more rapidly, so that after thirty-nine years, Nonsuch is covered with a young, mature forest, including a strain of disease-resistant cedar.

Formerly the site of a quarantine hospital for yellow fever, the island remained in desert condition after losing its evergreen forest in the 1940s, until 1962, when Wingate, inspired by the rediscovery of the rare Bermuda petrel, or cahow, was determined to bring it and other endangered bird species back by reforesting the island and providing the proper nesting conditions on the cliff side. During the first ten years, he planted over ten thousand trees and shrubs, basing his selection on earlier botanical studies culminating with *Flora of Bermuda,* written in 1918 by Nathaniel Lord Britton, then director of the New York Botanical Garden

To travel to Nonsuch with David Wingate by boat over choppy waters and, upon landing, ascend the steep path along an embankment of sea grape trees to the forest proper gives one the eerie sensation of following in the footsteps of the first settlers. The forest, where the wind whistles through a dense canopy of Bermuda palmetto, Bermuda olivewood, buttonwood, and Bermuda cedars (including tall skeletons of ravaged cedars that now support passion flower vines), creates a sense of place stronger than a restored historic house ever could. Unlike interior furnishings, which become questionable over time, nature, with its identifiable characteristics, textures, and fragrances is incontrovertible.

Once the canopy was established, shade-loving native ground cover, like sage brush, Bermuda sedge, yucca, snowberry, variegated mimosa, and the rare tufted grass, was introduced to the forest floor. Wingate also took advantage of two swales in the topography to create both a saltmarsh-mangrove habitat and a freshwater marsh like those that exist on the mainland. At least twenty-five species of migratory water birds now populate these areas, and the reward of patient observation behind a rustic bird blind is to watch a yellow-crowned night heron make a graceful landing with the turquoise sea beyond.

The largest tract of land where the prehistoric forest survives intact on the mainland is the Paget Marsh Nature Reserve, a twenty-five-acre oval area in Paget Parish owned jointly by the Bermuda National Trust and the Bermuda Audubon Society. The acidity of the peat, currently twenty to thirty feet deep, along with periodic flooding by rain water and high tides, has inhibited the growth of aggressive naturalized species that would have overwhelmed the native plant community. Its survival is considered something of a miracle, since other marshes on the island have been used as garbage dumps.

This ancient woodland casts a mysterious spell as one treads carefully along boggy trails through giant ferns, palmetto fronds, and fragile colonies of Bermuda sedge. Without destroying the primeval nature of the experience, the authorities, working with Jeremy L. Madeiros, Bermuda's new conservation officer, have devised a method of access that will preserve the wetland habitats. In the fall of 1999, following the excavation of a new pond at the entrance, a three-hundred-foot boardwalk was opened to the public (it now extends an additional hundred feet). Resting on flotation pontoons, the boardwalk meanders through five ecosystems, and the pond is now colonized by such water fowl as great blue herons, water thrushes, and wood ducks. The new six-foot-wide path passes through a red mangrove forest, along dense browny-green bushes of wax myrtle and across a saw-grass savannah until it reaches deep into the climax of the forest, the last surviving original stand of Bermuda cedars and palmettos entangled with Virginia creeper. Like the interior valleys first witnessed by the survivors of the *Sea Venture,* at the heart of the marsh is a prehistoric silence.

The Bermuda National Trust, which owns more than fifty properties, has played a pivotal role in the survival of the island's wetlands and nature preserves and in maintaining the gardens at its collection of historic houses. On the south shore, its twenty-four-acre Spittal Pond Nature Reserve contains the island's largest bird sanctuary and a trail through a series of dramatic landscapes that include a cedar graveyard, a salt marsh with white egrets, and high rocky cliffs overlooking the sea that bear the markings from 1543 of a Portuguese mariner.

At Verdmont Museum, the Trust's finest early eighteenth-century house, the gardens have been styled after the culinary and medicinal requirements of the colonists with an assortment of fruits and herbs as well as a high thick hedge of Surinam cherry seen throughout the island. A colorful double border leading to the front door combines roses with impatiens and calla lilies. And in St. George, the site of the island's original settlement, the Trust's old houses along narrow winding streets and alleyways are enhanced by small subtropical cottage-style or formal gardens tucked into courtyards and niches created by the butteries and other additions that give these white stucco houses with indigenous stepped rooftops their distinctive charm. Somers Garden in the middle of town, with stately palms, old roses, and hibiscus, commemorates the courage of Sir George.

Privately owned gardens opened to the public are also of particular horticultural interest, like the old Gibbons family estate, Palm Grove Gardens, on South Road in Devonshire Parish, with its collection of palm trees in a field set along the road with a Chinese moon gate of Bermuda stone. In a lily pond at the top of the hill behind the house, islands have been laid out in the shape of the map of Bermuda, and in the landscape garden beyond, more palm trees and hibiscus.

At the Bermuda Perfumery and Gardens in Bailey's Bay, where the flora originally provided scents for the perfume manufactured there and sold in their shop, Colin Curtis, the managing director, restored the six-acre gardens in the aftermath of Hurricane Emily in 1987, adding a nature trail. A series of hillside plantings were inspired by the famous Andromeda Gardens on the east coast of Barbados. With the oldest and largest tamarind tree in Bermuda and an entrance arbor covered with four flowering vines, the garden winds through steep terraces planted with heliconia, Hawaiian ginger, frangipani, crotons (ornamental shrubs with leathery, variegated leaves), and Lady of the Night. Working gardens below feature two fields of passionflower vines growing on wire mesh and, in season, another one devoted to Easter lilies. The final destination is a slat house (the subtropical version of a greenhouse) devoted to rare species of orchids.

All of the island's traditions are summed up and preserved in the Bermuda Botanical Gardens, the lovely thirty-six-acre public garden in the middle of the island that dates back to 1898. It incorporates the Camden estate with the official residence of the Premier (the elected head of the government), a two-story-veranda house with a formal rose garden.

One mission of the botanical garden is to preserve native and endemic plants that have lost their habitats and demonstrate the economic uses of plants on the island. Lisa Outerbridge, the curator, points out that the garden's five-acre woodland also protects early Bermuda species. The gardens' outdoor collections of cycads, conifers, and palms are extensive; others, like the hibiscus collection, are quite showy and spectacular. Although compact, the exhibits flow one into the other in the landscape: the visitor walks from a subtropical fruit orchard into a formal garden and out again into a grove of gigantic ficus trees. Within several slat houses protected by shade cloth are naturalistic displays of orchids as well as cactuses and succulents and other exotic plants. The setting on old estate grounds provides a pleasant walk through the history of Bermuda's botanical world.

New York Times, March 18, 2001

A Walk in the Park Around Jinji Lake

SUZHOU—This canal-laced city, famous for its courtyard scholar houses in stroll gardens built from the sixteenth to the eighteenth century, has long appreciated the pleasures of a waterside view. Now the largest array of waterfront parks and promenades in China has taken shape around Jinji Lake here, in the hope that what's good for the environment will also be good for business.

On the eastern outskirts of Suzhou and nearly the size of the old city, Jinji Lake has been the site of a major joint venture between Singapore and China to develop an industrial park. The 1,360-acre area, once covered with agricultural land and scattered fish ponds, has attracted prominent international businesses and light manufacturing. High-rise apartments, some housing the displaced farmers, adjoin cultural institutions, restaurants, and entertainment centers. But the value of the lake itself was not forgotten.

In the 1630s, in the first manual on Chinese-style landscape gardening, *The Craft of Gardens,* Ji Cheng wrote, "The level surface of the lake is a boundless expanse of floating light." Jinji Lake, with its two constructed islands, retains this pristine and rippling scenic feature.

To savor the pleasures provided by an historic lakeside stroll in China, one need go no farther than nearby Hangzhou, where lotus gardens and tree-lined causeways link the islands of its West Lake and provide views across the water to distant hills cloaked in summer haze. Out on the lake small craft with pagoda-like canopies ply the waters, transporting tourists. Ambling along, one could imagine being a lone traveler in a long Chinese scroll were it not for others enjoying the outing, a picturesque scene with women and girls carrying bobbing umbrellas in floral pastels against the sun.

"As China globalizes and modernizes, its intrinsic beauty is slipping away at an alarming rate," lamented Yi Lee, a landscape architect working in Shanghai. He is a senior associate at the San Francisco urban design and landscape architecture firm EDAW, which designed and built the recently completed parks and promenades that now surround Jinji Lake. The firm, which has six outposts in China, developed a sort of fusion cuisine that adapted contemporary design techniques to traditional Chinese landscape and horticultural traditions. It was a brave approach to take in China's most celebrated city of historic gardens.

The firm's mission in Suzhou began in 1996 when its president, Joseph E. Brown, and T'ing Pei, son of I. M. Pei, conducted a two-week workshop joining local architecture students and professional planners with experts from EDAW. Their purpose was to explore ways to improve the environment, particularly the water quality, and to restore economic vitality to this ancient city, which is northwest of Shanghai, with a population of 5.9 million.

Before accepting the commission to design the new Suzhou Museum, which opened in 2006, I. M. Pei, whose family's ancestral home was in the Lion Grove Garden here, had stipulated that the city first take steps to clean the canals. At the conclusion of the workshop Brown was invited to review the Jinji Lake development.

Throughout the decade-long, $47.7 million project for the Suzhou Industrial Park Committee, the landscape architects kept to the concept inherent in Suzhou's classical gardens. Visitors stroll through planned scenery that relates to the natural world and pause in pavilions or at outlooks to contemplate the watery view.

As a transition from high-rise buildings and urban streets, Millennium Plaza, an entry point to the Jinji Lake waterfront, is a hard-surfaced communal space of alternating concentric circles: black, gray, and rose granite inlaid with a clock whose large and small rectangles of lights denote the hours and minutes. A grand staircase leads down between berms to the lake, passing sweeping, curved basins of water. (The berms are exceptionally high to overcome a Chinese aversion to tomblike shapes.) On a lower level, ginkgo trees grow amid bright red and yellow flowers, which create the wide bands of color that are an important element in Chinese parks.

A long squared-off pergola walkway of wood and steel makes up the spine of the Harbor Plaza below. Here an immense granite surface with a shallow amphitheater of steps comes alive on Friday and Saturday nights, when some ten thousand people gather for a spectacular fountain display with colored lights and music at the water's edge. In early mornings groups practice tai chi; later in the day people stroll along boardwalks that frame shallow pools of water strewn with boulders: a very Zen and serene setting.

In the adjoining forest of camphor trees, an open pavilion of hardwood slats with a glass roof is a modern interpretation of the seating areas in the old gardens, where women often spend long hours visiting. Throughout the gardens, ubiquitous sweepers, dressed in yellow and green uniforms with straw hats, maintain immaculate conditions.

"We introduced promenading by the water to the region as a new suburban life style," said David D. Jung, one of the principal landscape architects on the project. To provide both exercise and display, a broad walk of black and gray granite stripes was designed, illuminated with an eerie glow at night by a crisp line of light poles. Slightly raised on the land side, low hedges with intermittent alcoves for benches are clipped in broad flat surfaces around trees, a style that is prevalent along roads in China. Music from loudspeakers well camouflaged in artificial rocks is a constant accompaniment, considered here to add a festive air.

Further along, the landscape becomes more natural, with river-worn limestone rocks from Anhui Province placed among the trees and along the embankments where visitors have direct access to the lapping waters. An occasional viewing platform juts out into the lake, sheltered by a taut white sail canopy.

In a more urban segment, three Suzhou canals that empty into the lake have been cleaned and planted with the customary willows, whose long fronds dip into the water or into underplantings of yellow iris and an occasional peach tree. With their half-moon bridges, the canals make a romantic vignette of old Suzhou.

More formal elements are used in the Arts and Entertainment district, like a sequence of three moon-gate fountains near the undulating Suzhou Science and Cultural Art Center; designed by the French architect Paul Andreu, its triple-layered lacy aluminum skin is based on a leaf design. In spring the wavy horizontal surfaces of alternating box and azalea hedges, growing under camphor trees, create a striped effect when the clipped azalea turns pink.

Earth has been sculptured into hills and dales for a red maple forest, where more than a thousand trees have been planted with intermittent paths and swaths of pink flowers streaming through. The current mayor of Suzhou, Jung says, loves maple trees and kept asking for more. The youngest still bear their bamboo supports, and gardeners continually pump excess water out of the clay earth at the base of these trees.

With boardwalk bridges over the canals and a modern tea house offering refreshment, a circuit of the red maple forest rivals a walk through any of Suzhou's classical gardens. Or, as Jung sums up the project more precisely, "Proximity to water may mean money, but it also represents good feng shui."

New York Times, September 16, 2007

Three

American

The Poetics of the American Garden

AMERICA WAS founded on the traditions of other cultures, and the customs and forms of those societies were transported to new soil. The great plantations of the South and the country estates of the North retained from their European antecedents either the axial formality of the seventeenth-century Renaissance garden or the serpentine contours of the eighteenth-century picturesque landscape. What altered these conventions in the course of time was an American idea about individuality and man's relationship to the vast wilderness; also, there was the memory of the tradition of subsistence gardening practiced by the first settlers, who planted seeds that were their treasures from the Old World. In nineteenth-century New England, where even the humblest house was set apart from the village by its own circle of green, a singular style of American garden emerged in a natural fashion. Without the protection of walls or courtyards, the house stood alone, facing the wilderness beyond, and the garden—a mixture of flowers, vegetables, and herbs—fringed the house and the dooryards formlessly, its outer edges merging with the open landscape of the countryside. These gardens were part of the domestic environment, a private domain planted for personal use and enjoyment, rather than for public approbation.

Writing less programmatically about Nature than did Alexander Pope in some of his *Epistles to Several Persons* in eighteenth-century England, nineteenth-century New England writers developed a poetics for a simplified and indigenous manner of cultivation by describing their own surroundings in es-

Facing page: Alan Ward, *Chinese moon gate, the Abby Aldrich Rockefeller Garden, Seal Harbor, Maine.*

says, novels, memoirs, and notebooks. The more complex civilization became, the more these writers recognized the plain beauty of informal compositions. Three of them—Nathaniel Hawthorne, Celia Thaxter, and Sarah Orne Jewett—are also connected by their summers on Appledore Island, ten miles off the coast of Maine. This was where Thaxter lived and carved out her garden from a scruffy seaside wilderness. For the visitors, Hawthorne and Jewett, that island in the Isles of Shoals contributed to their universal experience of the New England landscape—"this stern and wild scene, which has precisely the same characteristics now as two hundred years ago," Hawthorne wrote in 1852 in his *American Note-Books*.

For Hawthorne, the revelation about gardens had come ten years earlier, when he married Sophia Peabody and moved to the Old Manse by the river in Concord, Massachusetts. The gambrel-roofed house was set at the end of an allée of Balm-of-Gilead trees, and, wrote Hawthorne, "when we chance to observe a passing traveler though the sunshine and shadow of this long avenue, his figure appears too dim and remote to disturb the sense of blissful seclusion." Having already rejected the cooperative agrarian venture of the Transcendentalists after a year at Brook Farm, in 1841, Hawthorne thrived on the privacy of his "sacred precincts" where he observed the lushness of vegetation on his daily walks.

For Hawthorne, the apple orchard provided the transition from the wilderness to the garden: these trees of a domestic character had lost what he called "the wild nature of the forest-tree." He gives a detailed account of bean vines "with green leaves clambering up the poles," and went on to describe delicate blossoms and tender beans hiding in the foliage and how hummingbirds were attracted to the blossoms of one variety of bean. Summer squash became sculptures in the shapes of urns and vases with scalloped edges. He lists the procession of flowers: the first appearance of roses and a wild orchid, the pink Arethusa, that grows in the swampy meadows. On another occasion, he made a bouquet from the "amphibious tribe" of wildflowers at the riverside: a white lily, a blue pickerel weed, and a cardinal flower. Without design or form, the garden "that skirted the avenue of the manse" contained a collection of individual plants, and because they were few, each one became "an object of special interest." The toil of planting enhanced appreciation of and added zest to the harvest. And as for weeds, those tenacious enemies sown by the wind, he even wondered, in the modern ecological sense, whether "what we call weeds are more essential to the well-being of the world than the most precious fruit or grain."

Hawthorne left Concord after three years, but the garden at the manse was eventually transformed into the garden in his romance, *The House of the Seven Gables.* In that book, the restoration of the garden symbolized the renewal of the Pyncheon family and its reemergence into an era of good fortune. Set behind the house in Salem, Massachusetts (based on one lived in by Hawthorne's favorite cousin), this true American garden has been preserved in its literary form. Passages re-created from his *American Note-Books* provide a prescription for a harmonious mixture of fruits, vegetables, and flowers: damson plum trees and currant bushes; antique flowers including a white double-rose bush newly propped up; and summer squash, cucumbers, and rows of bean vines festooned on poles. What he elaborated on from memory was the attraction of hummingbirds to "a spiral profusion of red blossoms" belonging to a variety of bean (the Scarlet Runner) that the young hero had planted from old beans stored in the garret. "At times," he wrote in the novel, "it seemed as if for every one of the hundred blossoms there was one of these tiniest fowls of the air; a thumb's bigness of burnished plumage, hovering and vibrating about the bean-poles."

Although he completed *The House of the Seven Gables* a year before his visit to Appledore Island in 1852, there are important similarities between his fictional garden and Celia Thaxter's simple cutting garden, which spanned the full length of her porch (or piazza) like a colorful apron. Both, for example, featured a vine-covered structure that framed the view and created the sense of mysterious removal. In Hawthorne's description of the ruinous arbor or summer-house in his fictional garden: "The hop-vine . . . had begun to grow luxuriantly over the sides . . . and made an interior of verdant seclusion, with innumerable peeps and glimpses into the wider solitude of the garden." And, in her own words, at Celia Thaxter's garden, "The whole piazza is thickly draped with vines, Hops, Honeysuckles, blue and white Clematis. . . . Through the windows cut in this living curtain of leaves and flowers we look out over the sea beneath the moon—is anything more mysteriously beautiful? . . . [and] on the garden with all its flowers so full of color that even in the moonlight their hues are visibly glowing."

In the 1840s, Thomas Laighton, a former lighthouse keeper, opened a summer hotel on Appledore, the largest of the Isles of Shoals. After his daughter, Celia (who was raised in the Isles), married her Harvard-educated tutor, Levi Thaxter, she spent summers in her own cottage on the treeless ninety-three-acre island, where she created the fifteen-by-fifty-foot garden. Hawthorne, one of the many literary guests drawn to her flower-filled parlor, recalled seeing among her books a volume by the English aesthetician John Ruskin, who was a proponent of the natural setting.

The voyage out to Appledore, a path across waters marked by ringing buoys and lighthouses sitting on cushions of morning mist, remains an authentic nineteenth-century experience. From the island's small port, the Thaxter cutting garden, now reconstructed, can still be seen as a slash of color across the hillside. Although the cottage and the hotel burned down in 1914, what Thaxter called her "little old-fashioned garden" has survived according to the plan set down in her detailed memoir called *An Island Garden*, which she wrote at the urging of her friend, the Maine-born novelist Sarah Orne Jewett. (The illustrations by the Boston artist Childe Hassam, another summer visitor, are based on his Impressionist paintings of the seaside garden.)

The garden's rectangular beds and perimeter borders were arranged not for symmetry but to allow just enough space for one woman to turn around and work alone between them. This quintessential American garden was a private one, where, as in Hawthorne's, each planting was considered and recorded for its own merit. Although the space was minimal for such a mixed profusion of blossoms—sweet peas, dahlias, coreopsis—the plants grew to a great height, extending the garden upward into the air. One hollyhock grew thirteen feet high, "a stately column of beauty and grace," Thaxter wrote, and even today the hollyhocks spill beyond the corners of the board fence. And poppies of all varieties escaped from the garden on the wind and were naturalized along the island's granite ledges.

As part of her personal art, she cut flowers at daybreak and then spent hours making simple combinations in shades of one color: one row of arrangements would begin with snow white and rose tint and end in glowing crimson and deep maroon. These were lined up in glass vases that ranged from clear and white to pale green and a delicate blue. Although the house that contained this array is now a pile of stone rubble, the hop vine is still draped over the trellis arch that led from the porch to the garden.

In summer, with her women friends in tow, Celia Thaxter would explore the island, its high meadows and granite cliffs and ledges, in search of "the rarer wild flowers in their secret places," wrote Sarah Orne Jewett in a memoir celebrating her friend. The fellowship of these walks became a theme in Jewett's own writing, in which she portrayed the fragile balance and intermingling between the cultivated plot protected by the house and the wilderness, which sheltered a vigorous growth of its own. In 1896, two years after Celia Thaxter's death, Jewett published *The Country of the Pointed Firs*, her classic novel about the friendship of two women during one summer in a Maine coastal village. (The title refers, in her words, to "the long stretches of shore all covered by the great army of the pointed firs, darkly cloaked" and "sharp against the blue sky.") In describing the garden of Mrs. Almira Todd, Jewett stresses the idiosyncratic and personal nature of plantings that have no particular style except as a cherished expression of individual taste: "At first the tiny house of Mrs. Almira Todd, which stood with its end to the street, appeared to be retired and sheltered enough from the busy world, behind its bushy bit of green garden, in which all the blooming things, two or three gay hollyhocks and some London-pride, were pushed back against the gray-shingled wall. It was a queer little garden and puzzling to a stranger, the few flowers being put at a disadvantage by so much greenery; but the discovery was soon made that Mrs. Todd was an ardent lover of herbs, both wild and tame."

On one of their excursions, the two women go out to Green Island to visit Mrs. Todd's mother, where her house, "firm-rooted in the ground," is a step closer to the wilderness: "The front door stood hospitably open in expectation of company, and an orderly vine grew at each side; but our path led to the kitchen door at the house-end, and there grew a mass of gay flowers and greenery, as if they had been swept together by some diligent garden broom into a tangled heap: there were portulacas all along under the lower step and straggling off into the grass, and clustering mallows that crept as near as they dared, like poor relations."

The style of these gardens was not their form but their content, a catalogue of plants that were decorative and useful; the beauty of the gardens derived from the blend of the common with the rare and from the tension between the wild and the domesticated worlds. In Jewett's novel, Mrs. Todd leads her friend to a grassy meadow above a rocky cliff where she has discovered a rare pennyroyal ("as the rest of the world could not provide") and collects a few sprigs into a nosegay for her bag of aromatic herbs. But Celia Thaxter, at the end of Jewett's memoir, does not live to claim from the wilderness the strange white flower she discovers among the rocks on the island: "'This never bloomed on Appledore before,' she said, and looked at it with grave wonder. 'It has not quite bloomed yet,' she said, standing before the flower; 'I shall come here again'; and then we went our unreturning way up the footpath that led over the ledges, and left the new flower growing in its deep windless hollow on the soft green turf."

Design Quarterly, Spring 1993

1680 Formal Garden Discovered in the South

ARCHAEOLOGISTS WORKING in Virginia have discovered an English-style Renaissance garden dating from 1680 with a central broad walk of sand, the earliest documented formal garden in America. Last June, in the excavation of what was assumed to be a nineteenth-century garden, test holes turned up a concentration of seventeenth-century pottery shards, wine-bottle fragments, and seals. The distribution pattern of artifacts under the sand paths was uninterrupted, and the archaeologists realized that the fragments could have been deposited only at the time of construction. They had found a second, older garden.

According to Nicholas M. Luccketti, state archaeologist for the Commonwealth of Virginia's Division of Historic Landmarks, who has been involved in the project since its inception, "What we found is the largest, earliest, best-preserved, most sophisticated garden that has come to light in North America." The garden, an arrangement of six rectangular planting beds and outlying brick garden pavilions, covers an area larger than a football field. It is adjacent to Bacon's Castle, a 1665 high-Jacobean manor house that is itself the oldest datable brick house in the country. Deborah Nevins, a landscape historian and adjunct assistant professor at Barnard College, said, "The remains of the garden at Bacon's Castle may prove to be one of the most significant recent discoveries in garden history."

Bacon's Castle is twelve miles south of Williamsburg, across the James River at a village in Surry County called Bacons Castle, without an apostrophe. The dig was a joint venture of the Association for the Preservation of Virginia Antiquities, which acquired the house and forty surrounding acres from the estate of its last owner in 1973, the Garden Club of Virginia, which provided more than $100,000 for the final stages of the project this year and last, and archaeologists from the Commonwealth of Virginia's Division of Historic Landmarks.

A visitor walking along the central axis of the garden, which is 360 feet long and 195 feet wide, has a sense of the grandeur of its plan even when the ground is lightly covered with snow on a bleak winter day. William M. Kelso, the resident archaeologist at Monticello, first saw the garden from a helicopter last week and said, "It was similar to a bird's-eye view of a great English country house estate, and I had the impression I was looking at an active working garden, as if a veil had been removed after hundreds of years." Luccketti compared the garden's configuration to that of an early seventeenth-century English garden, such as the one once at Wilton near Salisbury, England, designed by Isaac de Caus in 1615 for the Earl of Pembroke.

Catherine Howett, a landscape historian and authority on southern gardens, who teaches at the School of Environmental Design of the University of Georgia, said: "The English Renaissance tradition that the Bacon's Castle garden represents was the dominant model for the high-style gardens that persisted in the South well past the middle of the nineteenth century. This garden's discovery dramatically illustrates the importance of landscape archaeology to the restoration of historic landscapes." Before last week, Middleton Place, near Charleston, South Carolina, laid out in 1741, was considered the earliest documented American landscaped garden.

Bacon's Castle's six raised rectangular beds, three on each side, measure approximately ninety feet long by seventy-four feet wide and are separated by a twelve-foot-wide central walk on the north–south axis and eight-foot-wide paths on the east–west axis. All of the paths, including the ten-foot-wide perimeter path, were of compacted sand. Bordering the sides of the garden are additional six-foot-wide planting beds. A foundation uncovered east of the garden may have been a small frame structure with a cellar used in connection with garden maintenance: fragments of seventeenth-century horticultural bell jars were found in the area. And finally, like the garden at Wilton, there is evidence of an arbor along the eastern perimeter path. It will be several months until soil samples sent to the University of Pennsylvania for seed and pollen analysis reveal the specific flowers or herbs.

The period of the garden coincides with the increasing prosperity and political influence of the plantation's owner, Major Arthur Allen, a native-born colonial. Built by Major Allen's father, who had come from England, Bacon's Castle, with its Flemish gabled ends and triple-diamond stack chimneys, is already an important architectural landmark. The name is derived from its use as a refuge during Bacon's Rebellion in 1676.

New York Times (front page), December 26, 1985

A Historic Colonial Plantation Recovered from the Rough

ON A RECENT misty morning in the Carolina low country, golfers teeing off at the fourteenth hole of the Crowfield Golf and Country Club were mindful that their golf balls could stray into an archaeological dig. A team of garden archaeologists, wielding root clippers, trowels, and whisk brooms between the fourteenth and seventeenth fairways, was investigating what has come to light as the earliest picturesque, or natural, landscape garden in America. Twelve miles north of Charleston, the twenty-three-acre garden was created at Crowfield Plantation by William Middleton in 1730. The land, including the golf course, is owned by the Westvaco Corporation, the paper, packaging, and chemical company.

"Crowfield is clearly the oldest ornamental landscape garden we know of in this country," said Jonathan H. Poston of the Historic Charleston Foundation, "and though now a ruin, its above-ground features are relatively intact." Crowfield's extensive ponds and canals, originally surrounded by profitable rice fields, predate by ten years the famous green, stepped terraces and butterfly lakes of Middleton Place, the garden nearby on the Ashley River that belonged to William Middleton's younger brother, Henry. William Middleton eventually inherited the family's property in England and returned there in 1754. Thereafter, Crowfield was sold to a succession of mostly absentee landlords. Its survival, even overgrown, was due partly in this century to its inaccessibility along back logging roads cloaked by 2,850 acres of swampy timberland that Westvaco bought in 1930.

Westvaco eventually decided to build a planned community for an estimated fifteen thousand people around Crowfield. For the future homeowners to qualify for Federal Housing Administration financing, Westvaco was required in 1986 by the National Historic Preservation Act to make an archaeological survey of the plantation site. Westvaco then proposed saving fifteen acres of the historic garden as the centerpiece of the golf course. Several holes on the course, which opened in December 1990, act as a natural buffer between the community and the garden. (This arrangement may be a trend: the Désert de Retz, a 1770s garden outside Paris, has also been preserved within a golf course.)

The existence of a 1730 American garden in this transitional style shows that the wealthy English in the Charleston area were in the mainstream of the

British fashion in gardens, and without the time lag usually associated with colonial culture. And the taste of that day was turning toward the natural over the formal and developed into the English-style landscape, reflecting literary ideas expressed by Alexander Pope and the Augustan poets and essayists in favor of naturalness. Although it is not known who designed Crowfield, English landscape designers were advertising in Charleston newspapers at that time, and colonists had access to books like Stephen Switzer's 1718 *Ichnographia Rustica* and John James's 1712 *Theory and Practice of Gardening.*

William Middleton was nineteen years old in 1729 when his father gave him the fifteen-hundred-acre plantation that was named for Crowfield Hall, the family's English seat in Suffolk. The Middletons, who were prominent in colonial government, were part of the Charleston community that had originally settled as sugar planters in Barbados in the seventeenth century. Born in the American colony, William cultivated the rice that was called "Carolina gold" because of the high rate of return that made the low country planters so wealthy.

In May 1743, on a visit to Crowfield, Eliza Lucas, a young colonist who pursued an interest in local agriculture, described the garden at its height in a letter to a London friend. She wrote of the plantings, the perspectives, and the "large fish ponds properly disposed which form a fine prospect of water from the house." This letter, the only reliable documentation of the way the garden appeared at the time, has been crucial to the restoration project. Massive live oaks draped in Spanish moss still line the old avenue to the ruins of the plantation house. The moon pond at the entrance, two hundred feet in diameter, lies just before the house. The house was abandoned in the early 1800s, and it has succumbed over the years to fire and earthquake, as well as vandalism to its handsome Flemish-bond brick work.

Some old magnolia trees are positioned behind the house near the section of the bowling green that has survived the golf course; in all, about eight acres of the original gardens were lost to development, the archaeologists' report said. And in the middle of the wilderness area, which may have had symmetrical plantings, a fifteen-foot-high hill, or viewing mount, indicates that the garden's features, like the ponds and the terraces, were meant to be surveyed from above. All of these features are more visible now after Hurricane Hugo felled many trees in September 1989.

The "fish ponds" that terminate the view are more precisely a central rectangular lake, framed on three sides by long canals. "There are few, if any other, gardens in America with authentic mounts or canals," said Rudy

J. Favretti, a consultant on historic landscapes from Storrs, Connecticut. It is conceivable that the ornamental lake and canals were also part of a system to irrigate the rice fields. (A flooded rice field is one of the water features incorporated in the design at Middleton Place.) In particular, Crowfield's plan, which included a Roman temple, resembles such English landscapes of the late 1720s as the water garden at Studley Royal in Yorkshire or the bowling green and serpentine walks at Claremont in Surrey.

In the most recent stage of garden archaeology, conducted in April by Michael Trinkley of the Chicora Foundation, a nonprofit heritage preservation organization, Westvaco acted with the advice of its consultants, Hugh and Mary Palmer Dargan, Charleston landscape architects who specialize in historic preservation. Although the archaeologists uncovered two brick foundations of garden structures, perhaps summer houses, and such artifacts commensurate with wealth as fragments of Chinese porcelain and glass goblets, the real work, as Trinkley saw it, "was to try to determine pathways and to study soil stains and topographical features that will guide in the garden's rehabilitation and restoration." During this dig, the team analyzed earth berms that elevated the pleasure ground and served as an invisible fence separating it from the cultivated fields. Team members were also able to determine areas where shallow top soil indicated grassy areas rather than deeply rooted flower beds.

Current plans call for the garden to be turned over to the homeowners' association when the houses encircling the golf course are completed. But Charles Duell, a Middleton descendant and president of Middleton Place Foundation, said he hoped that Westvaco would "donate a conservation easement on the property" to a consortium of preservation groups. This group could then control further archaeological research and restoration. So far, the site has been open only to researchers.

Although Crowfield is now only a beautiful ruin with classic water features edged with green lawns, it is evidence of how the first settlers transported high style to the New World. "It is the Mona Lisa of early American landscapes," Poston said.

New York Times, June 25, 1992

Fairsted: At Home with Frederick Law Olmsted

BEGINNING IN 1858 with Central Park in New York, Frederick Law Olmsted brought to American cities a version of the eighteenth-century pastoral and picturesque landscape parks that so impressed him on his travels in England. His singular vision remains fresh and fulfilling today, as witnessed by the many current restorations that are preserving the landscapes he designed all over the country—urban retreats as well as college campuses, private residences, and suburban developments—including that of Fairsted, his house and office in Brookline, Massachusetts.

Early in life, Olmsted perceived the powerful subconscious effect of natural scenery on the human mind. After years of touring scenic regions of the American countryside—often setting out with his father from the family house in Hartford to roam the Connecticut River valley or the Adirondack Mountains in New York State—he was prepared for the next stage, his journey to England and the Continent. Although he lacked a college education, Olmsted's sensibilities were tuned by these wanderings and his years as a farmer to appreciate the landscape revolution that had occurred in England, producing what he called the "green, dripping, glistening, gorgeous" landscapes he found there.

Already well versed in the eighteenth-century writings of William Gilpin (*Remarks on Forest Scenery,* 1791) and Uvedale Price (*Essays on the Picturesque,* 1794–1801), the seers of the British picturesque movement, Olmsted immediately absorbed the concepts of landscape gardening, as it was called in Britain by Humphry Repton, one of its main practitioners. Horace Walpole, whose famous essay, "On Modern Gardening," chronicled the new trends, described how "the living landscape was chastened or polished, not transformed" and "freedom was given to the forms of trees." Not only did Olmsted see the open landscape parks that had obliterated the formal parterre gardens, but he also visited in 1850, by a fortuitous chance, the country's first free-entry municipal park, designed by Sir Joseph Paxton on swampy land in Birkenhead across the Mersey River from Liverpool.

Working frequently on unpromising sites himself, Olmsted evoked rather than followed "the genius of the place" by importing natural materials, rocks and full-grown trees, to construct landscapes as rugged as a mountainous wilderness or as peaceful as a pasture for grazing sheep. He saw this as architecture, not gardening. Just as his eighteenth-century predecessors turned away from formal gardens to design rolling parks, he dismissed the profusion of plant species being cultivated in his time in favor of the totally green landscape—what Repton called a "unity of lawn or wood."

Scenery for Olmsted was not simply the aggregate of features that gave a landscape its character. Scenery for him was a voyage of the mind, a place so inviting that the eye could trace its contours as it traces the landscape in a Chinese scroll. "Domestic scenery" was the term he coined to convey an idea that went beyond simple gardening; for even in the leafy suburbs, modest plots of ground could be shaped and planted to recall the memory of majestic panoramas. On a more intimate scale, a short path through a boulder-strewn grove of trees, for example, could be made to seem like a walk in a wood, a retreat far distant from the nearby house.

Olmsted's concepts worked perfectly in public parklands extending over hundreds of acres, where he succeeded in creating the illusion of deep perspectives with undulating pathways leading toward a scenic horizon that was always green. Developing Fairsted, however, a farmstead and orchard encompassing less than two acres, was a true test of his genius. Ever since the National Park Service acquired the property in 1980 (when the successor Olmsted firm moved to a new location), landscape architects and horticulturists of the Olmsted Center for Landscape Preservation have been working to recapture a landscape of magical enclosures and greenswards that resembled a miniature Central Park.

Olmsted moved to Brookline in 1883 to establish his landscape architecture firm when he became increasingly involved in designing the Boston park system known today as the five-mile "Emerald Necklace" of greenswards linking parks and ponds along a parkway. He was devoted to the idea of suburbia as a place near the advantages of the city without surrendering rural life. His friend the architect Henry Hobson Richardson already lived in the town and was anxious that Olmsted should settle nearby. Earlier, the landscape gardener Andrew Jackson Downing had called the whole neighborhood a landscape garden of "open gates, with tempting vistas and glimpses under the pendant boughs [which] give it quite an Arcadian air of rural freedom and enjoyment."

Olmsted's Brookline property on the corner of Warren and Dudley Streets was first cleared as a farm in 1722, and the saltbox farmhouse was built in 1810 by the housewright Nathaniel Murdock. As the firm grew, Olmsted added wings behind the house for offices, drafting and printing rooms, and vaults to store the rolled plans for some 3,500 commissions including 650 public parks. These rambling additions, including a garden in which to test plants, were designed so as not to spoil the integrity of the simple farmhouse facade or the parklike setting that Olmsted created.

The property is surrounded by a spruce stockade with an arched rustic gateway weathered to a silvery gray that opens onto a circular drive that replaced a straight road into the property. The first view is of an island in the middle of this drive planted with Canadian hemlock and leafy shrubs, screening the landscape beyond. The first priority in the early 1980s was to restore the health and vigor of the existing plant material on the property—like a valuable *Cydonia oblonga* (common quince)—while developing a detailed master plan for the historic landscape documented by plans, planting lists, photographs, and correspondence. The goal was to work slowly in order to stabilize the landscape without risking the loss of important elements discovered during the research phase. Finally, the park service decided to restore the landscape to its appearance around 1930, when the Olmsted Brothers firm was at its peak. This necessitated removing features that had been added later and replacing others that were missing. (An unsightly swimming pool constructed near the house by later residents not associated with the firm was immediately demolished.)

A charming but little-considered fact about Olmsted is his name. It means "place of the elm" in Old English, and indeed the central element of the greensward remains the original towering American elm that has been miraculously free of Dutch elm disease. Like a monument on a village green, this tree, with its graceful branches extended balletically into space, is such an important symbol for this landscape that eventual replacement elms were cloned from the existing tree and are already growing to full height in the nearby Arnold Arboretum.

One of the ways Olmsted created an illusion of natural effects was by clearly separating passages of domestic scenery with curvilinear pathways that also increased the distances between points. An example at Fairsted is the route from the back of the house to the main feature of the landscape, the south lawn. Like the Sheep Meadow in Central Park, this expansive greensward recalls the pastureland that first became a pictorial element in the seventeenth-century pastoral landscapes of Claude Lorrain, whose canvases in turn influenced eighteenth-century landscape designers. (The landscape historian Mirka Benes makes the point that Claude's paintings themselves purposely reflected a change in land use at the Italian villas from vineyards to pasture.)

At the edge of the south lawn, the pastoral meets the picturesque in the gradual transition to irregular bays and headlands of dense plantings that climb a hillside, with ostrich ferns set against dark yews and higher up oaks, hemlocks, and Norway maples. What the suburban area offered in addition was the borrowed landscape of the neighbors' trees beyond and glimpses through them of their houses. Although it was probably not Olmsted's intention, his massing of trees and shrubs on the slope is reminiscent of the landscape at Katsura Detached Palace in Kyoto, Japan, where gardens and woodland also mimic in miniature actual scenic views either in other regions of Japan or in China.

The Olmsted scholar Charles E. Beveridge cites the "texture, color, play of light and shadow" of these massed plantings as representing for Olmsted "the highest kind of sensibility that a gardener should have." He also indicates that Olmsted's luxuriant style of plantings are derived as much from the English influence as from the rich tropical growth he observed while crossing the Isthmus of Panama in 1863.

At the southeast corner of the property, Olmsted transformed a hillock at the site of an old gravel quarry into a small wilderness area that achieved all the mystery found along the twisting pathways of the Ramble in Central Park. Called the rock garden, its narrow trail is banked with native Roxbury puddingstone, and the area is densely planted with mountain laurel, pine, birch, ash, cherry, and apple trees that form a canopy overhead. It fulfills that childhood dream of discovering a secret corner behind the shrubberies in the back yard, a dwelling place away from adult eyes.

To the left of the main entrance to the house, Olmsted added another characteristic woodland feature by carving out a hollow, or dell, from a natural slope. A flight of stone steps leads down into the dell with its profusion of plantings—vines tumbling over rock ledges, rhododendrons, cotoneasters, dogwoods, and other blossoming trees—and even a small grotto. During the restoration, it was important that the horticulturists match the actual species Olmsted selected, and this was accomplished with the help of the Arnold Arboretum.

One of the problems that preoccupied Olmsted in residential design was reconciling the formality of architecture with the irregularity of nature. At Fairsted, he made the transition by covering the house with a wall garden of *Wisteria sinensis* (Chinese wisteria) and *Actinidia arguta* (bower actinidia) supported by a grid of wire. According to the preservationist Karen E. Day, these twining vines "masked the angularities" of the architecture, as can be seen in period photographs of the simple farmhouse draped in vines. Although the vines were cut back during restoration of the house, the root stocks remain in place. The house itself was repainted the original shade of barn red that appears to glow in a New England sunset, and the louvered shutters and trim are a traditional black green.

Several new wire trellises have been made using cable and hooks that would have been available to Olmsted. The object is to install a trellis that will allow the vines to grow away from the walls of the house and that can be bent forward with the vines intact should the house require repair. This would be a revolutionary innovation because romantic vine-covered cottages are structural disasters, since the vines insinuate themselves under perpetually damp clapboards and shingles.

Protruding into the landscape from this mass of vines was a glass-walled conservatory that Olmsted designed as a room from which to view the major features of his park from the comfort of an indoor outdoor space. It was furnished in his time with wicker chairs set around a tea table. In lieu of restoring the space as a period room, the conservatory functions as an active reception area for meetings, and there is nothing so pleasant as spending an afternoon there overlooking the south lawn with sunlight glinting through the trees.

Although now a National Historic Site, the house and grounds are far from a period piece set in the past. Scholars and researchers flock to the old wood-paneled offices used by the Olmsted firm. At long drafting tables, they review with archivists the presentation plans and detail drawings of the parks and campuses they are restoring. After years of unfurling and inventorying some 140,000 rolled plans, the archives' staff is at the hub of landscape renewal projects rivaled in extent only by the original projects themselves. All of the pieces of the puzzles are there. Smith College, for example, a campus Olmsted Brothers designed as a botanic garden in the 1890s, retains the index cards with codes listing all the historic plantings. Their locations remained a mystery, however, until the Olmsted map providing the key was found in the archives. (The Olmsted papers and correspondence are held by the Library of Congress.)

While Fairsted is an important cultural landscape that has been restored, it also retains the intimacy of family life and the bustle of an office responsible for the good health of our cities by designing more landscape parks in America than there ever were in England. At the back of the house, the drying racks for prints are still intact, and in the archives a few shelves have been preserved with tightly rolled drawings in the mess they once were. As for the setting, it lives up to its name, Fairsted, or "place of beauty" in Old English. Although Olmsted designed distinct features in the landscape, he considered each composition as a blended whole. And if, as he wrote, "landscape moves us in a manner more nearly analogous to the action of music than to anything else," then viewing the domestic scenery of Fairsted is like listening to chamber music.

Antiques, August 1995

At Old Westbury, Gracious Gardens

IN 1905, the financier and sportsman John S. Phipps and his English-born wife, Margarita Grace Phipps, commissioned George A. Crawley to design an English-style country house with extensive gardens in the Long Island countryside. Completed in 1909, though continually modified over the years, the estate in Old Westbury was a gathering place for the large Phipps family.

This summer Old Westbury Gardens, as they are now known, mark the twenty-fifth anniversary of their opening as a public garden and arboretum. Crawley, an Englishman with a degree in history from Cambridge University, was not a formal architect; in fact, the Phipps mansion, built in the style of a Charles II Restoration manor house, was his only complete project. By designing the gardens as well, Crawley achieved a harmonious whole. The styles of the individual gardens in the fifteen acres immediately surrounding the house constitute a kind of visual history of English gardens: from rose garden beds in quatrefoil formation and an Italianate walled garden with trees espaliered in the seventeenth-century manner to herbaceous borders and a cottage garden of the late nineteenth century. The contours of the seventy-acre estate with lakes and ponds hark back to the eighteenth-century British landscapes of "Capability" Brown.

The original plantings, particularly the borders of annuals and perennials, have been changed over the years, but the axial lines, the grand vistas down long avenues of linden or beech trees and the proportions of the original gardens remain. The house, which is also open to the public, is furnished, as it was during the Phippses' residence, with eighteenth-century antiques. Very little has been done to alter the genteel, worn appearance. Fresh flower arrangements from the cutting gardens and greenhouses and a table laid as if for tea are intended to retain the sense of a home.

But just as an historic house undergoes subtle changes in becoming a house museum, a private garden undergoes a similar transition when it is opened to the public. Margarita Phipps, who died in 1957 (her husband died a year later), favored a relaxed, graceful appearance in the gardens—no sharp corners, as her former superintendent, George H. Wittlinger, put it. That meant that low boughs on trees were allowed to stay, and in closely planted beds drifts of flower colors melted one into another. As a public garden, this softening around the edges has given way to a more manicured appearance so that visitors have the impression of always seeing the garden at peak condition.

Also, because the Phippses usually spent their summers abroad, the twenty-six borders in the walled garden were only planned for spring and fall splendor. Now the garden staff, under the direction of the horticulturist Lemuel Hegwood, rotates the borders during the entire growing season, and for the sake of visitors, it is more a summer garden than it ever was before. And the once-narrow garden paths have been widened to accommodate larger crowds.

On Thursday evenings during July and August, visitors are welcome to view the sunset as the family once did, from the west terrace of the house, overlooking the embankment of rhododendrons and the boxwood garden, and to take leisurely twilight walks under the arbors and pergolas. Though the days of family polo matches on neighboring fields are gone, enjoyment is still the goal of Old Westbury Gardens, which were conceived for pleasure rather than for strictly botanical interest. Yet there is much for the observer to learn and to apply in smaller home gardens.

For example, as one walks the paths, the garden staff is available to answer questions about the rotation of the herbaceous borders and the care and cultivation of the magnificent rhododendrons ("Always keep the roots covered with mulch," Hegwood advises.). The boxwoods were already a hundred years old when they were moved to Old Westbury from Virginia, but it is only recently that some of the leaves have begun to turn brown. The problem, according to Carl A. Totemeier, Jr., the garden director, indicates that the roots have not had a chance to dry out properly because heavy rains have raised the water table on Long Island.

The rose arbor over the circular brick path around the rose garden was reconstructed last year using unstripped locust fence posts in a design that can easily be copied for the home garden, with nine-foot upright posts, eight-foot cross rails, ten-to-twelve-foot top rails, and three-foot braces. In replanting the arbor, the gardeners at Old Westbury have found the most successful varieties of climbing roses to be Don Juan (red), Golden Showers (yellow) and First Prize (pink), a climbing hybrid tea.

The formal pattern of the rose garden is based on that of Battle Abbey in Sussex, England, where Margarita Phipps's family lived. The idea for the ghost walk, a mysterious path bordered by towering hemlock hedges, also came from there.

Crawley's original watercolor drawing for the walled garden, with its brick corner summerhouse punctuated by an oval window, featured immense terracotta pots that remain in place today. The upper level of this garden displays borders of pastel colors, with pink lavatera and salmon lantana and touches of blue in the plumbago against the wall and in the delphinium by the rose-covered posts linked by chains. Deeper colors appear at lower levels— red snapdragons, orange zinnias and cosmos, and golden marigolds—with a foil of blue ageratum and white petunias. A lily pond at the end is backed by a pale green semicircular pergola with lattice-enclosed entrances that are twined with grapevines.

John Phipps was interested in the trees and would supervise the planting of a new pine in his pinetum. The estate became an outstanding arboretum with more than 350 different species of trees and shrubs, and stories still abound of the full-size trees brought in from the nearby Hicks Nurseries and planted either in solitary splendor or in long allées. The great variety of trees and their mature forms, particularly a beech close to the house, give the gardens a distinctive skyline, Totemeier said.

In 1969 three modest demonstration gardens, each the size of a typical backyard, were introduced at Old Westbury Gardens. They included a sunny garden, planted with formal beds of herbs; a green garden, emphasizing the texture and form of foliage, shrubs, and hedges circling around an old apple tree; and a secluded garden now planted in the Japanese style, with narrow paths around a pool and plantings of azalea, bamboo, and Japanese maple. These represent small-scale American landscaping at its traditional best, and lists of the plants are posted at the entrance to each garden so that visitors may note and reproduce the effects. In 1976 a contemporary vegetable garden with raised beds was added, and in 1978 a test garden for roses. It is one of twenty-four gardens that screen new roses for the All-America Selections program.

Old Westbury Gardens retains much of its original character, and memory plays a large part in this. The one who remembers best, and thus prevails, is the Phippses' daughter, Margaret Phipps Boegner, who is chairman of the board of directors. The president is Mary Phipps, a niece of John S. Phipps by marriage, and the youngest family director is Dita Amory, a great-grand-daughter and a specialist in botanical prints and books. She is the librarian at the Oak Spring Garden Library in Upperville, Virginia, the private collection of the landscape designer Rachel Lambert Mellon.

For the youngest niece, Anne Phipps Sidamon-Eristoff, the gardens came into their own in winter—truly the test of a great garden. "I recall with plea-sure those cold solitary walks, the wet and the frost, the dark green of the hemlocks, the open-work arches, the bare branches overhead in the allées, and the wall garden was always the secret garden of my dreams, my favorite place winter or summer."

Wittlinger remembers that when he was the superintendent, Margarita Phipps in later years would travel the paths in a battery-powered wheelchair with red spoked wheels, pruning shears in hand. Around the central fountain of the walled garden, a variety of white flowers still bloom—dahlias, Shasta daisies, and cleome. Amid the blazing colors, these were Margarita Phipps's signature, like the long strand of big pearls with an emerald pendant she al-ways wore around her neck.

New York Times, July 12, 1984

Stately Views: A 1920s Garden Inspired by the Villa d'Este

WHEN EDITH WHARTON wrote her book *Italian Villas and Their Gardens,* she was aware that the terraced hillside gardens of the Renaissance, with their clipped greens, cascading fountains, and elaborate stonework, produced an enchantment independent of what she called "flower-loveliness," so popular then in American gardens. She counseled her reader not to "content himself with a vague enjoyment of old Italian gardens, but . . . to extract from them principles which may be applied at home."

One of her examples was the Villa d'Este at Tivoli, where the cool dark green of towering cypress trees dominates the landscape. The view—through the edge of the *rondello,* a ring of cypress trees, up the stairways to spouting fountains along the garden's central axis, lined with boxwood and more cypress, to the balconies and arched entrances of the sixteenth-century villa's facade—provides one of the most distinctive and memorable vistas in the history of gardens.

The villa was visited on the Grand Tour from at least 1581 when the French essayist Montaigne called it "a very beautiful thing" and described "the gushing of an infinity of jets of water." In 1860, Goethe recorded his reaction to the villa in his *Italian Journeys:* "For the first time I can say that I am beginning to love trees and rocks."

Over the centuries, artists have stood by the *rondello* of cypress to draw and paint the iconic view—Jean Honoré Fragonard in 1760, Piranesi in 1765, the Englishman Samuel Palmer around 1837, and Maxfield Parrish, who illustrated the Wharton book. Thus, even for someone who has never been there, this vista is at once recognizable.

When, around 1920, the Philadelphia landscape designer Arthur Folsom Paul was called upon to draw up a plan for a twenty-two-acre wooded hillside estate in Maryland, he must, indeed, have thought of the famous Villa d'Este view and recognized the possibilities of the steep incline of the hillside that constituted the north vista behind the main house of the estate. While Paul had never been abroad, he would have been familiar with the Villa d'Este through photographs and paintings. As a 1903 graduate of Harvard, he was one of its earliest students of landscape design, a professional course introduced by the university in 1900. He also studied at Harvard's affiliate institution, the Arnold Arboretum in Jamaica Plain. There he learned a great deal about trees and their dramatic effects from Charles Sprague Sargent.

What Paul set out to create in Maryland was in keeping with Edith Wharton's further advice that, if the old Italian gardens "are to be a real inspiration, they must be copied, not in the letter but in the spirit." Certainly the spirit of Villa d'Este is preserved in the "Preliminary Study for the Extension of the Axis of the North Garden" that he presented to the estate's owners. The colored-pencil drawing in various shades of green, blue (for water), and brown is a flat rendition of the irregular progression of the planned steps that would first descend from the north porch of the estate's stone house, then pass through a boxwood allée to a ravine and then, crossing a brook, ascend a steep hillside on the other side to two intermediary landings, or fountain-terraces. Cresting the top of the far hillside would be a semicircle of trees. This is, in fact, the plan that was adopted and executed in the early 1920s, and that, sixty years later, has remained virtually intact despite the fact that the property has changed ownership. If anything, the trees, which are maintained by periodic pruning, have reached a graceful maturity, while the design has remained in scale.

In accordance with the tradition of landscape design that calls for orderly plantings close to the main house—and progressively wilder and more mysterious pathways as one wanders into the north vista—Paul planned formal gardens for either side of the then new east and west wings of the house, which gave a Palladian symmetry to the original structure. With their high, arched windows extending to the ground, these wings resemble traditional orangeries, and their interiors are, in fact, garden rooms.

The cobblestone entrance court of the house is surrounded by a high stone wall pierced by archways that lead to the east and west side gardens; overhanging one of these archways is a thick wisteria vine with spiraling lavender blossoms. The east terrace is a blue-and-white garden called the Della Robbia Garden by the present owner after the blue-and-white enameled medallions of the fifteenth-century artist. Beyond the west wing is a sunken pool with a fountain and plantings in stone urns, and from there, a rolling green lawn with majestic, solitary trees slopes down to a lake shore.

The central descent from the north porch begins with a staircase reminiscent of the horseshoe staircase around the Fountain of the Dragons at the Villa d'Este. The slope down to the boxwood allée is planted with pale pink and white azaleas. A few more steps lead into the formal boxwood garden with Japanese cherry trees anchoring the corners. The aromatic scent of the box, particularly after an early morning rain, distinguishes this as a Southern American garden. The boxwood now has the patina of age, the thickness and softness of line associated with centuries-old plants. The flagstone steps that lead into the ravine are lined with boxwood hedges, and the branches of tall trees cross, cathedral-like, overhead. In spring, the path is dappled with sunlight coming through the bare branches.

At the top of the ascent on the other side, which is lined with laurels and dogwood trees in a woodland setting, the thickly massed semicircle of fourteen tall cedar trees, pruned in the elongated fashion of Italian cypress trees, are like columns of a classical temple, and in the center a graceful white swan fountain spews a high spray of water, a feat of hydraulic engineering. The beauty of arriving in the midst of this perfect calm is heightened by the expectations generated by the long climb. As one looks back, the arched windows of the garden room above the cedars and boxwood are very like the Villa d'Este view. On the return trip, another path veers off from the central flagstone ascent and follows the rushing brook to a rusticated bridge crossing over to a narrow woodland path that circles back to the house.

This Maryland estate has one of the few remaining gardens landscaped by Arthur Paul. Another is his personal garden on a wooded hillside sloping down to an 1840s farmhouse in suburban Philadelphia, which has been restored by the current owners. It is a more intimate setting with boxwood, weeping cherry, a wisteria arbor, and a goldfish pond. This property adjoined the extensive Andorra Nursery, of which Paul became president in the 1940s after many years as a partner in various architectural firms in Philadelphia. The Andorra Nursery specialized in providing plant material for estate gardens, especially the great variety of large trees they required. In addition to his work in Maryland and Philadelphia—including plantings for Fairmount Park along the Schuylkill River—he designed gardens in Newport, Rhode Island, where his Philadelphia clients often summered. Few of these, however, are still maintained, and gradually the gardens are disappearing.

As one finally turns to make the passage downward from the *rondello* of cedar trees at the crest of the hill, one remembers Edith Wharton's description of a similar moment at the Villa d'Este: "The descent from terrace to terrace is so long and steep, there are such depths of mystery in the infinite green distances and in the cypress-shaded pools of the lower garden, that one has a sense of awe rather than of pleasure in descending from one level to another of darkly rustling green." On the Maryland hillside, though, on a spring day, there is certainly pleasure, too.

New York Times Magazine, April 15, 1984

Mediterranean Light: A Classic Italian Garden in California

WHEN, IN A letter to a friend, Pliny the Younger describes his Tuscan villa and its gardens on the lower slope of the Apennines, he succeeds in setting every detail of the estate before the reader's eyes: "A semicircle . . . densely shaded by the cypress trees; . . . roses grow there and the cool shadow alternates with the pleasant warmth of the sun." Centuries later, those vivid descriptions come to mind on the grounds of a villa in southern California, where the sharp contrasts of light and shadow, the glistening blue waters of the Pacific, and hills rising from the sea create a landscape that could almost be the Italy Pliny knew.

Halfway up a canyon on the Palos Verdes Peninsula, just south of Los Angeles, the Tuscan-style Villa Narcissa and its nine small guest cottages clustered along steep winding paths—only a hint of terra-cotta tile roofs shows through dense greenery—possess all the intimate charm of an Italian hill town. Although the villa and the plan for the surrounding landscape were created in the 1920s, it is owing to the present owner, Elin Vanderlip, a woman devoted to the conservation of art and architecture, that this complex of buildings and its restored gardens are now enjoying their finest moment.

Vanderlip is the founder and president of Friends of French Art, an American organization that has privately raised almost three million dollars in the past ten years to restore important works of French art and architecture in both France and the United States. In 1984 she was decorated a *commandeur des arts et des lettres.* This year, Jack Lang, the cultural minister of France, gave a fête in honor of her seventieth birthday. While shepherding her group through France, in an annual movable feast of a house party held at various chateaus and gardens, her eye has never been idle. The restoration of the Villa Narcissa reflects a personal taste informed by life and travels abroad.

Born and raised in Norway, where she still owns an island, Elin Vanderlip married her American husband, Kelvin Cox Vanderlip, in 1946. Her father-in-law, the New York banker Frank A. Vanderlip, had purchased the original 16,200-acre Spanish land grant of Rancho Palos Verdes in 1912 with the hope of developing the peninsula. But it was not until the 1920s that he established the early automobile suburb called Palos Verdes Estates, working with Olmsted Brothers of Boston as his landscape architects. Vanderlip's own villa, built in 1924 and named after his wife, Narcissa, was sited, with the help of a meteorologist, at an elevation above the fog that comes rolling in over the sea. Overlooking the surf at Portuguese Bend and, farther out, Catalina Island, the rustic villa in the form of a farmstead and courtyard was a guesthouse for a main residence that was never built.

But the grounds were grand enough as laid out by Frederick Law Olmsted, Jr., who built his own house nearby. Terraces and an orangerie at the villa were home to many exotic birds, and the call of peacocks remains a distinctive part of the ambiance. The major and still most dramatic feature of the landscape is a 268-step cypress allée that climbs a steep northern slope from the house. Two years ago Elin Vanderlip, who has been widowed since

1956, was finally able to acquire the upper half of the allée from other family members and begin a serious restoration of this landmark vista.

Ravaged twice by brushfires, the thick old cypresses brought over from Rome in 1920 recall the towering trees at the Villa d'Este as drawn by Fragonard from the foot of the steep ascent. In her book *Italian Villas and Their Gardens*, Edith Wharton captures the mood of the Villa Narcissa as she describes the view from the open loggia at the Villa d'Este that overlooks the Campagna: "From this upper terrace, with its dense wall of box and laurel, one looks down on the towering cypresses and ilexes of the lower garden. The grounds are not large, but the impression produced is full of tragic grandeur."

In front of a forest of avocados and pines and a peacock-proof walled garden, the old cypresses form a dense wall until one arrives at iron gates leading onto the open hillside. There, between newly planted cypresses, steps of crushed terra-cotta roof tile imbedded in a rosy concrete are held firm by railroad-tie risers, and a predominantly blue floral border rambles among the tree trunks. The wild profusion of plumbago, Mexican sage, cornflowers, white alyssum, fuchsia ice plants, freeway daisies, and wild poppies is also drought-resistant. On a plateau at the top of the steps, a Doric temple stands within a semicircle of oaks near a recently completed Greek amphitheater. There is a suggestion of Hollywood here: the Corinthian proscenium columns are salvaged fiberglass film props. The semicircular tiers of seats are rows of automobile tires half-buried in earth and covered over by a growth of ice plants. Another line of cypresses marks the wings. For a recent evening of amateur theatricals, family and friends came dressed as Olympian gods.

As one looks back down the hillside, the slopes are crisscrossed with new allées of olive and golden rain trees on one side and jacaranda underplanted with statice on the other. A circle of banana trees, Brazilian peppers, a shocking-pink geranium, and purple statice composes a living garden folly dubbed the Temple Eliana, in honor of one of Elin Vanderlip's granddaughters.

The guesthouses, which Vanderlip designed herself in the shape of towers or Italian roadside houses, also resemble garden follies. Private garden enclosures feature olive trees on stilts, a Chinese moon gate, and a canopy of burnt orange bougainvillea. Her own courtyard is a formal parterre of clipped box in circles with octagons. Terra-cotta pots with gardenias and roses are placed against the apricot-colored stucco of the wall.

On the south side of the house, columns of magenta bougainvillea frame the entrance. There the brick Hortensia Terrace facing the sea, patterned after a similar terrace of the Villa Aldobrandini in Frascati, displays pots of richly colored hydrangeas. Twisted marble columns terminate parallel rows of olive trees, whose lacy foliage dapples the sunlight over stone dining tables. At the other end of the brick terrace, a terra-cotta statue of Winter framed by winter jasmine presides over a rose garden with potted pittosporum shaped into parasols. Statues of all four seasons overlook a swimming pool surrounded by a hedge of white oleander, rosemary, and hibiscus. All of the statues were imported from Impruneta, the terra-cotta capital of Italy. The decorative pots came in the 1920s in a single shipment from the same source.

Much of the rest of the vast original Vanderlip property has lost its landscaping through the neglect of other owners, but in the present eleven-acre environs of Villa Narcissa, the tradition of the Italian Renaissance-style garden of the 1920s reigns supreme, with stone pines, parasoled magnolias, an herb garden, and hedges of jade. Just as Vanderlip single-handedly initiated the restoration in France of the Bouguereau ceiling in the Grand Théâtre de Bordeaux, the Brunetti staircase murals at the Musée Carnavalet in Paris, the mill at Pontoise painted by Cézanne and Pissarro, and the balcony in Renoir's *The Luncheon of the Boating Party,* she has applied the arts of conservation to her family property. The scale of this achievement is apparent from the first glimpse of the entrance drive, bordered with lavender geraniums and dark green pittosporum under an umbrella of pepper trees. As Edith Wharton wrote of the villa architects of Italy, Elin Vanderlip has obtained "with simple materials and in a limited space, impressions of distance, and sensations of the unexpected, for which one looks in vain in the haphazard and slipshod designs of the present day."

House & Garden, December 1989

Wethersfield: In the Style of an Italian Villa Garden

WHEN EVELYN N. POEHLER speaks of the ten-acre formal garden she designed in the classical style in the Taconic foothills in Amenia, New York, she might be describing the construction of an elaborate house. "The local people who built it were fine craftsmen working from a medieval point of view," Poehler, a landscape architect, said of Wethersfield, a privately owned garden. "There are four different kinds of stone in the design—granite, bluestone, shale, and red dog, a kind of rosy slag pulverized for walkways." In addition, she devised a complex hydraulic system that brings conserved rainwater from an upper terrace through a series of pipes to beneath the lower planting beds and the cutting garden.

Purely in the classical style, after the Italian villas of the seventeenth century, the garden is unusual in America. To transform the bucolic New York landscape into lush greensward, clipped hedges, and topiary forms, punctuated by stone balustrades, urns, and obelisks, meant starting from scratch. Poehler, who lives in Sharon, Connecticut, created the garden's dazzling serenity and formal order over twenty-five years beginning in 1947 on commission for the owner, Chauncey D. Stillman.

The planning that goes into such a project is indeed like the design of a house. A classical garden is arranged to extend the architecture of the house outdoors. Laid out on the same axis, it provides a sense of destination by drawing the visitor through roomlike enclosures and along green corridors to secret recesses and elevated lookouts. Instead of stone columns and porticos, there are topiary cones and balls to mark entrances, as well as cavernous hallways enclosed by clipped hedges. Unlike a picturesque garden that benefits from a certain careless appearance, these pristine forms in a classical garden require upkeep to maintain their architectural scale.

Poehler had a great advantage in working out her plan: a location with spectacular views. Near the Connecticut border, with an outlook to the Berkshires on the east and the Catskills on the west, the elevated site was formerly sloping pastureland and fields with an old apple orchard. From the crest of the hill one can survey the surrounding valleys, essentially wilderness land. Stillman had added twelve excavated ponds that appear completely natural, including one along the main drive, which is bordered by weeping willows.

When Poehler first saw the site, its Georgian Colonial brick and brownstone house, begun in 1939, had been completed. Set on an east–west axis, its main entrance is to the west. Designed earlier by the landscape architect Bryan J. Lynch, a courtyard terrace on the north side, partly enclosed by a brick wall, appears almost cloisterlike, with, instead of arcaded walkways, a long pleached beech arbor along one side facing a grapevine-entwined pergola on the other. A rill, the kind of narrow stone channel of running water favored in English gardens, brings refreshing sounds to this terrace. On an upper level, two knot gardens in intricate designs of green and silver-green foliage are offset by more informal plantings of standard fuchsias, roses, and pink geraniums in terra-cotta pots and blue-and-white Chinese porcelain planters, as well as by herbaceous borders around a central ellipse. This cozy inner garden contrasts with the formal garden rooms that lie beyond.

Poehler, originally commissioned to add a swimming pool, designed a graceful ellipse, which, when the water is still, serves as a reflecting pool surrounded by huge ball-like forms in yew. To establish the location of the pool, which is bisected by the east–west axis along which the main garden extends, she made a single benchmark outside the dining-room window. Her ten-acre plan was gradually laid out on that foundation.

From the inner garden behind the house one enters the outer garden through handsome gilded wrought-iron gates at the edge of the arbor. Standing guard are two marble cherubs—contemporary copies of the seventeenth-century style by the Pittsburgh sculptor Jozef Stachura—to prepare visitors for the transition to the classical world. The entrance to the garden yields a view of rich masses of pale green against dark green as the summer light, particularly in the late afternoon, strikes the various geometric forms at different angles.

Though the spaces flow easily one into the other, each elliptical or rectangular enclosure offers a different architectural experience. Stillman's close collaboration over the years with both Poehler and Stachura, who has embellished the grounds with sculptures based on classical myths, adds to the unity of the garden. It takes a horticulturist, groundsmen, tree men, and Stillman's attentive eye to maintain the correct proportions of these now-tall trees and large green masses.

Beyond the pool the second element was added, replacing the former orchard to the north: a 190-foot-long corridor of dense arborvitae twenty-three-feet high—all from the surrounding woods—that opens into an ellipse turned ninety degrees from the pool. A basin of baroque shape circles a naiad holding gilded fish that spurt water.

One morning at breakfast on the estate, Poehler said, she was looking out the dining-room window when the conception of the rest of the east–west axis, including the elevations and terraces, came to her. First there is the squared-off vestibule, which functions, as it does in a classical house, as an introductory area to all the pathways and gardens. To the east it leads into the main rectangular outer garden. Here a pathway around the inner lawn is bordered by dwarf viburnum; four dramatic weeping beeches stand at the corners.

A raised terrace on the north side was created by a ten-foot triangular cut into what was an old sloping cornfield. The solid shale wall, topped by a balustrade and with a niche enclosing a fountain, is a garden itself, with varieties of campanula, gypsophila, yellow sedum, and other small flowers. It is a masterwork of texture. Below this area is the original cutting garden.

Walking to the extreme eastern point and looking back, one sees the series of gardens opening and closing in various widths, with low hedges juxtaposed against cones and balls; only yew and arborvitae are used to create this green, sculptured panorama. The lines are softened by Chinese dogwood, which blooms in July, rhododendrons, azaleas, lilacs, wild roses, and urns of fuchsia. Many of the original plantings were purchased from a nursery and planted on the estate to be drawn on as needed.

Although Poehler especially admires such American gardens in the formal tradition as Middleton Place in South Carolina, most of the ideas she has gleaned over the years and used in this garden, she says, come from books. Trained some fifty years ago at the Lowthorpe School in Groton, Massachusetts, which was established to instruct women in horticulture and landscape architecture, she has had a career ranging from such large landscaping projects as schools, parks, and playgrounds to a pocket-handkerchief garden design for a town house in the East Fifties in Manhattan.

Beyond the garden's highly ordered spaces lies a landscape of pasture and woodland. Looking out, one realizes that only a small space has been tamed in a vast pastoral scene. A walk into the "wilderness" on the other side of the garden begins at the house on a lane bordered by two pairs of Stachura's seven-foot-high limestone mythical sculptures, on pedestals set into niches in a beech wall that has been trained around the statues. On the other side of the drive is a field that ends at a stone Palladian arch, and the clipped arborvitae below mark the close of the formal landscape.

Paths in the surrounding woodlands open up at clearings, where sculptures by Stachura stand—mixing the natural landscape with the classical in the manner of William Kent's park at Rousham, in England. A single jet of water cascading into a wide pool recalls the Emperor's Fountain at Chatsworth.

Climbing up a series of stairways at one end, framed by stone obelisks, one arrives at the fantasy ornament that crowns the garden—an open classical temple designed by W. Dean Brown. It is truly a belvedere, that perfect Italian composite of the Latin words meaning "to see" and "beautiful," for from its height one has a sweeping view over the garden and the surrounding valley—architecture in nature.

New York Times, September 27, 1984

The American Academy in Rome

FROM A HIGH terrace of the Villa Aurelia, part of the American Academy in Rome, Alessandra Vinciguerra looked out over the Eternal City bathed in the golden light of late afternoon. "Sometimes I think about how many people have planted here before us," she said, referring to the pleasure gardens from antiquity and the Farnese vineyard that later covered the hillside she looked down on, known as the Janiculum. Vinciguerra has been the coordinator of a transformation of the eleven-acre campus in anticipation of the academy's centennial this year.

Last June, the new fountain sent up a celebratory jet of water in the jasmine-scented courtyard, marking the official opening of the Mercedes and Sid R. Bass Garden, where the academy's fellows in fine arts and classical studies take their leisure, behind the recently-renovated august palazzo designed in 1914 by McKim, Mead & White. Charles Follen McKim, a partner in the New York Beaux-Arts architectural firm, was the American Academy's inspired founder. Twenty-four such foreign academies have been established in Rome since the French Academy was founded in 1666.

Adele Chatfield-Taylor, the academy's president, describes the new gardens as being "reimagined rather than redesigned," for there is little material authenticating the original landscapes surrounding the academy's villas on four sites separated by three city streets. The properties were acquired early on through the astuteness of the American financier, J. P. Morgan. The dazzling results, based on historical and aesthetic considerations, have restored to this residential district, just within the city walls, a significant swath of Roman Campagna as well as formal plantings inspired by such compact Italian Renaissance gardens as the Villa Lante.

In 1989, while attending a trustees' meeting at the academy, Laurie Olin, a Philadelphia landscape architect and former fellow, was dismayed by the poor condition of the grounds. "I saw that the landscape was ravaged and melting away down to a thin crust, but since it was happening in slow motion, no one else noticed," he explained. Also, many of the famous clipped ilex trees that were the academy's trademark were riddled with insects. In general, despite differences in style and period, the buildings had been forced to connect visually with miles of clipped hedges and climbing ivy that obscured iron grille fences and stonework facades.

Once Olin's firm, Hanna/Olin Ltd., came up with a master plan, including an historical report, the academy took drastic measures to stop the erosion and give a new vision to the landscape. Subtraction, simplification, and stabilization were the magic words used to reshape the gardens. Along with the removal of the tennis court and hedges, ivy vines were stripped from the courtyard and facade of the McKim, Mead & White building, leaving a clean open space that retains its majestic whiteness at night.

"The notion that you could walk through the cortile or inner courtyard of the main building and exit into a Roman Campagna that has otherwise been lost strikes me as moving," Olin said. The landscape was remolded into hills and concave valleys sloping down from the Casa Rustica, a picturesque building at the garden's rear, now used for offices and studios. Towering umbrella pines in clusters encircle the rural scene that is also dotted with cypresses, fig trees, and olive groves. A lone antique ruin supports a climbing rose.

Using two-thousand-year-old pruning techniques, the gardeners shape the olive trees to yield plentiful fruit for olive oil while retaining drooping branches for appearance's sake. The academy also maintains an orchard with apple and plum trees and an adjoining cutting garden with rows of iris, agapanthus, dahlias, and zinnias. Hawthorns and viburnum banked up against the outer fortifications built by Pope Urban VIII in the seventeenth century attract birds and butterflies.

One residence, the Villa Chiaraviglio, had acquired a garden cluttered with house plants and Christmas trees transplanted by departing fellows. An old aqueduct crossing this garden still feeds the rushing cascades of the Acqua Paola, the Baroque fountain in the street below. The garden's romantic character has been restored with informally clipped ilex trees and a serpentine path lined with citrus trees and roses facing a border of oleanders.

At the peak of the hill, lies the Villa Aurelia, built on fortifications constructed by the emperor Aurelian in A.D. 272. Once the headquarters for Garibaldi, the mellow gold and pink villa and vast formal garden were restored in the 1880s by Clara Jessup Heyland, an American heiress who left the villa to the academy in her will. The main features of this garden are green parterres with aerial hedges of clipped ilex trees around a central fountain. All but thirteen of the eighty-three trees were saved. Two freestanding ilexes on the lawn shaped like giant parasols are the symbol of the academy.

In place of a laurel hedge that obscured the villa from the drive, Vinciguerra has planted a low Mediterranean border, weaving together plantings of purple-leaved sage, creeping rosemary, and myrtle, interspersed with South African daisies in blue and white. Two long bay laurel tunnels complete the formal landscape. On the far side of the villa, below an archway of bougainvillea, terraces planted with plumbago and citrus trees slope down to the street in lush tropical profusion.

These gardens recall the memoirs of another American who came to live in Rome in 1894. Maud Howe, the daughter of the Boston suffragette Julia Ward Howe, often took rides near the present academy in the park surrounding the Villa Doria Pamphili, where fellows now jog early in the morning. In her 1904 book, *Roma Beata,* she described how the Tiber, the fountains, and the ilex trees "seem to whisper the secrets of the city." This certain atmosphere of Rome was the creative force behind these restored gardens. Respecting the character of each setting, these new landmark Italian landscapes will enhance the mission of the academy in its second century as a place of tradition and innovation. As Maud Howe concluded: "For men and women there is no school like Rome."

Financial Times, February 11, 1995

The Abby Aldrich Rockefeller Garden: A Blend of Far Eastern and English Inspiration

Part I: The Story of the Garden

Some moments are never eclipsed by others. Though many years have passed since I first entered the inner garden of the Abby Aldrich Rockefeller Garden in Seal Harbor, Maine, the vivid impression remains of walking from dark woods through the pagoda-like portal of the Chinese wall into a wild sod garden and then through the Bottle Gate, shaped like some giant inverted magic keyhole in a second wall, into a world of dazzling light and color, an immense rectangular sunken flower garden around a central greensward.

There was a literary counterpart. I felt like Mary Lennox in Frances Hodgson Burnett's 1911 story, *The Secret Garden,* when she turned the key, pushed open a formerly hidden door in the garden wall, and "stood with her back against it, looking about her and breathing quite fast with excitement, and wonder, and delight. She was standing *inside* the secret garden." (The only way Hollywood could adequately render this moment in the 1949 film of the book was to switch from black-and-white to Technicolor. I am sure that childhood memory also fed my impression.) The impact of that entrance has never lessened on repeated visits, nor have any other gardens, which have their own pleasures to offer, produced a similar effect.

The Secret Garden may not have been one of Abby Rockefeller's conscious references in creating the garden, but her son David Rockefeller, who now owns and oversees the garden with his wife, Peggy, remembers his mother giving him the book when he was a child. She loved solitude and would escape to solitary places, according to her biographer, Mary Ellen Chase, and David recalls that his mother went out to the garden often in the late afternoons just to sit by herself listening to the birds and looking at the flowers. She always insisted that her guests enter the garden through the Bottle Gate for that first startling view along the south-to-north axis over a reflecting pool set in a grass oval to the tall red spruce that anchors the north flower beds in front of a traditional Chinese moon gate set in the far wall. Behind the quiet moments of repose in this Oriental setting juxtaposed with a Maine interpretation of an English flower garden with its brilliant seaside hues is a richly documented history of the massive creative effort it took to build this garden at the top of a hill in a spruce forest—an effort of the principals and their architects, art dealers, contractors, gardeners, and stonemasons.

John D. Rockefeller, Jr., married Abby Aldrich in 1901, and they purchased The Eyrie, their house in Seal Harbor, in 1910. In 1908, acting for his father, Mr. Rockefeller began construction of a Japanese hillside garden with a teahouse near Kykuit, the family residence in Pocantico Hills, New York. Although they had this initial experience with an Oriental garden, and two Japanese landscape architects, clearly the galvanizing event in the couple's life was their four-month trip to the Far East in 1921, primarily for the opening of the Peking Union Medical College, which was supported by the Rockefeller Foundation. Yellowing newspaper articles pasted into a scrapbook chronicle their itinerary to Japan, especially Kyoto, and to China, where they visited the tombs near Peking, as well as to Korea and the Philippines.

A few days after the dedication of the college on September 19, 1921, the Shanghai *China Press* printed an interview with Mr. Rockefeller about the architecture of the college: "He explained the Chinese type of architecture adopted for the buildings as being an effort to make the Chinese feel at home thus expressing concrete friendliness and a desire to incorporate in the institution all that is best in Oriental life." Looking at *China Press*'s photographs of the tiled pagoda-style roof over the entrance to the chemistry building, one realizes that the architecture of the medical college became the architecture of The Eyrie Garden, as it was soon to be called.

What happened then is recorded in the hundreds of letters and drawings that went back and forth between the Rockefellers and their landscape gardener, Beatrix Farrand (the major correspondence, of great charm and *politesse,* was between Mr. Rockefeller and Mrs. Farrand, though it was always called Mrs. Rockefeller's garden), and that have now been preserved at the Rockefeller Archive Center in North Tarrytown, New York. Additional drawings and records, those specifically from Farrand's office, are deposited at the College of Environmental Design, University of California, Berkeley. The sheer quantity of material and intensity of focus make one wonder how any of them did anything else in their lives at this time. The Rockefellers' other accomplishments are well known. Farrand, preeminent in her field at age fifty-four, was a natural choice for them. She was Edith Wharton's niece, and Ogden Codman, Jr., who had collaborated with Wharton on *The Decoration of Houses,* had advised the young Rockefellers on the interiors of their town house on West 54th Street in Manhattan and no doubt told them of her early work. Also, between 1917 and 1921, she landscaped the Rockefeller Institute for Medical Research in Plainsboro, New Jersey. Finally, her own summer house, Reef Point, where she maintained an extensive native garden, was in nearby Bar Harbor.

During Farrand's own career, which spanned the years from 1897 to 1950 and included 176 gardens and landscape designs, mostly for residences and universities, she had designed one other mixed Oriental-European garden from 1914 to 1924 for Willard D. Straight in Old Westbury on Long Island. Her first letter to Abby Rockefeller was dated October 5, 1926, and it announced her fee of $100 a day "in the field or in the office," along with other charges, such as traveling expenses, a lower day-rate for her assistants' time, and a separate account for nursery expenses. She hired only women in her Manhattan office, including draftsmen trained at the Cambridge School of Architecture and Landscape Architecture for Women. Farrand herself trained with Charles Sprague Sargent, the first director of the Arnold Arboretum in Boston.

She already had in her file an article titled "Within the Moon Gate: The Gardens of China Are Made to Appeal to the Inner Eye of Contemplative Man," by Philip N. Youtz, from the March 1926 issue of *House & Garden,* illustrated by an old Cantonese moon gate. With the publication of the present article, fifty-nine years later, the ideas she gleaned then have come full circle to a new audience. Farrand never went to China, but she and Abby Rockefeller pored over books on Chinese architecture and sought the advice of a Mr. Nakagawa of Yamanaka and Co., dealers in Japanese and Chinese art objects in Bar Harbor as well as in Boston and New York. Most of the sculptures placed in the garden were purchased from him. With a small variation, Nakagawa's drawing for the Moon Gate dated September 19, 1928, was the one adopted. All of the gates and portals were first made up in cardboard and reviewed in place before actual construction.

In the contours of the garden, they sought that harmony of architecture in nature so important to the Chinese, who arrange each building or shrine in a rapport with the spirits of earth, wind, and air and vary the aspects of the garden to correspond with different moods. In one of her last letters to Mr. Rockefeller on the garden, dated September 6, 1950, Farrand recalls: "Mrs. Rockefeller always told me that we must not make the garden, vistas, or walks, or planting balance exactly, as the art of the Chinese in their gardens was almost always just enough asymmetrical so that the formality of true symmetry was not oppressive."

The rosy stucco-and-stone wall that curves around and encloses the garden on three sides is patterned after the red wall of the Imperial or Forbidden City in Peking. When part of the wall was demolished in China in the 1920s, the coping of yellow-glazed tiles was available for resale. The Rockefellers got the news and purchased ten thousand tiles for the coping of their own twelve-foot-high wall, as well as for the pagoda roof of the southwest portal. Farrand researched the exact shade of Chinese red for the wall and insisted that grass and wild sod be removed from its base so that it would rise directly from the road. And so it does.

The southwest portal opens onto the first axis established in the garden, west of the flower beds, called the Spirit Path. Placed along this path from the beginning was a double procession of seventeenth- and eighteenth-century Korean stone sculptures depicting military and civil officials. Positioned in descending order of size to increase the sense of a distant perspective, they are laid out according to the eighth-century Chinese custom of lining a walk to a noble burial mound, frequently marked by a stele, with two rows of statues. Farrand saw them as guardians of the entrance walk. The sixth-century stele at the path's northern end is in a small clearing that overlooks from its height the traditional wild north vista incorporated into many of Farrand's other designs, and a visual path has been cleared through the wooded hillside to open up a view of Long Pond below—what the English call a surprise vista.

Planted along the Spirit Path is a carpet of low-growing indigenous berry-producing plants—blueberry, cranberry, juniper, bunchberry, huckleberry, and bearberry—whose small points of deep color bring a richness to the solemn green. As one walks the length of the Spirit Path, small stone pathways diverge into the wooded areas to the west, where one can either contemplate a Chinese shrine, bearing a date in the T'ang period corresponding to 712, with a stone Buddha set in a niche, or sit on a stone bench by a clear pool of water next to one of several Korean stone lanterns and a most ingratiating stone frog poised on a granite ledge. Many of the stone sculptures among the trees have weathered in time to the colors of nature. They have become integral to their settings. Again, Farrand, in a 1930 letter to Mr. Rockefeller, credits Mrs. Rockefeller with having done "a really amazing thing in conceiving an idea which will permit the use of the old Chinese material in a new alien country without too exotic an appearance." Indeed, the two bronze Buddhas on lotus pedestals, one directly behind the Moon Gate and the other on a hillside on a line with the east gate of the garden, have made timeless temples of the Maine woods.

The major change in this series of gardens over the years has been in the central flower garden. What Farrand originally planned for the sunken panel, now a lush green lawn, was the Annual Garden, and for many years the central rectangle, divided by paths into unequal quadrants, was planted with annuals in circular formation. Essentially, this was *the garden* (and corresponds to the simple cutting garden that was the germ of the Rockefellers' first plan), and to the east and west, divided from the center by low stone walls, were the perennial borders.

One of the beds in the Annual Garden (on a plan corrected for 1932) was planted with *Nigella* 'Miss Jekyll', which brings up Farrand's great admiration for her English predecessor, Gertrude Jekyll, whose gardens she had seen on her trips to England and whose notes and papers she eventually purchased and added to her own collection, now at the University of California. The Annual Garden and the perennial beds reflect Jekyll's ideas about the compatibility of color and texture. One recalls two specific statements Jekyll makes in the chapter "The Mixed Border" in her book *A Gardener's Testament:* "For a border of some length it is found best to keep the ends cool in colouring, with a large amount of grey foliage, and to approach the middle through flowers and foliage of increasingly warm colour, with a gorgeous climax of strong reds nearly midway in the length"; and "For though it is undoubtedly best to treat flower borders with consecutive harmonies, yet the garden artist will know when and where to make exception."

Farrand did make a creative exception that adds subtly to the visual asymmetry of the garden: the east side of the garden was planted with blossoms of bright warm colors and the west side with pale cool colors, a distinction maintained rigorously today, while the north and south ends of the gardens have more neutral tones, especially in the green garden around the south oval lawn.

The Annual Garden was at a peak in 1935 when Abby Rockefeller decided to take over the management of the garden herself with Farrand available as a consultant. Sometime during the next few years, with increasing costs of maintenance, the Annual Garden was converted into a greensward with only an annual border below the original perennial borders as a memory of the former garden.

After the war, David Rockefeller says, his uncle William Aldrich, a Beaux-Arts-trained architect, suggested there would be better perspectives and vistas if the eye could follow a single line or path the length of the greensward to the spruce at the other end, and he recommended reinstating the cross paths, an idea with which Farrand was in complete accord. She wrote to the elder Mr. Rockefeller on November 27, 1947, that the grass panel "would seem less insistent in the design if the walk were allowed to cross it as it used to in its flower garden days."

After Mrs. Rockefeller's death in 1948, Mr. Rockefeller continued to work with Farrand on the garden—"We are fellow travelers along a lonely road," he wrote her on June 21, 1948. They softened the crosswalks of the greensward with borders at the corners where the paths met, and it remained until 1960, the year Mr. Rockefeller died. Beatrix Farrand, two years his senior, had died the year before.

Working with the landscape architect Robert W. Patterson, who had been an associate of Farrand's in Bar Harbor, David and Peggy Rockefeller restored the green panel to its present unbroken form. Those, like me, who have only known it in its present form would agree that the garden in its mature state, with the greensward at the center and the tall evergreens and deciduous trees as background, gives the floral borders that remain a restful setting that makes one appreciate all the more the individuality of each border segment.

Peggy Rockefeller is a plantswoman herself and has undertaken the annual review of the planting plans with her head gardener for more years now than her mother-in-law. Three years ago, the Rockefellers traveled to England and visited Sissinghurst and Hidcote along with other gardens in the Cotswolds. She made a list of two hundred English perennials, of which fifty have proven hardy in the Maine climate, and she is slowly introducing these to revive the perennial borders.

And in 1981, when David Rockefeller was in China, he visited the Tibetan temple called the Lama Temple, which had just been reopened, and noted piles of new yellow-glazed tiles on the grounds, the same as those used for the coping of the garden wall, which was in need of repair. He discovered then that the same factory which had made all the tile for the Forbidden City, and which had been making it for seven hundred years, was still in business. "They sent me a brochure in English and Chinese with samples of all the tiles. We needed replacements for fourteen different kinds and were able to get thirteen of the fourteen exactly the same as our two-hundred-year-old tiles." They were installed last summer, with an additional supply left over for the next fifty years.

After almost sixty years, the garden has never looked better or more brilliant. During the day last summer when I visited the head gardener, Gary Solari, a moment came when all the gardeners went to lunch, and I was left sitting alone in the garden. I closed my notebook and knew something of the peace that had attracted Abby Aldrich Rockefeller to its paths in late afternoon. This was a moment as unforgettable at that of my first visit.

Looking at a garden of such splendor, one must pay tribute to the devotion of those who have created and maintained it—a devotion not only to the garden, but to each other. As I combed the correspondence between the principals for details of the garden's evolution, I become aware of a personal story being told. It is the story of a couple whose quiet pleasures included reading together under the trees, as in the summer of 1944 when, according to Mary Ellen Chase's biography, Mrs. Rockefeller "had never loved her garden more as she tried to get it back to its former state of perfection."

In the summers following Mrs. Rockefeller's death, when Mr. Rockefeller returned to The Eyrie, there would be a bouquet of garnet-colored roses from Farrand. They were Mrs. Rockefeller's favorite, and he would place them under her portrait. Then he would write to Farrand, as he did on July 18, 1949: "I am delighted with the garden. It makes me yearn to have Mrs. Rockefeller there to enjoy it with me as formerly. But I am sure, though invisible, she is there. . . ." The story of the garden is a story of love and friendship.

Part II: Caring for the Garden

What one sees in radiant splendor in August will disappear in September—the Abby Aldrich Rockefeller Garden has no other season. But from the beginning and still today, the planning and the work proceed throughout the year. There is an infinite number of decisions: a perennial suddenly refuses to reappear, trees grow out of scale, stones crack, a favorite variety vanishes from the nurseries—and the list goes on. One can only smile at Beatrix Farrand's final comment in her first letter to Mrs. Rockefeller in 1926: "The office seems to be rather crowded this autumn so that I am rather hoping that you and Mr. Rockefeller are not thinking of any very drastic piece of work which would involve much time." Her letters did not stop until October 16, 1950.

Whether the topic was the depth of the topsoil (eighteen inches or two feet?), correcting the innumerable planting plans, or purchasing a few sashes for frames, the main decisions were discussed with Mrs. Rockefeller and confirmed with Mr. Rockefeller.

Beatrix Farrand to John D. Rockefeller, Jr.: We can . . . save the full cost of the frames by raising many of the young perennials which are needed for garden replacements. *August 16, 1934.*

His early comment on August 27, 1928—"As I was happy to tell you the other day, even I, unintelligent as I am, am beginning to see real beauty and charm in Mrs. Rockefeller's garden"—gave way later to an expert's understanding of the horticultural issues.

BF to JDR Jr.: Now as to the pruned maples. Your letter of the 31st is just what I should have expected from a fellow gardener. By all means let us cut out and take away the two maple trees on the east side of the garden and replace them with two red spruce trees. *November 4, 1949.*

JDR Jr. to BF: It was my intention to authorize the removal of all the remaining maple trees inside the east garden wall at the north end. I take it after the removal of the trees . . . you will be good enough to determine . . . where the spruces and cedars shall be planted in the area. This I shall appreciate. *November 15, 1949.*

BF to JDR Jr.: Although you are younger that I, yours is the wiser head. . . . You will be glad to hear that Mr. Young reports having already planted two new cedars and two new spruces to replace the intrusive maples . . . the plan is enclosed to you, to show that without having referred to the old plans, the new trees have been placed almost on the same spots as the old. *January 19, 1950.*

JDR Jr. to BF: These new trees are apparently well located.

Whether they will look lonely now because so small, it is difficult to tell
. . . best be left until next summer when we can review the situation on
the ground. *January 23, 1950.*

BF to JDR Jr.: It seems to me quite likely that with the new sunflowers and plants added that it will not look skimpy, though it will not
be as jammed and overcrowded as last year. *February 15, 1950.*

JDR Jr. to BF: I thought [a] few temporary cedar trees would
help to conceal . . . sunflowers, of course, grow quickly and make large
cover. They may accomplish just what you and I both have in mind. Cedars once planted do not need to be replanted each year and can be cut
out when they have served their purpose. *February 24, 1950.*

BF to JDR Jr.: You may depend on me to do what is possible to
further your wishes at Mrs. Rockefeller's garden, as we are both working
to try to improve the garden that was close to Mrs. Rockefeller's heart,
and with her spirit still helping us. *April 25, 1950.*

JDR Jr. to BF: I am delighted with everything about the garden, inside and outside. I do not miss any tree I cut down. The summer
flowers have grown so rapidly and so high I am in complete agreement
with you in having recommended our not planting any more cedar trees
inside the north wall even as a temporary measure. *July 22, 1950.*

So were the problems solved. Today, Peggy Rockefeller conducts her annual review with Gary Solari at the end of the season. Seven charts or planning plans corresponding to sections of the garden are kept in the office, a
small building in the woods behind the Moon Gate; and taking one chart at
a time, she and Solari walk the border together to review what changes they
want to undertake for the following year. When a substitution is made, she
considers all the variables of form, texture, color, and, most important, height
in making the new selections. The irregularity of height and of the shapes of
each individual bed of plants have made the garden's physical appearance full
of interest in its design and shape. There are no straight lines or square beds
in this garden.

"We have exaggerated the use of delphinium as tall accents, which give
the eye a visual pause, even more than my mother-in-law did," she says, "and
formerly, when the delphinium was over, it was over, but what we do now is
replace the early-blooming delphinium with new plants that were sown later
in the season, so we get two bloomings of delphinium to provide continual
accents."

Also, by introducing white flowers into the hot-colored side of the garden, she has made the deep reds and oranges less heavy in appearance. To plant masses of one color, or shades of one color, she selects three or four different types of plants with similar coloration but different textures, so color drifts or wanders across the beds. "An example would be a mauve flower in the lower bed like heliotrope; next moving up onto the wall, you have the same color, only it's clematis, then in the upper bed beyond, it might be delphinium. The idea is to carry the eye across the garden." Nowhere in the world does the purple *Clematis jackmanii* grow in such glowing health and beauty as it does on the walls of the garden, as it has ever since Beatrix Farrand planted it. Her attention to the wall gardens in between the borders unified rather than divided the gardens.

When the summer is over, Solari begins a new cycle of work with the six other gardeners. During the summer the grass panel is mowed twice a week and the flowers picked over daily while the gardeners wage a constant battle against the mildew of the Maine climate. The other enemy, in the harsh winters, is winter kill.

In the fall, they lift and divide some perennials and cut down others while they tear out the annuals, By November, the gardens are cleared out and covered with brush and leaves. They even take up all the gravel from the paths, which is screened in spring. "We feed the soil every three or four years and lime it every two years," Solari says. The soil is slightly on the acid side but close to neutral.

He orders the seeds himself in time to start the annuals in January, two or three weeks later than other greenhouses since they plan for an August garden. The staging area for the gardens including three greenhouses is around the harbor on another hill near David and Peggy Rockefeller's house.

The four hundred cedar flats for the seedlings, made by a carpenter on the premises, are branded mostly with the initials JDR Jr. A quantity of newer ones bear the initials DR. The dates of planting are recorded in ledgers: 1/7 begonia, oenothera; 2/6 penstemon; 5/1 calendula; 5/25 alyssum. And the greenhouses are filled with seedlings until April, when the tougher ones are moved to three cold frames. In season, most of the plants are moved to the garden. But one of the secrets of the Rockefeller Garden is that there is a second one, a cutting garden near the greenhouses, where a few flowers that might be needed later in the season as replacements are grown in regular rows along with the cutting flowers, including eighty rosebushes, vegetables, and strawberry and raspberry plants. It too has great beauty in its simplicity, especially the long rows of dahlias and purple monk's hood.

In a final walk in the garden one day last summer, I was reminded how important marigolds are in a Maine coastal garden, where on gray days they bring a golden light and have a special radiant glow at sunset. The name of one favorite of mine, at the northern end of the east annual border, sums up the entire experience of the garden: Marigold 'Color Magic'.

House & Garden, February 1985

Far East, Down East: A Classic Asian Landscape

SOME OF THE best traveling in the world can take place in a quiet room with a Chinese scroll depicting a mountainous scene in hanging mist with a small hut positioned precipitously on a high ledge. Hours can pass as the eye wanders through remote passes and winding trails to attain its restful goal at the little house, usually described as a scholar's retreat. Climbing a steep path along a rocky cliff on the Maine coast to an isolated cabin wedged into the granite under a pine can have a similar meditative effect, especially on a foggy morning when the music of buoy bells drifts across the water. According to one of the creators of such a Down East retreat—a small pavilion cantilevered out at the edge of a granite-bound garden at the couple's summer house overlooking a cove—no setting could be more conducive to concentration. For more than thirty summers the husband, a philosopher of science, left their house every morning at eight, walked through the woods to his secluded study-by-the-sea in Northeast Harbor, and settled in to ponder and write about questions of life and matter.

Inside the study, where one might expect to find a Buddha, hangs an engraved portrait of Voltaire, but outdoors next to the main house, a bodhisattva stands in a sanctuary of its own under the canopy of a laburnum. In a sense both sages are tutelary spirits of the surrounding garden, which, like other landscapes in that part of Maine (the Thuya Garden is a well-known example), harmoniously combines the Western tradition of colorful flower borders with Far Eastern features such as rock-rimmed pools and evergreens sculptured into hilly mounds that echo the contours of the mountainous landscape along the rugged coastline.

Besides evoking different cultures, this landscape embodies the passage of time. Much of the garden occupies the site of a sprawling turn-of-the-century summer "cottage," which had been torn down by the time the couple purchased the property in the 1950s. Only the massive cut-granite foundations survived as a romantic ruin. The new owners' architect, William Adair Bernoudy of St. Louis, who had trained with Frank Lloyd Wright for five years, designed a cedar-shingled house atop part of the ruin, but on a smaller scale than the original structure and set back farther from the edge of the bluff to make room for the garden. Deep overhangs give shade in summer, and horizontal lines are echoed by the low outstretched branches of trees that have been painstakingly pruned.

During the year following their acquisition of the property, the owners spent three weeks visiting the gardens of Kyoto where they immediately saw resemblances to familiar sights in Maine. Bonsai and other shrubs and trees shaped by human hands called to mind the pines and spruces that are similarly twisted and sheared naturally by heavy winds whistling along the wooded Maine coast. Inspired by what they had seen in Japan, the couple worked with Bernoudy and the Philadelphia landscape architect Howard S. Kneedler to reshape their own seaside terrain, which was then dominated by a single white pine. They began by clearing the rubble among the granite walls and added layers of soil for intimate planting areas; a series of natural hollows in the bedrock that filled with rainwater now serve as graceful reflecting pools across the garden.

The beautifully mellowed foundation walls—ranging in depth from two to eight feet—shelter flower borders which, in contrast to the angular masonry, follow a serpentine path that transforms the lower lawn into a swirling river of green. A knowledgeable botanist, the philosopher of science selected plantings appropriate to the Maine climate, but it was his wife who chose the glowing palette of pinks, blues, and purples—colors she associated with the memorable day in her youth when she first saw the windows of Chartres Cathedral. Viewed from higher ground or from inside the house, the precisely outlined beds of astilbe, delphinium, campanula, heliotrope, snapdragons, lilies, phlox, and artemisia can indeed suggest patterns in stained glass.

Few visitors to the landscape come prepared to find an allusion to medieval France, but then the element of surprise is one of the key lessons the owners learned from their experience in the Far East and imaginatively applied on home ground. There is, for instance, the enchanting surprise of roses nestled against a wall at the depths of a sunken garden and the unexpected drama that unfolds in the woodland that lies beyond the manicured landscape along the way from the family house to the scholar's retreat. What at first appears to be dense forest is in fact a cultivated wilderness, a rustic open-air cathedral with a nave of spruce leading to an elliptical apse of giant tree trunk pillars. At the focal point, positioned like a prehistoric altar or relics of Stonehenge, stand two huge granite monoliths that were unearthed nearby. Paths reinforce the sense of architectural cohesion, and much of the shady forest floor has been carpeted in moist moss and the lacy gray lichen that is the true flower of the Maine woods. The entire woodland garden is encircled by moose maple, whose fall foliage is so bright a yellow that it seems to bring sunshine into the dark grove on even the grayest day.

Convinced that no one should ever rush through a garden landscape, the owners stationed sculptures along the paths to encourage meditative pauses. In the woods a Japanese snow-viewing lantern and a pagoda from Kyoto, mementos of family travels, have both weathered to the same tonality as the granite bedrock of the cliffs. A terrace wall near the edge of a bayside bluff provides the pedestal for *The Three Graces*, a starkly handsome modern bronze by the German sculptor Gerhard Marcks, which the couple found on a trip to Heidelberg

Of course, there are plentiful reminders everywhere that a garden can never be a static work of art, subject as it is to changes imposed by nature. Year after year, the harsh maritime climate took its toll in the woods where the architecture of the cathedral-like design was altered by the loss of trees. When the owners lost the venerable white spruce next to the scholar's pavilion, they took advantage of the fortuitous clearing by planting a new garden of dwarf conifers.

Perhaps because they face extraordinary challenges in sustaining man-made landscapes from season to season, gardeners on the Maine coast take special pride in exquisite balancing acts. No horticultural feat demands so much skill and subtlety—or, when successful, appears so serenely inevitable— as the hybrid of Eastern and Western styles that has become a local specialty. On a summer day, nature and artifice can seem poised in perfect equilibrium. That this couple's garden remains one of the finest examples of the genre is a tribute not only to its creators' taste but also to their perseverance.

House & Garden, July 1993

A Cultivated Coast: The Garden at Somes Meadow

ON SUMMER days in Maine, there is a moment when stillness prevails. In her story about a coastal village, *The Country of the Pointed Firs,* Sarah Orne Jewett describes this as "the slack water period of the early afternoon" when the "very boats seemed to be taking an afternoon nap in the sun." Jewett's friend the poet Celia Thaxter wrote of a similar pause in *An Island Garden.* Looking out from her shady piazza, she gazed across her "happy flower beds" to "grassy, rocky slopes shelving gradually to the sea, with . . . blossoming grass softly swaying . . . against the peaceful, pale blue water."

Since change comes slowly to the coast of Maine, the scene remains almost the same a century later—especially at Somes Meadow, a property with a white clapboard Colonial house at the head of a meadow overlooking the village harbor at Somesville, Maine, where Beth Straus began creating her summer garden nearly twenty years ago. Currently senior vice chairman of the New York Botanical Garden and a volunteer there for over forty years, Straus has long been dedicated to the excellence of horticulture in the city. But she is also one in a distinguished line of women who appreciate that gardens in Maine are partners to the rugged beauty of the mountainous and rocky coast—the borrowed landscape beyond the garden fence. Besides Jewett and Thaxter, there were Beatrix Farrand, the landscape gardener, who lived at Reef Point in nearby Bar Harbor, and the writer and editor Katharine S. White, who gardened in Brooklin on Blue Hill Bay.

"There was so much beauty here that at first I thought a garden would be redundant to the meadow," Beth Straus recalls. "But I wanted a garden and finally tucked it in so as to enhance and retain the character of the landscape." She remembers early on looking out across the meadow in spring when it was a field of buttercups. Suddenly, the yellow flowers all took flight as a flock of goldfinches flew away. Now, in June, the tall spikes of masses of wild lupines, whose seeds Beth Straus scatters every year, make of the meadow a second ocean of purple blue as the morning mists rise above Somes Sound and Bar Island beyond. This view across the water, one of the few fjords on the East Coast, has an unexpected Nordic serenity.

Somesville preserves the independence and integrity of a year-round village, unlike neighboring towns that are mainly summer communities. The house at Somes Meadow, formerly a summer hotel with popular afternoon teas, is located near where the first permanent settler, Abraham Somes, landed on Mount Desert Island in 1761. Much of the surrounding wilderness has been incorporated into Acadia National Park. Although Beth Straus and her husband, Donald, live in Manhattan, they keep their Maine house open throughout the year, since Donald, a prominent arbitrator, is a trustee of the College of the Atlantic in Bar Harbor, a school dedicated to human ecology and environmental concerns. Beth Straus is chairman of the Asticou Azalea Garden in Northeast Harbor.

What is now the garden at Somes Meadow is actually a collection of gardens formed over the years on the edges of the wilder landscape. The first and largest is the eighty-by-sixty-four-foot vegetable and cutting garden, which occupies the site of the old clay tennis court. In feeling, it is very like Celia Thaxter's rectangular garden as portrayed in Childe Hassam's paintings, burgeoning with the brilliant seaside hues of poppies and roses against the silver gray of a weathered board fence. Because of strong coastal gusts, the rough cedar planks are spaced to lower wind resistance and keep the fence standing. The openings also offer glimpses of the garden to people walking up the hill from the landing.

The large central bed of the garden, planted in utilitarian rows, is framed by granite curbstones quarried and cut locally. From the garden gate, the main axis across this bed, a narrow path through a double row of marigold 'Lemon Gem', leads to a weathered garden bench backed by a lacy wall of sweet peas, twigged up, as they say Down East, by fine birch branches gathered in the woods. From the grass walk around the central area, views extend across the panorama of bright colors and regimental rows of mixed flowers and vegetables of various heights; nasturtiums, zinnias, snapdragons, beets, lettuce, and shallots, to name a few. Almost all the annuals and perennials are grown from seed, beginning with delphiniums in February. Coming home to Maine from trips to other regions or abroad, Beth Straus often arrives with small envelopes of seeds to add to her mixture. She has been guided in this endeavor by Paul Ritter, a retired neighbor from New Jersey, who has gardened with her during the past ten years. "We taught each other how to garden," she says.

Regardless of the season, there is a sense of balance, a richly multicolored striped carpet across the sound from Norumbega Mountain. Along one perimeter bed, roses and dahlias rise above a frilly edge of parsley, and two smaller rectangular beds encompass a strawberry patch and the herb garden with lovage, mint, sorrel, dill, and scented geranium. Elsewhere, rosemary topiaries grow in terra-cotta pots. Raspberry canes and five kinds of high-bush blueberries are screened from the birds by a light nylon mesh, and pole beans provide a tall green filigree along one edge of the garden.

Warm colors give way to cooler passages—pink, white, and lavender with a touch of yellow—in planted areas away from the water, particularly in the shade garden, raised above a stone wall with columbine, astilbe, and thalictrum. In a small cottage garden around a Lord & Burnham greenhouse, a preponderance of silver foliage offsets the pale colors. Both of these gardens blend into a meadow of wild grasses and daylilies, with a few old apple trees beyond. Only a swath of meadow around the house is mowed once a year in September, and a path from the harbor cuts across the grassy slope on the waterside through a screen of spruce trees that partially shields the dark green-shuttered house and its long deck.

When it comes to cutting and arranging flowers, Beth Straus agrees with Celia Thaxter's notion that "they look loveliest . . . when each color is kept by itself." Of the five major arrangements in the living areas, one may be all of white, with lilies, petunias, and phlox, and another a mixture of magenta dahlias and purple asters. Beth Straus used to specialize in spare oriental arrangements for her modern New York apartment, but now the Maine cutting garden has inspired these generous bouquets of many different flowers. But what is most Maine is the intimacy of the dooryard garden. Seen from afar as a fringe of color above a stone wall, this sunken border across from the main entrance includes artemisia, hosta, nepeta, thalictrum, and *Sedum* 'Autumn Joy', with a honeysuckle tree at one end. Laid out in a great semicircle, the artfully simple border is not unlike one described by Jewett in her story: "There grew a mass of gay flowers and greenery, as if they had been swept together by some diligent garden broom."

House & Garden, September 1991

On Maine's Coast, Vistas Are Cast in Stone

LIKE THE grandeur of the West, the mountainous coast of Maine was viewed in the nineteenth century as a vast, untouched wilderness, even though the lands had been well trodden and shaped by Native American populations. Scattered travelers and government expeditions were overwhelmed by the ruggedness and austerity of natural forms of scenery, and their appreciation for what may be called the American Picturesque ultimately led to the creation of the national parks. Artists and chroniclers found Maine's coastal views particularly uplifting when enhanced by the dramatic rhythms of rough surf and spectacular sunsets.

This summer, visitors to Maine have the unusual prospect of absorbing the nineteenth-century experience through a fine exhibition of landscape paintings in Rockland and of then continuing up the coast to view the same majestic land formations as preserved in Acadia National Park on Mount Desert Island. Along the way, it is also possible to see man-made landscapes and gardens that draw on the traditions of Maine and enrich local community life.

Flying into Rockland over the coastline, one observes the long fingers of water emptying into inlets along the irregular shoreline and the isolated villages on the extreme points of the peninsulas, their white church steeples marking the terrain. Maine is a rural state, and even the meadows along the airstrip are filled with weedy wildflowers.

This summer's special quest for Maine scenery begins in Rockland at the Farnsworth Art Museum, which specializes in American art. In an engaging exhibition titled "Inventing Acadia: Artists and Tourists at Mount Desert," the curator, Pamela J. Belanger, shows how landscapes painted by pioneer artists as early as the 1830s attracted urban dwellers to explore these majestic regions on their own. As a result, summer colonies grew to such a proportion later in the century, threatening idyllic views, that wealthy, established summer residents took measures to preserve the landscape. The eventual result, the establishment of the 35,000-acre Acadia National Park, incorporating most of the landmark mountains that sweep down to the sea (the "sleeping giants" recorded by the artists), as well as the tip of Schoodic Peninsula across Frenchman Bay and some offshore islands, including Isle au Haut in the Atlantic Ocean.

The park's name recalls the earlier French claim on this region as a colony extending from Maine into the coastal regions of Eastern Canada—the "Acadian land" with the "forest primeval" made famous by Longfellow's poem *Evangeline*. The Portuguese explorer Esteban Gomez was the earliest European to enter Mount Desert's Somes Sound, sailing from Spain in 1525 in search of the Northwest Passage to the Pacific. But in 1604 the French navigator Samuel de Champlain became the first to chart the island, acting on behalf of Pierre du Gua, Sieur de Monts, who had a royal land grant from Henri IV for "La Cadie," from the Native American name meaning "The

Place." Champlain named the island l'Île des Monts Déserts, the island of barren mountains. Their silhouettes form an undulating landmark when seen from the sea.

In the Farnsworth exhibition catalogue, Belanger and other essayists document the migration of the Hudson River School painters to coastal Maine and place their work in the social, cultural, and aesthetic context that explains the popularity of these "artist-explorers," who provided a kind of salon entertainment in cities where the large canvases were viewed as vicarious voyages into seemingly uncharted territories.

Artists often manipulated scenes by adding symbolic traces of human settlement—deserted houses or abandoned boats—that further enticed viewers by placing them psychologically within the frame. On the whole, though, the painters accurately portrayed the lone lighthouses, islands scattered across the bay, and rocky headlands under violet-streaked skies. Then as now, a patient gaze was required to capture the subtle and transitory atmospheric changes that altered one's perception of the Maine landscape.

Thomas Cole and his student Frederic E. Church were prominent among the artists who made expeditions to the island. The two often painted the same scenes—images that have since become iconic views of Acadia. Both Cole's *Sandy Beach, Mount Desert Island, Me.* of 1844 and Church's *Coast at Mount Desert Island (Sand Beach)* of about 1850 capture the contrast between jutting boulders of pink granite and the only smooth sand on the island. Cole's 1845 scenes of waves crashing against rocks in Frenchman Bay and Church's sunset paintings of the 1850s, one including an imaginary distant view of Mount Katahdin inland, are testaments to the extraordinary artistic response to the variety and inspiration offered by Mount Desert Island.

Cadillac Mountain, the highest on the island, figured frequently among the painters' subjects, and Sanford Robinson Gifford even places an artist sketching on a rocky perch at its summit, looking out toward the horizon. In 1896, Childe Hassam portrayed the mountain in an Impressionistic haze from the vantage of Frenchman Bay.

While most artists worked on land, Fitz Hugh Lane painted and sketched on ship deck, capturing statuesque masts and sails and luminous effects on water. His 1852 *Entrance of Somes Sound from Southwest Harbor* depicts the deep channel of water formed during the ice age there, a rare fjord on the East Coast and the location in the 1760s of the first permanent colonial settlement on the island. Very little had changed when Richard Estes painted

A View of Somes Sound in 1995, more than a hundred and forty years later, and that is the principal point of the show—the scenic experience of Maine has been preserved.

This view is substantiated after a morning's visit by walking into the museum's new gardens. In recent years, when the Farnsworth converted the white church across the street into a center to showcase the Maine work of the Wyeth family of artists, the decision was also made to build an extension to the main building and reorganize the grounds into a campus that includes the 1850 Farnsworth Homestead and carriage house.

Now enclosed on the street sides by a white wooden fence with tall posts and plantings of white rugosa roses, the entire property has been given the domestic scale of a series of village gardens by the landscape architect Clara Couric Batchelor. Between winding paths, low stone walls, a semicircular hornbeam hedge, and tree plantings of gnarled crab apple and white birch, Batchelor has planted mixed borders of homegrown plants like black-eyed Susans, creeping phlox, and Joe Pye weed. She also saved two specimen lilacs on the grassy slope by the carriage house.

On an afternoon drive along the coast to Mount Desert, the visitor can stop in nearby Rockport at Avena's Herb Gardens, where a remarkable woman, Deb Soule, has created an apothecary garden. Here the leaves and colorful blossoms are harvested and dried for tinctures, teas, salves, and oils— organic compounds that are known for their wide-ranging healing effects and that are sold by catalogue. In a Maine tradition of female herbalists that goes back to the Native inhabitants, Soule has planted an ornamental garden that also benefits her rural neighbors. A split-rail fence and a row of sunflowers barely contain massive beds of *Calendula officinalis* and *Echinacea purpurea* planted around a thyme-covered central circle with radiating paths, one passing beneath a cedar pergola draped in hops vines and hardy kiwi. All of the flowers and herbs are botanically labeled.

Passing next through the coastal town of Camden, with its immaculate summer cottages and lawns and a village green designed by the Olmsted firm, the visitor should pause at the bend in the road next to the Camden Library for a view of the horseshoe amphitheater designed around 1930 by Fletcher Steele. To experience the full impact of this powerful plan, which takes advantage of local mineral and plant materials, one should leave the library through the children's area at the lower level and turn immediately left. With tiers upon tiers of granite steps interspersed with grass and boulder ledges, clumps of hydrangeas, and the strong vertical lines of white birch trees—a Steele signature—this steep outdoor theater has been beautifully maintained for community events like concerts, plays, and graduations. The permanent show takes place in the active harbor beyond, and at night tall classical wrought-iron tripod light fixtures, each with a slight variation, cast a soft glow over the landscape.

From there the drive is a straight run to Mount Desert Island, the twelve-by-fourteen-mile island connected to the mainland by a causeway. No sooner does a visitor cross over than cedar signs appear with directions for entering the protected park lands. With the paintings in mind, one is cognizant of the efforts made by those who recognized the impending threat to the pristine landscapes. Once a wilderness area is engaged by man, it ceases to be in a natural state. Its future hangs between those who fight to protect it for its beauty and from the encroachments of civilization.

By 1900, fearing the consequences of the latter, Charles W. Eliot, president of Harvard University and a summer resident of Northeast Harbor, took his case for conservation to local village improvement societies. These societies, which still exist today, were already establishing and protecting Maine's woodland and mountain trails. Realizing that his mission required an entity with funds to purchase land, he followed the advice of his landscape architect son, Charles Eliot, Jr., and in 1901 formed the Hancock County Trustees of Public Reservations (HCTPR) with himself as president and his Boston friend George D. Dorr as director. Dorr was a fortunate selection; until his death in 1944, he devoted his entire life and financial resources to establishing and maintaining the park.

When the Maine legislature withdrew the charter of the HCTPR in 1913, Dorr, with undimmed determination, sought government protection in Washington. Although he made his approach at a difficult stage of World War I, on July 8, 1916, President Woodrow Wilson signed a proclamation establishing the Sieur de Monts National Monument. Only weeks later, on August 25, the National Park Service was founded, and Dorr grasped the opportunity to designate Mount Desert's conservation areas a national park. With political savvy, he supported the name Lafayette National Park for a country currently defending France, and the park was established by an act of Congress on February 26, 1919. The name was changed to Acadia National Park in 1929.

During my summers in Maine, I always begin with the sweep of the Ocean Drive, a segment of the circular park road that begins just outside the town of Bar Harbor and offers immediate access to the landscapes that figured prominently among the nineteenth-century artists. The sand beach of Cole and Church may be densely populated with bathers on a good day, but one can still appreciate its curved outcropping of granite and the nearby rock chasms that invite crashing waves. The road passes by Otter Creek, where Church painted a lone figure on a rocky beach, and proceeds along coves and inlets, the view opening out to the glittering sea with bobbing lobster buoys before coming under cover of woodland. The best view of Frenchman Bay and the Porcupine Islands is from the Shore Path, the public walkway along the coast back in Bar Harbor.

At the heart of the park, the Abbe Museum, filled with local Native American artifacts, maintains its original Spanish Colonial Revival building, now complemented by larger premises in Bar Harbor. The Sieur de Monts Spring covered with a Florentine-style canopy near the museum in the park was dedicated by Dorr to the man who established "New France" in North America. Further on, the Wild Gardens of Acadia bring an assortment of native plants to the public eye in a very straightforward arrangement.

Driving across the island, one observes clusters of cars parked here and there, their owners having taken to the trails throughout the park. These paths are beautifully maintained and clearly marked, making it difficult to lose one's way. All of the park roads lead to Mount Cadillac. From its heights, one can see expansive views of the sea, the distant hills, and the island's unusual rock formations, which derive from its complex geological origins.

There is nothing more suggestive of future possibilities than a Maine sunrise seen from the peak of Mount Cadillac, when the first gleam of light pours over a watery horizon and turns the world briefly into a blush of pink. In that quiet moment under a streaked sky, time appears to expand into timelessness. It was moments like this that inspired a generation of painters to make palpable the wonders of the Maine landscape and benefactors to preserve the experience for future generations.

> *New York Times,* July 16, 1999
> (with additional material from a later version in *Site/Lines,* Fall 2009)

Autumn in New England

WHENEVER I sit down for a cozy reread of a favorite book, invariably a few dry but still brightly colored pressed leaves spill from its pages into my lap. Each one recalls a happy autumnal trek through New England to view the fiery reds and brilliant yellows of the spectacular fall foliage. What New Englanders call leaf peeping is no casual matter; in advance of the season, from the last week of September to mid-October, local newspapers print road maps of rural New England marked with weekly forecasts about the peak of color, from the scarlet and orange of sugar maples and oaks to the golden hues of beeches and birches.

Last year I spent three days in Maine, mostly in the rain, hiking through woodland along the coast and marveling at the abundant moose maple whose large leaves turn so bright a yellow that on the grayest day, like hanging lanterns, they bring a radiance to dark trails. Back in the villages, the streets were slick with a mosaic of colored leaves that had fallen prematurely in the storm. And in the Japanese-styled Asticou Azalea Garden in Northeast Harbor, a range of manicured trees and shrubs, planted for their array of autumnal color, was reflected in the still waters of a serpentine pond.

What drew me to Massachusetts this year was my memory of *The Oxbow*, a panoramic landscape painted by Thomas Cole, one of the artists of the Hudson River School. On a trip from New York State to Boston in 1833, Cole stopped in western Massachusetts and went to the top of Mount Holyoke to sketch that famous silvery bend in the Connecticut River. Forty-two years later, Henry James placed one of the early scenes of his novel *Roderick Hudson* on the same "grassy elevation studded with mossy rocks and red cedars" above the "great shining curve" in a valley of "elm-dotted river meadows."

On just such a day as James describes, "when summer seems to balance in the scale with autumn," I drove there with friends along back-country roads lined with fields of dry corn husks bordered by rows of drooping sunflowers. On the wide green lawns of village houses, the freestanding maples were the first to turn, like massive fountains of fire. These are the ones I knew best in my childhood as I walked to school in a small town, scuffing my way through piles of dry leaves. We passed pumpkin stands that sold apples as well and saw by an old stone wall a crimson burning-bush, the native *Euonymus alatus*.

Along the winding ascent to the summit of Mount Holyoke, the woodland that closed in on either side was filled with yellowing ferns and the rich burgundy leaves and red berries of native dogwood. Above these, the pale yellow leaves of white birch appeared like sunlight trapped under a taller darker canopy. Then, as we approached the top, the woodland terrain gave way to a granite shelf above the dramatic view, the curve in the river and a valley of tilled fields ringed by a blue mountain range—all curiously recognizable after a hundred and sixty years. Cole himself felt that the American landscape, without ruined towers or classical temples, evoked the future, and his "village spire" still gleams white amidst green foliage tinged with crimson.

On the way down, there was a profusion of that other roadside harbinger of autumn, the lavender gray of wild *Aster novae-angliae* that in England has been hybridized into the Michaelmas daisy. These were also prominent the next day as I continued my leaf tour on Martha's Vineyard, an island off Falmouth, Massachusetts. In Trudy Taylor's seaside garden enclosed by a low stockade fence, the asters were clustered with hydrangea, already turned a greenish pink, and late-blooming magenta cosmos—a muted combination that was a welcome contrast to the high color.

Bartholomew Gosnold, a ship captain from England (Otley Hall, in Suffolk) allegedly named Martha's Vineyard for his daughter in 1641, and ripe grapes draped over tunnel-like arbors add to the fragrance of autumn on the island. The distinctive place to see color there is Beetlebung Corner, where a grove of beetlebung trees is the first to turn brilliant scarlet. (Beetlebung is the native *Nyssa sylvatica,* cultivated in England since around 1750.) In 1961, Polly Hill, a local amateur horticulturist noted for her varieties of stewartias and azaleas, gathered seeds from Beetlebung Corner and planted them along a path by her stone wall. The twenty trees are pruned high up like a hedge on stilts, and the view beneath them stretches out across her arboretum on an old sheep farm.

I flew back to Boston in the copilot's seat of a small plane that felt like a chariot riding over the islands—a red-streaked sunset on one side and the harvest moon piercing the clouds on the other. I thought of Henry James and his fictional description of the river valley visit: "This is an American day, an American landscape, an American atmosphere."

Gardens Illustrated, December 1993–January 1994

Four

British

The Painted Garden: William Kent's Rousham

ON A GENTLE slope rising above the winding river Cherwell near Steeple As-
ton, in Oxfordshire, England, a woodland path at the edge of a close-cropped
bowling green, north of a Jacobean stone house, runs into a small park. The
path widens through a series of sun-dappled glades ornamented with urns
and statuary green with lichen and the patina of time, past arcades and small
classical temples, cascades of water spilling over stone grottoes. A serpentine
rill—a stream in a stone bed—follows the curving line of a gravel path and
empties into a clear, dark octagonal pool hidden in the midst of the woods.
The long view extends upriver to a medieval bridge, then across the meadow
on the opposite bank to a Gothic ruin and beyond to a rustic stone arch on
a distant hill. Walking along the path and coming upon the surprise views in
the soft early-morning English air, one understands the beauty and mystery
of great parks everywhere.

Rousham Park, as landscape historian Christopher Hussey wrote in 1946,
is a "unique document of garden art; the earliest surviving ancestor of all the
landscape gardens and parks in the world." Last year marked the tercentenary of the birth of the man who created it, William Kent, whose innovative style not only set a pattern for the great private parks of England (some
of them later landscaped by "Capability" Brown, who notably became head
gardener at Stowe) but was the forerunner of many of our most cherished
nineteenth-century urban American parks. Of the several eighteenth-century
parks Kent designed, Rousham is the only one that survives unchanged—and
in the same family—since its completion in 1741.

Facing page: Lanning Roper, *Herb garden, Scotney Castle, Kent.*

In the second decade of the eighteenth century, whenever the literati of London dined together, by the time the port was served the fashionable gossip was likely to have been dismissed for more serious topics—among them the principles of gardening. Such eminent writers as Alexander Pope and Joseph Addison talked and wrote passionately on the subject of gardens. Seeking to abolish the French tyranny of geometric formality in gardens like Versailles, and the labored artifice of the ever more outrageous shapes of topiary admired by the Dutch, they penned essays with wit and vehemence in favor of what was to become the quintessential English style: the natural, or picturesque, landscape—a landscape born of the neoclassical taste of the Augustan poets and essayists, who encouraged notions of an easy naturalness, of grace and civility as opposed to stateliness and pomposity.

"Our British gardeners . . . instead of humouring Nature, love to deviate from it as much as possible," wrote a disapproving Addison in the *Spectator* in 1712. And in *An Essay on Criticism* (1711), Pope uttered his now famous battle cry, "First follow Nature . . . / At once the source, and end, and test of Art." Cultivating his own garden at Twickenham on the Thames, Pope practiced what he preached with notable flair and became an example and mentor to his friends and neighbors.

By 1720, one dined best on architecture and gardens at Burlington House (where Pope was a frequent guest), the London residence of the third earl of Burlington and of his protégé William Kent, architect, designer, and painter. Kent, who was born into modest circumstances in Yorkshire, as a young man of great charm and talent had been taken up by wealthy patrons and sent to study abroad. In Italy, Lord Burlington befriended him, As a result of their Italian sojourn, Lord Burlington became the prime promoter of Palladian architecture in England, and he and Kent also brought back a taste for the Italian Renaissance garden in the softened form captured in seventeenth-century paintings of classical scenes by Claude Lorrain and his contemporaries.

William Kent had distinguished himself early on as an architect and designer of furniture as well as an artist (he illustrated Pope's enterprising translation of the *Odyssey* with some head- and tail-pieces), but after 1730 he emerged as the greatest practitioner of the new landscape style that epitomized Pope's edict: "All gardening is landscape painting." In the two decades before his death, in 1748, Kent oversaw the creation of a series of such landscapes, among them Lord Burlington's at his Palladian villa, Chiswick House, which earned Pope's praise in the concluding stanza of his 1731 "Epistle IV" to Burlington:

You too proceed! make falling Arts your care,
Erect new wonders, and the old repair;
Jones and Palladio to themselves restore,
And be whate'er Vitruvius was before:

It was in the same Epistle that Pope made his famous declaration:

Consult the Genius of the Place in all;
That tells the Waters or to rise, or fall,
Or helps th' ambitious Hill the heav'ns to scale,
Or scoops in circling theatres the Vale;
Calls in the Country, catches opening glades,
Joins willing woods, and varies shades from shades;
Now breaks, or now directs, th' intending Lines,
Paints as you plant, and, as you work, designs.

Kent's achievement was set down for posterity by another man of letters, Horace Walpole, in his landmark essay "On Modern Gardening" (begun in the 1750s, not published till 1780), which places this period of English garden design in historical perspective. "At that moment appeared Kent," Walpole wrote, recognizing the bold genius of the mind that had fused painterly principles of light and shade, the curved contours of nature, and elements of classical architecture to create a new form of landscape.

For an immediate understanding of Kent's radical accomplishments, a walk along the winding paths and balustraded lawns of the twenty-five-acre park at Rousham—"the most engaging of all Kent's works," according to Walpole—still provides an experience very like that of the day 245 years ago when the last turf was laid and the waterworks turned on. Only the trees have grown taller and more dense.

Recent generations of Rousham's Cottrell-Dormer family have been as devoted to the maintenance of this historic treasure as Lieutenant General James Dormer and his cousin and heir, Sir Clement Cottrell, friends of Lord Burlington's, were to its formation between 1738 and 1741. Their voluminous correspondence has been bound and preserved, along with drawings and early plans and views of the garden. In the preindustrial age, the creation of such a garden was a massive engineering feat, sometimes employing 140 men at a time to level terraces into slopes and create valleys from small declivities. The men frequently had to wait for instructions from Kent, who would often not appear until late spring. During one stretch of turbulent weather, at least forty men were kept idle, according to one letter, unless "the water sinks, the weather mends or Mr. Kent comes."

Kent was working with a preexisting garden plan executed by Charles Bridgeman; his genius was to map out a new pattern, a natural succession of open and enclosed spaces, each with its own feature, so that anticipation of the unexpected is built into every turn of the garden. Not only does each clearing offer its own classically pictorial composition, giving one the sense of walking from room to room in a natural museum, but the continuous change of scene provides a depth of perspective as one catches a glimpse of the next opening or from a new vantage looks back on a clearing just passed.

For the gentry who visited the finished garden in 1741, Kent designed a special entrance, a Palladian door near a crenellated lodge on a road west of the house. The path to the garden was separated from the outlying meadows by an ingenious ditch, or "ha-ha" (so called for the exclamation of surprise it is supposed to have elicited from anyone coming upon it), devised around that time to make a physical but invisible separation between the garden and pastureland beyond, where prize-winning English longhorn cattle now graze.

"But of all the beauties he added to the face of this beautiful country, none surpassed his management of water," wrote Walpole. "Nature abhors a strait line" was Kent's ruling principle. The Cherwell was naturally winding, and the garden took its overall shape from a sharp bend in the river's course. But to circulate water through the pools and the cascade of the Vale of Venus, he had first to devise a system of conducting water underground, then overground, along the narrow serpentine rill which flowed through the woods, spilling at one point into the octagonal bathing pool. A statue of Venus with two swans presides over the upper cascade of water pouring into a stone grotto above a lily pond that is the source for the water trickling down a fern-encrusted lower wall. The sounds are natural and refreshing.

The clearings merge gracefully with woodland areas as the trees thin out at the forest's edge, and plantations of individual trees form the background for the architecture and for classical statuary (Bacchus, Mercury, and Ceres). Conifers, introduced by Kent and mixed in with the beeches, oaks, limes, and elms, recall the shapes of trees in classical landscapes. Except for wildflowers in spring, there is no color but the rich, deep contrasts of green. (Only in the older walled garden east of the house are there herbaceous borders and a patterned rose garden, separated from the newer Kent park by a thick yew hedge.) The prospect is particularly fine as one looks toward the greensward along the elm walk, which ends with a heroic statue of Apollo.

Perhaps the most masterly aspect of the overall design is its integration of architecture with landscape. Derived from the Augustan taste for classical ornamentation in natural settings, like the quiet presence of the hillside temples in the paintings of Claude Lorrain, Kent's garden structures are mostly open to the air and are smaller in scale than their classical models—fragments of architecture that fire the imagination into a fanciful world of the past.

It is exciting, then, to come across the arcade called the Praeneste (Latin for Palestrina, the ancient resort near Rome), set into the hillside, with its even pedimented archways opening into a shallow interior. The recesses of the arcade provide both shelter from inclement weather and a place to look out at the splendid views formed by the arches. Kent's original garden benches, painted gray and embellished with acanthus-leaf carving, are still there, set against a pale-yellow back wall. A simple experience, yet it suggests a more palatial scale.

Where the garden comes to a point, near its end, Kent placed the Temple of Echo, a small rustic Doric replica facing upriver toward Heyford Bridge, built by the monks of Eynsham Abbey around 1200. The interior is like a vestibule, an anteroom to beyond; from inside, a trick of perspective makes the river and the bridge seem at a greater distance viewed through the columns.

A similar example of classical architecture in a natural setting that predates our great urban parks is the early nineteenth-century American garden cemetery. The great classical, baroque, and gothic mausoleums along serpentine ponds in cemeteries like Spring Grove in Cincinnati and Green-Wood in Brooklyn are the same miniaturized versions of architecture in a flowing landscape.

Even more tantalizing—and romantic—are the invented ruins, or "follies," at Rousham that focus the view at some distant point in the landscape. An old mill has been dressed up with a protruding Gothic facade, a large window, pinnacles, and flying buttresses jutting out in relief from the long building. The Temple of the Mill, as it is called, is a paean to the agrarian structures integral to British pastoral landscapes. And equally striking, on the skyline at the crest of a hill, is the Triumphal Arch in the gothic style, a single gable with triple arches—"the Eye Catcher"—which crowns the whole visual experience. Beyond it, until woods grew up in later years, only the watery English sky showed through the arches. The present guardians of the park,

Charles Cottrell-Dormer and his wife, Angela, hope to persuade their neighbors to fell the woods and let the sky show through once more.

The aura of the sham ruins does not diminish on close inspection, even as the corn grows high around the Triumphal Arch. From that vantage, one looks back toward the park, as it flows into the surrounding landscape, presided over by the great battlemented house, and one understands clearly what Walpole meant when he wrote of Kent, "He leaped the fence, and saw that all nature was a garden."

Vanity Fair, April 1986

Painshill Park: Charles Hamilton's Folly Garden

TODAY'S THEME parks, with fairy-tale castles and elaborate gardens, are meant to evoke the romance of faraway places. Historically, they derive from a far subtler form of landscape park in England, which, in the eighteenth century, also promoted make-believe to visitors, who were expected to tip the gardeners for the privilege. Among the originators of that style of illusion in nature was Charles Hamilton, the ninth son of the sixth earl of Abercorn. In 1738, he began by leasing some 125 acres of scruffy moorland in Cobham, Surrey, along the River Mole, only twenty miles from London, and until he ran out of funds in 1773, he transformed the land—eventually 250 acres—into one of the most imaginative and fashionable landscape gardens in England, Painshill Park.

Armed with an Oxford degree and accompanied by a well-heeled friend—Henry Fox, the future Lord Holland—Hamilton went to Italy on an extended grand tour and later studied painting at the academy in Lorraine, France. Painshill Park became a summation of these formative experiences, for no scene or mood that he had observed in art or landscape was left unexplored in the architecture of the park. He drew inspiration from the ruins of the Roman campagna and from the brooding wilderness depicted in the seventeenth-century paintings of Salvator Rosa. In transforming the landscape to create intimate settings for temples and architectural follies that recall an older Europe, he also became a horticultural innovator by introducing plants and trees from America, and by laying out gardens in a new fashion that combined the last vestiges of the old formality with a foretaste of the picturesque.

No eighteenth- or even nineteenth-century garden guide or travel diary was without a lengthy description of the wonders of Painshill. Alighting from their pony chaises, visitors flocked to this pleasure ground to follow the rustic paths of a three-mile circuit that trailed through woodland glades around a serpentine lake and were so contrived as to conceal and then reveal a variety of views. As described by the Irish visitor Sir John Parnell in 1769, the "thick plantations . . . artfully prevent the eye from seeing all at once and make the whole appearance doubly large." Dramatic vistas opened up across the water and into the hills, and took in distant temples and ruins, bridges connecting islands, and densely planted hanging woods, as they were then called. One writer suggested that the view was a feast with the delicacies tantalizingly out of reach. The experience of the park has been compared to a linear voyage as portrayed in a Chinese scroll.

Among the fashionable visitors was that most intrepid of garden tourists, Thomas Jefferson, garnering ideas for his Virginia estate. On April 2, 1786, while minister to France on a diplomatic mission to London, he escaped to Painshill, by then an even larger affair in the hands, since 1773, of a new owner, Benjamin Bond Hopkins. Jefferson's guide was Thomas Whately's *Observations on Modern Gardening* of 1770, and he wrote in his own account book: "Paynshill . . . three hundred and twenty-three acres, garden and park all in one. . . . A Doric Temple, beautiful." John Adams, Jefferson's counterpart in London, who went two months later, declared, "Paines Hill is the most striking piece of art that I have yet seen."

Painshill Park (the name perhaps lent by Richard Payn, a thirteenth-century Cobham landowner) was preserved more or less intact into this century. It began to be seriously overgrown and affected by commercial forestry in the 1930s and was sold off in separate lots after World War II. At the instigation of the Friends of Painshill, the local Elmbridge Borough Council rescued the park by 1980, purchasing 158 acres encompassing the original pleasure grounds. With initial funding from preservation organizations and private donors, the Painshill Park Trust is proceeding, like Hamilton, in the hope that the fund-raising will keep pace with the restoration. Today the gardens and follies of Painshill are slowly reemerging as a site of great horticultural and architectural merit, attracting serious garden devotees and the patronage of the Prince of Wales. In the end, the park will look "natural" again, or as described by another period visitor, "you are sometimes in doubt whether you are looking at a garden or an ordinary landscape."

While Painshill was created during the great period of the English landscape garden, it nevertheless stands out as a completely original idealization of nature according to tenets of the Augustan poets and essayists. In his *Epistle IV to Richard Boyle, Earl of Burlington* of 1731, Alexander Pope advised fashionable improvers: "In all, let *Nature* never be forgot . . . / Consult the *Genius* of the *Place* in all, / that tells the Waters or to rise, or fall." Unlike other gentlemen, who watched from their country houses as William Kent, Lancelot "Capability" Brown, and other professionals improved their grounds, Hamilton was his own improver, and the result is a uniquely personal vision.

What he developed one by one were individual sets to evoke, say, the atmosphere of Italy or the wild scenery of the Alps, and to transport the visitor into imaginary worlds outside his everyday experience. And because Hamilton became a leading exponent of using trees and plants to reinforce the atmosphere created by the architecture, the follies, albeit of rather flimsy construction, were made to feel like real places. "Mr. Hamilton," cites one hand-book, "was as careful in the situation and grouping of his trees as in the arrangement of his temples."

The structures were in turn set in a larger landscape composed of elements best described by Horace Walpole in his essay "On Modern Gardening" as "the garden that connects itself with a park, into the ornamented farm, and into the forest or savage garden." He defined the last, the "alpine scene," as "composed almost wholly of pines and firs, a few birch, and such trees as assimilate with savage and mountainous country." He writes on: "Mr. Charles Hamilton, at Pain's-hill, in my opinion has given perfect example of the mode in the utmost boundary of his garden. All is great and foreign and rude; the walks seem not designed, but cut though the woods of pine; and the style of the whole is so grand, and conducted with so serious an air of wild and uncultivated extent that, when you look down on this seeming forest, you are amazed to find it contains a very few acres."

Hamilton was a courtier to Frederick Louis, Prince of Wales, and even a member of Parliament in the 1740s, but his true occupation was to fulfill Pope's pronouncement that "All gardening is landscape painting." Sir Uvedale Price, one of the foremost protagonists of the emerging picturesque style, even said of Hamilton that he had "not only studied pictures, but had studied them for the express purpose of improving real landscape." Hamilton took as examples the seventeenth-century classical landscapes of Claude Lorrain and Nicolas Poussin as well as the more savage visions of Salvator Rosa, two of whose paintings he owned. Painshill Park itself quickly became the subject for artists, whose paintings, drawings, and engravings now provide a record of its appearance and of the gentry and gardeners who brought the stage to life. Even Fredrik Magnus Piper, an architect who became the garden designer to King Gustav III of Sweden, made drawings at Painshill, including one of the Turkish tent that conveys that sense of exotic decor in a rustic setting.

These pictures, the archaeological evidence, and archival materials have given the present restorers a foundation for one of the most monumental and experimental undertakings in English garden design. In a way, only Hamilton could grasp the magnitude of the venture, for in restoring the park Janie Burford, the landscape architect who is the director of the Painshill Park Trust, and her staff are, as it were, re-creating the original eighteenth-century experience. The dilemma is to determine to what period the ruined garden should be restored and how to protect its underlying structure and architecture. As valuable as the remaining buildings are seven 240-year-old cedars-of-Lebanon.

Hamilton's library, which survives, indicates how firmly he was grounded in horticulture and classical architecture. He began the park in the 1740s by cultivating a vineyard on the south slope that conjures up the French countryside. In the 1750s he received advice on the cultivation of vines and winemaking in a correspondence with Abbé Nolin, the garden adviser to Louis XV at Versailles. Hamilton's vineyard produced grapes for sparkling wine "superior," as he wrote, "to any *Champaign*." However, he admitted that "such is the prejudice of most people against anything of *English* growth, I generally found it most prudent not to declare where it grew till after they had passed their verdict upon it." Judging from the spectators viewing the vineyard from across the lake in a painting of the 1770s, its regular rows (soon to be replanted) were a picturesque agricultural complement to the Ruined Abbey adjoining it, which was the last of the follies Hamilton built. Resembling the ruined abbeys of Yorkshire, it conceals an abandoned brickworks Hamilton instigated as a commercial venture.

The centerpiece of the park—the major illusion—was a serpentine lake with a cluster of islands in the center. Because of its contours, the entire lake was never visible at a glance, making it appear larger than it was and sometimes like a river passing beneath the bridges. Water was channeled from the River Mole to a water wheel, a kind of engineering folly, which raised its level so that it could spill over a cascade into the lake. As his last work in the park, in 1773 Hamilton extended the lake to the abbey and vineyard for a total of fourteen acres of water.

Beyond the overlook to the vineyard was the first set piece—a green amphitheater of trees and shrubs where, in the style of the period, evergreens
were displayed in a formal, graduated manner rather than in informal drifts.
To restore this effect, Mark Laird, the historic planting consultant, based his
plan on a detailed layout of 1737 for the Duke of Norfolk's estate at Worksop
in Nottinghamshire. Low-growing vinca in the foreground gives way to viburnum, holly, and finally tall pines.

At one end of the amphitheater stands a stone plinth that once supported
a lead copy by Jan van Nost of Giambologna's marble *Rape of the Sabines* in
Florence. Soon to be reinstalled in a new casting, the lead statue is symbolic
of both the Renaissance and ancient Rome, two narrative threads that are
woven throughout the park. At the far end of the green amphitheater is the
Gothic Temple, a wooden building originally painted to look like stone, that
stands now in a field of daffodils overlooking a great sweep of lawn to a distant view across the lake. This was the first of Hamilton's original vistas to be
opened up after trees were felled to begin the restoration. The ten-sided castellated pavilion with quatrefoil windows and ogee arches was probably based
on prototypes in Batty Langley's *Gothic Architecture* of 1747. The temple
has been restored to the fantasy it once was: the timbers have been stabilized
with resin and strengthened with stainless-steel lath, and a rose-colored fan-
vaulted ceiling protects a patterned stone floor from the weather.

Below, by the lake, on a peninsula that leads to the Chinese Bridge, Hamilton experimented with the new plants, such as rhododendrons and azaleas,
that John Bartram was sending from Philadelphia to the plant collector Peter
Collinson in Middlesex. In contrast to the regimented order of the amphitheater, these beds of colorful and fragrant deciduous plants—roses, honeysuckle, and jasmine—were laid out among evergreen shrubberies along
serpentine walks. The bridge in the stylized Chinese Chippendale style that
leads to Grotto Island has recently been rebuilt. Today, although the central
chamber lacks its roof, the grotto has the atmosphere of a glittering kingdom
under the sea. With dark damp caverns, fluorspar and lavender crystalline
walls, and floors of cockleshells, the grotto chambers, built by Joseph Lane in
the 1760s, are magical and otherworldly.

Another bridge, based on a design by Andrea Palladio, crosses from Grotto Island to the mainland and figures in an engraving by William Woollett that
became one of the most popular contemporary views of Painshill. It was one
of three scenes of the park chosen for the famous Green Frog service decorated with views of Britain that Catherine the Great ordered in the 1770s

from Josiah Wedgwood and Thomas Bentley for the Chesmenski Palace near Saint Petersburg that she called La Grenouillière.

In a clearing on the south bank of the lake stands the Mausoleum, a kind of Roman triumphal arch once alive with urns and antique sculpture, set in a somber grove of yews to evoke a feeling of melancholy. This folly, engraved by Woollett, also appeared on Catherine the Great's service.

No eighteenth-century theme park should be without its hermitage, here a small wooden house with Gothic windows and a thatched roof built high on a hill of alpine woods. It had a comfortable parlor from which to muse on the river below, and for a while Hamilton even hired a hermit to inhabit it as an amusement for his visitors. The Hermitage has yet to be rebuilt, along with the Turkish Tent and the Temple of Bacchus, which have also disappeared. Much copied in Sweden, the tent, designed by Henry Keene in the 1750s, was draped and swagged with blue and white canvas over a brick shell and overlooked sheep grazing in the meadows above the lake. (The sheep, a special breed of eighteenth-century Jacob's sheep, have been returned to the park, where Hamilton had used them to fertilize the grounds.)

What Jefferson most admired, the Doric Temple of Bacchus, was perhaps the most finished structure in the park, a kind of Maison Carrée with a portico at each end and bas-relief entablatures inside and out. A copy of the Apollo Belvedere was in one of the niches flanking the facade, and a seven-foot-tall statue of Bacchus that Hamilton acquired in Rome was displayed inside. The ceiling was said to have been designed by Robert Adam. Bright, cheerful plantings reinforced the temple's role as a banqueting house and a place for general revelry. From a distance it had the quiet aloofness of the classical buildings in a painting by Claude.

At the highest point in the park rises the castle that ends the quest in every fairy tale. This four-story Gothic Tower with a turret and battlement serves as a belvedere with a view over the nearby eighteenth-century gardens at Claremont and Woburn Farm and as far as Windsor Castle. Within the tower the Painshill Park Trust has installed an exhibition of various works of art relating to the garden.

Today, the tower also overlooks the A3, the highway to London. As civilization has encroached to the very portals of Painshill, this encapsulated world of the imagination has increased in significance. Perhaps the reason this kind of landscape has become so important to the twentieth century is because, as an early visitor observed, "In no place that I ever saw has so much been done for Nature as at *Pains-hill.*" Nature remembered in Alexander Pope's sense has become as important a link to the past as architecture. This may be the new theme of Painshill Park.

Antiques, June 1991

The Waterways of Castle Howard

> From ev'ry Place you cast your wand'ring Eyes,
> You view gay Landskips, and new Prospects rise,
> There a Green Lawn bounded with Shady Wood,
> Here Downy Swans sport in a Lucid Flood.
> Buildings the proper Points of View adorn,
> Of *Grecian, Roman* and *Egyptian* Form.
> —Anonymous, *Castle Howard* (c. 1733)

AS HE LOOKED out the window of Castle Howard onto the newly pristine surface of the North, or Great, Lake and its adjacent ponds, the Honorable Simon Howard exclaimed, "We had one of the greatest views in England and couldn't even see the main lake." He was referring to the tangle of reeds and rampant trees that had gradually overcome the ponds and destroyed the fragile banks since early in the twentieth century, finally obscuring the view. Fortunately, in 1987, three years after taking over the estate following the death of his father, he began a process of repair and recovery that has restored to this palatial house the smooth sheet of water to the north and, to the south, the glittering ribbon of light that is a mile-long waterway into the countryside.

Even without visiting Yorkshire, viewers of the 1981 televised production of Evelyn Waugh's *Brideshead Revisited* will remember the spectacular bird's-eye view of this domed Corinthian pile located fifteen miles north of York and framed by the Howardian Hills. But to walk the grounds today is to appreciate the evolution of one of England's greatest country houses, which has survived many vicissitudes, including fire. It is in splendid condition because of the devoted collaboration between generations of the Howard family and the architects, landscape designers, and artisans of their day.

The story begins in 1699 when Charles Howard, third earl of Carlisle, met Sir John Vanbrugh at the moment Vanbrugh was turning from drama to architecture. The earl commissioned him to replace a ruined castle in the village of Henderskelfe. It was Vanbrugh's first commission and became his most outstanding contribution to English architecture. Armed with the book he called his "Palladio," he followed the Italian master's classical style as introduced to England by Inigo Jones. Early on, Vanbrugh began consulting on practical aspects of building with Nicholas Hawksmoor, who had trained in London with Sir Christopher Wren.

In the beginning, the main feature of the landscape was a sixty-four-acre wooded hillside known as Ray Wood just east of the house, where a valuable collection of trees was interspersed with a labyrinth of walkways, classical statues, and arbors as well as fountains, cascades, and a reservoir filled by a stream, or beck, that ran from the neighboring village of Coneysthorpe. By 1724, an immense rectangular basin of water called South Lake had been built southeast of the house, causing Hawksmoor to write to the earl, "Your Lordship may also see by this lake (as it is at present) how Beautiful a Body of Water at Connysthorp would look to ye North Front." However, the north area was not flooded until the time of the fifth earl in 1797.

A terraced walk leading obliquely from the house past the South Lake followed the route of the old village street of Henderskelfe to Vanbrugh's final work, the Temple of the Four Winds, which he designed in competition with Hawksmoor. Based on Andrea Palladio's Villa Rotunda in Vicenza, it was completed nevertheless by Hawksmoor in 1739, after Vanbrugh's death. Hawksmoor himself received the commission to design the family mausoleum further into the distance, a domed rotunda, reminiscent of the Pantheon, surrounded by a Doric colonnade and frieze, that sits majestically on a hill above a collection of mock fortifications.

By 1744, maps of the estate show another water course called New River (dating from the 1730s) that was separated from the bastion wall of South Lake by a belt of trees and was traversed midway along by a rusticated bridge with three Roman arches built by Daniel G. Garrett. This combination of bridge and temples set in an Arcadian landscape recalls the great scenes set in the Roman campagna painted by French artists of the seventeenth century, such as *The Massacre of the Innocents* (Dulwich Picture Gallery, London) by Charles Le Brun. In this painting, the round Mausoleum of Hadrian (now the Castel Sant'Angelo) is juxtaposed with an arched bridge and a temple in a manner very like the constellation at Castle Howard.

Following a visit to Castle Howard in 1772, Horace Walpole wrote to a friend, "Nobody told me that I should at one view see a palace, a town, a fortified city, temples on high places, woods worthy of being each a metropolis of the Druids, the noblest lawn on earth fenced by half the horizon, and a mausoleum that would tempt one to be buried alive."

These were the fixed elements in the landscape when George William Frederick Howard, seventh earl of Carlisle, a bachelor, took up residence at Castle Howard with his mother and two of his sisters. Shortly thereafter, on October 29, 1849, he invited the landscape architect William Andrews Nesfield for a consultation. Nesfield is rarely listed in the canon of celebrated British landscape improvers like William Kent, Lancelot "Capability" Brown, Humphry Repton, and John Claudius Loudon; nonetheless, he was the most sought-after garden designer of his day, with more than two hundred commissions to his name. Before coming to Castle Howard, Nesfield was already engaged at the Royal Botanic Gardens at Kew in creating the great vista to Syon House across the Thames, the Broad Walk, the Pagoda Vista, and the parterres of the Palm House terrace, which have basically remained intact.

Equipped with a portfolio of seventeenth-century French designs for parterres, *The Theory and Practice of Gardening* (1709), the treatise by Antoine-Joseph Dezaillier d'Argenville on the French formal style practiced by André Le Nôtre (translated by John James), and ideas gleaned from *Essays on the Picturesque* (1794) by Uvedale Price, Nesfield created designs that blended the formal with an appreciation of the natural. However, he always claimed, particularly with regard to water, that an artistic landscape had to be either artificial or natural, but never both. He once described landscape gardening to Sir William Jackson Hooker, the director of the Royal Botanic Gardens, as "the Art of painting with Nature's materials."

It is not surprising to learn that when Nesfield served with a regiment in Canada under the command of Sir Gordon Drummond during the War of 1812, the experience that left the greatest mark, once hostilities ceased, was the assignment to make a large-scale drawing of Niagara Falls, a scene that he also painted more than once and that made a lasting impression on his own designs. He later wrote, "To describe the grandeur or terrific appearance of this phenomenon in such a manner as to convey the most distant idea of it to a person never having seen the Falls is, I conceive, impossible." Although on a much smaller scale, a similar rush and foam of cascading water lend drama and vitality to the water gardens at Castle Howard.

According to Christopher Ridgway, the present curator of Castle Howard, very few archival plans remain to document the improvements made during the Nesfield period, but an extensive correspondence and accounts survive that trace the progress of the collaboration between the landscape architect and the resident agent, John Henderson. Nesfield admitted early on to "being more anxious about my reputation in connection with Castle Howard than all my other places put together."

Work began in 1850 on the North Lake with the enhancement of a small island and the creation of the Reflecting Pond beyond the existing Dairy Pond. Both ponds were divided from the lake by a low promontory of land that encircled them. This was completed in time for a visit from Queen Victoria in August 1850.

The major creation for Castle Howard during the 1850s was the immense, two-tiered Atlas Fountain with the kneeling Titan shouldering the world surrounded by four Tritons spouting water from shells and by innumerable other shell motifs The fountain was designed as the centerpiece of a grand embroidered parterre with scrolls, volutes, and scallops set within a balustraded enclosure across from the south facade of the house. This was the first stage of the waterworks that required sophisticated planning among Henderson, Nesfield, the sculptor John Thomas, and the engineer James Easton, who refined the steam engine that pumped the water from Coneysthorpe beck up to the new reservoir in Ray Wood. Taking advantage of the ample downhill water pressure, Nesfield was engaged at the same time in designing a second fountain, also gravity fed, at the center of South Lake. In October 1853, Georgina Dorothy, Dowager Lady Carlisle (née Cavendish) and her daughters Harriet Elizabeth, duchess of Sutherland and Mary Matilda, Lady Taunton, were invited to the unforgettable first demonstration of the two fountains, which appears to have been a rousing success, according to the letter Nesfield sent to Lord Carlisle appropriately embellished with charming drawings and schematics of the fountain configurations and the trajectories of the water jets: "I am proud to state that we arrived at a most satisfactory result not only as to individual form but to general effect, so much so that the Committee of Ladies considered that matters could not be improved—Lady Carlisle particularly wished me to give your Lordship a line which I do with great pleasure because the whole affair exceeded my expectations—The supply of water is so ample that we were able to introduce in addition to the principals 8 subordinate jets in the shells which materially conduce to the richness & action of the whole." The drawings indicate a sixty-foot-high single jet in South Lake with four minor jets on either side. Known as the Prince of Wales Fountain, the feathery plumes of water, jetting in three directions, reproduce the feathered emblem associated with that title.

After Victoria's visit in 1850, Carlisle commissioned Nesfield to paint a view of Castle Howard from the Mausoleum as a gift for the queen, and this watercolor, which was completed in 1852 and is still in the Royal Collection, became an important element in imagining the further step of joining the water features to create a single piece of water from South Lake to New River. In Nesfield's romantic view, the Atlas Fountain and the Prince of Wales Fountain are correctly conceived, and the South Lake with quadrant corners has a small sluice pouring forth from its bastion wall. A marshland with trees separates the lake from New River and its bridge with water tumbling through the arches. It appears that Henderson was the first to suggest intermediate waterways that would create a continuous flow to direct the eye from the house towards the long vista culminating with the Mausoleum a mile in the distance.

A decade later, in 1863, Nesfield refined Henderson's proposals and added a stepped cascade fed from the small Frog Pond at the southeast corner of South Lake. The water gushed down another drop to fill a basin with quadrant corners, the one-hundred-foot-long Temple Hole. That, in turn, climaxed in a waterfall that tumbled into New River West and flowed under the New River Bridge and over a plateau into New River East. The formal water features ended at the river, which meandered on in serpentine fashion across the countryside, terminating below the Mausoleum at the crescent-shaped Eastern Dam, where it continued its flow as a beck called Lowdy Gill. The beck completed its circuitous route through the pastoral landscape at Low Gaterly Pond and the mill there that predates Castle Howard. This is the true terminus of the South Waterways. Nesfield got the dimensions just right to create the illusion from the house of a level piece of glistening water running from South Lake to New River Bridge, despite a drop of forty feet. In 1864, Nesfield and Henderson completed their grand design, and in December of that year Carlisle died, thus bringing to a close another era at Castle Howard.

Like the enchanted woods in the fairy tale *Sleeping Beauty*, the vistas both north and south of Castle Howard were obliterated in time by the extensive overgrowth of trees and aquatic plants. Perhaps the seeds of their destruction were planted just a year after Carlisle died, when his nephew George James Howard, the future ninth earl of Carlisle, arrived one day to visit accompanied by his young wife, Rosalind Frances (née Stanley). She immediately expressed her distaste for the formal gardens, which in time were deemed so costly as to rob the tenant farms of much-needed improvements. In 1893, within four years of becoming the countess, she replaced the parterres with the lawns and yew hedges that exist today. But she also had earth transferred from the gardens to soften the slopes and banks of South Lake and Temple Hole, where she planted trees and shrubs that, along with yews to the east, eventually obscured the view of the Mausoleum. At the same time, as Ridgway writes in his report, "the South Waterways became silted up and overgrown, as did the ponds on the shores of the North Lake, and the fountains fell into disrepair." Thereupon followed a century of neglect and a landscape lost to time.

To reclaim the views required the kind of inspired detective work associated with historical archaeological excavations. (Simon Howard has also preserved the ten-thousand-acre estate in forest and farmland without giving in to the production of rapeseed that has covered much of England with Day-Glo yellow.) Without drawings or plans, the only options were to study the land itself for clues to the configuration of the waterways and to seek confirmation in descriptive letters stored at Castle Howard and other archives. In lieu of a period restoration that would have required selecting a given moment, it was decided simply to repair the waterways after a thorough investigation on the ground. Work began with clearing reeds and self-sown trees from the shoreline of the North Lake, reinstating the clean line of the ponds and adding a third one—Simon's Pond—to balance the other two.

Before the South Waterways were drained for conservation, the Ray Wood Reservoir was refurbished to restore its half-million gallon capacity, and the Atlas Fountain, which had leaked from the start, was rebuilt from underground up and fitted with a waterproof liner. With the jets repaired and the zodiac signs that girdle Atlas's globe regilded, South Lake was drained and cleared of lily roots, a fragile operation because the clay bottom did not permit the use of heavy machinery. Very little was known about the hydraulics for the Prince of Wales Fountain, since no one alive had ever seen it working. Although the main jet was known to be supplied by the Ray Wood Reservoir, the cast-iron pipes for the subsidiary spouts, long bent out of shape, had to be traced through the mud to discover their source in the overflow water outlets of the Atlas Fountain. All the pipes were so thoroughly rusted that the first time the fountains were turned on the sprays were a shade of bright red.

Once the Frog Pond was repaired, the decayed stonework of the Cascade was replaced with particular attention to the horizontal ridges, which, given sufficient water power, produce a white water effect devised by Nesfield as a nod to his memory of Niagara Falls. Temple Hole itself was dredged to a depth of two or three feet, and a steel dam was inserted behind the Waterfall at the eastern end to prevent seepage through the wall. The original stone finials and globes, which Nesfield had so carefully copied from Vanbrugh's designs for the roofline of Castle Howard, were recovered in the mud below and reinstated on top of the Waterfall wall.

To give water a shape and direction is one of the greatest challenges of garden design. To do it well reaps many rewards: water reflects the light of the sky into the landscape and provides acoustical pleasures in its trickle and flow, and even roar, to say nothing of freshening and cooling the air. To follow the waterways at Castle Howard, the visitor pauses at the serene ponds of North Lake before turning up the long pathway to the Reservoir in Ray Wood. If it is February, there will be a field of tender snowdrops lining the way to the top, and in spring blooming rhododendron and azaleas that are part of the rare specimen collection introduced to Ray Wood beginning in 1968 by the plantsman James Russell. At the center of the Reservoir stands a solitary plinth embellished with carved water creatures.

The South Waterways begin at the Atlas Fountain, where from certain angles the water jets bouncing off the figure of Atlas create a cloud of mist that outlines the Portland stone figure and his globe in a whitish light. To walk along the edges of this water garden through daffodils in spring and appreciate each architectural detail in a bucolic landscape, with a swift course of water running through it, is to understand the meaning of landscape architecture. Arriving finally at the Mausoleum at the top of a windswept Yorkshire moor, the visitor looks back on a vista of open country to Castle Howard and to New River, the bridge with Roman arches, the Waterfall, Temple Hole, the Cascade, and the feathery plumes of the South Lake fountain to marvel at what Nesfield called in the end the "great picture."

Antiques, August 2003

Reclaiming Noble Gardens of the Towy Valley

WILD WALES, with its naturally picturesque landscape, gnarled trees, and trickling water, has come into its own in the garden world. With the founding last year of the Welsh Historic Gardens Trust in Llandeilo, in the county of Dyfed in South Wales, there is a new focus on recovering abandoned and ruined gardens and parks, many survivors of great country houses. Two formerly neglected gardens, which recently opened near Llandeilo, inspired the formation of the gardens trust, which will encourage restoration and provide expert advice.

The newly-opened places are Middleton Hall's late eighteenth-century woodland water garden with cascades and a weir, now reestablished, near Llanarthney; and Aberglasney, a cloister surmounted by terrace walks in Llangathen that dates to the seventeenth century, perhaps even earlier. Aberglasney is a romantic ruin on a small site, overrun with vines and inviting restoration.

The 250-acre Middleton Hall estate has been chosen by the trust as the site of the new National Botanic Garden of Wales. The hope is that it will join the Royal Botanic Gardens at Kew near London and the Royal Botanic Garden in Edinburgh as one of the three major botanic gardens in Britain. Kew Gardens and Dyfed County Council will help found it and assist in the design of a master plan.

A third newly-opened area is the seven-hundred-acre Dinefwr Park, a National Trust property in Llandeilo, that includes a mansion and the ruins of a thirteenth-century castle. The park, originally a private deer park established in 1660, is enhanced by landscaping added in the eighteenth century by "Capability" Brown.

What is notable about all three sites is that they retain the mystery and romantic aura of their past. Although the park, along with its castle and house, has historical significance as a once princely realm of Welsh kings and noble families, the impressive feature now is the preserved landscape. At both Middleton and Aberglasney, too, the landscape surpasses in importance the great house that gave birth and reason to its plan. As the cultural remains of different periods, these gardens and parks now represent a survey of the philosophy of landscape design for more than a century.

Wales already has more than two hundred historic gardens and parks, many of them restored and open to visitors. But with the planned national botanic garden, the restorations, and the presence of the gardens trust, Llandeilo in the Towy Valley could become the garden capital of the Principality. Ghillean T. Prance, the director of Kew, has already endorsed what he calls "the great potential of using our present knowledge to begin a contemporary botanic garden that will also benefit from a special historic site that includes a five-acre double-walled garden and waterworks leading down the valley." Furthermore, he stresses, "Wales now has the opportunity to develop its own themes including an emphasis on regional botanic forms and the interrelationship of local flora." He suggests the botanic garden as the appropriate location for a national collection of daffodils—the daffodil is the Welsh national flower.

As a traveler to Llandeilo, one feels akin to the inveterate seekers of the picturesque in the late eighteenth century, like William Gilpin, the English clergyman who cherished the woodlands, rocks, and ruined castles of South Wales—the elements that defined the rugged picturesque landscape. Approaching by narrow roads that wind through hilly, sheep-grazing meadows and hedgerows of hawthorn with a touch of yellow gorse or wild plum, one sees first from a considerable distance the two great clumps of trees that mushroom above the town from the highest hill, crested by the ruins of Dinefwr Castle and its park. When Gilpin recorded his views of Dinefwr Park in his 1782 *Observations on the River Wye, and Several Parts of South Wales,* he wrote, "I know of few places where a painter might study the qualities of surface with more advantage [and] that the woods were clumped with greater beauty."

According to Richard G. Keen, the historic buildings representative for the National Trust of South Wales, in the mid-1770s "Capability" Brown, the champion practitioner of the naturalistic landscape in England, wrote this after he had been to Dinefwr: "I wish my journey may prove of use to the place, which if it should, it will be very flattering to me. Nature has been truly bountiful and art has done no harm." What art he is assumed to have added to the existing medieval oak forest and meadows high above the Towy River, which snakes through the valley, are the majestic clumps of beech trees that were his signature. These sculptured clusters of trees are planted to look natural in the park.

Brown's plantation of trees is a transition from cultivated fields below to denser woodland and wild nature on the way to the castle ruins. The castle is a loose circular enclosure with a thirteenth-century keep, an inner parapet and outer battlements, and an eighteenth-century belvedere that commands a fine view over the park. Plas Dinefwr, the seventeenth-century mansion with its ornate gardens, was built on the site of a medieval settlement, gothicized in the nineteenth century with castellated turrets and surrounded by a ha-ha (a ditch-cum-wall). Of its own garden, only a few fruit trees remain.

The National Trust may soon occupy part of the house, which is privately owned, and the Venetian Gothic–style conservatory and the garden. In addition to installing historical exhibitions relating to the park, the National Trust hopes to bring to Dinefwr the National Eisteddfod, the annual contest of Welsh poets and musicians that dates to medieval times.

But now, nature is ascendant, and, if one stands in an open glade beyond the house, the design of the undulating parkland is clear. The house overlooks the water meadows just below the open pastures, where a herd of 140 deer is on the move (soon to be rejoined by the white cattle traditional to the park). A slow turnaround reveals a view of the castle above and, somewhat lower, the eye catches Brown's clumps of beeches. Although the combination is centuries old, there is the spirit of renewal in the violets and pale yellow primroses luminous against the mossy roots of ancient trees. One scholar calls it "a pastoral Westminster Abbey."

Beyond the hill and dale of the Welsh countryside are distant landmarks associated with the two other gardens, Grongar Hill near Aberglasney and Paxton's Tower, a folly overlooking Middleton Hall. The Welsh poet John Dyer was born at Aberglasney in 1699, in the house tucked away in a low-lying region east of the hill and that he describes as "a poet's home" in "The Country Walk," written in 1726:

> See her woods, where Echo talks,
> Her gardens trim, her terrace walks,
> Her wilderness, fragrant brakes,
> Her gloomy bow'rs, and shining lakes.

The recently rediscovered gardens at Aberglasney may no longer be trim, but all the elements he describes are still there. According to the British garden historian John Dixon Hunt, the three-sided cloistered courtyard and terrace walks above may be the only surviving example in Britain of this kind of Italianate Renaissance garden feature. Hunt, who is director of studies in landscape architecture at Dumbarton Oaks in Washington, D.C., believes some of the stonework may date to the sixteenth century and certainly to the seventeenth century, before the Dyer family acquired the property.

What is left of the early house with its nineteenth-century Ionic portico is near collapse and no longer as significant as the remains of the parapet garden. Encrusted with thorny rose vines and wildflowers growing in rock crevices, the terraces of Aberglasney are the quintessential romantic ruin, what Hunt calls a memory of the "inside-outside and up-down Italian garden terraces of the sixteenth century," rather than a copy of any specific model.

Rising to a height of more than twenty feet, the terrace walks, where evening strollers would have taken the air above the darker, more melancholy garden below, were reached by stone steps at either end, and structural remains hint at two summerhouses at the junctures where the side terraces meet the central one. A lower terrace overlooks a pond and evidence of another one to complete Dyer's "shining lakes." Outside the cloistered area is a large open garden, perhaps a kitchen garden, and, extending from the other side, a typical stone Welsh longhouse, no doubt for animals. Just steps away are the "gloomy bow'rs," a dense yew tunnel of centuries-old trees whose branches crisscross tightly above the tunnel's inner hollow. And on the pathway out is an intriguing Gothic-style stone arch that was perhaps a gateway to a sixteenth-century fortified manor or folly. The ensemble of all these rare elements at Aberglasney offers an ideal opportunity for archaeologists to determine the true dimensions of a style that would have come to Wales later than England but was eminently suited to its rugged terrain. One hopes that its mysterious beauty will not be lost in restoration.

Once scholars and archaeologists study archival and on-site evidence and measures have been taken to protect the infrastructure of the garden and its architecture, one of the quandaries facing restorers of ruined gardens is to determine what period in the past constitutes the appropriate state for the future of the garden. Middleton will be particularly challenging because the current 250 acres of the estate will be incorporated into the new National Botanic Garden of Wales, making its eighteenth-century setting of a water garden and park unique among botanic institutions. Middleton reached its height as an estate in the late eighteenth and early nineteenth centuries, when Sir William Paxton, a wealthy nabob who had been Mint Master in Calcutta, retired to the property and hired the architect Samuel Pepys Cockerell. In addition to the neo-Palladian mansion, Cockerell built a splendid eye-catcher, Paxton's Tower, on the top of a hill, where it could be seen from Dinefwr Park. The tower was dedicated to Admiral Lord Nelson. A three-story triangular structure with parapets and crenellated towers, it looks at home among the genuine ruined castles of neighboring hills.

In 1930, on Halloween, Middleton Hall burned to the ground, leaving only the servants' quarters and a handsome stable block. A new building, the design of which has yet to be decided, is planned at the site of the house to serve as the headquarters of the new botanic garden. The now vacant double-walled garden across the road offers splendid opportunities to the designers. At one time, it is thought espaliered fruit trees lined the facing walls and an herb garden was planted within a semicircular extension of the wall.

What is remarkable about Middleton was the development of the newest technologies of running water for both utilitarian and ornamental uses.

Crisscrossing the estate were terra-cotta aqueducts carrying cold water to the fountains and heated water to the conservatory. Just below the mansion, in a hilly, densely wooded area, the remnants of the entire network of a woodland water garden were rediscovered in the 1980s during a local forestry project. Water can take many shapes depending on speed and height, and here no effect has been neglected in restoring the conduits and cascades and setting them in motion again. As one walks on narrow trails through a thick forest of beech, ash, and hornbeam with sunlight filtering through the leafy canopy, this is magical space. Each water feature is an independent link in a chain of running brooks and channels with stone beds. A weir of dammed water is as smooth as glass, before water shoots through a sluice, then glides under a stone bridge and over a waterfall. A three-tiered cascade ends in a rush of water channeled through embankments incorporating fragments from the portico of Middleton Hall. Black Pond above is a smooth lake reflecting the low boughs of trees and yellow flag irises.

This is also a world of butterflies and wildflowers—celandine, wood anemones, and moschatel, a little flower called locally the "the town hall clock," because the delicate blossom faces four ways. Here the visitor can explore one of the goals of the new botanic garden: to recognize the role of the botanical sciences in the harmony of the natural environment.

For inspiration, the founders of the National Botanic Garden of Wales are harking back to seventeenth-century metaphysical poets like Andrew Marvell, who advocated a return to "where Nature was most plain and pure," for what distinguishes Welsh gardens is the quality of the natural landscape in which they are placed. This is where one finds the true picturesque.

New York Times, July 8, 1989

Classic Garden Tames a Fierce Welsh Crag: Powis Castle

THE SERENE beauty of the storybook castles that, like Powis Castle, rise above rolling green hills on the English-Welsh border, seems to belie the bellicosity of their past. The Marches, as the borderlands were known, once were a perennial battleground for marauding exploits between Welsh princes and Anglo-Norman knights.

After repeated destruction under siege and subsequent rebuilding, however, Powis Castle finally evolved in more steady times from an enclosed and forbidding fortress, on the site of a stronghold dating from the late eleventh or early twelfth century, into a stately country house with elegant furnishings and a garden carved from the barren cliff that once was the castle's chief defense. The formal terraced garden, with its ancient yews and box, its mellow red-brick retaining walls, and its architectural detail in the Italian style, is the oldest and grandest garden of its kind in Britain.

Sir Walter Scott, writing about twelfth-century Wales in one of his *Tales of the Crusaders* ("The Betrothed"), described the frontier as having been "fortified with castles" by rulers "thus making good what they had won." He introduced a "Prince of Powys," Gwenwyn, who in 1187 exercised "a precarious sovereignty over such parts of Powys-Land as had not been subjugated." For the Feast of Easter, Scott wrote in 1825, subjects and vassals were "invited in large numbers to partake a princely festivity at Castell-Coch, or the Red Castle, as it was then called, since better known by the name of Powis Castle."

"The architectural magnificence of this noble residence," Scott wrote, "is of a much later period than that of Gwenwyn, whose palace, at the time we speak of, was a long low-roofed edifice of red stone, whence the castle derived its name; while a ditch and palisade were, in addition to the commanding situation, its most important defenses." The castle Scott described in 1825 as a "noble residence" is the castle that stands, though greatly transformed, on a rocky bluff overlooking the Severn Valley a mile southwest of Welshpool, in the modern county of Powys (the correct spelling for the county). The sixth earl of Powis, in his early eighties, is still in residence, but the public areas and state rooms are on view.

Little of the twelfth-century Red Castle remains. By the thirteenth century it had become a complex of both stone and wood, but it was destroyed twice in local struggles, in 1233 and again in 1275. There was then a real Gruffyd ap Gwenwynwyn, whose son, Owain, was granted the remains of the castle and its lands as an English barony on condition that he give up his Welsh titles. He undertook the extensive rebuilding that by 1300 gave the castle its rambling, romantic form. His daughter, Hawys the Hardy (so called for defending her rights of inheritance), married an Englishman who added a moat, a drawbridge, and crenellated drum towers and battlements of the same red gritstone as before, highlighted by pink mortar.

That barony died out in 1551. Sir Edward Herbert bought the castle in 1587, beginning an era of possession by the Herbert family that lasted (with one gap) until the fourth earl of Powis gave the property to the National Trust before his death in 1952.

By the mid-1600s, the palisade falling steeply away from the ramparts had been in service as a defense for more than five hundred years. After 1644, when the castle fell to the Roundheads during the Civil War, defenses against siege were no longer needed. In the late seventeenth century, the first marquess of Powis began excavations to turn the palisade into a garden, and the result was not unlike the miraculous blossoming of the pope's staff in the finale of *Tannhäuser.*

Influenced by the sixteenth-century Italian terraced garden, as it had been interpreted in France and Holland before arriving in Britain, and probably advised by the architect and landscape designer William Winde, the first marquess created four stepped-down limestone terraces in the classical style, each two hundred yards across, parallel to the ramparts on the southeasterly aspect.

The Herbert family lost the castle in the late seventeenth century, after political reversals, to an illegitimate son of William III, the earl of Rochford. Lord Rochford may have continued work on the terraces, but it was not until after 1722, when the second marquess of Powis reacquired the property, that the terraces and plantings were completed. The orangery on the main terrace, with its eighteenth-century sash windows, was completed at the same time. A 1742 engraving by Samuel Beck, hanging in the long gallery, shows the castle and garden as they were supposed to look when all the plantings were in scale. There are some differences now, of course. The topiary yews along the top terrace, originally pyramid-shaped, now resemble enormous gumdrops, thirty feet high. The slope below the main terrace, a bare embankment in the engraving, is now overgrown by old apple trees, japonica, cotoneaster, mountain ash, dogwood, and Japanese maples—its high color in autumn has become a major attraction. A wilderness area was added in the eighteenth century. And the engraving shows a baroque fountain, on what is now the great lawn, that either never was built or has since been dismantled.

But the yews' shapes now are comfortable, and they have the soft, velvety texture of age. The plantings on the slope are spectacular through autumn. A narrow walk along the ridge of the wilderness area offers one of the finest views of the terraces. And the terrace garden does remain, the bare bones of its classical design intact, thanks in part to benign neglect during the eighteenth-century era when elsewhere in Britain formality went out of style. Several eighteenth-century paintings of the castle indeed show the garden in an overgrown state, and Lancelot "Capability" Brown, who did away with some of the best parterres in Britain in favor of the so-called natural park, is reputed to have suggested a return to bare rock. But he did not prevail, although one of his disciples, William Eames, created the wilderness. The garden, as it has developed with its fantastical yews and the controlled overgrowth on the slopes, is quite simply a style unto itself.

A countess of Powis, the wife of the fourth earl, reestablished the garden beds and borders (all lime-tolerant species) early in this century, and the National Trust has made further improvements. The trust also has provided a plant store in one of the stables and an excellent plant book and guide.

A good place to start is below the terraces. Looking up at the towering castle, one can see red stone crenellations silhouetted against blue sky. Then follow the paths that ascend along ancient yews, mounting the four hundred feet from terrace to terrace. Clematis, roses, and espaliered pear trees climb along the terrace walls. Vines and fragrant herbaceous borders are beautifully maintained, and planned for seasonal effects.

In the garden's architectural details—the gritstone balustrades with their mounted urns and lead statues of Arcadian figures, probably the work of the sculptor John Nost; the arcaded loggia on the second terrace—there are striking resemblances to the ornamented retaining walls surrounding the water garden behind the early seventeenth-century Villa Aldobrandini, on a steep hillside in Frascati. The proximity of the formal garden to a nearby wilderness area, a relaxation of the strictly classical convention, is another similarity.

North of the great lawn is the old kitchen garden, once a bowling green. Here are rows of apple and pear trees, pruned to pyramidal shapes, in an orchard first cultivated in the 1890s. Several trees have recently been replaced, offering an opportunity to see the stages of growth. Circling back to the castle through the wilderness area, developed for the most part in this century, one finds oaks predominating, as in all the best of Welsh woods, mixed here with yews and rhododendrons. The path passes an outdoor pool, once restricted for use by the ladies of the castle, where the presence of gardeners was not permitted after 11 A.M. A short distance up the valley is a 179-foot Douglas fir, thought to have been the tallest tree in the British Isles until a gale took off five feet about ten years ago.

Inside the castle courtyard, the warm red stone enhances the sense of enclosure. Architecturally, Elizabethan themes dominate the inside of the house: in the long gallery, with its wide oak floorboards and plasterwork ceiling design of fruits, flowers, and nuts, added by Sir Edward Herbert in 1592, and in the areas restored by the architect G. F. Bodley early in this century. The tastes and acquisitions of successive generations of the Herbert family have produced a comfortable mélange of Sevres china, military memorabilia, and paintings and furniture collected by the Lord Clive who conquered India for the British and served as governor of Bengal.

Lord Clive's son was created Earl of Powis after marrying Lady Henrietta Herbert, whose brother died without an heir, and after serving as governor of Madras. He brought many of his father's treasures to Powis Castle, among them Bernardo Bellotto's *View of Verona,* with the Castel San Pietro in the center, which hangs in the Oak Drawing Room near a portrait of Charles II by Sir Godfrey Kneller. The family later changed its name to Herbert.

In the dining room, once the common hall where soldiers and retainers ate, there is a portrait of Lord Clive by Nathaniel Dance. There also are paintings by George Romney and Sir Joshua Reynolds. Reynolds apparently added a hat to his portrait of Lady Henrietta Herbert after it was finished, to conceal what had become an unfashionable hairdo.

The main staircase hall and the library have early eighteenth-century ceiling and wall paintings by Lanscroon, and elsewhere there are tapestries from the Mortlake factory outside London, depicting the life of Nebuchadnezzar. The sumptuous State Bedroom is the only bedroom in the Louis XIV manner surviving in Britain. It has a gilded railing separating the bed from the part of the room where the King's guests might be expected to stand during a levée, as at Versailles. The room's tapestries from late seventeenth-century Brussels show scenes from the life of Suleiman the Magnificent.

Leaving the castle, at the end of the drive through the deer park, a visitor should pause to admire the luxuriant hedgerows that line the public road. They bear close study. Hedgerows in Wales are a dense, occasionally blossoming mixture of trees and shrubs—hawthorn, blackthorn, hazel, ash, oak—trained into shape by bending, crisscrossing and pruning. The technique is called "laying a hedge." Because of the automatic shearing machines now in use by local highway authorities, however, and a lessening of interest in the art, quality has been deteriorating. Hence a lobby for hedge preservation has been formed.

The view of the castle from this quiet road is medieval, romantic, and splendid.

New York Times, July 6, 1986

Buckhurst Park: From Humphry Repton to Edwin Lutyens and Gertrude Jekyll

THE COUNTESS De La Warr has learned that happiness often comes disguised as duty. In 1972, she was invited at the last minute to fill out a foursome at a bridge party in London. Rather than beg off, she graciously accepted, and at the party she met her future husband.

In 1988, he came into his title as the eleventh Earl De La Warr. Part of his inheritance was Buckhurst Park, the 2,200-acre country estate in Withyham, East Sussex, a property of woodland and farmland that had been in the family since the eleventh century. (One Lord De La Warr was the first governor general of Virginia.) While the sixteenth-century manor house required some attention, the gardens had been sadly neglected, with crumbling structures overgrown with weeds.

There is no way to prepare for the moment of inheritance. The couple had been living in London with only weekend visits to their cottage on the estate, and Lady De La Warr had never so much as handled a rake. Nevertheless, she offered to oversee the daunting task of restoring the gardens. "I did not know anything about gardening when I undertook the project, and I made many mistakes," she says, "but I have found it fascinating and interesting the more I learn."

Today, the gardens of Buckhurst spread out in rich and beautiful order, and the countess's achievement is all the more impressive for the fact that she was given stewardship over one of the most historically significant patches of greenery in England. For the Buckhurst gardens comprise a unique compendium of several of the signal British landscape design styles.

For generations, the plantings on the estate—originally called Stonelands—had remained pretty much as they were when the earl's ancestors in the Sackville family took possession in the eleventh century. Then, beginning in the early 1800s, the grounds became the object of successive improvements by some of the country's greatest garden planners. The first to visit, in 1805, was Humphry Repton, the day's leading landscape gardener to the gentry. Influenced by the picturesque school, Repton admired "wild" (yet, of course, carefully planned and maintained) vistas, and was particularly taken with scenic possibilities in a string of small lakes on the estate. The manor was the subject of one of Repton's famous before-and-after design guides, known as the "Red

Books," titled *Hints, Plans and Sketches for the Improvement of Stonelands* (preserved at Yale University's Beinecke Library).

The next designer to leave his mark was Lewis Kennedy, a fashionable landscaper who had worked at Malmaison for the Empress Josephine. He came to Buckhurst in 1819 and made ambitious plans, which he also laid out in a book, still owned by the family, called *Notitiae.* It includes several archetypical Romantic garden designs, most notably plans for such landscape "vignettes" as a rustic wooden Swiss bridge that spans a dramatic waterfall.

Last, in 1903, Buckhurst came to the attention of the famed landscaping team of architect Sir Edwin Lutyens and garden designer Gertrude Jekyll. Their major and lasting contribution was a gorgeous series of three stone-walled terraces—formal gardens, as the countess describes them, "dropped into a wilderness"—that descend down a hillside, framing wonderful views into the valley below. By the late 1980s, these terrace gardens were unplanted and collapsing. Like their predecessors, Jekyll and Lutyens left behind extensive plans and drawings—Jekyll's planting plans were rediscovered in a drawer at Buckhurst, and Lutyens's drawings were consulted at the Royal Institute of British Architects.

Soon after moving into the manor house, the countess restored the Swiss Bridge to Kennedy's specifications with new logs and rebuilt the rockery below the cascade. Following Repton's plans, she thinned out the woods along the lakes—a process aided by the huge windstorm of 1987 that blew down many overgrown trees—to achieve a broken and therefore lighter reflection in the water. Today the scene, with clumps of trees and black-and-white sheep grazing in green pastures, looks remarkably like one of Repton's "after" illustrations. Lady De La Warr also planted wild cherry trees on the banks of the lakes. As they have matured, the trees cover the landscape with clouds of blossoms.

Restoring the terraces has been the most complex and time-consuming task. Encompassing the mixture of architectural and planting features that made the Lutyens-Jekyll collaboration so important to the Arts and Crafts period, the terraces create a visual surprise. When visitors begin at the top, each level of the garden only reveals itself as they descend sets of rounded staircases. The upper terrace features a lily pool enclosed by flower borders; on the second and third levels, massive stone buttresses form pockets to protect flowerbeds from strong winds. On the lowest terrace, Lutyens set a grottolike domed fountain into a wall, and flanking the terraces, like wings at either side, are two stone-columned pergolas, which the countess intends to plant with roses, wisteria, honeysuckle, and other vines for continuous blooming. Visually, they embrace the Reptonian landscape in the valley below in one of the happiest confluences in an English garden.

When executed, this scheme will be one of many ways the countess has made her own mark on the gardens. She planted the terraces in the spirit of Jekyll, with lavender, nepeta, salvia, alchemilla, gorse, and digitalis, but has focused, she says, on "all the roses I love, and that grow so well in the clay Sussex soil." She will continue to experiment and make changes, she says, because she believes that only the architectural framework should remain unchanged. In addition, the countess oversees a kitchen garden, two greenhouses, and an orchard. One of her loveliest touches has been to train climbing roses across the facade of the house—a gesture that unites Buckhurst's past with the present.

Looking over the grounds on a Sunday morning, as the bells of the Sackville family chapel toll in the distance, one feels certain that Humphry Repton would compliment the countess as he did her predecessor some two hundred years ago: "Her Grace's good taste confirms my [hopes for] rescuing the art of landscape-gardening from the hands of ignorance, or mistaken fashion."

Gardens Illustrated, 2011

Lanning Roper's English Gardens with a U.S. Flavor

THE WORLD of English landscape gardening is an area of enterprise as closed to outsiders as are the gardens within their protective walls. Yet, for more than thirty years, one American was able to penetrate the secret and sometimes sacred garden doors of England. That man was the late Lanning Roper.

Roper, born in West Orange, New Jersey, in 1912, and a 1933 fine-arts graduate of Harvard, came to be recognized as one of England's preeminent landscape designers and horticultural journalists. His landscaping and architectural skills, which helped plan the formal gardens of aristocratic estates, the herbaceous borders along country cottage walks, and the terraces of London town houses, were sought worldwide. In the United States, his work can be seen at Ludwig Mies van der Rohe's Farnsworth House along the Fox River in Plano, Illinois.

Roper succeeded in creating nearly 150 quintessential English landscapes that bear his mark of quiet profusion: distinctive borders with lavender spilling onto pathways, walls covered with a tangle of vines, endless varieties of old-fashioned roses, and a preference for silver-gray foliage as a useful foil for flowers. What appeared as romantic informality derived, nevertheless, from the precision of certain knowledge sharpened during years of study and training.

At the height of Chelsea Flower Show week in London, Roper's numerous former clients, associates, and friends will gather for the opening of the Lanning Roper Memorial Garden behind Trinity Hospice, a hospital for the terminally ill in a group of eighteenth-century town houses on Clapham Common North Side. Prior to his death last year in London, Roper had advised on a plan for the restoration of these gardens, an almost two-acre parklike area of stately trees, sweeping lawns with hilly contours, and undulating paths with flower borders in muted shades.

Roper grew up in Closter, New Jersey, a town near the Palisades, the high stone cliffs along the Hudson River. "I had a series of gardens there," he once wrote, "and spent much time roaming wooded slopes that stretched from our house to the Palisades collecting wildflowers . . . gardens and flowers were the great interest of my life." Although he planned on becoming a landscape architect after his graduation from Harvard, his final career was delayed by the Depression. For a few years he taught at the Buckley School in New York and frequently traveled in the summer as a tutor. "Newport [Rhode Island] is where I got my first taste of grand gardens," he reported. Finally, in the late 1930s, he traveled to the Continent and then to England, where he fell in love with English landscapes, architecture, and gardens.

During World War II, he commanded a troop of ships in the U.S. Navy that participated in the first landing on D-day. By coincidence, for the next six weeks he was stationed near Exbury, the great Rothschild estate near Southampton famous for its rhododendron gardens. "Here I had my first introduction to English rhododendrons," he wrote, "and could not have been happier in the evenings roaming through the great gardens and woodland." The romance was sealed.

After a brief sojourn in business following the war, he returned to America for a serious talk with his investment-banker father, Willet Crosby Roper, and then took the plunge. He trained as a student gardener for two years at the Royal Botanic Gardens, Kew, working in the rock gardens and the nurseries, and mastered the practical aspects of gardening while he learned the complete collection of plants. He spent another year at the Royal Botanic Garden at Edinburgh, specializing in rhododendrons, and then visited every important garden in the British Isles and on the Continent. The personal style he developed included underlying references to Italian and French gardens in the classical tradition that he also admired.

During four years as assistant editor of the Royal Horticultural Society's journal, he developed his skills as a horticultural journalist. By 1956, he was writing for *Country Life* and other journals. For thirteen years, beginning in 1962, he was the garden correspondent of the *Sunday Times,* and the columns were popular because they so obviously sprang from his direct contact with a wide range of gardens and the great variety of English soils. In the introduction to his *Sunday Times Gardening Book*, he wrote, "I make it a rule to select personally the plants for my designs, and, whenever possible, I supervise the planting and often do a good deal of it myself."

There were five other books, either descriptions of famous gardens he admired or practical guides based on his experience: *Royal Gardens* (1953); *Successful Town Gardening* (1957); *The Gardens in the Royal Park at Windsor* (1959); *Hardy Herbaceous Plants* (1960); *The Gardens at Anglesey Abbey* (1964). What makes all of them appealing is their clarity. In the appendices to *Successful Town Gardening,* for example, he has specific directions for pruning some seventy-one different genera of trees. There are always long waiting lists for these books with both American and English rare-book dealers.

The tradition Roper embraced was in a direct line with the work of earlier landscape designers—the contoured "natural" landscapes and water features of Lancelot "Capability" Brown and the later improvements of Humphry Repton that brought formal gardens closer to the manor houses. Roper's mixture of certain colors and his love of silver-gray foliage came from Gertrude Jekyll.

Roper advised on the restoration of important country estates that belonged to titled hands; other gardens were his own creation; and often he was called upon to make a large garden smaller and more labor-saving. He had a tactful way of suggesting an idea that made an owner feel it was his as well.

Although Lanning Roper was not a draftsman, his closely typed reports were rare documents that made a garden visible. The four or five pages he wrote after a first visit to a garden summarized the existing layout and spelled out his plans for future changes. Some of his headings were "The Long Rhododendron Border," "Contouring," and, simply, "Fragrance." "I rate fragrance high," Roper was known to say. The reports were then made periodically, with maintenance schedules.

He had no office or permanent staff, except for an excellent secretary, Anne Terry, preferring direct contact with the estate gardeners and local nurserymen with whom he unfailingly struck a good rapport. In later years, he worked out of his maisonette at 29A Clarendon Gardens near Little Venice, where he maintained a small terrace garden that included fragrant lilies. During his marriage, which lasted until 1965, he lived with his wife, the artist Primrose Harley, at Park House, off Onslow Square in South Kensington; their courtyard and garden were integral to his work and his writing.

The special beauty of Lanning Roper's herbaceous borders derives from giving each plant its own space so that form and color have equal significance. He had a preference for grays and blues, and in one typical planting in Lord and Lady Gibson's garden at Penns in the Rocks, Sussex, he alternated beds of blue rue, santolina, and box with pear trees growing in beds of pink rugosa roses. Yellow toned down by white was another favorite combination.

"When I let my thoughts wander to the perfect garden," he wrote, "roses are the first flower that always comes to mind. How I love them . . . in all the gardens . . . including the cottage gardens of country lanes, where climbers and bushes grow over the sheds and walls, through the trees and even in the hedgerows."

Roper traveled widely in a sweep from Ireland, where one garden at Glenveagh Castle was once owned by his Harvard classmate Henry P. McIlhenny, to France and the Aga Khan's residence in Gouvieux, and on to Geneva for the lakeside garden of Prince Sadruddin Aga Khan. He also returned often to America, and in the fall and spring of recent years, he came to oversee work on two very different landscape plans.

The first he called the "river landscape," by Mies's Farnsworth House, owned by London property developer Peter Palumbo. He replaced the direct driveway that bisected the meadow behind the house with a winding road through a new oak and maple allée a distance from the house. He then restored the meadow in the fashion of an English park. Also English-style are the "pools" of daffodils of different varieties; in spring, those nearest the glass-and-steel house bloom first, starting a succession of ever-widening circles of gold.

The second American garden is at Ananouri, the country house of Mr. and Mrs. Constantine Sidamon-Eristoff that perches on a cliff overlooking the Hudson River in upstate New York. Here he began by extending the lawn to the cliff edge, the better to view the river from an English-style bench. The new library terrace is planted with lavender and clematis, and a former solid wall of several varieties of rhododendrons has been divided by a stairway that makes the configuration a formal gateway to the outer meadows.

When Lord Snowdon asked Lanning Roper to design his London town house garden, it was, he said, "much like getting 'Capability' Brown to do a window box." But all gardens, especially those in town, were a challenge, and Lord Snowdon's is a junglelike green garden in the Caribbean manner, and one that makes an excellent backdrop for Snowdon's fashion photographs.

There are other urban landscapes as well. Churchyards in London are places of respite, like vest-pocket parks in Manhattan, and Roper transformed the yard behind Christopher Wren's 1679 Church of St. Stephen Walbrook with a mahonia tree, camellias, rhododendrons, scillas, and daffodils. He was consulted on the plantings for the roof garden of the new Ismaili Center, across from the tower of the Victoria and Albert Museum. He also drew up a landscaping plan for a new London square, Mansion House Square, which is projected to go next to a proposed office building which Mies designed in 1967. In this plan, Roper emphasized the importance of hardiness, fragrance, and seasonal color and the patterns of light and shadow from leafy trees. Even in estate landscaping, he retained a fondness for gingkos and honey locusts, the New York street trees he used to pass in his young teaching days.

"Among the charms of London," he wrote in *Successful Town Gardening,* "are the numerous parks and squares with their landscaped lawns, well kept paths, fountains, flower beds and trees and shrubs. The houses which overlook them, in a few cases with gardens adjoining, have a feeling of spaciousness which it is impossible to achieve in any other way in built-up areas save possibly by a river view."

Finally, he consulted on the landscaping of the Sainsbury Centre at the University of East Anglia in Norfolk, on the gardens of the Royal Horticultural Society at Wisley and on properties of the National Trust. Among these were Chartwell and Scotney Castle, where he created a circular herb garden around a Venetian wellhead and against the picturesque ruins of the old seventeenth-century castle.

Besides the Lanning Roper Memorial Garden in London, a second, though private, garden of remembrance has been planted in America. By the Mies house in Illinois, a small wooden sign announces "The Lanning Roper Wild-flower Walk" at the entrance to a woodland path. Here, Palumbo and friends planted, among many varieties originally suggested by Roper, trillium, Dutchman's breeches, columbine, hostas, and honeysuckle in a natural arrangement and labeled with their botanical names. Wire mesh around a few trees trains the clematis to climb. Here one remembers the boy who began by collecting wildflowers on the Palisades overlooking the Hudson.

New York Times Magazine, May 13, 1984

Machine in the Garden: Charles Jencks's Garden of Scottish Worthies

*U*NLIKE ARCHITECTURE, which requires solidity to provide shelter over time regardless of style, landscaped gardens are ephemeral by nature. They may possess a degree of flamboyance and fantasy expressive of the philosophical tone of their times and their creators without concerns for function. This is particularly true among the rolling hills of southwest Scotland, where in Portrack, just north of Dumfries near the English border, Charles Jencks, the American theorist, architect, and (increasingly) landscape architect, and his late wife, Maggie Keswick, created a thirty-acre garden on a family estate that engages both the mind and the senses. Known as the Garden of Cosmic Speculation, it was completed for the most part in 2002. Every landscape design by Jencks, no matter how bucolic in appearance, incorporates a symbolically loaded theory, since for him traveling and creating gardens is a challenging and liberating intellectual pursuit.

In this pastoral setting at Portrack, however, suddenly one hears the long drone of a train whistle as freight cars rattle by just beyond the garden. Although Keswick's father had screened out Railtrack's right-of-way across his property with a double row of poplars that rustle soothingly in the wind, the London–Glasgow line makes its presence felt as trains speed along the garden's edge before crossing the River Nith.

When Railtrack, now Network Rail, announced in 2002 that the 1845 bridge over the Nith and a sandstone viaduct leading to it were dangerously weakened by heavier loads of coal freight, Jencks was faced with the company's proposition to move the tracks ninety-eight feet farther east, still on the property. With his customary ingenuity, Jencks offered, and Network Rail accepted, a counterproposal: He, along with engineers Scott Wilson Group, would design the new bridge across the river if the company would construct and fund a two-linear-acre garden for him along the original tracks using the detritus from the old bridge and the railroad bed. This garden would encompass the spirit of Leo Marx's "noise clashing through harmony," from his book *The Machine in the Garden* (1964), where he quotes Ralph Waldo Emerson's journal entry: "I hear the whistle of the locomotive in the wood. Wherever that music comes it has its sequel. It is the voice of the civility of the Nineteenth Century saying, 'Here I am.'"

Jencks sees the rail garden as a continuation of his adjacent Garden of Cosmic Speculation, only on a new theme. For the earlier garden, Jencks devised the Snake and Snail grass mounds (the latter wrapped around with pathways in the form of a double helix) interpolated with paisley-shaped lakes. (Similar mounds surrounded by ponds are also features of his designs at the Gallery of Modern Art, Edinburgh, and a the new Parco Portello, Milan.) Reflecting Keswick's expertise in Chinese gardens, a series of seven fanciful, bright red bridges cross the streams and rivulets channeled into this former swampland.

For the theme of the new garden, Jencks pays tribute to his adopted country by saluting the events and forces responsible for the evolution of Scotland from a bellicose clan culture into an autonomous region with sophisticated urban centers. After reading Arthur Herman's *The Scottish Enlightenment: The Scots' Invention of the Modern World* (2002), he discovered, he writes, a "narrative adequate to the impact of trains on social progress"—hence, the Garden of Scottish Worthies. Jencks took his cue from William Kent's Temple of British Worthies at Stowe in Buckinghamshire (c. 1734), a Roman-style masonry screen with sixteen busts of Whig heroes set in niches.

One need only travel through the Dalveen Pass in Scotland on the way to Jencks's garden to perceive how the soft green hills sloping into valleys have created a mound culture. In lieu of niches and busts, Jencks has constructed seventeen moundettes on the old rail bed parallel to the new one, each a tribute to a man or woman who influenced the Scottish Enlightenment. They contributed to the rational, creative, even poetic aspects not only of Scottish society but the world at large from the eighteenth to the late twentieth century. Planted with yellow-blossomed mahonia japonica, each animal-like mound is secured by a boulder head, a concrete beam, and ballast shoulders. A red flange element from the old bridge supports a raised, ten-foot, brushed-aluminum sign where the name, dates, and a saying of the worthy are laser-cut in open letters and read against the sky. Taken together, these "epigrams" compose a single train of thought over time. At the head of this chain of progress, a petite yellow, green, and red engine, contributed by Network Rail, appears to be pulling the mounds and their "passengers" into the landscape. The philosophers Frances Hutcheson and David Hume and the political economist Adam Smith lead off, followed by the poet Robert Burns (who lived near Portrack), the industrialist Andrew Carnegie, and the writer Rebecca West.

Pathways wind down from the mounds—the high road—through green slopes to the original screen of forty poplar trees along the low road. Dangling from each tree is a red aluminum banner with a plain aluminum cut fringe demarcating events over seventeen hundred years, which Jencks calls The

Bloodline—blood referring to clan and tribal vendettas and later warfare, as well as intermarriage. He begins with the slaughter of Caledonians by the Roman general Agricola in A.D. 84 and ends with the opening of the new Scottish Parliament in 1999. Behind this scholarly history is the myth of Scota, the daughter of an Egyptian pharaoh, who brought the sacred stone to the Promised Land east of Ireland.

As the culmination of the garden's design, the first moundette gradually transmutes into two long, sloping mounds like legs that terminate in a hillock-cum-derrière, a lookout point over the swift-flowing Nith and the new railroad bridge. A splendid piece of industrial architecture, the single-span arches and zigzag trusses of the 295-foot-long bridge are painted rust red, as are the massive fluted concrete piers on land, relating them to the small bridges in the Garden of Cosmic Speculation. A remaining section of the old bridge, also painted red, cantilevers out as a walkway over the river, offering views of the natural contours of the Scottish hills beyond with their symphony of blended greens that Jencks believes are reflected in the Scottish tartans. The true rail garden, with a crisscross of rusted rails in a field of red ballast and interplanted with zigzag rows of wild strawberry plants, is on an incline between the two bridges. The restored nineteenth-century sandstone viaduct, with its four arches along a meandering stream, lives on for Jencks, like a ruin in the Roman campagna of Poussin's paintings. A third bridge, a new red flange connecting two berms, serves as a gateway to open meadows and the new fishhenge Jencks was required to build lower down the river for local fishermen. In addition to a small hut, the riverside site features another Jencks installation, a deliberate scattering of stones representing a cross-section of the galaxy with superclusters and a Stonehenge-style summer solstice moment.

With all these endeavors, Jencks acknowledges the assistance of his head gardener and master craftsman, Alistair Clark. In framing the theoretical concept behind the garden, Jencks refers to landscape historian John Dixon Hunt's *Greater Perfection: The Practice of Garden Theory* (2000), in which he defines the three natures of gardens, based on Cicero and later Italian humanists: first the wilderness, then farming and husbandry, and finally the development of the art of gardening. To this sequence, Jencks adds a precursor, the underlying laws of nature, and a successor, today's landscape of industrial waste. By artfully using and reshaping the remains of the railway, and incorporating rather than camouflaging the speeding trains into the pastoral setting, he designed the new rail garden to complement in structure and technique his earlier achievements. As evocative as the garden is of Scotland and its industrial landscape, Jencks clarifies his goals, saying, "I don't do ornament, I do symbolism." He has delved so deeply into the character of place that he seems to have adopted the epigram of one of his worthies—Sir Walter Scott's "This is my own, my native land."

Architectural Record, July 2009. Reprinted with permission from *Architectural Record* © 2009 The McGraw-Hill Companies. www.architecturalrecord.com

Sitting in the Garden: A History

IN *The Portrait of a Lady,* Henry James knew how to draw his reader's eye into a view by conjuring up "the lawn of an old English country-house, in . . . the perfect middle of a splendid summer afternoon. . . . The shadows on the perfect lawn were straight and angular; they were the shadows of an old man sitting in a deep wicker-chair near the low table on which the tea had been served." In scenes like this, garden furniture becomes movable architecture. Unlike its structural cousins—stone walls, gates, pergolas, and arbors—that enclose areas of the garden and give it form, seating becomes a prop on a outdoor stage, modulated by light and shadow.

In paintings and prints of landscapes and gardens, garden seats, so nearly like human figures, appear to populate gardens; and as ornamental fixtures, they may even become organically entwined with the plant life around them. In a seventeenth-century view of the gardens at Ham House in Richmond, near London, shell-backed *sgabella* chairs, usually found in halls, alternate with Versailles planters to form an outdoor corridor for the Duke and Duchess of Lauderdale, who are about to begin their procession through the formal garden.

What we think of now as garden furniture developed with the English landscape movement in the eighteenth century. Previously, in formal gardens a marble bench or exedra at the end of a crosswalk provided respite on a promenade. But the openness of a naturalistic landscape without symmetrical limits invited society to move around and to pause, preferably seated, and gaze out on picturesque views. Often a gathering would take place right outside the house, with tables and chairs brought from inside onto the lawn along with an Oriental carpet that defined the space as a room, as hedges had previously done.

On a summer day in 1752, Sir Joshua Vanneck, a newly created baronet, and his family posed in such a manner for the English artist Arthur Devis outside Roehampton House near London. In a popular "at home" portrait or "conversation piece" of the period, Sir Joshua, a prosperous financier of Dutch descent, stands by a tree with nine members of his family on his terrace overlooking the Thames River. In this composition, the gray seats both define the limits of the group and echo the linearity of Putney Bridge. The straight-legged benches with a hint of ears at the ends of the crest rails are in a simplified rococo style. The small pedestal table appears to be the tilt-top variety, making it handy and portable for use in the garden.

In the beginning, most outdoor furniture repeated or suggested counterparts in the *salon*, but one chair, the Windsor, evolved in England around 1720 specifically to be used outdoors by the upper classes. One of Sir Joshua's daughters is seated in a Windsor; identifiable by the spindled back and the upward scroll of the crest rail visible behind her satin-draped shoulder. Generally, as this portrait indicates, furniture made for the outdoors tended to be painted in colors that blend with stone or bark.

In his portrait of members of the Maynard family, Devis includes a Windsor settee with elaborately turned legs and a child's seat as an extension of the right arm. The lightness and versatility of the Windsor, its strength and durability, and the many possible decorative variations made it ideally suited to use outdoors in England and the American colonies, where it also flourished.

The idealized landscapes that garden designers were striving to achieve in England in the eighteenth century were natural to America. One of the most picturesque landscapes in America to this day is to be seen from the columned piazza behind George Washington's house, Mount Vernon, in Virginia, so beautifully sited overlooking grassy slopes, clustered trees, and a great swath of the Potomac River. According to Kathryn R. Meehan, acting chief of horticultural services at the Smithsonian Institution in Washington, D.C., "The late eighteenth century is when the garden began to be used in America, when people began to sit and enjoy their land and their prosperity as they looked out on natural vistas." George Washington, who oversaw most of the purchases for Mount Vernon himself, took advantage of his vista in 1796 by ordering a number of Windsor chairs from the Philadelphia chair-making brothers Robert and Gilbert Gaw, and placed them along the piazza for his guests. (In correspondence, Washington called the Windsor a chair for "common sitting" when he ordered his first one from a London agent.)

When the inventory of Martha Washington was taken after her death in 1802, there were still twenty-four Windsors aligned on the piazza, which continued to be the center of the family's social life from early spring until late autumn. In a rare watercolor, the architect and artist Benjamin Henry Latrobe captured the family there one afternoon at tea. Washington peers at distant ships through a telescope, while his wife presides at the tea table before a steaming urn. She sits in one of two Windsor armchairs, both of which have the upholstered seat cushions she preferred. The Windsors lining the piazza today, more recent versions, may not be upholstered, but sitting in them vividly imparts what life was once like at Mount Vernon. Times may have changed, but the view, remarkably, has not.

Isolated in a landscape, garden chairs became decorative objects on their own, offering both a destination on a promenade and the hope of repose. In an 1801 watercolor, the English landscape gardener and theorist Humphry Repton gave equal status in a vista to a classical urn and two Windsor chairs on opposite banks of a lake at Wimpole, the seat of the earls of Hardwicke. Repton painted this scene for the Wimpole Red Book, one of his handsome presentation manuscripts bound in the red Morocco that gave these unique volumes their name. "There are certain situations in which some object is absolutely necessary to break the monotony of green," Repton wrote, "and it is nowhere more desirable than in these dark recesses of water where it may be doubled by reflection. . . . A Painter's eye will instantly be aware of the great importance which may be derived from an Urn so placed or even a garden chair upon the margin of the water."

A particularly magical rendition of a Windsor chair in moody isolation is found in a Repton drawing of the cast-iron Gothic pavilion he designed, but never built, for Plas Newydd, the great Welsh country house on the Isle of Anglesey overlooking the Menai Strait. Casting a long shadow in pale moonlight, the chair is witness to a trysting couple. In Repton's characteristic before and after views of his own cottage in the village of Hare Street, Essex, a Windsor in an after view becomes a humble and homey spectator to the flower borders.

In the exhibition "An English Arcadia, 1600–1990: Designs for Gardens and Garden Buildings in the Care of the National Trust," now traveling around the United States, several views of Stowe in Buckinghamshire demonstrate how garden seating was integral to formal sightseeing. Like Louis XIV, who used a stately mobile chair at Versailles to view the gardens, Lord and Lady Cobham are seen in an engraving by Jacques Rigaud and Bernard Baron being wheeled in what appears like oversized Windsors rigged up on platforms with large wheels. Oddly, this engraving was commissioned by the landscape gardener Charles Bridgeman and not by Lord Cobham, who looks a bit melancholy as he contemplates the temple at Stowe, designed by Sir John Vanbrugh.

By the time Thomas Rowlandson sketched at Stowe, William Kent had made his naturalistic improvements, and his Temple of British Worthies, viewed from across the Elysian Fields, has a relaxed and bucolic atmosphere. More to the point, the two benches with curved arms, most likely designed by Kent himself, take on different roles. The one placed in the middle of the semicircular temple, with its display of important busts, has a ceremonial role, almost like an isolated throne, while the one across the water is a companionable participant in a day of picnicking and sightseeing. At Stourhead in Wiltshire, on the other hand, visitors making the historic circuit around the lake to view the Temple of Apollo and the Palladian bridge were probably happy enough to come upon a round rustic seat at the edge of the woodland path.

That agreeable hour "dedicated to the ceremony known as afternoon tea," as Henry James called it, was a theme of nineteenth-century drawings made outdoors. None perhaps is as famous as Sir John Tenniel's illustration of this passage from Lewis Carroll's 1865 *Alice's Adventures in Wonderland* that begins: "There was a table set out under a tree in front of the house, and the March Hare and the Hatter were having tea at it. . . . 'No room!' they cried out when they saw Alice coming. 'There's plenty of room!' said Alice indignantly, and she sat down in a large arm-chair at one end of the table." Tenniel's armchair for Alice is an outrageously large tufted concoction exuding the commodiousness and comfort of a Victorian interior.

In contrast, the straight-backed chairs in Kate Greenaway's drawing of three young ladies in white taking tea in the garden enhance the primness of the occasion. She has brought the indoors outdoors, creating a tidy room within the garden against a tapestry of flowers.

In *The Open Air Breakfast,* William Merritt Chase has created another outdoor room, this one in his Park Slope, Brooklyn, New York, backyard, peopling the scene with members of his family against a backdrop of shrub roses and a wooden slat fence. Among exotic props from his studio decorating the scene, including a Japanese screen and two rattan chairs, the ubiquitous Windsor chair looks as much at home here around 1888, draped in a paisley shawl, as it did a century earlier.

French gardens and public parks of the late nineteenth century were enhanced by the lightweight and graceful metal chairs (best when painted pale green) that became their hallmark. In a painting of his brother sitting in his garden in 1878, Gustave Caillebotte captured the quintessential corner with two oversized Versailles planters and four of these chairs with a matching table. The chairs, with seats made of spokes radiating out like rays of the sun and backs of slightly ballooned rungs, represent another form that has been translated over the years into newer versions that have never lost the connotations of the original. Stacked up in a Parisian park after a first snowfall, they become an important graphic element offset by rows of bare trees and children at play in a 1955 photograph by Edouard Boubat. In this country, they are a main feature of the terrace at Chesterwood, the restored home in Stockbridge, Massachusetts, of the sculptor Daniel Chester French; in the American version, the seat pattern is usually repeated on the back.

As seen in an old photograph, when Claude Monet painted his long, horizontal canvases of the water lilies at Giverny in France, he brought his garden bench inside the studio, thus completing the garden view. These benches, now painted bright green, continue to be an attractive feature of the restored garden.

In the nineteenth century, garden seating became whimsical. In England, lightweight, reeded, wrought-iron benches were made with segmented backs in circles and scrolls that would appear from a distance like fine tracery in white against green hedges. These, and heavier, cast-iron benches in patterns of ferns and tree branches, were painted white and became formal objects in the garden, as ornamental as urns. In America, these cast-iron seats, incorporating twining grapevines or medallions in seasonal motifs, were frequently placed like monuments in the nineteenth-century cemetery parks that were the American equivalent of the English landscaped garden. So realistic did these castings become that tree-trunk stools could be fashioned that were almost identical to the real thing.

At the turn of the century, architects and garden designers began to create garden furniture along with walls and trellises. According to garden historian Jane Brown, the English landscape designer William Robinson once wrote, "It is rare to see a garden seat that is not an eyesore." That was before he met the architect Sir Edwin Lutyens, who designed for him a six-bay seat around a tree at Gravetye Manor, Robinson's garden in Sussex. From Lutyens's sketch it appears to be a graceful addition to the garden, with its back composed of rungs that recall the old Windsors. Lutyens also injected humor in a design he made for a wheelbarrow garden seat that added handles and a wheel to a garden bench.

What is known though as the Lutyens garden seat is a distinctive broad bench with a curved crest, horizontal splats, and roll-over arms that was probably created around 1905 for Hestercombe in Taunton, Somerset, where Lutyens collaborated with Gertrude Jekyll in designing E. W. B. Portman's garden. Jekyll was against using "tyrannical" white and preferred instead to let the natural wood weather, as it has in her own photograph of a Lutyens seat placed under the half-timbered gallery of her house, Munstead Wood. Against the wall, it becomes integral to the architecture of the house, rather than the garden, and it offers seclusion in a recess under the clematis vine. (She was not against purely rustic seating, as can be seen in another of her photographs of a garden seat made of encrusted tree trunks.)

Her counterpart in America, the landscape gardener Beatrix Farrand, also sought seclusion by tucking a bench she had designed under the vine-draped eaves of Reef Point, her house in Bar Harbor, Maine. To date, this example, with masterfully turned spindles, was a unique design, which only now is being reproduced in limited quantity. As a truly American bench, it could rival the Lutyens bench as a fixture in American gardens.

In another American vignette, in a parlor chair of no particular but pleasantly massive design, President William McKinley's wife, Ida, sits in a secluded bower in the glass conservatory at the White House in a photograph taken in 1900. Long gone, the conservatory was once a major attraction on the grounds of the White House. In general, the social life of the garden determined its ornamental furnishings. For example, as croquet became a popular pastime on American lawns, a specialized spectator bench was devised with a folding tentlike awning, making it one of the most practical and alluring inventions for the out-of-doors.

America contributed heavily to garden furniture styles during the era of the great camps in the Adirondack Mountains early in this century. In addition to rustic chairs and benches fashioned of interlaced twigs and branches, a chair was invented that has become as American as the picket fence. Known as the Adirondack chair, it is as popular and pervasive on front lawns now as the Windsor chair once was. Since about 1930, this chair, with its elongated back legs, high slanted and fanned-out slat back, and wide arms for drinks (not tea), has become the icon of American summers. Fairfield Porter captured its essence in his painting *July:* a wide expanse of lawn, a stand of evergreens, and three gleaming white Adirondack chairs in profile with their legs lunging out like ballerinas. The Jamesian lawn is still there, but the set has changed over the years.

Antiques, June 1992

Five

French

The Gardens of Versailles

> *En sortant du château par le vestibule qui est sous*
> *la chambre du roy, on sera sur la terrasse . . .*
> On leaving the chateau by the vestibule under the King's
> bedchamber, go out onto the terrace . . .
>
> —Louis XIV, *The Way to Present*
> *the Gardens of Versailles*

THUS BEGINS Louis XIV's walking tour of the gardens of Versailles. Never published in his lifetime, the six versions of this tour, recorded either in his own hand or by secretaries between 1689 and 1705, were used as guides to lead official visitors through the groves and around the fountains of one of the most complex and extensive architectural extravaganzas of the seventeenth century. Like any host, the king wanted the satisfaction of showing his guests the gardens through his eyes.

On an August day in 1700, Louis XIV walked through the gardens himself, probably along the preordained route, in the company of André Le Nôtre, whose vision since 1662 was responsible for the brilliant arrangement of *bosquets* (open-air rooms surrounded by high hedges), parterres (ornamental flower beds), and waterworks. This was Le Nôtre's last walk in the garden, for he died the following month at his house in the Tuileries Garden in Paris, where he had been First Gardener to Louis XIII even before Louis XIV was

Facing page: François Halard, *Column house, Le Désert de Retz, Chambourcy.*

born. At his death, he left the fruits of this lifetime collaboration to his great-grandson, Louis XV.

The gardens and park of Versailles and the Trianon—more than two thousand acres in all—have both evolved and deteriorated since the early 1700s, reflecting the innovations and renovations decreed by the taste of succeeding epochs. However, the strong lines of Le Nôtre's plan have remained relatively intact so that visitors today can follow the map in the current guidebook with a copy in hand of Louis XIV's recently reissued tour, *The Way to Present the Gardens of Versailles.*

The conservation of the chateau and gardens of Versailles was long overseen by a single architect, and anyone following the restoration of the chateau knows that boiserie and regilding have been high on the list as newly resplendent interior suites have been unveiled to the public. But by the fall of 1989, with the scholarly Jean-Pierre Babelon at the helm as director, and with many of the trees dangerously overgrown or diseased, the decision was made to divide the responsibilities for the buildings and the gardens. On February 1, 1990, Pierre-André Lablaude, a chief architect of Historic Monuments and a native of the town of Versailles, assumed the task of restoring the gardens. The next night a dramatic storm felled at least fifteen hundred trees at Versailles and devastated a great swath of the Île-de-France. The storm alerted the country to its garden heritage and stimulated a new concentration on treasures long neglected.

At Versailles, it is invigorating to be in a garden that appears to be beginning all over again. Although the tall, iron grille gates to the bosquets can be opened by remote control from Lablaude's Renault rather than with the large keys once used by Louis XVI's inspector of buildings, Lablaude's inspection tours to oversee the work of contractors in the gardens, now denuded of trees, have the feel of a seventeenth-century enterprise.

"At one time," said Lablaude, "gardens were considered like the sauces in *grande cuisine,* but now we approach their restoration with the same rigorous methods we apply to the great cathedrals." The architectural historian Vincent Scully makes a similar comparison between the seventeenth-century constructed garden and the Gothic cathedral: "To those cathedrals the gardens of the seventeenth century are linked in many ways: in plan, in the ideal geometry of square and circle, and in the common objective of shaping the fundamental harmony of the universe around the ritual of the French crown. . . . Paradise itself . . . moves back outdoors to the space of nature."

The most memorable portrayals of the park at Versailles in our time are in the photographs taken by Jean Eugène Atget in the early 1900s and exhibited in this country since 1968 when the Museum of Modern Art in New York acquired a large collection of his works purchased after his death by the American photographer Berenice Abbott. (Also, this past spring the Musée des Arts Décoratifs in Paris displayed their newly restored Atgets of Versailles.) His portraits of venerable trees and his stark views of staircases, urns, and pathways peopled with statues have a desolate beauty that hints at future decay.

To evoke the gardens as they were between 1662, when Le Nôtre began planning them, and the end of the eighteenth century, an exhibition has been mounted in the chateau of more than eighty paintings, drawings, and prints of the gardens. To see this exhibition of static views is to experience the park through the eyes of Louis XIV himself, for Simone Hoog, the chief curator of the Musée National des Châteaux de Versailles et de Trianon, has written in her introduction to the king's walking tour that the tour "is a succession of pauses and viewpoints. Standing in just the right place, the visitor has only to admire a vista or some specific décor." If Louis saw the landscape as a series of still pictures, Le Nôtre was the filmmaker, fashioning a landscape designed to move people through the gardens, towards the surprise awaiting them in each bosquet. Subsequent to the exhibition, a walk in the gardens was enriched by its visual history and storehouse of lost images superimposed on the memory.

Versailles was only a royal hunting lodge with some formal parterres when Louis XIV and his queen, Marie-Thérèse, were feted on August 17, 1661, by Nicholas Fouquet, the king's superintendent of finances, at Vaux-le-Vicomte, Fouquet's opulent new chateau and gardens. Unfortunately—among other sins—Fouquet had built more grandly than the king, creating in the open countryside what became the first fully formed landscape in the French classical style. For his pains, Fouquet was imprisoned. The king then moved Fouquet's formidable team of Le Nôtre, the artist Charles Le Brun, and the architect Louis Le Vau to Versailles.

The state of education in the seventeenth century led to the state of architecture in the garden. Geometry as applied to geography—to design fortifications that surveyed the horizon—created the technique for garden terraces stretching out to a distant perspective. Le Nôtre studied geometry, drawing, and architecture as well as art in the studio of Simon Vouet, where he first met Le Brun. His genius was to enlarge and elongate distant shapes, viewed in foreshortened form, to create the optical illusion of symmetry in the landscape. His brilliant plan and the contributions in both the arts and the sciences from sculptors, water engineers, and gardeners made of these gardens an outdoor fantasy palace that was home to the mythological gods—especially Apollo, who came to symbolize the reign of Louis XIV, the Sun King.

A 1662 watercolor map of the park before Le Nôtre began work shows the walled village of Trianon, which the king razed to create the Trianon de Porcelaine in 1670, which in turn was replaced by the Grand Trianon in 1687. Another plan from 1714 is of the gardens as Louis XIV last knew them. The strength of old plans like these is that they help the eye remember configurations in the same way a map of a foreign city gives a traveler a first unforgettable image and sense of place. In the plan of 1744, all the elements of the garden are clearly marked, and the park is situated in the surrounding countryside. To the east, the town of Versailles is drawn toward the chateau along the goose-foot formation of main boulevards. Clearly delineated are the main bosquets or groves west of the chateau and the Fountain of Apollo at the foot of the Grand Canal, whose northern arm leads to the Grand Trianon. Also the reservoirs that provided water to the fountains can be seen at their various locations. Though the interiors of the bosquets have changed over the centuries, traces of their designs have survived.

A revealing feature of a plan from 1847, a hundred years later in the reign of Louis-Philippe, is the number of paths that radiate in starlike patterns from a central point, symbolic of the monarchy and in contrast with the remaining parallel and perpendicular allées. The Ministry of Defense now controls some of the land adjoining the bosquets, and a dispute is raging over whether land so close to the garden can be sold for development. The vicomte de Rohan, the president of the Société des Amis de Versailles, has questioned whether the government even has the right to sell land at all.

So enamored was Louis XIV of his garden that he commissioned large paintings of the interiors of the bosquets for the Grand Trianon, where they hang today, giving the imposing long gallery in which they are displayed the feel of an intimate garden pavilion. As the artists generally took some license with details, the scenes evoked in the paintings cannot be depended upon for complete accuracy for the purposes of restoration. Among the painters of these pictures was Jean Cotelle, who also painted twenty corresponding gouaches, all from the aerial viewpoint of the gods he depicted looking down from the clouds. His gouache of the bosquet de l'Encelade is of particular interest, since this clearing in the grove behind the Fountain of Apollo is today undergoing an extensive restoration, including the rebuilding of the elaborate octagonal trelliswork gallery. At the center of the fountain, the mythological giant Enceladus struggles to free himself from the pile of rocks cast down by the gods to keep him from reaching Mount Olympus. In the painting, Jupiter strikes him with lightening, to which Enceladus responds with a seventy-five-foot-high jet of water.

The trelliswork was removed by Louis XIV in 1704, and to find the footings Lablaude carefully superimposed plans of the bosquet from different periods. As a prototype, one of the trelliswork triumphal arches has been rebuilt using strips of distressed wood wired together—the seventeenth-century method of making rustic trelliswork. The trelliswork is painted the original bright yellowish green as determined by archival research. This is probably the most intricate and sumptuous trelliswork at Versailles, and already covered in vines, it includes such classical motifs as triglyphs in the cornices.

The Hall of Antiquities, in the bosquet adjoining that of Enceladus, was painted by Jean Joubert about 1700, before its transformation. Furnished is the word that comes to mind when observing this line of statues set on pedestals in long canals, white against dark green. High, parallel jets of water, like transparent fluting, suggest a columned interior. Chestnut trees replaced the statues in 1704, but the round pool in which Narcissus observes his reflection in Joubert's gouache survives in what is now known as the Salle des Marronniers, or Hall of the Chestnut Trees.

In another painting of the same period, the *charmilles* (high hedges of hornbeam that are the distinctive feature of the Versailles bosquets) appear to have the solidity of stone. And like stone, their sculptured surfaces are modulated by light and shadow. As part of the restoration over the coming decades, many of these hedges will be replanted with trees behind them that will be removed as the hedges attain their full growth. The Salle des Festins (now called the King's Garden) was a complex design of fountains, pools, bridges, and, in the center, the Royal Isle.

The most powerful sculpture at Versailles is Jean Baptiste Tuby's Apollo in his horse-drawn chariot emerging from the waters in a fountain at the foot of the Grand Canal. Against a distant horizon of low hills, the sun god appears to be rising up over the edge of the world, shedding his light along the main eastwest axis formed by the Grand Canal and the Royal Avenue (also known as the Tapis Vert, or Green Carpet). In the background of an early eighteenth-century gouache of this scene are the small frigates and battleships ordered by the king to disport on the Grand Canal.

The group representing Apollo being bathed by his nymphs at the end of the day, sculpted by François Girardon, was in the grotto of Thetis until the grotto was replaced by the north wing of the chateau about 1684. It was then proposed that the Baths of Apollo, as it is called, be installed under three canopies set against a *charmille*, with Apollo and his nymphs under a central canopy flanked by his horses under smaller ones. Only the central canopy was built, and a maquette of it on view was beautifully detailed with a valance of fleur de lis.

From 1778 to 1781, the official designer of Louis XVI's gardens was the artist Hubert Robert, whose paintings and drawings suggested ideas for how to ornament architecture with landscape settings in the picturesque manner. He entered into royal and aristocratic circles as a designer of gardens in the popular Anglo-Chinese style. He was commissioned by the comte d'Angiviller, the superintendent of buildings, to incorporate the Baths of Apollo into a grotto once again. In his pen-and-ink drawing on view of the grotto supported by rustic columns, a kind of templelike cave, Apollo and the nymphs are recessed in a cavernous hollow above the horses on ledges of caves below. A rush of water cascades over the rocks into pools. Sunset for Apollo comes at the opposite end of the garden from where he dashes up as the rising sun and in a romantic setting originally quite out of keeping with the classical garden, but now very much a part of it.

In one of the most telling canvases shown, also by Hubert Robert, the trees on the Tapis Vert are being chopped down in preparation for replanting the bosquets in 1775 and 1776. (When the trees grow too tall, they obstruct Le Nôtre's intended perspective view from the terrace in front of the chateau across the gardens to the park and the distant horizon. Thus, the trees have been replanted every hundred years, the last time in the 1870s.) In Robert's idealized scene, as in his romantic evocations of ruins in a decaying landscape, children seesaw on one of the fallen tree trunks while at the right Marie Antoinette and her children look on. Louis XVI is just a few paces behind wearing a rose-colored frock coat. In the background at the left is the colonnade designed in 1684 by the architect Jules Hardouin-Mansart within a bosquet.

Even before the recent storm, the authorities at Versailles knew that the time had long gone when the trees should have been replanted. The storm sounded the final alert. In restoring the gardens to their late seventeenth-century appearance, the administration of Versailles is supplying funds for new plantings of trees and the over-twenty-foot-high hornbeam hedges that hang like curtains enclosing the bosquets, while the interior decor of each bosquet is being restored with private funds raised by the Société des Amis de Versailles. During the next twenty years, more than twenty thousand trees will be replaced around the bosquets. There will be no oaks, only a few chestnuts, but lots of maples, lindens, and hornbeam. Trees whose full height is no more than about forty feet will be selected to reflect the appearance of the gardens at the end of the seventeenth century. In time, the new plantings will be thinned as the canopy of mature trees reaches full growth

Without trees, it is apparent that the town of Versailles is at the very edge of the gardens near the Fountain of Neptune. In the eighteenth-century plan on view by Pierre Prieur, the Fountain of the Dragon, which has the highest spout of water at Versailles, is just beyond the Fountain of Neptune. Flanking it are the two bosquets currently under restoration: the bosquets of the Three Fountains, which had intricate waterworks, and the Arc de Triomphe, whose three-bay pedimented arc in gilded ironwork was set above a waterfall cascading over three marble steps. Both are devoid of their original decor, although a drawing of 1714 shows the bosquet of the Arc de Triomphe as it once was. Before the interiors are replanted, new rusticated trelliswork is being installed around both bosquets. In Louis XIV's time, on his whim, overnight the gardeners could change an entire garden from red to white roses. In the twentieth century, Lablaude must struggle with contract terms and scheduling, but the results are immensely satisfying as the bosquets, with their fountains and sculpture renewed as well, take on their early appearance as outdoor rooms—equivalent, as Lablaude sees it, to the restored rooms in the chateau.

The parterres of the Orangery, south of the chateau, viewed in the exhibition in a painting attributed to Jean-Baptiste Martin, are set between the two grand staircases called the hundred steps. With its round arched windows, the building in which the trees spend the winter looks like an immense Romanesque hall and is now used in summer for special entertainments. Orange, lemon, and pomegranate trees are again being placed along the parterres in *caisses*, known to the garden world as Versailles planters. Although they were painted white at the end of the nineteenth century, paintings from the eighteenth century show them as a grayish blue-green—a shade re-created after many experiments for Lablaude's approval before the planters were painted last spring. The patterns formed by the parterres are still those shown in the Martin view, and they are now planted with campanula, poppies, and foxglove within double borders of boxwood.

As they were on the Grand Canal, mock battles were conducted on the Swiss Lake that terminates the gardens on the south, beyond the Orangery. In a view of one painted by Nicolas-Marie Ozanne, the three young princes are in attendance at the lake's edge. The lake is so called for the Swiss Guards, many of whom lost their lives to the marsh gas that was released as they dug the lake.

As suggested in Louis XIV's tour, outings to the Grand Trianon were best made on the Grand Canal on board the royal sloop, as seen in a painting during the time of Louis XV. This past spring, the Jardin Français between the Grand Trianon and the Petit Trianon was restored to the form given it in 1786 by Richard Mique, an architect who made major contributions to Versailles at the end of the monarchy. An earlier eighteenth-century view shows the Pavillon Français at the center before the Petit Trianon was built. In the cruciform plan attributed to Mique, the parterres, punctuated by pools of water, extend the length of the garden on either side of the Pavillon Français. It is called the Jardin Français to distinguish it from the Anglo-Chinese landscape garden created for Marie Antoinette on the other side of the Petit Trianon, which also included her rustic hamlet.

Seeing the Jardin Français replanted makes one feel part of the young Versailles. Every tree and flower is in perfect order, but it is all new and full of potential for its future form. The 350 Dutch linden trees planted along the paths will be clipped in round arches in the *marquise* style, and around the six miniature bosquets, a four-foot hedge of hornbeam encloses plantings of hornbeam trees that will eventually be more than seven feet tall. Parterres and round beds are filled with old varieties of flowering plants, including lilacs, roses, carnations, phlox, and lilies. A solitary tree was planted to commemorate the spot by the Petit Trianon where Marie Antoinette had her *jeu de bague*, a chinoiserie precursor of the carousel.

The classical formality of the Jardin Français is indeed a contrast to the picturesque landscape Mique created around the Belvédère and grotto he built for the queen between 1777 and 1781. Illuminated at night for the visit by the Holy Roman emperor Joseph II in 1781, an occasion recorded in a painting by Charles-Louis Chatelet, the Belvédère glows like a jewel in the dark and brooding landscape.

In 1704, Louis XIV opened the main bosquets at Versailles to the public— a custom not maintained by Louis XV. Today, bridal parties, joggers, and ball players lend a festive air to the gardens on Sundays. Kings no longer reside at the chateau, but curiously, work goes on in the garden in a grandly royal way. And when the fountains are turned on and illuminated at night (even Louis XIV monitored them carefully so as not to waste water), the transparent walls of light and froth bring a new dimension to the gardens, as magical under a dark sky now as during the royal marriage fêtes of bygone days. As Louis XIV himself suggested, "Walk along the embankment with water jets on either side and go round the great pool; at the far end, pause to gaze at the sprays of water, the shells, basins, statues, and porticos." It is all still there today, tended by seventy gardeners.

Antiques, September 1992

An Echo of a Memory: Recultivating the Tuileries

LIKE HIS father and grandfather before him, André Le Nôtre, the seventeenth-century garden designer, lived next to the Tuileries Garden in Paris—in spite of Louis XIV's offer of a house at Versailles. Though he was the third generation of gardeners working on its parterres, the new configurations and terraces he devised between 1666 and 1671, at the king's behest, have been the most enduring.

Today, at the northwest corner near where his house once stood, a concentrated hush reigns daily over the sandy terrain under the horse chestnut trees. There men, who call to each other in the mellow accent of the Midi, take turns tossing balls in a skilled game of boules. Also located at this corner is a new, temporary glass house of the sleek utilitarian sort, shaded within by white scrims, which served as an exhibition hall for a remarkable show on the past and future of the 2,500-foot-long garden. This straightforward installation documents the complex evolution of the sixteenth-century royal garden that was the earliest public park. In modern Paris, its central allée is the first segment of the triumphal route linking the Louvre with la Défense.

Beyond a small courtyard behind the greenhouse is a simple shed structure for the office overseeing what the French call the "continuation" of the Tuileries as part of the final stage in the creation of the Grand Louvre. Continuation—as opposed to restoration or renovation—because the new plan represents only another layer in its four-hundred-year history, and it comes at a moment when decay has endangered much of the garden's terrain.

There is also continuity in the architectural process. When I. M. Pei, the architect of the Louvre's expansion plan, comes to this garden office to confer with the Tuileries' designers, the meeting in a sense recreates scenes from the collaboration between Le Nôtre and Louis Le Vau, the architect who renovated the Tuileries Palace in the 1660s. Also, the comparison has frequently been made between the similar roles played by Louis XIV and François Mitterrand, the president of the Republic, in determining the future of the Louvre and the garden.

Although the enlargement of the Louvre, one of Mitterrand's Grands Projets, began in the early 1980s, it was not until 1989 that the Tuileries was included in the plan. Following a storm that year that felled three hundred trees near Versailles, a preoccupation with gardens and the environment took hold of the official imagination, even creating rivalries between government ministries. Mitterrand is now described by his adviser on cultural affairs, Laure Adler, as an "homme de la terre" (a "man of the earth") who prides himself on his knowledge of trees. He frequently walks in the Tuileries, like the rest of Paris, just to get a breath of air. The idea for the renovation was born on an early morning outing the president made to the park in the company of his country neighbor Marc Simonet-Langlart, a historian who is restoring an Henri IV chateau garden in Burgundy. Simonet-Langlart was the original coordinator of the Tuileries project.

From the outset, the president called for a renovation that would not erase the physical traces of the garden's historic past. To that end, in 1990 the cultural minister, Jack Lang, called for a competition (dubbed a "consultation") among eight teams of landscape designers to determine different ways of achieving the ultimate goal of architectural preservation with the reinvigoration of plant life. These eight proposals with drawings and models constituted the core of the exhibition in the greenhouse. Set alongside plans and illustrations of the Tuileries dating from the sixteenth century to the present, these proposals stimulate broad-reaching ideas about a cherished public space. Using elements that range from the rigid geometry of Baroque gardens in Italy and France to the free-flowing greens of the English landscape movement, the exhibits encapsulated a historical overview of European urban parks.

Still on view is the final plan, not one of the proposals per se, but a composite of the ideas of two different teams, as expressed in their entries and in the spirit of their established work. At the time the selection was made, Mitterrand and his advisers made the decision to divide the project into its two historic parts: the Tuileries and the Place du Carrousel. The former was assigned to the young French team, Pascal Cribier and Louis Benech, and the latter to the Belgian Jacques Wirtz working with his son Peter. In order to create a transition between the two spaces, the avenue that now separates them will be rerouted underground, allowing for a new terrace—a belvedere overlooking the Tuileries—which will be lowered to an earlier level. As architectural features, the terrace—the Cour du Carrousel—and a monumental staircase into the garden will be designed by Pei Cobb Freed & Partners.

Of course, what is missing today, and can never be replaced, is the building that gave definition to these gardens—the Tuileries Palace itself. Catherine de Médicis had the palace built in 1563 on the site of the old tile (*tuile*) factories from which it received its name. It was burned down by insurgents during the Commune uprising of May 1871, and today many Parisians cannot say exactly where the palace was or what it looked like. Even missing, its placement is an important element in the perception of the two gardens. Were it there today, the palace, running north–south, would close off the Place du Carrousel from the street. What survives of the complex are the Pavillons de Flore and de Marsan, which now terminate the two arms of the Louvre.

Although the palace remained unfinished for years, by 1578 the plan for the vast walled garden across the road appeared as fully conceived in engravings. Its central allée was on direct axis with the main pavilion of the palace, and it was terminated by a semicircular echo wall that reflected sound. Within, parallel and perpendicular walkways created a network of rectangular and square parterres in the Italian Renaissance manner, several planted quincuncially, with trees in formations of fives. In addition to a popular labyrinth, one allée, overseen by the grandfather Pierre Le Nôtre, was covered with a trelliswork tunnel created for a royal wedding feast.

Thus, long before André Le Nôtre was born in 1613 and raised in a house built into the garden wall, the Tuileries was already thriving and developing with use. During the reign of Henri IV in the early seventeenth century, a raised terrace of mulberry trees had been planted on the north terrace in an attempt to introduce an active silk industry. And by the time André began working in the garden officially at age twenty-two, the elaborate *broderies* of arabesque and foliate designs were in full sway. Probably executed in curvilinear plantings of dwarf box seen in relief against colored sands, these were a feature of the parterres opposite the palace facade and of the rear courtyard, the better to be seen from windows above. More recently, this courtyard, now part of the Place du Carrousel, is remembered as a sculpture garden where in 1964 André Malraux, then cultural minister, placed the eighteen Aristide Maillol bronzes that had been presented to France by the artist's model and executrix, Dina Vierny, bringing a fresh contemporary note to the foyer of the Tuileries.

Although visually this transitional space between the Louvre and the Tuileries now appears seamlessly linked to both, its history as an interior court has been extremely varied. In 1662, the *broderies* of the 1650s gave way to a parade ground where, in honor of one of Louis XIV's favorites, the cavalry performed in set formations a tournament in the Italian style called a carrousel—a recurring event that eventually gave its name to the place. And in 1806, long before the palace was destroyed, the Arc de Triomphe du Carrousel, designed by Charles Percier and Pierre Fontaine to celebrate Napoleon's victories, was constructed in the middle of the enclosure. Now, of course, out in the open it is the gateway to the triumphal route on axis with the Arc de Triomphe de l'Étoile and the Grande Arche de la Défense.

Trained in drawing, geometry, and architecture, as well as in practical gardening, Le Nôtre was able to assimilate the decorative forms of the Baroque and Mannerist periods of the French formal garden and to distill these into layouts and patterns of a purified and lasting style. He did not create the French classical garden; he clarified it. This is important to see now because the plan proposed by the two landscape designers selected to continue the garden also represents, rather than innovation, even further clarification of the style but in contemporary terms.

As with music of the period, the court provided both stage and audience for garden design; and like the other arts, it was raised to a theatrical level. Earlier at Vaux-le-Vicomte and at Versailles, where Le Nôtre started fresh on a broader canvas, he was able to work out ideas on linear perspective relating architecture to landscape that prepared him for his assignment at the Tuileries. The Tuileries represented the greater challenge because he had to work around an already established design that was integral to the social texture of Paris.

Le Nôtre began the alterations by removing the east wall and, as they are doing once again, by eliminating the road between the palace and the garden in order to create a terrace with steps leading down, thus opening the garden to its surroundings at the edge of the city. In general, he simplified the texture of elaborate surfaces and let the eye escape down a widened central vista to a vanishing point along the tree-lined path that became the Champs Élysées.

Seen in context, Le Nôtre's genius was to discover freedom within convention. In brief, there were fewer parterres in his design, and by enlarging those on the south side, he created the illusion of symmetry. Two major *broderies* that unfurled before the palace were in the pattern of a St. Andrew's cross around basins of water with a third, central basin at the apex. (This pattern may have been suggested by a plan for an ideal garden drawn by André Mollet, whose family formed the other gardening dynasty of the Tuileries.) Arranged in alternation, the parterre and bosquet designs were elegant configurations of turf and trees, the classical green garden that was Le Nôtre's gift to the French. And at the far end, in place of the echo wall, he extended the garden beyond a formerly private one to create the great octagonal basin and horseshoe ramp. The new south terrace along the river replaced the wall and the house of his birth.

There are few pleasures as instructive as leafing slowly through a 1670s or 1680s album of engravings of the Tuileries Palace and Garden by either Israel Silvestre or Gabriel Pérelle—no photograph can convey the same amount of detail. The garden was fresh and young again with spouting fountains, and, seen in all profiles and from every direction, it is clearly a magical place of manicured parterres extending into the countryside with windmills on the horizon. One Silvestre view from across the Seine takes in the whole sweep of the palace and beyond to the few city streets. The tree cover of spruce, horse chestnut, and yew and the low shrubberies, so recently planted, make the present garden in comparison appear worn and antiquated.

Also, in these engravings the garden is the site of fashionable promenades, for it was the first instance of a garden outside the confines of a chateau or townhouse made for public life. Louis XIV's finance minister, Colbert, wanted to close the garden to all but royalty to prevent its decay. However, Charles Perrault, whose fairy tale scenes suggest the palace and its verdant park as he saw them late in the seventeenth century, prevailed upon him to keep it open to all but soldiers, lackeys, and people in rags, according to the storyteller's memoirs. Perrault was in charge of royal buildings.

The Le Nôtre design remained intact until the Revolution and into the nineteenth century, when certain alterations were incorporated that resulted in the plan of the garden that exists today. In the 1850s, Napoleon III did what no other sovereign had done before. By surrounding the near parterres of the Tuileries and their mirror basins with fosses, or ditches, he carved out a private garden for the palace that excluded the public. These parterres were planted in the manner of an English landscape of the period with a variety of trees and shrubs and with beds of flowers along green lawns.

Since the shape of the garden is its history, these descriptions of the past become the tools for the continuity and rehabilitation of the Tuileries and the Carrousel. For Americans in Paris, the view of the Tuileries usually begins with the Louvre, especially since I. M. Pei's pyramid in the entrance courtyard has become the new first element of the triumphal axis. Pei's man in

Paris, the architect Stephen L. Rustow, has adopted the French term *espace minéral* to describe the cold materials of glass, steel, and stone that furnish this plaza and the adjoining *rond-point* in the middle of the traffic passage that links the wings of the Louvre. This is the location of the second, though inverted, pyramid, a skylight for the underground passageway to the museum from the eight-hundred-car garage under the Cour du Carrousel. Rustow sees the new Parterre du Carrousel as the foil for this hard-edged space.

Because of construction, there is nothing there now. But even a frequent visitor to Paris is hard put to remember the Cour du Carrousel as anything but a pleasant green setting for the Maillols. It was always a surprise to have that extra distance to walk on the way to the Tuileries. Perhaps the reason Mitterrand and his advisers chose to make this a separate garden was to distinguish it from the Tuileries, with the rose marble Arc de Triomphe a giant keyhole opening the door to Paris for the flow of people leaving the Louvre.

Clipped trees and clipped hedges are the major ingredients of a French classical garden. Jacques Wirtz may be from Belgium, where he works from his house and garden in Schoten near Antwerp, but he has had long experience with private French gardens and is a plantsman at heart. One photograph in the exhibition from his own garden is of undulating hedges dusted with snow in winter, and this image becomes the basis for a conceptual language in the garden.

Giving the Pei pyramid its more literal Egyptian interpretation—rather than relating it to the visionary drawings of Étienne-Louis Boullée—the Wirtzes recalled an image of Akhenaton and Nefertiti with the sun radiating above their heads. By making the Arc the concentrated source of power, they have planned a spread of rays that begins in stone under a planting of horse chestnut trees, and that, in the form of undulating yew hedges, fans out over an inclined lawn in pairs, three on each side of the Arc. In fact, the iconography is also very French: it could be the sun's rays around the head of Apollo, the symbol of Louis XIV, the Sun King. This may be one reason Mitterrand is not keen on them.

In garden terms, these radials are a version of the goose-foot plan (also attributed to André Mollet), like the three-pronged avenues into hunting forests or the radiating allées at Versailles. Graphically, these hedges, contoured like twisted ribbons, appear to be a graceful design; densely planted, the several varieties of yews will make a blend of vivid greens. Periodic cuts through the hedges will allow pedestrians to pass back and forth, and from a cross path, the view will extend back between the rows to where the hedges appear nearly to intersect. On either side of the Arc are square "rooms" defined below by clipped hedges and above by an aerial hedge of clipped linden trees. Beyond these, elliptical enclosures of high hedges will provide settings for some of the Maillols. Dina Vierny, now in her eighties, will have final control over the placement of the sculptures.

In a brilliant gesture, the decision was made to recall the presence of the vanished palace by placing a pair of long canals over the footprint of the building, thus restoring the context and division of the two gardens while introducing a new classical water element. The idea was first proposed by François Houtin in another entry to the Tuileries competition. In the Wirtzes' drawing of one canal, two Maillol statues are disposed along the banks with the same elegance that makes Maillol's *The River* so memorable in its position leaning into the pool of the sculpture garden at the Museum of Modern Art in New York. With the Paris installation set against a background of clipped lindens and the mansard roof of the Pavillon de Marsan, one concludes that if not the palace, at least a palace garden would be restored. The path dividing the canals would provide the proper pause from which to see the Tuileries Garden as if one were standing in the entrance of the imaginary palace. So much for good ideas: as of this writing, Mitterrand has approved a new proposal eliminating the canals.

While the cost of the canals was underestimated, there was also some concern for their appearance in winter, though the Tuileries' own basins have survived beautifully. Mainly, the decision was made to minimize divisions between the two gardens so that the Carrousel will remain a transitional space rather than a more distinctive interior court. Pei's terrace, paved in *terre stabilisée*—the combination of sand, gravel, and earth that evokes the look of French parks—will make a neutral divider. In summer, this terrace will blossom into an orangery with tubs of orange trees, and late-eighteenth-century urns will decorate the staircase into the Tuileries.

Working in the Tuileries, Pascal Cribier and Louis Benech explain their task as wearing the shoes of the distinguished gardener, and they have studied the views and plans of Le Nôtre's garden in the late seventeenth-century engravings of Silvestre and Pérelle. The two-dimensional plan on paper, they say, resembles a geometric mandala, one they have meditated on to create their own scheme. What Cribier and Benech have understood in their work, in collaboration with the architects François Roubaud and Patrick Écoutin, is that even the purely classical element is transformed in time by what they describe as the *force végétale*—the vigor of plants. Without being slavish to the past, they have succeeded in translating seventeenth-century forms into a contemporary setting through a fresh horticultural interpretation. This modernity, like Le Nôtre's own version, will bring a new cohesion to the garden in the next century.

What was once a formal landscape in a country setting is now a park surrounded by the city. As light slants low across Paris in the mornings and early evenings, the central axis of the Tuileries becomes a channel for the flow of sunlight that separates the bosquets within the larger garden. Cribier and Benech see the mystery and poetry of the Tuileries in its dense forest of trees and in *clair-obscur*, the contrast of light and shadow. For the visual promenade—the view at eye level—the most important element of the Tuileries, according to Cribier, is its horizontal unity. This he describes as that open band of light above the clipped hedges and below the tree canopy seen far into the distance. The interiors of the bosquets are to be lowered so that new plantings will not intrude on this horizontal unity. The now-declining health of the Tuileries plant materials can only be considered an opportunity for the designers. After all, even the treasured corridors of horse chestnut trees that were planted for their fast growth and luxuriant blossoms were not in the seventeenth-century plan. These will be restored by replanting slowly row by row over the next quarter-century, to create a continuous frame that casts a dark shadow in contrast to new plantings of sycamore and maple that dapple the sunlight.

Mitterrand was specific in wishing to retain the exuberance of the nineteenth-century plantings in the once-private Imperial gardens, where flower beds in the style of an English park will arc around the basins and enclose areas of lawn open to the public. Benech, who was trained in an English nursery, knows how to select the quintessential herbaceous border. Interspersed with shrubberies and trees in a more casual arrangement than the rest of the park, this area will balance the openness at the far end around the horseshoe ramp. The grand transversal axis that cuts across these lawns will remain an outdoor gallery for the 150 or so statues and urns from the past four centuries, including many copies of antiquities. The round basin in the middle will continue its function as Paris's number-one water course for toy sailboats.

The rest is the Le Nôtre plan with centuries of overwriting by others that has not altered its basic integrity. Unlike the restoration of a historic building—the Louvre, for example, whose function changes over the years—a park will always serve as an outdoor respite for public promenades. On paper, the new schematic is almost identical with Le Nôtre's.

While retaining his formation of sixteen bosquets, with four planted solidly in trees and another in the classical theater formation of the old Salle de Comédie, Cribier and Benech will devote others to botanically systematic plantings organized according to soil types. This innovation is in line with their admiration of the Jardin des Plantes and a beauty that is achieved in quantity and regularity. The linear design of the clipped-hedge enclosures seen in sharp silhouette against the sandy soil will hauntingly recall the seventeenth-century plan.

Another layer of the garden to be preserved includes the two marble exedra with classical statues created during the Revolution. These areas will be reestablished with basins planted as botanical water gardens. In comparing the dark beauty of a period gouache of one exedra with a rendering by François Roubaud of the project now, one cannot help but judge that the Tuileries will be enhanced by its new floral displays that will in no way diminish the cool green of a French park. Alongside the twin galleries of the Orangerie and the Jeu de Paume, on the raised terraces next to the Place de la Concorde, flowers will be planted in rows like agricultural fields to create bands of color interspersed by yew topiaries. (The Jeu de Paume was recently renovated by the architect Antoine Stinco, who, by reinserting glass into the arches of this nineteenth-century Egyptian temple, gave the building a new transparency appropriate to a garden pavilion.)

Looking down from these terraces surrounded by linden trees, one will be able to see the single detail that will read from above like Le Nôtre's drawn plan: the truncated triangular parterres of box with the great swirls of volutes cut out at the corners. In this area around the octagonal basin at the foot of the ramp, the green merges with stone, and shadows are cast by statues rather than by trees.

This is the Tuileries as a classical garden. But it exists for people, and all the traditions from years of use will be acknowledged, including the diagonal paths that cross the garden as shortcuts. A dozen new and simplified kiosks will be erected, and the children will have their carousel and Punch-and-Judy shows. And the men from the Midi will have their boules—but now they can count on the sandy soil being regularly raked and moistened as it was in the eighteenth century. Already there is a new organization to protect the future Tuileries and a dispute over whether a noisy traveling carnival should be allowed to take up periodic residence on one of the terraces.

It may be thirty years before the Tuileries is whole again, but the growth will be gradual since the modest plan is simply, as the designers wrote, "to continue the garden." Pascal Cribier and Louis Benech concluded their proposal with the hope that this century would see an end to the opposition between history and modernity, and that, counter to the dictates of fashion and the media, the way to defy time is simply to know how to grow. It sounds very French, but the Tuileries, like the best gardens everywhere, will continue in the future to tell stories that echo the past.

Design Quarterly, Spring 1992

The Formal Farm: Pascal Cribier's Vision of Rural Geometry

IN THE Seine Valley of Normandy, winds from the Channel sweep across the landscape, and a faint mist hangs over miles of apple orchards. Alongside fields of flax alternating with pastureland stand half-timbered houses where the same families have lived for centuries. One domain northwest of Rouen, near the Commune of Limésy, has been in the same family for six hundred years, but not since the eighteenth century have its gardens and surrounding parkland played so prominent a role in life on the estate.

In the 1700s, Toustain de Frontebosc, an ancestor of the Bagneux, the present owners, wrote a scholarly manuscript concerning the principles of Norman horticulture and agriculture, including tenets he practiced in the environs of his own chateau. With all due respect to the spirit of Frontebosc's treatise and to the venerable French tradition of plantings based on clarity and geometry, Pascal Cribier, a thirty-four-year-old landscape architect, has staked out a fresh interpretation of these ideas on the Bagneux property to create a veritable garden for the twenty-first century.

Adalbert and Anne-Marie de Bagneux retreated to a four-room farmhouse on their domain, La Coquetterie, when the eighteenth-century chateau burned down after World War II. Using the regional vernacular of half-timbering with decorative brick infill and high sloping roofs with massive chimneys, they expanded the house but kept its charm intact. Adalbert de Bagneux was mayor of Limésy from 1929 until his death in 1973, and since then his wife has carried on to complete their projects at La Coquetterie.

Pascal Cribier's office in Paris is at the edge of the Luxembourg Gardens, with a view over the tops of the radiating allées of horse chestnut trees that give this park its distinctive quality. The view in autumn, with its rows of golden to bronze leaves, is particularly symbolic of Cribier's favorite theories about the effectiveness of planting in quantity, with a composition that relies on slight variations of a repetitive motif instead of major contrasts. He also understands the spirit of a working domain where, as Madame de Bagneux says, "gardeners like best to mow lawns and clip hedges and would rather tend vegetables than flowers." It is Cribier's ability to grasp the genius of place and express it in a modern design idiom that has inspired an ever-increasing demand for his work.

Madame de Bagneux's basic requirement for La Coquetterie was clear: a garden close to the house that would be beautiful year-round and easily maintained. Cribier, however, characteristically takes the position that gardens around a house make the structure itself too important. "Instead," he says, "the garden should be a collection of variables of which the house is only one element." And in a little sketch to make his point, geometric shapes spin off and away from the main house.

Within a large graveled stable yard in front of the house, framed at one of its far corners by cow sheds, Cribier has laid out an enchanting *potager*, or kitchen garden, called the Jardin des Carrés. In the traditional potager, like the one in the re-created Renaissance garden at Villandry, the carré, or square, is the basic form for the entire series of beds, each planted with only one kind of vegetable or herb. At La Coquetterie the potager consists of thirty-six 2.5-meter squares set in a grid of twelve rows of three across. Here, too, vegetables, flowers, herbs, and low evergreens are distributed, one variety per carré, each square a miniature version of single-crop agriculture. (Like any crops, some vegetables will be rotated yearly to keep the soil fertile.) Whole fields of lavender or tobacco waving in the wind are the sort of image Cribier has in mind when he says that "in large quantities, in a kind of saturation of plants, each one becomes more valuable as part of a whole." Each square is framed with what must be the rarest paving blocks in France—stone recently removed from an inner courtyard of the Palais-Royal to make way for contemporary stone and marble columns by the sculptor Daniel Buren.

Under soft gray skies and amid a sea of gravel paths, this arrangement of squares appears cool and spare, and the muted shades of greens, grays, blues, yellows, and whites have a luminous quality. Squares of similar colors, like the beds of purple petunias and lavender, seem to call out to one another. Contrasts of texture—stiff blades, floppy leaves, and rigid stalks—are as important as color in modulating the regular grid. The sum of these parts is as satisfying as the enclosed gardens of the Renaissance, and yet it feels refreshingly new, modern, and open.

No other area near the house is left simply to be neutral—not even the gravel space for parking. Here twelve linden tress set out in a rectangle will be pleached and clipped over the years so that their branches form a floating hedge, suspended above the family cars (sometimes as many as twenty-five) that assemble on weekends and holidays. In front of a laurel hedge on the lawn bordering the potager is another example of what Cribier calls *la force végétale* (the natural vigor of plants): here he has trained three triangular pylons from living hornbeams, their supple trunks, three together, bent and tied into forms Madame de Bagneux calls her Eiffel Towers. Crowned by bushy leaves and braced with cut branches, these have become living stakes for tomato vines.

A dirt gardener himself, Cribier enjoys the sense of taming these forces of nature and of containing both the wild and the ordinary in a strict geometry of space. Along the piers of the cow sheds he has placed terra-cotta pots filled with immense bouquets of wild grasses and herbs. And in the entry court to the house, twenty-five box clipped into small globes appear to have sprouted up between the typically Norman sandstone pavers, like sentinels in military formation—a disciplined rank that nevertheless allows for diagonal paths to the doors. From this courtyard one can survey the entire potager seated in comfort against the sword-shaped leaves of one of Claude and François Lalanne's fanciful patinated-bronze benches. (The design was originally commissioned for the Lila Acheson Wallace garden at Colonial Williamsburg.)

Around the corner of the house, the pinks of apple blossoms in spring and hydrangeas and standard roses in summer marry well with the mellowed bricks of the house set in traditional patterns. And along one side, Cribier has planted a border in a sculptural composition setting off the rigidity of clipped box against the shiny leaves of camellia trees and the soft texture of ferns and masterwort. The plants may be common, but the arrangement is not, with its distinctive clarity of form.

To protect the swimming pool on the back lawn from the constant winds off the Channel, Cribier has set a tall hedge of yews within an existing low stone wall. He is making adjustments as well in the family's long floral border at the bottom of the lawn that along with the hedge behind creates a strong horizon at the end of the garden—beyond which are fields and woods. In summer and on into autumn this border glows with the richer hues of zinnias, asters, and cosmos—and dahlias donated by the village curé.

At a time when most contemporary architecture in France appears to be striving for the boldly new, Pascal Cribier belongs to a school of young landscape designers who prefer to crystallize images for the present from the art and architecture of the past. Although the resulting forms may appear minimal, they evoke the richness of centuries of French culture.

What also touches Cribier's work directly are visits to such favorite haunts in Paris as the concentric oval beds of the École de Botanique in the Jardin des Plantes, where more than ten thousand kinds of plants are classified for the public. Cribier regularly exchanges ideas with colleagues such as the architects François Roubaud and Patrick Ecoutin in the kind of collaboration of friends that has always stimulated French artists. After Cribier briefly described the proposed Jardin des Carrés at La Coquetterie to Roubaud, the latter sketched the imaginary grid of squares, conveying in spirit all the texture and magic it now has in reality.

Curiously, these Parisian designers tend to see the history of French gardens through the eyes of the California landscape architect Barbara Stauffacher Solomon, whose influential book *Green Architecture and the Agrarian Garden* Cribier keeps close at hand. In an imaginative combination of drawings and photographs of European landscapes, this American observer conveys the essence of the tradition that Toustain de Frontebosc wrote about centuries ago and that has again beautifully come to life at Limésy.

House & Garden, February 1990

The Désert de Retz: Cultural History Through Architecture

IN OBSERVING the bicentennial of the French Revolution this year, there is a tendency, because of its pattern of violent change, to see it as an abrupt demarcation between the old and the new regimes. Yet certain intellectual and philosophical developments engendered on the eve of the Revolution survived if, not necessarily intact, at least as fragments with a continuity of their own. An example is the late eighteenth-century French landscape garden, which embodied both the art and literature of Romanticism. Even out of fashion, these gardens went on, fragile and overgrown, recalling not only the earlier age of their classical follies but the spirit of a society on the threshold of change. Gardens, in a sense, may be timeless, but as repositories of ideas, they become true barometers of an age.

Such is the Désert de Retz, a rambling, picturesque landscape garden a dozen miles west of Paris near the town of Chambourcy on the edge of the Forêt de Marly. After two hundred years it had until recently the appearance of the enchanted wood in *Sleeping Beauty:* "a vast number of trees, great and small, bushes and brambles, twining one with another," as the fairy tale goes. In place of the hidden towers of the princess's storybook castle, concealed behind the mysterious curtains of green were architectural follies evoking ancient ruins, which had, in time, become ruins themselves.

In 1774, at the age of forty, François Racine de Monville, an amateur in the best sense of the word, purchased the first parcel of land for his hundred-acre *désert* (in the French seventeenth-century meaning of a country retreat) in what was then the village of Retz. At twenty-six and already a widower, de Monville had inherited a great fortune from his maternal grandfather. Tall and handsome, an expert archer, a good dancer, and an accomplished harpist (he even played with the composer Christoph Gluck), de Monville was not strictly speaking a man of the court. Yet his exquisite if eccentric taste, especially in the Désert, was sought after particularly by the ladies of the court and by fashionable artist friends who promenaded along the winding paths to experience the surprising views so beautifully calculated by their host.

Little seems changed now in the French countryside as one approaches the Désert on a rain-soaked June day. After driving through lush orchards, where even the fences lining the road are espaliered with apple trees, one enters the Désert along a footpath leading from a cluster of old farm buildings. During the ancien régime, the king could enter the Désert from his domain at Marly-le-Roi by passing through a still-extant rock outcropping that resembles a grotto.

Some forty years ago, Sidonie Gabrielle Colette wrote of her first visit to the Désert on just such a pale gray day with water dripping through the thick branches of rare specimen trees: "By having made the acquaintance of Le Désert on a stormy June day, I shudder to think of it altered, deprived of its excrescences, affronted by the glamour of its own renewal. . . . The abundance at Retz is that of a dream, a fairy tale, an imaginary island." Colette's fear of a restoration that would strip the Désert of its character seems now unfounded. Its two current owners are restoring the architecture and landscape but are taking into account the additions, especially horticultural ones, gradually made by subsequent owners. Curiously, even as the property has changed hands over the years, the landscape garden has retained its integrity. De Monville sold it to an Englishman, Lewis Disney Ffytche, in 1792, but the revolutionary government confiscated it in 1793. In the nineteenth and early twentieth centuries (albeit with a few chicken coops) it was the home of a bourgeois family. Later it became a dilapidated ruin in which, in the 1950s, the surrealists, led by André Breton held masked revels. As resurrected, the Désert will evoke the theories of Jean Jacques Rousseau and the landscape paintings of Hubert Robert with their Roman ruins.

Ironically, in France the royal domains planned by André Le Nôtre and others, with broad formal avenues and geometric stateliness symbolic of the monarchy, were long ago restored. But only in recent decades have the French recognized their own rich tradition of natural landscaping—a tradition that came later to France than to England, but like England's stemmed from literary sources.

Long before the 1740s, when first William Kent and later Lancelot "Capability" Brown created the quintessential English park by carving out picturesque landscapes that imitated nature itself, poets and essayists such as Alexander Pope and Joseph Addison had heralded the new taste in gardening that opposed artificial formality. Horace Walpole summed up the particulars of the new taste in his essay "On Modern Gardening," first published in 1780 and translated into French in 1785 by Louis Jules Mancini-Mazarini, duc de Nivernais, formerly the French ambassador to London. Walpole explains that when the French adopted the English landscape garden they attributed its origins partially (and mistakenly, he adds) to the Chinese, thus calling the new fashion the Anglo-Chinese garden. In fact, in France the English landscape garden merged with firsthand accounts of the emperor's gardens at the summer palace outside Peking, in which there were "pavilions and grottoes" and a "winding piece of water."

Even more influential in France were the writings of Rousseau, especially his popular epistolary novel *Julie, ou la Nouvelle Héloïse*, of 1761. Among other virtues, the novel celebrates those of a garden called the Elysium, created by the heroine of *Julie* at Clarens, an estate near Lake Geneva with "winding and irregular walks bordered by these flowery thickets and covered with a thousand garlands of woody vines." This appearance of wild nature "leaves behind a melancholy idea of solitude," Julie says. In championing the completely natural, Rousseau takes issue with both the Chinese and the English for forcing the ensemble of elements in the picturesque garden. Of Richard Temple, first Viscount Cobham, and Kent at Stowe in Buckinghamshire,

England, he writes: "The master and creator of this superb solitude even had ruins, temples, and ancient edifices built here so that times as well as places are gathered together with a magnificence that is more than human."

Rousseau died in 1778, while he was the guest of Louis René, marquis de Girardin, at Ermenonville, another extensive landscape garden, and his host erected a classical tomb for his remains on an island encircled by poplars designed by Hubert Robert. Robert quite easily transferred his ability to paint canvases of classical ruins and rustic abodes in bucolic landscapes to designing such settings for the aristocracy, including a pastoral hamlet for Marie Antoinette at the Petit Trianon at Versailles.

Illusion was the key to the intellectual environment in France during the years preceding the Revolution, and it was in this atmosphere that de Monville devised the Désert and its seventeen *fabriques,* or follies. (The French word at that period better suggests how the ornamental structures and fake ruins were placed in a landscape to create a seductive illusion of reality, the same way artists composed landscape paintings of historical scenes.) As former Grand Master of the Water and Forests of Rouen, de Monville was no stranger to horticulture, and with two neoclassical houses in the Faubourg Saint-Honoré in Paris, designed for him in 1764 by the visionary architect Étienne-Louis Boullée with interiors reminiscent of a Turkish fantasy, he had original tastes in architecture. Although he was assisted early on by the architect François Barbier, there is little possibility that the Désert is anything but de Monville's own conception—a history of culture through architecture to reflect a century of enlightenment and of categorical knowledge discovered through archaeology and travel. At the same time, it is most probable that the Désert represents a romantic view of the past in the face of the harsher realities surfacing in France.

In this small, undulating valley crisscrossed by winding paths, de Monville established his first residence in the Chinese House—a decorative, two-story teak building with a pagoda roof that was the only private house in the Chinese style in Europe. Built in 1777 and 1778, it was set by a pond and had an enclosed garden of its own in which there were other small pavilions and fountains. The Chinese House has unfortunately crumbled away. Already by 1950 Colette described it as "subsiding into the center of the lake like moist sugar . . . its panels of fretted wood . . . yielding to the pressure of dog-rose and elder."

The house de Monville lived in after 1782 was still more ingenious—a four-story Doric column fifty feet in diameter and eighty feet high, broken off at the top as if it were a remnant of one of Hubert Robert's colossal temple columns or the relic of an earlier civilization. The Column House may have been a symbolic ruin, but the appointments were the epitome of refined eighteenth-century taste, and the interior of the massive stone building retained the airiness of a garden pavilion because of the many mirrored surfaces that reflected the green landscape by day and candlelight by night.

Set around a central spiral staircase, the rooms were nearly oval. On the ground floor alone there were a vestibule, salon, dining room, and bedroom. Sun poured through a conical skylight and nourished rare plants placed between the balusters and that trailed all the way down the open core of the staircase. The three tiers of windows set into the flutes of the column establish a dynamic rhythm: French windows at the base, then square ones, and finally ovals at the top. Inventories made after the Revolution mention the sleeping alcoves and windows curtained in toile de Jouy, carved seats painted gray, white marble fireplaces, a painting by Hubert Robert, and busts of Benjamin Franklin and George Washington. America was part of the eighteenth-century equation: included in the list of more than one hundred exceptional trees still standing in the Désert are oaks, walnuts, and sequoias brought from North America.

Although clusters of trees once artfully isolated have grown into woods, one ancient linden next to the column house has itself become architectural—a dense shelter of many twisted trunks and branches. Those follies which still stand have created their own clearings. The Temple of Pan, the god of woods and fields, for example, is a circular structure ringed by Doric columns and containing a small room that was well suited for the assignations of which de Monville, a great ladies' man, was reputed to have had many. No matter how small the folly, the magic is to be inside. Even the icehouse in the stark shape of an Egyptian pyramid has a cryptlike interior below the twin staircases.

Among the follies now vanished were a Tartar tent, a classical frieze with urns below a natural stage for a theater, and assorted obelisks and altars. These monuments of melancholy in the rustic landscape were destinations for those walking out from the Column House. In 1783, de Monville brought a genuine ruin—a thirteenth- or fourteenth-century Gothic chapel in the parish of Saint Jacques de Roye, which adjoined his land. Although only a shell with delicate window tracery, it has survived better than the fake ruins.

Besides the views of the Désert preserved in period watercolors and engravings by artists such as Louis Carrogis (known as Carmontelle), and later photographs, details of all the original structures survive in two sources. First, after King Gustav III of Sweden visited the Désert on July 14, 1784, in the company of Louis-Philippe-Joseph d'Orléans, duc de Chartres (whose own landscape garden is now at the Parc Monceau in Paris), he asked de Monville for a set of plans for the Column House and the Chinese House. They were conveyed to him in 1785 and eventually given to the Nationalmuseum in Stockholm. Also in 1785, George Louis Le Rouge, the geographer to the king of France, published twenty-four engravings of the follies in the Désert in Cahier XIII of his *Détail de nouveaux jardins à la mode,* which is a survey of the Anglo-Chinese style in France, England, and Germany.

In addition to the specimen trees that make the Désert a rare arboretum, the heated greenhouses, one resembling an *orangerie,* contained an extensive botanical collection which was removed after the Revolution and placed in what is now the Jardin des Plantes in Paris. Although there may have been larger landscape parks and gardens during the period, none could equal the Désert for range of accomplishment in the field of landscape design.

The Revolution brought this way of life to an end, although de Monville himself survived to die a natural death in 1797. The Passy family which owned the Désert for the longest period thereafter—eighty years—included the economist Frédéric Passy the first winner of the Nobel Peace Prize in 1901. But for the last fifty years or so, the Désert has been left to itself and the forces of nature. The follies were classified historic monuments in the late 1930s, but little was done to protect the Désert, as witness Colette's plea: "A little longer and Le Désert de Retz will be no more than a poem in the style of an epoch. And yet, may it not be a fine thing to preserve even a poem from an epoch?"

In 1966 André Malraux, then minister of culture, singled out de Monville's creation when speaking to the National Assembly in support of a law for the preservation of historic monuments. "The Désert de Retz," he said, "where are found . . . the most important remains in Europe of eighteenth-century chinoiserie, has an owner who would sooner sell off the trees and let the rest collapse not just into ruin but into dust, while the government stands by completely helpless." But even with the law passed, and the government offering to pay half the cost of the restoration, no significant progress was achieved with the unwilling owners of the Désert.

The two present owners are not only restoring the Désert but bringing it alive as a research center for the study of historic parks and gardens. Olivier Choppin de Janvry, an architect, discovered the Désert in 1963 when, as a student at the École Spéciale d'Architecture, he drew up a restoration plan for the garden as a study project. The other owner, Jean-Marc Heftler-Louiche, a Paris banker, was introduced to the Désert by Choppin de Janvry in 1982, and in 1986 they bought it for the Société Civile du Désert de Retz, of which they are the directors. The initial stage of the restoration will cost $1.8 million, and they are still seeking about $300,000 to be matched by the government.

A most instructive exhibition devoted to the Désert in the cultural context of its time was mounted at the Musée du Parc de Marly nearby. And work has begun to restore the follies and open the vistas by cutting out all but the exceptional trees and reshaping the crowns of the remaining ones. However, the restoration will only be complete when visitors once again promenade along the paths of the Désert, as Marie Antoinette did several times, as Madame du Barry did with her friend the artist Elisabeth Vigée-Lebrun, and as Thomas Jefferson did in 1786, commenting about the Column House, "How grand the idea excited by the remains of such a column!" The concept of the interior later turned up in Jefferson's unrealized designs for the United States Capitol and his plans for the rotunda of the library at the University of Virginia in Charlottesville.

With the restoration of the Désert de Retz a new generation will experience the ideas of the eighteenth century that also became a common ideological ground for America and France.

Antiques, March 1989

Six

Japanese

Autumn in Japan

LONG BEFORE the International style in architecture gave cities all over the world a similar look, garden designs spread over the centuries from country to country. Without traveling at all, a garden aficionado could visit Italian terraces, French parterres, or English borders. Even George Washington's garden at Mount Vernon has been recreated in Bath, England. Yet there is no substitute for going to the source, because gardens as originally conceived are wedded not only to a place but to a culture.

Before my recent sojourn in Japan, I believed that I knew something about Japanese gardens. Every spring I visit the Brooklyn Botanic Garden's Japanese garden at cherry blossom time and walk along its manicured paths lined with clipped azaleas. And in Maine, where I summer, moss gardens with snow lanterns are a common genre along the coast. But to see gardens in Japan, particularly in Kyoto, is to observe unexpected details that are as powerful as they are simple: images and sounds that bring vividly to life landscapes that pale when reproduced without this cultural overlay.

First, in the stillness of Saiho-ji Temple, as visitors ritually dip brushes into ink to write on wooden panels before entering the moss garden, there comes from outside the rhythmic sound of sweeping. Inside the garden, this sound pervades the autumnal air. Its visual accompaniments include the implements used to sweep the leaves—rustic brooms and woven winnowers that scoop up the piles—and the sweepers themselves dressed in faded indigo stripes and plaids. Also unexpected here, at the height of autumn color, is the juxtaposition of the crimson canopy of Japanese maples fanned

Facing page: Jerry Harpur, *Japanese Zen garden by Marc Peter Keane, Kyoto.*

out over the ponds and nearby hedges of pink camellias in full bloom. At 35 degrees north, Kyoto is on the same latitude as Tunisia and North Carolina.

Seasonal rituals dominate the entire culture in Japan, especially in small galleries which rotate their collections. Hanging scrolls with poems brushed in calligraphy are embellished with branches of autumn leaves. At the Hatakeyama Memorial Museum of Fine Art in Tokyo, a place devoted to the tea ceremony, a wooden tea caddy is stored in a silk sack in autumnal colors and a water container from the Momoyama period is decorated with migrating geese. The traditional flower arrangement at the tea ceremony during this season is a single camellia bud with a branch of dry leaves.

On the autumn holiday called Culture Day, women coming and going to the teahouses in the Hatakeyama stroll garden wore kimonos in patterns depicting the flowers and leaves of autumn. And on the lawn, surrounded by bamboo hedges, grasses, and shrubberies covered in red berries, lunch was prepared at long low tables covered in festive red felt and protected by a red parasol, creating a genre scene like a print from the Floating World.

Persimmons are the true color of autumn. Their smooth orange-red skin glows from trees and from neighborhood fruit stands like shimmering carp in garden ponds. Just outside the garden wall at Shinju-an, an old Zen monastery, a tree with only a single persimmon remaining signals the season's end. At the same moment as this becomes visible, the visitor hears from an inner courtyard the repeated hollow knock of the *shishi-odoshi,* the bamboo pipe that strikes a rock each time it empties of water and swings up, marking the passage of time.

Pervading all the gardens is the utilitarian but texturally beautiful black twine called *warabinawa.* Lashed around the joints of bamboo fences or the wooden stakes that stabilize young trees, the twine weathers to earthy shades of brown. It also holds together elaborate arbors created to support ancient cherry trees, as well as bamboo lattice pergolas for wisteria vines. In a tea garden, a simple stone tied with the mundane twine signifies a path that is off limits.

Japan is a land where uneven numbers are preferred for their asymmetry—especially seven, five and three (totaling fifteen), as can be seen in numerous sand gardens, such as Ryoan-ji, with their clusters of rock islands. Stepping stones along garden paths are laid out in sets of these numbers; some are placed perilously uneven on purpose, as in the Imperial garden at Katsura, to force visitors in traditional dress to look down—then leveling out again to draw their gaze over a special view of the misty landscape.

In a country where perfection rules, some have a taste for *heta,* roughly translated as that imperfection that adds zest. At Ryoan-ji, for example, the visitor sits at the edge of the pavilion to view in complete Zen tranquility the raked gravel that swirls around the rocks. What no postcard shows is that lined up under the ledge on the other side of the Temple are nine bright red plastic pails in case of fire. This is *heta.*

Two final images. In a scene from the old tale of the warring Genji and Heike clans at the Kabuki, a military commander sits in a pavilion in his inner garden. When the *shoji* screens behind him are opened, the stage garden revealed is an exact duplicate of a Kyoto garden in autumn. In spring, it probably changes to cherry blossoms. On my last day it rained. Out on the street, a long line of schoolgirls walked closely together in unison. In uniform, they looked like a navy blue wave moving along over a white line of socks, but bobbing above them were umbrellas in every pastel hue imaginable—a harbinger of another season and a floating world if ever I saw one.

Gardens Illustrated, February–March 1994

Japanese Screens and the Gardens of Kyoto

SO ACCUSTOMED are we to the notion that museums are the guardians of our cultures that we forget at times that objects artistically displayed for their individual merits had social significance in their original milieu. By the time these objects are acquired by museums, the places and events that gave them meaning have themselves undergone transitions so that, in a sense, they no longer belong to their past. In "rescuing" these art objects, scholars attempt through provenances and comparisons to piece together their history, and in doing so they occasionally restore to them their original aura.

This is what occurred in a recent exhibition of painted wall panels at New York's Metropolitan Museum of Art titled "Immortals and Sages: Fusuma Paintings from Ryoan-ji and the Lore of China in Japanese Art," which injected fresh perceptions into the complex iconography of Japanese art. First of all, like medieval European tapestries that were hung to insulate great stone halls, Japanese paintings in the form of *fusuma* (sliding panels) were integral to their architectural settings. In separating and restoring a set of four double-sided panels, their original setting became known to the Met's conservators. Old bills and receipts used as backing for one of the panels identified them as partitions between two adjoining rooms of the *hojo* (the abbot's six-room apartment) that overlooks the famous dry garden at the Zen monastery of Ryoan-ji in Kyoto, Japan.

As I had just returned from visiting Ryoan-ji when the exhibition opened, I was particularly sensitive to the implications of their findings that these sumptuous gold-leaf paintings at a temple represented samurai influence in monastery culture at the beginning of the seventeenth century during the Momoyama period (1568–1603). That fact alone sent me back to my notes and observations of the many temples and gardens I saw during my stay in Kyoto. Like others, I traveled to Japan armed with garden guides but soon realized that the Zen gardens are but the external manifestation of interior decors with comparable images and symbols derived from Chinese culture. Fortunately, evidence of these spare but elegant interiors is extant in Kyoto, a city that remains green, with parks and gardens surrounding clusters of temple pavilions.

Although many of Kyoto's temples and gardens have been altered over time, there are great rewards in seeing them in light of the analysis made by Met research curator Hiroshi Onishi. Temple records dated the Ryoan-ji fusuma to 1606, and their placement was confirmed by a detailed description in a guidebook of 1799. They are the earliest known fusuma painted for a Zen monastery in the elaborate polychrome and gold-leaf manner, which succeeded the ink monochrome panels found in monasteries of the Muromachi period (c. 1330–c. 1570). Onishi follows the transition of these decorative displays that first adorned samurai castles and then monasteries in a merger of the social and religious communities. Having visited several places he selected as examples, I could suddenly see in these temples and one major castle the life reflected in their art.

The oldest surviving hojo in a Zen monastery is in the sub-temple of Shinju-an at Daitoku-ji, one of the largest temple precincts in Kyoto. Built in the late fifteenth century and since reconstructed, the wooden buildings at Shinju-an, joined by verandas and surrounded by gardens, retain the essence and simplicity of the early monasteries. Because the sliding panels enclosing the main rooms of the hojo open up onto gardens, the spaces inside and outside are linked visually for contemplation and meditation. The original sliding panels painted in the late fifteenth century by Soga Jasoku, a layman who studied Zen, are still in place and depict in ink monochrome either birds and flowers or simply landscapes of the four seasons.

These dreamlike scenes in the Chinese style stretch out into an infinity of mist-enshrouded mountains looming over water inlets with a solitary boatman gliding across the surface. Tucked into valleys or perched on outcroppings in groves of bamboo trees are rustic pavilions for meditating scholars. Movement through space and time is conveyed by the changing seasons or a shift from daylight to moonlight as the eye travels along a path across the landscape. Onishi sees in these themes the Japanese admiration for natural beauty and an affinity with the supernatural. The naturalistic panorama may also represent a cosmic view, a Zen way of watching life move on.

An extraordinary moment in experiencing Japanese temple art and architecture comes in being seated on the floor, as is the custom, at the base of the painted landscape with the mountains towering above. And then, by a slight shift, to view the east garden at Shinju-an, legs dangling over the ledge of the temple pavilion above the landscape attributed to Murata Shuko, the founder of the tea ceremony. Here miniaturized mountains surrounded by water are conveyed by rocks artistically arranged in auspicious, asymmetrical clusters of seven, five, and three in a sea of moss. From a nearby courtyard, one can hear the hollow knocking of the *shishi-odoshi* or deer-chaser, a bamboo pipe that strikes a rock each time it empties of water and swings up, marking the passage of time. Beyond this timeless scene at Daitoku-ji, where once the hills of Higashiyama rose in the distance, now only buildings and city streets form the visual boundary.

How the swirling mists suggested by a few brushstrokes of ink in earlier fusuma, like those at Shinju-an, came to be replaced by such richly ornamental gold-leaf and polychrome paintings in the late sixteenth century is a story of conquests, wealth, and castles that culminated eventually with the first appearance of these ornate panels at Ryoan-ji and other monasteries. In a sense, this period of Japanese art invokes the spirit both of Louis XIV's Versailles and of the Napoleonic Empire in France, where innovations in the decorative arts combined with borrowings from a classical past served to centralize power. Opulence based on cultural legitimacy, from China in the case of Japan.

While the Zen temples traditionally propagated the Chinese themes in painting, those themes were first celebrated in many colors and gold leaf in the castles built by the samurai. Three years after the great samurai chieftain Oda Nobunaga secured the military victory that unified Japan for the first time in 1573, he began constructing his seven-story castle on Mount

Azuchi overlooking Lake Biwa northeast of Kyoto. Completed in 1579, it was reported to be of an unusual splendor for that period, and the new architectural spaces required an equally bold and lavish decorative treatment. In his descriptions of Far Eastern art, Sherman E. Lee points out that castle interiors were in a perpetual twilight since "the small exterior windows and the post-and-lintel construction characteristic of East Asian architecture tended to make the great rooms rather dark."

By the time Nobunaga appointed Kano Eitoku as the chief painter to oversee the decoration of the fixed and sliding wall panels, the artist's work had already evolved from the ink monochrome style in favor of a faint gold wash for the sky. A grandson and pupil of Motonobu, he was a direct heir of the Kano decorative tradition, and in his late style, richly colored tree trunks and branches with bright green leaves by pools of blue water with craggy rocks stood out against swirling clouds of gold leaf applied to the stretched paper. Unlike the panels painted with vast monochromatic landscapes that gave the illusion of depth and distance, this new "flatter" style can be compared to a stage set with a background of gold—more like a formal park setting peopled with ancient Chinese sages and immortals acting out Confucian and Taoist themes from a mythic past. And the large areas of gold leaf gave a subtle glimmer to the dimly lit interiors.

All of this disappeared in six years, when a rebellious vassal murdered Nobunaga and burned down the castle. But his avenger and successor, Toyotomi Hideyoshi, continued to employ Kano Eitoku to decorate his own castles with a large team of collaborators including the artist's sons, Kano Takanobu and Kano Kotonobu. Unfortunately, all of these castles were destroyed as well, along with Eitoku's art, by the Tokugawa family, which emerged as the ruling power in Japan not long after Hideyoshi's death. (Momoyama, the name given to this period retroactively, means Peach Hill and describes the peach trees planted on the site of Hideyoshi's castle at Fushimi after it was demolished by Tokugawa Ieyasu, who established the Tokugawa shogunate in 1615, thus ushering in the Edo period.)

Nijo Castle in Kyoto was originally built from 1601 to 1603 by the shogun Tokugawa Ieyasu and eventually included some structures transferred from Fushimi Castle. Its wide moat and massive stone fortifications belie the peaceful precincts within, where the aesthetics of a Momoyama castle have been preserved in the central structure, Ninomaru Palace. Its succession of reception rooms, audience chambers, and private quarters is reminiscent of the long enfilade of ceremonial rooms at Hampton Court Palace in England during the reign of William and Mary at the same period. As one approaches the grand chambers along the famous nightingale floor (so called after its construction with nails and clamps that squeak in birdlike song), the visitor today senses that its rooms sum up the lavishness of the other castles destroyed from the Momoyama period.

Just as the main audience hall at Azuchi was splendidly decorated with Kano Eitoku's painting of trees and birds in polychrome and gold leaf, his grandson, Kano Tanyu, employed similar themes at Nijo, where a single massive pine tree on a gold ground decorates the main audience room. To one side, sliding panels to an inner room are marked by long red ties and tassels against dark green pine and gold. Although blossoming cherry trees with pheasants were painted in an inner audience chamber by Kano Tanyu's younger brother Kano Naonobu, it is the older brother's panel of a pine tree with gnarled branches supporting two hawks that symbolize the strength of the Tokugawa regime. With one branch measuring more than thirty feet, this panel was painted for the room where the Shogun's spears, swords, and other weaponry were stored. (As an aside, at a Kabuki performance in Kyoto last year, the curtain opened on just such a stylized pine tree with low branches in brilliant green stretched out across the gilded ground of the backdrop.)

Outside Ninomaru Palace, the stroll garden attributed to the renowned tea master and landscape architect Kobori Enshu was also laid out in 1603 around a large central pond. As in the decorative panels within, water is glimpsed beyond massive rocks in extraordinary sizes, shapes, and colors that are grouped along the banks to resemble miniature mountainous landscapes. In the center of the irregularly shaped pond, three islands—Crane Island, Turtle Island, and Island of Eternal Happiness—add to the visual complexity of the landscape, as if one were moving across an ink monochrome landscape scroll. From outside, the palace structures with tiled roofs and upturned eaves give the impression of quiet temple architecture.

Were it not for clues revealed during conservation of the Ryoan-ji screens at the Metropolitan Museum of Art, in light of the above history and because of their immense size and bright coloration, they could have been identified as fusuma for one of the samurai castles. In addition to receipts identifying Ryoan-ji, the panels were numbered, with the highest number 16, the exact total of panels along the west, north, and east sides of the middle room in a hojo where ceremonies and rituals were performed. The room was open on the south side to overlook the garden. This meant that the panels on the reverse would have been the first four panels in the adjoining patron's room on the west side. The eighteenth-century guidebook that confirmed the Met's discovery described the panels after a disastrous fire at the temple from which they were rescued.

What surprised the curators was the sudden shift at a monastery away from the meditative tranquility of ink monochrome landscapes to the lavish and festive portrayal of the "Chinese Immortals" and "Four Elegant Accomplishments," Confucian and Taoist narrative themes that survived from the Tang dynasty in the early tenth century. During the samurai conflicts of the last quarter of the sixteenth century leading up to the Tokugawa regime, temples like Ryoan-ji, already the crucibles of Zen culture, became under samurai patronage open meeting places for artists, nobles, merchants, and tea masters. These gatherings were celebrations of the tea ceremony and poetry, including poems inspired by paintings created for the occasion and based on Chinese motifs. Artists of the Kano school would be among those present.

The taste exhibited in these temple interiors was symbolic of the mutual dependence between Zen monks and their samurai patrons—the former seeking support and the latter cultural enlightenment. When Ryoan-ji's samurai patron, Hosokawa Yusai, commissioned the paintings for the hojo, perhaps from Kano Eitoku's son, Kano Kotonobu (active during the early seventeenth century), he saw the qualities portrayed in the fusuma as those essential to ideal gentlemen. According to Onishi, the resulting ensemble was "a vision of what might be called the utopia of the ruling elite." The figures in the paintings, moving in orderly gardens, merged with the elegant guests in the temple and its own idealized garden.

In the *shicchu*, the central ceremonial room, the scene in the four panels of "Chinese Immortals" portrays the moment when Resshi (the Chinese immortal Liezi) rejects worldly ties and flies away into golden clouds—a miracle that astonishes the others whose robes are whipped by the strong wind. Although the narrative extends across all four panels, each one is a composition that can stand alone. And what appears as a dense gold cloud field, opens up with puffy edges to reveal fantastic rock formations and pine trees. The high fence lashed with rope is like many still visible in Japanese gardens.

The reverse of those fusuma composed a wall of the *dannanoma* (the patron's room) and depicts the scholarly art of painting, one of the "Four Elegant Accomplishments" that also include the arts of music, calligraphy, and *go*. The Met's panels show sages and their attendants admiring a long scroll painting while in the fusuma immediately to their left, an inebriated old man is supported by two young companions. He is probably the popular Tang-dynasty Chinese poet, Li Po, symbolizing a free spirit. Although these two sequences are similar in their formality, in the second the cloud cover partially obscures a more extensive landscape including rooftops, perhaps of a temple, near a woods; a long trellis fence with a climbing vine covered in red blossoms; and a pool of dark blue water lapping over a rock ledge. Adjoining panels in both rooms, some of which have been identified in other museums since the Met's discovery, reveal similar incidents executed by the same hand.

Having myself contemplated the fifteenth-century dry garden at Ryo-an-ji, with its clusters of fifteen moss-edged rocks surrounded by waves of raked sand, I can imagine the sensation of standing on the veranda of its hojo with luminous golden rooms behind me—a startling contrast between Zen austerity and bourgeois opulence. But the scene would have struck the desired festive note, especially during a gathering in spring when the weeping cherry was in bloom behind the clay wall on the far side of the contemplative garden attributed to the painter and gardener Soami.

In keeping with its name, Peace Dragon Temple, today Ryoan-ji is decorated with fusuma dating from the 1950s that portray fanciful dragons in the monochromatic palette. During the gold-leaf period, the fusuma in the *reinoma* (entrance room for visitors) displayed the traditional theme for this room, "Tiger and Bamboo," symbolizing the strength and endurance of the samurai.

A fine example of this theme in Kyoto today is found in the temple of Nanzen-ji, where a set of fusuma shows one tiger drinking water from a stream and another walking stealthily through a forest of green bamboo. These were executed by Kano Tanyu and are an excellent example of how well the gold ground emphasizes the bulk of the tigers' silhouettes. Tigers were important in Japanese iconography—their roar summoned the wind of the West—even though artists knew them only through their pelts. Nanzen-ji also houses a rare example of fusuma painted on gold leaf by Kano Eitoku, probably near the end of his life in 1590, on the theme of "Chinese Immortals"—only his flying immortal, Oshikyo (Wang Ziqiao in Chinese), departs this world on the back of his friend the crane rather than on the wind.

Though later in style than other gardens described here, the landscape at Nanzen-ji (dating from the early Edo period, c. 1610–1867) combines aspects of architecture and nature that symbolize all the arts of Kyoto. It begins in the foreground with raked sand and graduates to a series of rocks laid out in diminishing size amidst plantings of azalea and other shrubs clipped in rounds. A massive rock at one end suggests the garden's name, the "Leaping Tiger Garden." In linear formation rising above the garden is first the tile coping of the wall and beyond a complex of angled rooftops with upturned eaves. This tight composition at Nanzen-ji, of garden and architecture, along with the fusuma of the interiors, is a visible embodiment of what Ryoan-ji must once have looked like—an image that began to unfold with the discoveries made during the restoration of the fusuma at the Metropolitan Museum of Art.

Antiques, September 1994

Balancing Act: A Contemporary Garden for Kyoto's Oldest House

IN THE COUNTRYSIDE surrounding Kyoto, autumn is a mood as well as a season. On the side of a mountain of rice fields, under a flaming yellow ginkgo tree, stands the oldest existing residence in the precincts of the city, built for a samurai family in 1657. To welcome guests on an early November afternoon, the smooth stones in the courtyard, worn with age, have been dampened with water—a sign of hospitality in the Zen world of tea. John McGee, a tea master at Urasenke Foundation in Kyoto, has lived in this house since the mid-1980s. A native Canadian, he first came to Japan as a guide at the 1970 Osaka World's Fair.

In the gardens adjacent to the house, a red-leafed maple tree, the red berries clustered on the heavenly bamboo *Nandina domestica,* and a lone persimmon clinging to a branch evoke an autumnal melancholy that is reinforced by the gathering shadows under the low overhang of the thatched roof. In traditional Japanese houses, only sliding screens separate the inside from the outside. Together they create an aesthetic unity.

The gardens on the surrounding acre were designed by Marc Peter Keane, the thirty-nine-year-old landscape architect who has lived in Kyoto since 1985. Born in New York State, he received his degree in landscape architecture from Cornell University before going to Japan to live. "My boyhood images of Japan came from souvenirs my father brought home from the war in 1945," he recalled. "I remember reading classic children's stories printed on paper made with silk in Meiji-period books covered in kimono fabric with ivory clasps." To discover the connecting themes and the balance integral to Japanese culture, he became a research fellow at Kyoto University and immersed himself in local theater, art, graphics, food, and fashion, as well as the art of Japanese gardens. A year before he was called upon to redesign John McGee's gardens, he began absorbing the Japanese aesthetic by studying ink-brush painting and calligraphy. "Only then did I feel comfortable enough to bend a path in a Japanese garden," he confesses.

In a country where the craft of gardening is usually handed down from grandfather to grandson, Marc Keane had to teach himself about the arrangement of rocks and plants. With his designs for John McGee's gardens, he mastered the traditional themes suitable for an old country house without being afraid to contribute innovations that still embraced the basic aesthetic. With the help of Englishman Colin Cameron, he constructed three distinct spaces within the acre around the building. In creating a Zen dry garden in a courtyard along the west side of the house, he took as his theme the natural spiral form of a Japanese maple tree. Set in a snug harbor by a half-buried mountain rock with ferns growing in its cracks, the spiral form of the tree trunk appears first to spin out into a spiral moss garden. Then, from the depths of a declivity at the roots of the tree, like a smooth stream of water, a broad curving stripe, raked counter to the straight ridges of the fine gravel field, circles out and back upon itself to echo the spiral shape of the tree. And to add to the drama, the whole "ocean" of raked gravel rises into a swell with the swirl, as if "a whale were about to break the surface," Marc Keane says. Each time this gravel mixture is raked, it is leveled with a flat rake before the ridges are re-shaped in ceremonial fashion into wavelike patterns by the teeth of a wooden rake the width of an English foot, or one *shaku*.

Inspired by the great dry garden at the nearby Zen Buddhist temple Ryoan-ji, this garden also encourages contemplation as the visitor sits at the edge of a moon-viewing platform, a slatted veranda off the *kura* or storehouse. From the far corner behind the maple tree, the musical trickle of real water can be heard dripping from a bamboo spout into overflowing bowls carved into an upright rock. Marc Keane sees this *chozubachi,* or laver—a rugged stone bearing the imprint of man—as the epitome of the balance in a Japanese work of art. The wetness flowing down the rock into a bed of river-stones forms a broad dark stripe like the one suggestive of water raked into the gravel. At the opposite end, a smooth river-stone with a water-filled depression becomes a receptacle for a single cut flower.

When evening descends and the air becomes brisk, a warm glow washes across the garden in stripes of light. Marc Keane allows that "except for points of light from oil lamps placed in stone lanterns, illuminating a garden after dark is a new idea in Japan." Here the light works its magic on the scarlet leaves scattered across the ridges of sand and accentuates the curved roof tiles that frame the garden. As one sits in contemplation, the garden is revealed as a perfect combination of motion and stillness.

While the garden as a whole is a contemporary interpretation of an ancient form, the old garden in the south courtyard may well date to the early years of the house in the seventeenth century. It also provides the ritual entrance to the tea ceremony. When Marc Keane began working in this area, he cleaned out the weeds and installed a new bamboo fence and drip edge. Just outside the fence is the *tsukubai,* a basin-shaped stone sunk into the ground. In a purifying ritual, participants rinse their mouths and wash their hands with cool water from this small pool before walking along the garden's stepping stone path to enter the formal sitting room or *shoin.* Many of the plants and shrubs, like the *Camellia sasanqua* and the twin evergreen oaks, are centuries old. Marc Keane has added wild herbs and mountain flowering plants, cultivated for the spare seasonal flower arrangements that accompany the tea ceremony. Viewed from the house, this part of the garden is a mass of dense green, with a variety of leaf textures and patterns, punctuated by a few trees—Japanese maple, black pine, and *Camellia sasanqua.* Here and there a small stone sculpture or stone lantern nestles into rocks surrounded by carpets of moss.

In the third garden, east of the house, where an old barn once stood, host and guests gather for afternoon English tea in the shade of lush wisteria vines growing overhead on trellises of bamboo bound together with the distinctive black Japanese twine called *somenawa.* These trellises are arranged in the flying geese pattern made famous by the configuration of the structures at Katsura Detached Palace in Kyoto. Reed screens, hanging between the posts, emphasize the distinctive layering of Japanese architecture.

This is a true summer sun and shade garden. In a mass of variegated miscanthus, water drips down an old grinding stone into a pool, the source of a small rivulet at the gateway to the garden. Crossing the water marks a spiritual break between house and garden. Surrounded by cutleaf maple, hydrangeas, and a low-growing grass called dragon's beard, *Ophiopogon japonicus,* a table set for guests is often covered in the brilliant red felt that makes outdoor entertainments so festive in Japan. Soaring above this intimate enclosure is the borrowed scenery of the mountain itself. For Marc Keane, this combination of wild and controlled nature establishes the true harmonious beauty of the Japanese garden.

Gardens Illustrated, October/November 1997

Tea and Empathy: The Japanese House, Shofuso, in Fairmount Park

WHAT IS MORE ephemeral than a show house? Like playhouses, they present enticing possibilities to the curious who drift through them, offering the promise of a painless fresh start. After a few months, having inspired some and titillated many, they disappear forever. But one such temporary structure, the Japanese house with a teahouse and garden that drew record crowds to the Museum of Modern Art in the warm months of 1954 and 1955, has gone on to have a real life of its own as a permanent cultural center in Philadelphia, in Fairmount Park, the swath of green that rambles for miles through the western part of the city. The public goes not just to look: cultural activities this month include a tea ceremony and a traditional "moonviewing" and Japanese dinner.

To see the house today full of vitality, it is hard to believe that in 1954 it arrived in New York from Japan for a "limited engagement," in 636 crates, like so many numbered Lincoln Logs. On a summer Sunday, as about thirty guests gathered to share in green tea and sweets, the stillness of the late afternoon was broken only by water splashing over artfully placed rocks in the Japanese-style pond. On a small island reached by an arched wooden bridge, a gnarled Scotch pine, almost horizontal, looked like a scene from an old scroll. A school of golden carp swarmed, as they do in temple ponds in Kyoto. In this dreamlike setting, Philadelphia seemed far away.

The Japanese house began life as part of a series of exhibition houses that were displayed intermittently in the Sculpture Garden of the Museum of Modern Art from 1949 to 1959, mainly to show off new technology or to offer novel aesthetic experiences. The program was very popular with New Yorkers, and the decision to place the houses outside gave them a sense of reality. Dwarfed by the cityscape, their apparent miniaturization added to their appeal.

Of the three architects represented—Marcel Breuer, Gregory Ain, and Junzo Yoshimura—it was Yoshimura's traditional Japanese house that drew the biggest crowds. Almost a thousand people a day walked across the tatamis in rice-paper slippers.

The earlier Breuer and Ain designs had demonstrated housing solutions for American suburban families that combined economy of space with elegance of form. The Ain house in particular featured sliding walls that made it possible to expand and contract its rooms. What became clear to Arthur Drexler, then the curator of architecture and design, was that the principles incorporated in these modern houses—curtain walls and open interiors—had been formulated by the Japanese three hundred years earlier.

So for the third exhibition house, he selected Yoshimura, a Japanese architect. In 1941, working under Antonin Raymond, a Czech-American architect who had offices in Tokyo, Yoshimura was the project manager for a Japanese-style beach house (now owned by Ralph Lauren) in Montauk, Long Island. Yoshimura later designed the Japan Society's sleek building on East 47th Street, completed in 1971.

Drexler and Yoshimura traveled together throughout Japan to study traditional houses that had survived World War II, many of them part of temple compounds. Yoshimura then worked with craftsmen in Nagoya to devise a design that included a garden with a main house and teahouse connected by a wooden walkway. The house was constructed of lightweight cypress columns that supported a massive curved roof covered with layers of cypress bark. The interior spaces were made flexible by sliding panels, and exterior walls were made of either translucent white paper or thin unpainted wood.

The garden included a pond, a waterfall, a symbolic mountain representing the Buddhist image of paradise, and a contemplative sand garden featuring raked wavelike designs symbolizing water. Tansai Sano, who designed the garden, was descended from seven generations of gardeners at Ryoan-ji, the famous temple in Kyoto. He helped select rocks with sculptural qualities in the mountains surrounding Nagoya. Plantings of weeping cherry, Japanese maple, bamboo, ferns, and mosses were selected by a consultant in the United States. Following the opening of the house in June 1954, the *New York Times Magazine* commented on its "serenity in proximity to the blaring noises of 54th Street." The *Syracuse Herald-Journal* hailed the house as the "granddaddy of ranch style."

Concerned about the house's future after its second season, the museum entered into negotiations with the Fairmount Park Commission, which oversees the 3,500-acre park along the Schuylkill River in Philadelphia. It was reconstructed in the park in 1958. In a sense, Fairmount Park has become an outdoor museum of historic houses, eleven in all, ranging from a 1740s Quaker farmhouse to an 1802 Georgian mansion, all separated from one another by large expanses of land.

The Japanese house was bestowed with a name—Shofuso, or Pine Breeze Villa, taken from characters on a scroll that had adorned its main room. Because of the fragility of its materials, the house had to be extensively renewed in 1976, in a renovation paid for by the Japanese government. In 1982, the Pennsylvania Horticultural Society undertook the rejuvenation of the garden. Now, the Friends of the Japanese House and Garden are raising money to repair the cypress-bark roofs.

Over the decades, the house and grounds have become a place to celebrate Japanese culture. One of the guides, Gretchen Sturm, came to Pine Breeze Villa by way of lessons in martial arts. Dressed in pleated black hakama pants, she said, "As part of my training, I wanted to study the different Japanese arts."

The house, teahouse, and garden have lost none of their magic. The spareness of the furnishings is offset by the richness of the wooden beams. The earth-floor kitchen displays its old storage chest; in the bathroom, a traditional wooden tub is invitingly placed just below a window, to take advantage of the view. A channel of water running under the house provides coolness in summer.

In the teahouse, a single scroll hangs near a meticulously executed flower arrangement. Its meditative message is contained in a single Japanese character, meaning "nothing." In the Zen tradition, this signifies "everything." A paradox? No more so than the way a dream house takes on a real life.

New York Times, August 1, 1996

Rice Paddy in the Sky:
Rooftop Garden at the Mori Center

AS TRAVELERS speed through the Japanese countryside on the bullet train, they glimpse the glittering surface of submerged rice paddies surrounding villages and towns. Men and women wearing indigo farmer's clothes and straw hats or *tenugui*—patterned cotton towels—wrapped around their heads stand silhouetted against the landscape, planting or harvesting the crop according to season. Even in congested residential Tokyo, a back street will suddenly open onto a small square, in its entirety a watery expanse reflecting the sky with green shoots penetrating the surface.

No dramatic scene demonstrates more clearly the cohesive role of Japan's rice culture than the closing moments of Akiro Kurosawa's film *The Seven Samurai,* when the young woman who strayed for romantic adventure is bound once more to the community through the haunting rice-planting song as she bends to her chore with the others.

These are the images of rural life that Minoru Mori remembered from his boyhood in Nara Prefecture, his family's seat southwest of Kyoto, where he was evacuated from Tokyo during World War II. As part of his visionary "Urban New Deal," Mori, a real-estate developer, has recently recreated a microcosm of that rural life on a rooftop in his twenty-nine-acre massive complex of high-rise commercial and residential buildings called Roppongi Hills (think Beverly Hills), which opened last spring in the Roppongi district of Tokyo, known for its razzmatazz nightlife and quiet residential neighborhoods. From the street, Roppongi Hills is a multilevel hub of exclusive shopping malls, cinema complexes, a luxury hotel with stylish restaurants, and ubiquitous video billboards featuring the cartoon designs of the resident artist, Takashi Murakami. Tied together by grand stairways and escalators and a hyperactive street life that would make Jane Jacobs cheer, the development's tallest building, Mori Tower, is crowned by a modern art museum.

Comparisons to Rockefeller Center come easily, although Roppongi Hills covers almost six acres more. And like Rockefeller Center's architect, Raymond Hood, who believed the city architect could no more neglect rooftops than the country architect plantings around a house, Mori has overseen the greening not only of Roppongi Hills' ground-level gardens and tree-lined streetscapes but also of the rooftop terraces (with English-style gardens for apartment dwellers designed by Dan Pearson of Britain). The rice paddy garden, dear to Mori's past, was designed by Yoji Sasaki of Ohtori Consultants, a former Harvard University visiting scholar and the master landscape architect for the entire development.

Set on top of the seven-story glass-sheathed Keyakizaka cinema and boutique complex, the 155-square-foot rice paddy garden combines tradi-tional Japanese motifs like stepping stones and rock formations with con-temporary twists like a metal—instead of a bamboo—fountain. Rainwater is collected and recycled for watering. In an overall view, diagonal stone paths crisscross two major rice paddies and lawns with a vegetable garden planted at one end. Perimeter paths of irregularly cut stone bands merge with a long wooden deck, and each corner features trees identified with a particular season. The garden reflects what Mori calls "the heart of Japa-nese culture."

True to the phrase *rus in urbe* (the country in town), coined by the Latin poet Martial to describe a friend's palazzo in the Roman hills, the rice pad-dies in Tokyo conjure up country scenes. But also, as Mori acknowledges, the symbolism of this high-in-the-sky rice paddy is not new. The imperial family has held rice planting festivals for the past thousand years or more, paying homage to rice and prosperity for the people. With several farmers instructing them, local elementary school pupils planted the rice in May and harvested it in early September, in a festival of their own, for a yield of nearly 135 pounds of both organically grown Koshihikari and sticky rice-cake rice. The rice straw, left to dry in sheaths, will later be used to weave slippers.

"Edges are the most important aspect of approaching space in a Japanese garden," said Sasaki. To prepare for the mind-altering experience in contrast to the urban world below, he explains, the visitor follows the perimeter path, walking head down over the cut stone pavers under a shade tree promenade. The view then opens to the expanse of lawn and the rice paddies set in trap-ezoidal beds; stone paving blocks at the far end become stepping stones across a crescent pond. A wooden plank bridge leads to a lily pond that at-tracts birds and dragonflies, while bamboo trellises support vine-growing vegetables in the kitchen garden. True to advanced technology, the garden would also serve to dampen vibration during an earthquake.

In celebrating the seasons, the garden marks the passage of time with ephemeral moments like the scattering of cherry blossoms in spring. Summer, when the rice shoots are green, is the time for outdoor tea ceremonies. And finally, when the maple grove turns crimson and the persimmons ripen in autumn, people gather on the rooftop to view the moonrise to the east through the tree branches—and through the latticework of the Tokyo Tower beyond.

New York Times Magazine, March 7, 2004

Plum Blossoms: The Third Friend of Winter

The two plum-trees:
I love their blooming,
One early, one later.
—Buson

AS ONE WHO marks the seasons with rituals of her own, I have long been drawn to Japan, where the entire culture is attentive to nature and its cyclical adornments. With the same pleasure and regret for the ephemerality of cherry blossoms and the scarlet hues of autumnal maples, I have cherished the experience of walking the paths of temple and shrine gardens with hundreds of others, making a pilgrimage through time. In 1999, while visiting Kamakura in May, the season of clipped azaleas, I first discovered the temple Hokai-ji and its spectacular allée of glossy green trees. When I learned they were plum trees, I made a mental note to return someday to see them in bloom.

In Japan, the plum tree flowers just as winter tantalizingly heralds spring. More than 350 varieties of flowering plum (*Prunus mume*) with white, red, or pink blossoms bloom from late January through March, making it difficult to pinpoint an optimum moment for viewing. As the years passed, I instead encountered plum trees mostly through art—primarily on the four sliding door panels or *fusuma* installed in the *shoin* or Japanese reception room at the Metropolitan Museum of Art in New York. The panels are collectively titled *The Old Plum* and attributed to Kano Sansetsu, around 1545; I began visiting them regularly to marvel at the tree's thickly gnarled trunk, crooked branches, and wispy white blossoms set against gold leaf.

And in my catalogue of Rimpa art from the Idemitsu Collection in Tokyo, I frequently study the famous pair of six-fold screens of blossoming red and white plum trees, attributed to Ogata Korin and painted around 1712. In quintessential Japanese style, the branches of the red plum twist and turn, contrasting with the linear branch of white. Both are starkly etched into a gold background above a stylized river in black.

In January this year, a winter exhibition at the Kaikodo gallery in New York titled "Let It Snow" featured a nineteenth-century hanging scroll by Okada Tamechika, *Fujiwara Kinto with Blossoming Plum*. Under the snow-laden branches of a red plum, a portly imperial official in black robe and headdress holds a sprig of plum blossoms and a fan. He is composing a poem for the emperor as he shuffles back to court through drifts of snow. An irresistible image: plum blossoms in snow. When I arrived in Japan in February, I found a country celebrating plum blossoms in every aspect of daily life.

I began my pilgrimage at the Hatakeyama Memorial Museum of Fine Art in Tokyo, founded in 1964 by Issey Hatakeyama, who collected unusual tea ceremony utensils and related art objects with seasonal themes that are displayed at appropriate times. In the winter exhibition, featuring plum blossoms and camellias, the vigor and beauty of the three friends of winter traditionally depicted together—pine, bamboo, and plum—were captured in underglaze blue on a seventeenth-century bowl and lid from the Ming Dynasty in China. This delicate bowl was a reminder that the plum tree was a native of China before it arrived in Japan in the seventh century.

In one of the twelve paintings of birds and flowers by Sakai Hoitsu from the Edo period, a bright pink camellia is entwined in a white plum with a Japanese nightingale poised on its bough. Unlike cherry blossoms, which burst into flower simultaneously, the plum blooms gradually along a branch and is portrayed in art with both full five-petaled blossoms and tight buds at the end of each twig. This iconography establishes an air of expectation, of future potential—the same sensation I felt later standing in groves of plums. Even on a small ceramic incense burner on view by Ogata Kenzan (Ogata Korin's brother), the decoration of a heavy twisted branch combines full white blossoms with buds. As is customary, the visit to the museum concluded with bowls of green tea whipped to a froth and sweets in the shape of plum blossoms. Each guest held a different bowl with individual characteristics worth studying.

Little preparation for this voyage was required. My friends in Japan embraced my quest, taking me to view plum blossoms in several regions and milieus. Amy Katoh, whose books and Tokyo store, Blue & White, seek to preserve traditional rural crafts and the indigenous indigo culture, had prepared for the season in her inimitable style a bright pink-and-white booklet titled *Pickled Plums & Friends*. Among stenciled designs of plum blossoms for *tenugui* (a Japanese hand towel-cum-sweatband) and evocative haiku is a mélange of history, customs, and recipes, especially for the tasty pickled plums called *umeboshi*. (A popular Japanese proverb—"Pickled ume and friends, the older, the better"—gave Amy the title.) Here one learns that in the relatively peaceful Edo period, the crossing of natural varieties yielded a wide variety of plums with fruits that are smaller and more tart than their European or American counterparts. Some large orchards, planted for the fruit alone, are dazzling when in bloom.

Armed with historical and horticultural information, I set out with Amy for the Shimane Prefecture, on the Sea of Japan, and the town of Omori, with its narrow streets of restored wooden houses, shops, and shrines along a river valley north of the famous Iwami Ginzan silver mine. Last year the entire region, which dates to the sixteenth century, was designated a UNESCO World Heritage Site. We stayed with her friends the Matsubes in their home, Abe Ke, a rambling Japanese courtyard house, one of the largest in town. Its succession of rooms separated by shoji screens and fusuma surrounds interior courtyard gardens with verandas. Shoes were removed and placed on the packed dirt floor of the entrance hall.

During the first night, I left the warmth of my futon bed and slid open the inner screen and an outer glass one to watch a heavy snowfall on the courtyard garden with its stone snow lantern. The next morning, I walked into the front garden and there, gnarled and stunted with age, was a white plum tree in blossom with glistening snow piled high on its branches and in its crevices. This was the reason I had come to Japan. Later I would see many others, planted along the river that meandered through the town under high arched bridges. Camellia hedges with red blossoms were equally encrusted with snow.

Indoors, outdoors, in nature and in art, the plum seemed ubiquitous. During the day, we visited the Matsubes' store, Gungendo, managed by their daughter, Yukiko. Installed in the entrance was a seasonal display of blue and white ribbon streamers with stylized paper plum blossoms. Immediately inside there was a pink obi with a plum blossom design. At Abe Ke itself, where the mother, Tomi Matsube, oversees a Life Style Study Center, ceramic jars with a few sprigs of plum blossoms were placed strategically for the best aesthetic effect. And along the wintry town streets, cut-off bamboo stalks tied to the exterior latticework of houses were filled with plum blossoms.

One afternoon we made an excursion to view a nearby dry garden with exquisitely pruned trees and clipped shrubs along a river of stones. We also visited the Izumo Taisha Shrine, the oldest Shinto shrine in Japan, with its signature crossed bargeboards at the peak of the gabled roof. On the way back, by chance, in an enclave of old houses with tiled roofs, we passed by a classic vignette of the season: a massive plum tree with dark pink blossoms at the edge of a rice field covered in snow. And the snow continued to fall.

Dinner at a long table in the commodious kitchen of Abe house was a communal, neighborly affair. For the occasion, bottles of plum wine were opened and shared with guests. On wooden shelves in an immense storeroom behind the kitchen stood large jars of *umeboshi* from the crop of the previous summer. Visitors to the Study Center are encouraged to borrow an in-house digital camera to record images of the town as a visual essay of their own impressions. One of the guests from Osaka showed me the sequence of photographs she had made in the fresh snow, including one of the gnarled plum tree. Since I choose to describe images only in notes, she generously offered me a disk of her photographs as a souvenir.

We then left these wintry scenes behind, continuing on to Kagoshima, on Japan's southernmost island of Kyushu. There we visited Kobo Shobu, a residential craft center where adults with Down syndrome and autism create traditional and original crafts. The change in temperature was striking. The drive into the city was lined with what another traveling companion, Susan Cohen, dubbed "corduroy" tea-fields after the long green ridges of tea plants. The plum trees in this warmer clime were in full bloom; our host, Kobo Shobu's director, was particularly proud of the white plum that loomed over his garden; I saw the tree at twilight, which gave it an eerie glow.

The next day we traveled to a mountainside on the coast overlooking a large expanse of bay toward Japan's dramatic volcano, Sakurajima: deep green slopes on a peninsula, with wisps of steam rising from the crater. In a sweeping garden on the land side, plum trees with pale pink blossoms were interspersed among palm trees in the foreground, a subtropical view.

Back in Tokyo, my plum blossom walks became more serious under the guidance of the writer Sumiko Enbutsu, author most recently of *A Flower*

Lover's Guide to Tokyo: 40 Walks for All Seasons. In it, she tells the story of the ninth-century Kyoto scholar-statesman Sugawara Michizane, much favored at court for his command of Chinese classics and poetry in this early period of Japanese literature. Falsely charged by rivals, he was exiled to Kyushu in despair, leaving his beloved pink plum tree with this farewell poem: "When the east wind blows, / emit thy perfume, plum-blossom; / Because thy master is away, / forget not the spring."

His death soon thereafter was followed by a stream of natural disasters, bringing about his swift posthumous restitution and deification as Tenjin, a "god of heaven." Shrines dedicated to him and planted with plum trees are found all over Japan. As the first blooming of plums coincides with the dates of university entrance exams in January, aspirants who seek support from this scholarly god hang thousands of wooden plaques at the shrines, inscribed with wishes for success. Examination results are announced around the period of full bloom.

On a Saturday morning, Sumiko gathered a few friends to join the throngs visiting plum gardens at Zen temples in the eastern section of Kamakura. (A former capital of Japan [1185–1333], today Kamakura is a residential quarter on Sagami Bay, southwest of Tokyo.) While the rest of the city was out doing the weekly shopping, a steady stream of visitors wound through the neighborhoods that separate the temples. Private gardens yielded plum blossoms in all hues—some weeping to the ground—plus red camellias and pine trees pruned into exotic forms. Sometimes the path followed the banks of the Namerigawa River.

For anyone who treasures Saiho-ji, the moss garden in Kyoto, the visit to Zuisen-ji in Kamakura is revealing. Muso Soseki, who designed Saiho-ji's lush landscape as the temple's first abbot in 1339, began designing in Kamakura, twelve years earlier, as the first priest at Zuisen-ji. Beyond the temple and its plum trees, Muso carved out caverns at the base of a steep cliff above a pond. In his time, a dramatic waterfall cascaded over the cliff and into the pond below, completing the composition, but even today the dark caverns in the rock—with water below and sky above—are an arresting sight.

Though the grounds of the temples I visited were not extensive, each was distinctive in the color and arrangement of its plum trees and the preservation of its landscaped features. At the entrance to Sugimoto-dera, the oldest temple in Kamakura, an ancient white plum was supported by stakes in the manner the Japanese do so artfully. A pink plum in the same grouping was set off by a yellow witch hazel that bloomed simultaneously. Well-placed stepping stones surrounded the thatched-roofed temple, and to the side stood a small pavilion with effigies of Buddha wearing ritualistic bibs made of colorfully designed textiles. Of Hokoku-ji, one remembers the woven bamboo fence, the dark pink plum near the entrance, the raked gravel and camellia trees leading to a dark and mysterious bamboo grove, like a forest of organ pipes, and caves again in an overhanging cliff. And of Jo-myo-ji, the rounded forms of tea hedges surrounding the gardens and the combination of white, pink, and red plums gradually coming into bloom.

We climbed the Genjiyama Hill overlooking Sagami Bay for lunch in an old farmhouse in the sturdy architectural style developed for northern regions. The farmhouse had been relocated here and restored, its massive beams and loftlike upper rooms creating a sense of amplitude and purpose.

Rested, we moved on to Hokai-ji, and there I finally achieved the fulfillment of the wish I'd first had on that May visit, years earlier: the overarching entrance allée of plum trees bore myriad buds and fragrant pink blossoms. Further along stood a majestic weeping plum with wooden supports that appeared integral to its natural form. Other images I still recall: the straw hats of the gardeners, and a large ceramic bell. I ended at the great Shinto shrine of Tsurugaoka Hachiman with the double lotus ponds that were in flower on my earlier visit. The shrine is grander and more ornate than the temples, and the plum blossoms on either side of the steep stairway leading up to it were equally impressive.

Sumiko and Amy teamed up to plan my last day, in Hino City, on the western outskirts of Tokyo. The highlight would be a visit to Keio Mogusa-en Garden (no. 37 in Sumiko's book). Afterward we would attend the fire ritual at Takahata Fudo, a nearby temple of esoteric Buddhism, and visit the antiques fair on the temple grounds (a natural coupling in Japan). As we approached the garden, graphics of plum blossoms on pink-and-white banners attached to streetlight poles announced its nearby presence. But nothing prepared me for what I saw as I ascended the stone steps and emerged from a wooded hillside: eight hundred plum trees of every pastel hue and at various stages of bloom. In the middle of the garden, by a thatched-roofed farmhouse, stood an old white plum that had been planted there by a nun three hundred years ago. Because plum trees are pruned and hacked back to create fuller blooms, the branches develop in contorted directions, like the tree in the Met fusuma or the one in the Korin screen. Over the course of time—they can live for centuries—they develop their picturesque gnarled trunks.

Originally the site of a temple called Shoren-an, the landscaping here is enhanced by ponds that reflect the trees, and bridges guide visitors along a circuitous route over the water for a full experience of the garden. Interspersed pines, elegantly pruned into cloud formations, are decoratively protected by taut ropes—like the ribs of bamboo umbrellas but with the practical purpose of preventing accumulated snowfall. This garden was the pinnacle of plums.

When we arrived later for the fire ceremony in the fourteenth-century, smoke-blackened Fudo Hall, just a few places were left inside, and we squeezed in before the incantations began. A central fire had been lit for the burning of stacks of prayer sticks, seeds and beans, and other plants. Carefully tended by the priest, the fire conveyed a sense of purification. After the congregants rose to circle between the fire and the central altar to leave monetary donations, they settled back on the floor, and the priest began to speak. Even though I do not know Japanese, his tone expressed an openness to the communal aspects of the ceremony, and he had special words for a mother holding an infant, beautifully dressed as if for a baptism of sorts.

Once outside, we mingled among the flea market merchants and their assortment of antiques laid out on the ground or on low shelves. Amy, as always, sought out blue and white ceramics and textiles. I wandered over to a rack of old kimonos, always in ample supply since clothes are discarded at death in Japan. Rummaging through, I was intrigued by one the merchant said was from the 1950s. Against a solid ground the color of rosé, a design in white combined sprigs of plum blossom—both flowers and buds—with bouquets of autumnal chrysanthemums. It is unusual in Japan to mix seasons in a design, since women wear only what is appropriate to the season. Yet there was its message: the first and last flowers to bloom in the year. I purchased it for five dollars.

We moved on to the rustic Sanko-in convent for a vegetarian lunch in the Take-no-Gosho style of Kyoto. We were served exquisitely presented steamed turnips, potatoes, and seaweed, reconstituted tofu, and other delicacies; the carrots were shaped into five-petaled plum blossoms. And for our final stop, we passed by the Jindai-ji temple for a charming view of its thatched front gate flanked by pink and white plum trees. That evening, at dinner with Amy at Shabusen in the Ginza, the dessert, *yoshino-koubai,* was the real thing: a Japanese plum, slow-cooked in honey and served in a glass of clear jelly.

316

Seven

Flower Shows

Courson: French International Flower Sale

BEFORE I SETTLED in for this year's Chelsea Flower Show, I crossed the Channel to attend the increasingly popular plant sale known as the *Journées des plantes de Courson*. What began in 1982 as an informal plant exchange between members of the Association des Parcs Botaniques de France has blossomed into one of the most exciting horticultural events in Europe, due to the gracious hospitality of Hélène and Patrice Fustier, the owners of the seventeenth-century chateau of Courson, thirty-five kilometers south of Paris.

Twice a year, in May and October, more than twenty thousand people cross the chateau's moat and pass into the stable yard to enter the landscaped park and arboretum where more than 150 nurseries from France, England, Holland, and Germany spread out their young plants, many of them rare, on the lawns or under trees. The beauty of Courson is its informality. Even in teeming rain, it is a festive market scene that has the advantage of blending in with the landscape. With trellises and arbors set around the perimeters, along with several white marquees for dining, the setting seems like a permanent installation, a kind of garden fair where friends might meet every day on patches of lawn between plant displays to discuss their gardening hopes. Judith L. Pillsbury, an art dealer from Paris, bypassed conversation to make a beeline for the *Nicotiana sylvestris*. Nicotiana, it appears, is difficult to find in France, despite the fact that it is named after Jean Nicot, who introduced tobacco to the French Court in the sixteenth century.

Armed with capacious baskets, members of the aristocracy, many accom-

Facing page: Jonathan Player, *Landscape architect Mark Anthony Walker and his seventeenth-century French classical garden, Chelsea Flower Show, London, 1994.*

panied by their gardeners, select their plants. The marquise de Ravenel drove a hundred kilometers to visit the stand of Michel Rivière, whose family has cultivated peonies for six generations, a national collection with more than six hundred varieties under cultivation near Montélimar.

Business was also brisk at the stand of Pépinière de la Foux, a garden center near Toulon that specializes in salvias. Since 1982, the collection has been increased from a dozen varieties to the current 150 with the help of botanic gardens in France. The object was to promote salvias for more unusual summer plantings along the Côte d'Azur. The New York public garden designer Lynden B. Miller was delighted to discover a blue *Salvia guaranitica* for the Connecticut-style garden she has designed at this year's International Festival of Gardens at Chaumont-sur-Loire.

Many plants are loosely displayed to suggest combinations to gardeners, particularly for borders. Cuckoo Pen Nursery, which traveled to Courson from Oxford, created both sun and shade gardens by banking potted plants in small groupings at various heights. And André Gayraud created a naturalistic but striking effect by arranging, under an existing grove of trees, a woodland garden consisting of a vast collection of white hydrangea plants interspersed by a single red rose bush.

The *treillage* or trelliswork pavilions that Bertrand Servenay brought to the show were painted in the same blue-gray that has become the new historically based color for the orange tree planters at Versailles. With a bit of frou-frou to decorate the trellis roofs, the austere classical pavilions can be transformed into rococo or chinoiserie creations. And Bruno Caron of Damblemont was at the ready to give the history of the French garden seats he displayed against instant walls of moss and ivy. Closer to architecture than to furniture, these massive historic forms, some with flat balusters in the seat back that date back to Marly in the seventeenth century, were shaped to shed rather than to retain rain water. The weather cooperated in the demonstration.

The prize-giving ceremony outdoors was a jovial event under a sea of umbrellas with Hélène Fustier in her trademark felt fedora making everyone feel like a personal guest. I was particularly alert to the Blérancourt prize for the best specimen of an American plant. Named after the museum outside of Paris which promotes French-American friendship, the prize this year was awarded to a beautiful *Heuchera* 'Rachel.' In 1993, the Courson event itself was awarded the coveted Veitch Memorial Medal by the Royal Horticultural Society.

But the real hit of the show was an English item called a Bosbag—or maybe it was the way French women can make any utilitarian item look chic by the way they carry it. Nancy de la Selle bought one to fill up with plants for her garden near Chartres, and the commodious bag in spring green blended beautifully with the stalks of young columbine peeking over the top. Stiffened with ordinary curtain wire, the Bosbag is perfectly designed for its purpose of carrying plants, and unlike the bright Kelly green which manufacturers believe is suitable for gardens, the pale yellowish green bags became as much a part of the Courson landscape as old French garden baskets.

Gardens Illustrated, August–September 1994

At Chelsea Flower Show: Gardens in Romantic Ruins

LONDON—THROUGH THE decades, the Chelsea Flower Show has been the world's most comprehensive and influential gardening exhibition, a kind of National Gallery of the flower world.

This year, seven hundred exhibitors are participating, on twenty-seven acres of gardens behind the imposing symmetrical wings of Sir Christopher Wren's 1692 Royal Hospital on the banks of the Thames, in Chelsea. There, along avenues of pink-blossoming horse chestnut trees or under a three-and-a-half-acre white marquee with candy-striped awnings, new varieties of plants are introduced and appear side by side with traditional ones in brilliant displays. There are rows of orchids, rows of roses, and, this year, a display that features broken glass, of all things.

How did it crash this genteel event?

One picturesque aspect of eighteenth- and nineteenth-century British gardens was the way Romantic ruins, usually fake ones, were gently incorporated as follies into the landscape, to simulate antique or medieval settings. Several landscape designers at Chelsea this year have discovered ideal matériel for garden ruins in the detritus of their own age. Using the decay of contemporary structures has turned into a trend, as other gardeners have found that disused common objects can indeed turn into picturesque sights in a garden.

Stephen Woodhams, a garden designer, recalled that last summer, as he was arranging flowers for a wedding at Donhead Hall, in Dorset, he wandered through an old blue door and into a walled garden. There he found a Victorian greenhouse in an elegant stage of decomposition. "It was a magical moment to see how nature had overtaken the man-made," he said of his first view of the broken moss-encrusted frame.

Seeing that the building was obviously not being used, he asked permission to transport the remains to Chelsea—shards of broken glass, old brick wall, clinging ivy, and all. Here, seen in a soft English rain, it is a truly Romantic and enticing sight, a crumbling ruin in a re-created garden, complete with arches of hornbeam, a sixty-year-old pear tree trained against a wall, and a sweet-smelling rose called Boule de Neige. The tools of Donhead's old gardener, James Maidment, who worked in this greenhouse from 1915 to 1955, lie at the ready.

Another unusual setting at the show is a long-disused railway ticket-seller's cottage, complete with a section of track below the platform; it provides an opportunity to demonstrate how quickly an abundance of wildflowers can overtake a swampy railroad bed. Iris, poppy, vetch, and thistle are only a few of the scattered plantings tucked in around the railroad ties, thereby converting utilitarian remnants into natural garden enclosures.

Julian Dowle, who designed this native garden and the terraces around the cottage, said he discovered the beauty of deserted railroad tracks on long walks in the mountainous Snowdonia region of Wales. Transformed into public footpaths or greenways, these old lines evolve into lush habitats for indigenous plants twined among the ruins. (Indeed, the introduction of weedy gardens and lawns for their own sake may represent the greatest innovation at Chelsea over the last decade.)

Not to be outdone, Isabel and Julian Bannerman designed an abbey garden that incorporates architectural remnants borrowed from no less grand a place than Salisbury Cathedral, now undergoing restoration. Herbaceous borders of nineteenth-century cultivars, including irises, sweet peas, and roses, create a fringe along the garden wall. The brick wall itself, with insets of Gothic stonework, is softened by climbing roses and wisteria. More ruinous than the wall or even the castellated summer pavilion that is part of the display is an old gnarled mulberry tree supported by a crook in the middle of the broad lawn.

"It was like a miracle, the day we saw the tree in the middle of a farmer's field in Somerset," recalled Isabel Bannerman as she described the excavation of the six-ton root ball. The tree will find a new home on the grounds of a factory after the show ends tomorrow. For now, it gives character to a scene that could not be improved upon by Jane Austen or Anthony Trollope.

One landscape architect, Mark Anthony Walker, did without ruins: he even looked across the Channel for his inspiration. To create a seventeenth-century French classical garden with old statuary and urns, Walker, a landscape architect for Clifton Landscape and Design, in London, transported six mature linden trees from near Bologna, Italy. Their branches create a ready-made pleached or woven canopy to shade the garden walk. Behind the clipped yew hedge at the back, taller trees give the illusion that the garden sits at the edge of a small grove. Arched openings in a rose arbor frame views of spiral topiary in a box-edged parterre that is planted with salvia, lavender, and other fragrant plants. A still-water canal next to the arbor provides the obligatory reflected light. It is Versailles in a nutshell.

According to Sir Simon Hornby, the new president of the Royal Horticultural Society, who toured the show in his tweeds and green Wellington boots, the scale of gardening has changed in Britain. "As ownership of the larger landscaped gardens passes from private hands to organizations like the National Trust," he said, "there is a greater concentration on gardening well in small areas." He has also noticed an increase in the variety of plants in English herbaceous borders and in the quality of small nurseries as demonstrated by the many unusual plants displayed among the acres of roses under the marquee. He applauds what he calls "a remarkable effort among growers to preserve old varieties that has led to the creation of certified national plant collections."

As an example of energetic horticultural activity, the Barbados Horticultural Society arrived with thousands of boxed blooms to show off the talents of their private growers. For example, while five years ago there were only fifteen varieties of heliconia, now there are almost a hundred in varying shades of yellow to red. Despite a major drought on the island and five previous flower shows this year, the Bajans produced a display around a small rum shop that appeared as brilliant in color as exploding fireworks in fan-shaped patterns. Red, not green, is the dominant hue of both flowers and foliage.

At the other end of the color spectrum, both subtle and rare, is Carol Klein's moonlit garden for her nursery Glebe Cottage Plants in Devon, where she specializes in species plants or hybrids that are self-made. She has arranged the plants from whites to pale yellows as if to reflect moonlight emerging from behind a cloud. And this year, she introduced several new plants, including two varieties of polemonium, 'Glebe Cottage Violet' and 'Sonia's Bluebell'.

Although gardening is a national pastime, what gives Britain its true character are the miles of hedgerows that border fields and country lanes. They are fast disappearing due to neglect and lost maintenance techniques among the farmers. Therefore, a small exhibit at Chelsea on the Great Hedge Project may also be one of the most important for preserving the traditional landscape. Sponsored by Plantlife, the only charity organization in the United Kingdom devoted to saving wild plants and their habitats, the booth displays what could be a medieval hedgerow with seven woody species including hawthorn, buckthorn, Guelder rose, and viburnum that bloom in spring and produce berries in autumn.

The age of an old hedgerow is gauged by the number of species in a thirty-yard segment multiplied by one hundred. Properly trained into thick masses, they are periodically pruned with the leafy branches woven through. "We are trying to reach community groups to preserve the Anglo-Saxon hedgerows that define their parish boundaries as a way of gaining local support for our program," says Tim Rogers, the project officer.

By tomorrow, 200,000 people, including the Queen, Prince Philip, the Queen Mother, and Princess Margaret, will have walked through the show grounds and seen the modern ruins and other horticultural splendors. The present owners of Donhead Hall, who thought they had seen the last of their derelict greenhouse, were so taken with the sight of it at Chelsea that they have decided they want it back as a ruin in their own garden, shards and all. Is that the ultimate compliment?

New York Times, May 26, 1994

Free to Grow Bluebells in England: British Prisoners Win Gold Medal

LEAVING BEHIND their confines for a temporary stay in the open air, seven prisoners from Her Majesty's Prison Leyhill in the Cotswolds won their second gold medal last week at the Hampton Court Palace Flower Show, the Royal Horticultural Society's summer extravaganza. Their show garden, "Take a Walk on the Wild Side," included a woodland garden of wildflowers and grasses under linden and beech trees, with a stream flowing under a stone bridge.

"It is one thing to make a garden, and another to mimic nature," Adrian Foulkes, a prisoner, said of the difficulty of forcing bluebells and wild garlic into bloom and weaving them into the grasses. Foulkes, who is thirty-nine and is nearing parole on a life sentence for murder, heads the prison's garden committee this year.

The flower show, which ended last weekend, is an annual event on the grounds of Hampton Court Palace, in the London borough of Richmond-upon-Thames, on the Thames River. The show, which attracts horticultural groups and garden designers, uses displays that are designed so that visitors can walk through them. The prisoners' exhibit, situated on the banks of a long canal with spouting fountains, seemed like a real woodland in which one could rest on a willow seat under linden trees.

The prize also honored the prisoners' kitchen garden display: carrots, onions, parsnips, and runner beans, enclosed by cordoned apple and pear trees and a rusty fence overgrown with blackberry bushes from the prison's grounds. The kitchen and woodland gardens were designed by Gareth Goundrill—not a prisoner, but the eighteen-year-old son of Jeff Goundrill, who oversees Leyhill's business enterprises. Gareth Goundrill made the designs as his final exam for a high school course, and the prisoners planted the flowers, vegetables, and trees with the help of the prison farm foreman, Martin Brookes.

Leyhill, a minimum-security prison, has participated in Royal Horticultural Society shows at Hampton Court and Chelsea since 1991. "It is a real pleasure to work with the Leyhill team," said Stephen Bennett, the director of the shows. "They have become good friends. They provide much pleasure to the gardening public, and their skillful use of plants—all grown at the prison—makes a valuable contribution to horticulture and the community." Leyhill is in the town of Wotton-under-Edge in the Cotswolds, one of England's best-known garden belts, about a hundred miles west of London. The institution, on about 250 acres, with ornamental gardens and three acres under glass, is surrounded by crumbling stonewalls.

"In order to work as a gardener," said Tom Williams, the prison's warden, "a prisoner needs no horticultural experience. But he must be quick to learn, work hard, and have a sense of humor under pressure." Williams himself painted the watercolor rendering of the show garden for the leaflet distributed at Hampton Court.

Leyhill's grounds include an arboretum with more than one thousand specimen trees and a stately home, Tortworth Court, a sixty-room mansion that was built in 1853 and is the former seat of the earls of Ducie. Henry John, the third earl, created the arboretum from 1853 to 1921. The arboretum has been managed by Leyhill since the prison acquired it in the 1940s. Leyhill also maintains pastureland for raising rare Gloucester cattle and runs a museum of old farm machinery in the prison's Tortworth Visitors' Center, which also includes a farm stand.

The prison's gardens have become a serious moneymaking enterprise over the last five years. This year, Leyhill has supplied a million carpet-bedding plants to nearby towns, and it distributes organically grown vegetables to twenty-seven other prisons. "If a prison serves a bad meal, it sours the whole atmosphere," said Colin Lennox, the farm manager. And the prison takes the word "organic" seriously. Pests are controlled by their natural predators instead of by sprays and pesticides. A computer monitors the prison's nine greenhouses along with irrigation and fertilization.

There is an additional enterprise for the Leyhill gardens: they provide organic salads and sandwich fillings for British Airways Concorde flights originating at Heathrow Airport. For all the efficiency of the prison's garden operation, there is one drawback: as Jeff Goundrill said, "The best gardeners are always being released."

> New York Times, July 16, 1998
> Greenfingers (2001), a feature film written and directed by Joel
> Hershman, starring Helen Mirren and Clive Owen, was based on this
> article.

A Garden Festival in Lausanne

NESTLED ALONG the northern shores of Lake Léman, Lausanne, Switzerland, is surrounded by a countryside of steeply terraced vineyards and, across the lake, the borrowed scenery of the Alps. This summer, to add to these majestic landscapes, the narrow streets of the old quarter, the broad esplanades, and even the embankments of the Métro are flourishing with thirty-four newly-installed gardens that represent some of Europe's freshest ideas on urban landscape design. Mayor Yvette Jaggi sees the International Festival of Urban Gardens, called Lausanne Jardins '97, as an opportunity to rediscover this city now woven together by innovative green architecture.

Most of the gardens are unconventional and contemporary in spirit. As the quarter hours strike from the town's myriad clock towers, the sound of crystal chimes and gongs wafts over sculpted hedges and beds of catmint and sage that undulate along the Esplanade de Montbenon overlooking the lake. Beside the quay on the lake, a fence of white slanted boards, recalling wooden rafts or *jangadas* on the Amazon, encloses a garden composed entirely of the solanaceae or nightshade family—potatoes, tobacco, tomatoes, and various garden flowers and weeds. Inaccessible and visible only through angled slats, the interior becomes a natural sanctuary where plants, permitted to grow wild, will exceed their boundary and overflow the openings. Illuminated at night, it has the eerie presence of a hidden world.

Vertical structures for vine gardens placed along the alleyways and hilly terraces around the cathedral are extensions of the picturesque houses that line the streets. Across three terraces, a post and beam scaffolding of chestnut poles, planted with twining Scarlet Runner pole beans, nasturtiums, and morning glories, creates a delicate labyrinth of arbors. Along one incline, an arcade and walls of wire mesh covered with hop vines trace, like a memory, the configuration of houses that long ago disappeared. In one conceptual display, fifteen cubic cages house segments of gardens, some densely grown, others spare or with a single tree, that force the viewer to imagine the larger contexts they represent.

Landscape designers, artists, and architects were assembled and given their sites and assignments by the festival director, Lorette Coen, who discovered the life of gardens one day while sitting in a park in Basel. In addition to the temporary gardens, the city has profited from major restorations of some of its existing gardens—for example, the Casino garden, a formal display surrounded by hedges in which a few clipped "windows" have been wittily crisscrossed with wires to create a woven tapestry of vines.

Gilles Clément (a designer of the Parc Citroën in Paris) undertook the most ambitious and lasting of the permanent projects, in which he planted a string of gardens in a sequence of colors to be viewed from the above-ground Métro windows. With this summer display, Lausanne has stepped out front with its concept that in urban gardens of every stripe horticulture and design must be equal partners.

New York Times, July 20, 1997

Epilogue

A Winter Garden of Yellow

ON DRIZZLY WINTER MORNINGS, I often stand at a corner window, hot mug of milk in hand, looking down on Park Avenue. The moment has to be right, a little after eight o'clock. Suddenly, moving slowly up and down both sides of the center islands, school buses and taxis fill the slick dark avenue with chrome-yellow shapes that gleam in the rain. I move away for an instant, then, when I look again, this world in a mist seems transformed into a stream in an old Kyoto garden where golden carp weave in and out of dark waters, their backs glistening as they turn. In another moment, the children have disembarked at the school next door, and Park Avenue is gray again.

During the drab months between holiday lights and the first blooms of spring, what sparks the gloom of cityscapes is the winter garden of industrial colors—particularly, in New York, yellow. Invented at an educators' conference in 1939, "National School Bus Yellow" was selected for its high visibility that led to safety. Although New York City's taxi fleets originally maintained their own company colors, by the 1970s yellow became the industry's standard for medallion cabs. Seen from above, a single yellow cab gliding through the snow in Central Park carries with it a world of warmth.

In London, red is dominant thanks to the omnibuses, a few old telephone booths, and pillar boxes of the Royal Mail. But it was not always so. In Oscar Wilde's poem "Symphony in Yellow," he wrote how "An omnibus across the bridge / Crawls like a yellow butterfly . . . / And, like a yellow silken scarf, / The thick fog hangs along the quay." Even in rural Vermont, the poet Sydney

Facing page: William John Kennedy, *Taxi in wintry Central Park, New York.*

Lea observed in "Annual Report": "In mind, the school bus was a mobile jonquil, / giant bud in February's gray."

The once stylish yellow rain slicker also brings a sunny presence to New York's sidewalks—the patrol officer at the school swings in hers butterfly-like as the schoolchildren cross the street. At a women's college in the 1950s, slick-ered students crossing the commons in winter looked like daffodils bobbing on the horizon. In his book *For the Union Dead*, Robert Lowell described the progression through the rain of two cops on horseback in "their oilskins yellow as forsythia."

Frequently in the city I catch special glimpses of winter yellow. Once, in a dusk magically glowing, I watched a school of rush-hour taxis through the chain-link draperies at the Four Seasons, just off Park Avenue, where I was waiting for a friend. This calls to mind an old Chinese scroll with golden fish rising through swirls of water, and an obi sash embroidered with carp darting through glinting waves. Not far away, at the Asia Society, a porcelain jar from the Ming period, decorated with eight goldfish swimming through aquatic plants, was captioned "a symbol of harmony."

Matisse captured the look in a maquette for a stained-glass window called *Chinese Fish* made with orange yellow cutouts swimming across a grid.

This is the height of the season, a cold gray city adorned with the glow of metallic yellow, as if a goldfinch had alighted on the bough of a wintry tree. Only weeks away, nature's colors will take over again—red tulips and pink cherry blossoms on Park Avenue's islands—and this poignant yellow of winter again will fade.

New York Times, February 27, 1995

330

Afterword

John Dixon Hunt

PUBLIC INTEREST and awareness of garden-making and garden-visiting are more extensive and probably better informed than ever before, fuelled in part by an increasing concern with environmental issues. Books, magazines, articles, exhibitions, garden festivals, and radio and television broadcasts, not to mention the ubiquity of garden centers and visitable historical sites, make gardens everywhere a prime topic of inquiry, tourism, and amateur design and horticulture.

Yet there seems sometimes a striking divide between this widespread public interest in gardens and the work and pronouncements of professional landscape architects. This has several explanations: a studied suspicion of "gardens" by professionals, who feel their skills are better employed in large-scale work and activities such at the newfangled "landscape urbanism"; their nervous sense that gardens are "elitist," even when so much popular visitation and attention is nonetheless focused upon them and speaks to the contrary; a need by professionals to distinguish their own activities, not just by designs legitimized by their legal status as registered practitioners, but by contributing to what they tend to call its "discourse," commentary that (often in academic situations) seeks to elevate the work of place-making from what is traditionally seen as a merely pragmatic activity by discussing it in terms borrowed, more often than not, from modernist architecture and cultural studies, along with much of its endemic jargon.

This divide, while unfortunate, is not necessarily permanent or inevitable. There are occasions in which informed, intelligent, analytical, and widely knowledgeable commentary can make garden culture, on the one hand, suddenly richly significant and intricate, and, on the other, reveal professional skepticism as misplaced and professional writings as either ignorant or beside any point but their own. Paula Deitz provides one example of such a commentator. In book and catalogue introductions and in an astonishing number of sustained journalistic pieces (often, but not exclusively, in the *New York Times*) she has extended the scope and depth of our understanding of gardens, garden-making, and garden-experience. It is a selection of these important contributions that are published here.

Of Gardens may be read as a book, where a historically alert commentary unfolds through a series of visits, biographical analyses, and accounts of foreign travel. But it is also available as a series of meditations on what their author considers prime achievements in the creation and maintenance of designed landscapes. These can provide an enthralling series of perspectives, opening, like the prospects in some well-designed parkland, as a reader wanders at random through the different sectors.

The two supreme virtues of good journalism are accessibility—the skill of talking to that old but still plausible creature, the "general reader"—and research. Paula Deitz displays both these qualities. In the first case, her writing, subtly modified for the occasion (the magazine or newspaper), is clear, evocative, and informative. In the second case, her display of information, never overbearing or showy, always apt and relevant, is based upon wide reading and a historical imagination. The range of references—the variety of sites in many countries that she has visited, the designers (both historical and contemporary) that have been the subjects of her essays—put most professional landscape architects and critics to shame: many of them could benefit from her subtle understanding of historical precedent, modern exigency, and design challenges and achievements. Indeed, the analysis of designs, of sites, and of larger cultural landscapes is extremely skilful, surrendering nothing to the local readership, yet ensuring that both historical context and appreciative comprehension of technical matters, horticulture, and ground work are fully presented and clearly explained. Jargon is avoided, but nothing conceptual or theoretic that is needed for understanding a site is absent, let alone watered down. Furthermore, while the original publication of many of these essays involved photography to an extent not feasible here, the essays remain a wonderful exercise in presenting topics verbally; indeed, the rhetorical skill often achieves more than could their visual supplements.

Welcoming this collection of essays into the Penn Studies in Landscape Architecture is both a personal pleasure—I have appreciated Paula Deitz's writing for many years—and, more important, it serves to affirm a cluster of essential themes, which the series attempts to foster by including a deliberately varied repertoire of research and writing. Paula Deitz's contribution is above all to remind us that gardens are the source and founding inspiration

of all landscape architecture; that contemporary landscape architectural practice and criticism must be historically alert and well grounded; and that the
better and more availably the garden is discussed in public forums like the
journals for which Paula Deitz has written, the better and more fruitful will
be the practice and the experience of our society's garden culture.

Acknowledgments

ON ONE of our long drives to our summer house in Maine, during which we had memorable conversations, my husband, Frederick Morgan, commented that whenever we visited an exhibition together or traveled to a new place, I invariably made unexpected connections that threw an original light on the situation. He suggested that rather than let these thoughts dissipate over time, I should try to write them down. I began that very summer with my first garden article about the fictional garden in Nathaniel Hawthorne's *The House of the Seven Gables* and a synchronistic event relating to the Scarlet Runner beans that were planted there and attracted hummingbirds. I sold it to a magazine and received more mail than for any article since—everyone wanted to know where to order Scarlet Runner pole beans. Not only did Fred strongly encourage my writing career, he also served as my best editor, for no piece was submitted without his prior perusal. I owe my greatest debt to him for his generous spirit.

In truth, I write for editors and learn constantly from the pleasurable give and take with them. When, after biding my time, I thought I found an appropriate topic for the *New York Times,* I telephoned Nancy Newhouse, then the editor of the Home section. Not knowing me at all, she requested five Polaroids and a five-hundred-word précis, and I got the assignment. To her I owe my many years as a regular contributor to the *New York Times,* later under her aegis as the discriminating Travel editor. She was followed at Home by Dona Guimaraes, the kind of hard marker who brings out the best in a writer, and who had a mind overflowing with information that stimulated ideas. At *House & Garden*, Denise Otis's expertise in American gardens guided my writing about several prominent ones in Maine; at the *Magazine Antiques*, Allison Ledes encouraged long historical essays, especially on British and French gardens; and at *Gardens Illustrated* in London, the founding editor, Rosie Atkins, was a powerhouse of facts coupled with nuance, who gave me a British audience and a stint with my own column. There are many more successive editors who offered valuable encouragement, each of whom contributed to my development in a unique way. Often I made proposals, but mostly I benefited from assignments that led me literally along new paths, expanding my horizons.

Although I began by writing on weekends, mornings soon took up the overflow, and on a deadline day I might never show up at the *Hudson Review* office at all. And so I deeply appreciate the tolerance coupled with enthusiasm that my colleagues have always shown me, especially Ronald Koury, the magazine's managing editor for the past twenty-five years. As my writing and research files became voluminous, I engaged a series of part-time student archivists, whose assistance in maintaining order made information readily available. Among them, Suzanne Pratt, the first, and Isa Loundon, the current one, stayed beyond their student days, providing the invaluable gift of continuity. For their steadfast friendship throughout the years as good listeners and critics, a special thank-you to Susan Cohen and Emily Grosholz.

By proposing this book, the landscape historian John Dixon Hunt gave me the valuable opportunity to bring order to disparate articles written for a variety of publications over many years. As a great admirer of his own manifold contributions to landscape architecture as a dedicated teacher and writer of brilliant volumes on garden history, I am indebted to him for the time and thought he gave to selecting these essays from a much larger pool. To Jo Joslyn, the University of Pennsylvania Press editor who made this book a handsome reality, and to all her colleagues, my deepest gratitude always for their understanding and expertise. And finally, to the landscape architects, owners, and overseers of the places that are the subjects of these essays, I am grateful for their gracious welcome.

Index

Photography Credits

A special note of appreciation to the following photographers or their representatives for providing permission to reproduce these photographs that enhance this edition.

Title page: Fred R. Conrad, *Pleached crab apple tree arbor, Oak Spring Farms, Upperville, Virginia. The New York Times*/Redux.

Introduction, page xii: Eugène Atget, *Versailles, coin de parc, 1902,* albumen print. Courtesy of George Eastman House, International Museum of Photography and Film.

Prologue, page xviii: Walker Evans, *Detail of a Frame House in Ossining, New York, 1931.* Copyright © The Museum of Modern Art/Licensed by SCALA/Art Resource, NY.

Landscape Architects and Designers, page 6: Hervé Abbadie, *50 Avenue Montaigne, Paris.* Michael Van Valkenburgh Associates, Inc.

Parks and Public Places, page 76: Cervin Robinson, *IBM Garden Plaza, New York.*

American, page 166: Alan Ward, *Chinese moon gate, the Abby Aldrich Rockefeller Garden, Seal Harbor, Maine.*

British, page 220: Lanning Roper, *Herb garden, Scotney Castle, Kent.* RHS Lindley Library.

French, page 264: François Halard, *Column house, Le Désert de Retz, Chambourcy.* Trish South Management/trunk archive.com.

Japanese, page 292: Jerry Harpur, *Japanese Zen garden by Marc Peter Keane, Kyoto.* Harpur Garden Library.

Flower Shows, page 318: Jonathan Player, *Landscape architect Mark Anthony Walker and his seventeenth-century French classical garden, Chelsea Flower Show, London, 1994. The New York Times*.

Epilogue, page 328: William John Kennedy, *Taxi in wintry Central Park, New York.* Copyright © 1987 by William John Kennedy. All Rights Reserved.